D1572521

America Classifies
the Immigrants

America Classifies the Immigrants

FROM ELLIS ISLAND TO THE 2020 CENSUS

JOEL PERLMANN

Harvard University Press

Cambridge, Massachusetts · London, England

2018

Library of Congress Cataloging-in-Publication Data

Names: Perlmann, Joel, author.
Title: America classifies the immigrants : from Ellis Island to the
2020 census / Joel Perlmann.
Description: Cambridge, Massachusetts : Harvard University Press, 2018. |
Includes bibliographical references and index.
Identifiers: LCCN 2017037497 | ISBN 9780674425057 (alk. paper)
Subjects: LCSH: United States. Bureau of the Census—History. | United
States—Emigration and immigration—Government policy—History. |
Race—Classification—History. | Ethnic groups—Classification—History. |
Race—Political aspects—United States—History. | Ethnic
groups—Political aspects—United States—History. | United States—
Race relations—Political aspects—History.
Classification: LCC JV6483 .P45 2018 | DDC 325.73—dc23
LC record available at https://lccn.loc.gov/2017037497

For Rivka, with love

Contents

PART FOUR
Incorporating the Legacies of the Civil Rights Era and Mass Immigration from the Third World

America Classifies
the Immigrants

Introduction

IN 1881, IMMIGRANTS arriving in the United States exceeded half a million in number for the first time. They first exceeded a million in 1905; then the number of annual arrivals *averaged* over a million for a decade. The immigrants came mostly from Europe, although those from China and later Japan were a target of American hostility far greater than their proportion in the immigration would have suggested. Moreover, by the mid-1890s, the changing sources of immigration *within* Europe—from northwest to southeast—also led to unease about immigrants. British, Irish, German, and Scandinavian arrivals gave way especially to southern Italians, Slavs, and eastern European Jews.

Federal officials had begun to collect basic information on immigrant arrivals in the early nineteenth century. As questions about immigration increased over the decades, so did the range of information these officials gathered and reported. By the 1890s, age, sex, country of origin, literacy, prior occupation, funds on hand, and health were all subjects of inquiry in varying degree of detail. Indeed, these reports on immigrant arrivals had some of the same social functions that a national census did. The ways in which new arrivals were classified were influenced by the big social questions of the time, questions that reflected hopes and anxieties about the direction of society. These questions include: Were young men coming alone or with whole families? The former might well be a less permanent and law-abiding group. Was the number of illiterates growing? And even if it was

1

declining, was it still too high for an ever-more advanced economy? Was the personal merit of arrivals decreasing along with self-selection now that the quality of ships made the journey across an ocean less forbidding than before?

But no topic seemed more pressing than immigrants' origins—origins, that is, like race and nationality. Would any Asian immigrants at all be tolerated? Which European races were suited to become Americans? How would the qualities of different races change America in the near term—its economic output, its standards of living, health, and crime rates? And how, over the long haul, would the descendants of various new arrivals affect its ability to survive as a democratic republic? Especially important for thinking about this latter issue were the particular mental traits that the descendants of immigrants would exhibit. Would these be determined mostly by the qualities immigrant peoples transferred to their descendants, especially through the blood, or would the assimilative processes of the republic transform the descendants enough to make them unrecognizable, mentally and spiritually, from their immigrant forbearers?

Today we would describe the use of terms like race and nationality in this context as attempts to capture historical, or ethno-racial, origin. There were multiple reasons these kinds of origin characteristics received so much attention. First, virtually all the other qualities that were enumerated—population profiles by age, sex, literacy, occupation, and health—seemed to many Americans to be strongly associated with, and perhaps rooted in, an individual's group of origin. Second, the languages of many new groups were unfamiliar in America and their religions unpopular, including Catholicism, Eastern Orthodoxy, and Judaism (to say nothing of Asian beliefs). And third, many Americans came to believe that crucial qualities of character that could *not be* enumerated—for example, self-discipline, intelligence, initiative, and suitability for self-government—were in fact dependent on these very racial or national origins. Various social theories competed to explain *why* classification by race, nationality, people, or religion revealed these differences across the groups. Once in place, the particular kinds of classification also helped channel discussion to particular kinds of hypotheses to explain social differences. Too many immigrant arrivals from the wrong races and nationalities might produce excessive poverty or crime in the short term and might be expected to bring the degradation of republican institutions in the long term.

Despite such claims, terms like "race" or "nationality" were difficult for Americans—including the officials charged with classifying immigrants—to define with much precision. What exactly did these categories of origin explain, and how powerful were these explanations? What was the appropriate way to understand the links between historical origins and the behavior of the immigrant encountered on the street? What did race in particular really mean? What was the relation between *immigrant* races and America's *"other* race problem"—as the problem of America's freedmen, a mere fifteen years from slavery in 1880, were often described in immigration debates.

In general, large-scale immigration, especially from a wide diversity of countries, is likely to be perceived both as deeply consequential to a nation and as something the state can restrict or encourage. Consequently, it is likely to be something over which groups struggle. And the discussions about new classifications for historical origins can often reveal assumptions about how origins are thought to matter for the human potential of the immigrant and consequently how the arrivals will influence the host society. The intellectual history of these connections forms one feature of this study. The other concerns the social and political context, how particular groups—in this study typically federal officials, politicians, and ethnic advocacy groups—interacted in wielding the ideas embodied in the classifications, and why some actors prevailed and others lost out or why particular imperfect compromises emerged from these actors' struggles.

Most of this book deals with the introduction of such successive new origin group classifications, or with the uses of classifications to direct immigration policy. The rest deals with the major intellectual reorientation, especially between 1920 and 1960, about how origins relate to character. The study covers the century and a quarter since the late 1890s, beginning in the mass immigration of that time.

Part I tells the story of the List of Races, soon renamed the List of Races and Peoples. In the late 1890s, two energetic immigration officials at the Port of New York created the List in order to provide a new and better classification of immigrant arrivals. They took up this task on their own initiative, but they soon convinced the top official at the Bureau of Immigration to adopt their new system. Its principal value was to classify *European* immigrants into some three dozen *distinct races*. These races included, for example, the English, Irish, Scotch, German, Northern Italian, Southern Italian, Hebrew, Croatian and Slovenian, Magyar, and Scandinavian. The Bureau of Immigration immediately made the List the primary basis on which statistics of immigrant arrivals were recorded and published; it remained in use, applied to every immigrant arrival, for more than half a century.

A few years later, Congress created the United States Immigration Commission (1907–1911) and charged it with producing an authoritative report on immigration trends and future policies. The commission adopted the List of Races and Peoples as the basis of its own work, in forty-one long volumes of reports. Both the bureau's annual reports and the commission's tomes tended to assume, and certainly allowed readers to assume, that the characteristics of immigrant groups differed as a result of something inherent in each group. Moreover, the commission extended the reach of the List. Its studies were not limited to arriving immigrants, but covered the later lives of immigrants in America and also the lives of their American-born offspring. Finally, the U.S. Immigration Commission also pressed to make the List the basis of a new race question on the upcoming 1910 U.S. census. That classification scheme, on the republic's most authoritative population survey, would have presented the many groups of European immigrants (and their children) as racially distinct from each other.

At all three of these government agencies—the Bureau of Immigration, the U.S. Immigration Commission, and the Census Bureau—criticisms of the List forced a revealing self-consciousness about the usage of terms and meanings. It also modified that usage on several occasions. The criticisms came from a decidedly narrow base—from Jewish organizations protesting the presence of a "Hebrew" race category. These organizations represented the most middle-class, well-connected, acculturated, and politically articulate American Jews of the period. Looking back from our own times, with the Nazi era between then and now, it would be easy to assume that the Jewish organizations were arguing against the idea that Jews constituted a race. In fact, their objections to the List would have been, and eventually had occasion to be, just as strong against classification of Jews as a "people," "nationality," or "ethnic classification." They insisted that the Jews were a *religious* group, and they argued that the constitutional separation of church and state prohibited federal scrutiny of an individual's religious preference. Not all Jewish groups supported the protests; in fact, those who identified their Jewishness in terms of cultural or political nationalism publicly condemned the protests against the List. Nevertheless, the most influential Jewish leaders of the day were nearly all united on the side of consistent protest to the highest federal officials they could reach. Throughout this book, I refer to their criticisms and efforts to marshal evidence and expert opinion as *the Jewish protest* over the List. As early as 1900, these protests pushed the Bureau of Immigration to drop a newly introduced question on immigrant religion. In 1903 an additional protest stimulated the U.S. cabinet secretary who oversaw both the Immigration and Census Bureaus to undertake a remarkable internal (secret) review of the issues the Jewish groups had raised. Memos from both of these bureaus as well as the Departments of Justice and State went back and forth. That review convinced the government that it could defend the List.

The dynamics of the 1910 protest to keep the List off the U.S. census were more complex, with results that differed between the Census and Immigration Bureaus. At first it appeared that the Jewish protests would successfully block the List from the census. But then other ethnic leaders—Slavs in particular—protested that without some kind of addition to the census, their people would appear only in terms of the empires that oppressed them—for example, Czechs, Slovaks, Poles, Bosnians, Ruthenians as Austrians or, in other cases, as Russians or Germans. Congressional committees and the Census director were forced to find a solution that would calm diametrically opposed groups. Eventually, the director followed the advice of a Russian Jewish immigrant, a left-wing intellectual long employed at the Census Bureau. The director kept clear of racial terminology by taking up the conceptualization followed in Central and Eastern Europe for such matters: he proposed a new census question on "nationality or mother tongue." Here was the first effort by the American census to explore mother tongue, and it had nothing to do with support for, or opposition to, a multilingual republic. But in that same year, the Bureau of Immigration reaffirmed the use of race and now clarified explicitly that "race" meant "blood."

Consequently, for the next several decades the two bureaus, Immigration and Census, described European immigrant peoples with these very different terms. Moreover, *both* bureaus' usage shifts in 1910 came as reactions to the Jewish protest over the List's Hebrew category.

We are immensely fortunate to have both verbatim transcripts of interactions in many of these episodes, as well as relevant private correspondence. In order to understand more fully still what race, and the related terms of origin, actually meant to contemporaries, it is also helpful to focus on more systematic and detailed, but still politically relevant, formulations about race and immigration. This is accomplished through a close look at the detailed and explicit arguments of Henry Cabot Lodge, among the best-educated, most articulate, and most influential senators over a period of thirty years. Not all his particular formulations were shared by others of course, but questions that his use of race was meant to address and his assumptions about historical origins groups were widely shared. How his formulations differed from those that came somewhat later, in the writing of Madison Grant or Harry Laughlin, is also important to appreciate.

The discussions that shaped the List of Races and Peoples, supplemented by the analysis of Lodge, Grant, and others, provide a lens through which to reconsider legislative restrictions of the early 1920s (Part II); that remained in effect for forty years. One reconsideration concerns the influence of the two broad kinds of racial thinking just mentioned, those articulated by Lodge and Grant, and particularly about how much of a push Madison Grant's full-throated biological determinism provided for congressional action. Another is to highlight just how explicit the Senate in particular was in recognizing that the relevant legislation, The National Origins Act of 1924, used "national origins" simply as the best workable proxy for "race."

A third major issue about the 1924 law has reverberated through American race and immigration history before and since its passage. Race was applied to differences among Europeans but also to differences between Europeans and others—that is, between whites and nonwhites. In other words, there was a difference in the kinds of race differences discussed. Both of these kinds of race differences need to be understood, and both were enacted into the 1924 law. Did contemporaries even realize that they were invoking two different kinds of race difference? To the extent that they were conscious of invoking this distinction, just how did they articulate what distinguished between these two kinds of race differences? Of course, intellectual formulations were by no means all that mattered. Whatever the intellectual understandings, the operation of different kinds of racial boundaries in society—among Europeans and between blacks and whites, for example—is ultimately a more fundamental question. But surely, intellectual underpinnings are a part of that larger question and deserve careful exploration. Part I and especially a full chapter of Part II therefore track this difference in race differences not only in the 1924 act but also in other discussions that linked race and immigration policy in the 1920s.

Part III deals with the uneven intellectual evolution away from "race" to the usage of "ethnic group" that emerged among American sociologists between the 1920s and 1960s. This transition has often been noted, and it stands as a summary of the rejection of biological determinism in the study of American immigrants and their descendants. Less understood is that both terms—race and ethnic group—were already available in the nineteenth century, and at that time both terms could be used in connection with biological processes for transmitting group differences. Other terms, too, such as "nationality," played a role in the evolution of thinking between the 1920s and the 1960s. Moreover, much of the movement away from biological determinism was accomplished while still using the race term to discuss immigrants and their descendants. Finally, the diffusion of self-consciousness about the terms and their meanings turns out to have been decidedly limited through the early 1950s, among academics and even more so among highly educated federal officials.

Another feature of the changing thinking about ethno-racial life during those decades concerned the increased focus on the tension between the persistence of ethnic groups and the dissolving social forces of assimilation. During the preceding years of mass immigrations, it was natural for most people to be thinking instead about the challenges of absorbing diverse peoples into a unified society and polity. Moreover, the support that ethnic persistence was believed to draw from biological processes heightened the perceived challenge. It would be misleading to say that the concern with the losses of group distinctiveness only followed the 1920s; several influential authors had taken it up by the start of that decade. Nevertheless, later—after restriction followed mass immigration, the second and third generations followed the first, and the notion of biological determinism lost favor—the questions about ethnic survivals in the face of America's assimilative social dynamics loomed larger. This same tension between ethnic group persistence and assimilative tendencies that preoccupied some social scientists would reverberate through the successive efforts to reform federal ethno-racial classifications since the 1960s.

The classificatory changes since that decade were defined by two legislative watersheds: first, the peak of the civil rights acts and, second, the near-simultaneous immigration act that eventually created a new mass immigration, this time from the third world. The civil rights acts brought a sea change in the relation between the federal government and minority groups—most especially blacks but also others (especially Hispanics, Asians, and even the "white ethnic groups" who had become well known by the end of the 1960s). One issue involved defining "Hispanics" and "Asians" as "pan-ethnic" aggregates of familiar national origin groups (Mexican, Puerto Rican, etc., or Chinese, Vietnamese, etc.). Less appreciated has been the way the new classifications conceived of ethnic persistence: they tracked immigrant group origins across unlimited generations of descendants, as had always been the procedure for races (such as African Americans and Asian Americans). Now, for the first time, new census questions related to Hispanics and even Europeans in this way. These changes came about to address a civil rights concern relevant to families who had resided in the United States for generations, in particular Mexican Americans in the Southwest (but also, with less conviction, the grandchildren of Southern and Eastern European immigrants). The civil rights concern was essentially historically oriented, focused on the extent to which socioeconomic parity was incomplete for these groups and that cultural distinctiveness among them persisted too. This perspective shaped the Hispanic Origin and Ancestry questions introduced in 1980 and it offered renewed justification for Asian race enumerations. However, the other giant transformation of those decades, the tens of millions of new arrivals from Latin America and East Asia, ensured that most of the people counted in the new classification scheme as Hispanic and Asian were actually immigrants themselves or (later) their children. The original late-generation target of the counts became an afterthought. But a tendency emerged to understand distinctive features of the population captured by Hispanic origin or Asian race categories by reference to membership in that particular group rather than as experiences common to most new immigrants.

By contrast, the second major classificatory reform of the post–civil rights era permitted individuals to record their origin in more than one race (introduced in the 2000 census). It tended to tilt the balance between group persistence and assimilation somewhat towards the latter side of the scales. Finally, by 2017 the Census Bureau proposed a third set of changes in federal ethno-racial classification, to be introduced in the 2020 census. It would reshape the initiatives of the 1980 reform—most especially by creating a single question that would include both race and Hispanic origin. It would not make Hispanic origin a race, but it would recognize that this grouping had become a co-equal category with the already listed races, however each category might be defined now. Each of these three reforms in post–civil rights era classification was initiated by different actors and each followed its own complex political path to federal adoption. Each shifted understandings about group origin and current condition.

PART ONE

The List of Races and Peoples

~

CHAPTER 1

Creating and Refining the List, 1898–1906

THE LIST OF RACES endured for over a half century, but the story of its creation will not serve as a model for the ideal enactment of public policy—deliberative discussion by high elected officials, a careful procedure of review by their administrators, consultation with experts on racial classification, testing of forms and responses? None of these apply. But neither was it the product of smoke-filled rooms and cynical politicians serving powerful economic interests or the prejudices of patrician nativists. The List's beginnings were more humble and contingent. And its initial purposes were more benign. Eventually, the List was embraced by nativists, many of whom relied on racial arguments to explain why certain European and other immigrants were undesirable. But it did not emerge as a result of such views. Indeed, it did not emerge as a result of political pressure of any kind, whether from nativists or economic or other special interests.

The federal government had been classifying immigrants by their country of origin for three-quarters of a century; the results were listed and discussed in the *Annual Report of the Commissioner General for Immigration*. Then, in 1898, that *Report* announced that henceforth immigrants would also be classified by race. That the List's races were nearly all Europeans reflected the composition of the immigrant flow. Mass immigration had been increasing fairly steadily through the decades since 1820, and the vast majority of arrivals had always been European. This would remain true until the immigration restriction laws of 1921–1924 ended a century of mass immigration to the United States for four decades. It is easy to lose sight of the European origins of the immigrant arrivals of 1820–1924 when we look back from our own time—that is, the new era of mass immigration that began in 1965 after a further change in immigration law.

It is true that not all of those earlier immigrants had been European. Between 1850 and the early 1880s, an immigration of moderate size (numbering about a quarter million in all) also had arrived from China. These Chinese immigrants were concentrated in California and had been met with fierce opposition there, eventually leading to the 1882 Chinese Exclusion Act. By the turn of the twentieth century, a moderate number of Japanese arrivals (a total of 155,000 by 1908) began to reach the United States, and particularly California. Like the Chinese before them, the Japanese immigrants were met with great hostility, this time resulting in President Theodore Roosevelt's "Gentlemen's Agreement" with the Japanese Empire (1907; not a law or formal treaty). The agreement greatly reduced the number of Japanese laborers permitted to emigrate west. Further steps to exclude East Asian arrivals would come between 1917 and 1924. The only noteworthy immigration of Latin Americans during the century before 1924 came from Mexico. Indeed, small settlements of Mexican immigrants in the Southwest had long preceded the arrival of Anglos, and they—perhaps a total of some 50,000—were absorbed into the United States after the War of 1846 across the vast territory then ceded by Mexico. For decades thereafter, people crossed the border between the two countries informally in both directions. A noticeable, permanent northward movement of consequence came only with the construction of a north–south railway line in Mexico during the 1890s, and especially after 1910, when people fled the desperate conditions created by the Mexican Civil War (185,000 came between 1910 and 1919). To put these numbers from Asia and Mexico into perspective, consider that between 1820 and 1924, the federal government recorded about 36 million immigrant arrivals, and of these nearly 34 million came from Europe or Canada. Indeed, during the great immigrations of 1880–1924, only 3.7 percent of arrivals came from Mexico or elsewhere to the south. Another 2.5 percent came from Asia. All the rest, some 94 percent of the immigrants, came from Europe or Canada.[1]

But if the immigrant arrivals between 1820 and 1924 were overwhelmingly of European origin, their places of origin *within* Europe changed dramatically during that period. Especially important for the creation of the List of Races were the changes that occurred after 1880. Prior to that date, most immigrants had come from Great Britain, Ireland, Germany, and Scandinavia, that is, from northwestern Europe. During the 1880s, and especially the 1890s, great numbers of immigrants, especially Italians, eastern European Jews, and Slavs, began to arrive from southern, central, and eastern Europe—well over a million of these three groups had arrived by 1890, 4.6 million during the 1890s, 9.4 million in the first decade of the new century. Five million more came between 1910 and 1924, despite the disruptions of the World War I years and the imposition of quotas soon after. The relative magnitude of these immigrations underscores why so much of the discussion about racial difference between immigrants and the older-stock Americans concerned the new European peoples.

An Improbable Pair Create the List

In 1892, Edward F. McSweeney was leading a Massachusetts shoemakers union. That year, he undertook to help the Democratic nominee, Grover Cleveland, in his campaign for a second presidential term. Cleveland won, and soon after he appointed McSweeney to be number two at Ellis Island, as the assistant commissioner of immigration for the Port of New York. McSweeney thus became one of many labor leaders who attained important posts within the U.S. Bureau of Immigration.

Although he was the assistant commissioner, subordinate to the commissioner, McSweeney tended to take charge of Ellis Island affairs. He survived there for nearly a decade, until Theodore Roosevelt initiated a "good government" review of the Bureau of Immigration. Whatever the politics of the review, McSweeney had run a loose ship. And yet, he was a curious, inquiring official. In fact, he was perhaps too curious, as Roosevelt's investigating committee eventually exposed the assistant commissioner's sins. One was that he had conducted investigations of issues at government expense without authorization, and on occasion simply to intrigue his friends with the findings.[2] At any rate, our concern is with a McSweeney initiative that long outlasted his or even Theodore Roosevelt's administration.

In this initiative he worked closely with his able subordinate, Victor Safford, a surgeon at Ellis Island. Safford may appear to be the more studious professional of the pair, but of course, like McSweeney, he had no formal training in a social science. Moreover, McSweeney was by no means merely the public voice for Safford; they both gave thought, time, and energy to the work. And there is every reason to believe that they thought of themselves as introducing an improvement that would help all concerned.

Congress had long mandated that certain information be recorded in connection with each arriving immigrant. This information was recorded on a form known as the *Passenger List*. For the overwhelming majority of immigrants who arrived by sea, the Passenger List was itself part of the *ship's manifest*. Blank copies of the form were provided to the steamship companies, and the ship's captain was ultimately responsible for the form's completion. Over the years, Congress increased the information called for on the Passenger List. Indeed, by the 1890s the list was as detailed as a census schedule and included similar questions.

> The full name, age, and sex; whether married or single; the occupation; whether able to read or write; the nationality; the last residence; the seaport of landing; the final destination; whether having ticket through to such destination; who paid his passage; whether in possession of money; and if so, whether upward of $30; whether going to join a relative; and if so, his name and address; whether ever before in the United States; whether ever in prison or an almshouse; whether under contract to perform labor; and what is the immigrant's health, mentally and physically, and whether deformed or crippled.[3]

Steamship companies were ordered to fill out the forms before a ship departed its port of origin. This procedure increased the chances that any traveler who was likely to be barred under American law would be caught and removed from the vessel. Moreover, the steamship lines had to bear the cost of returning any individual barred at the American end of the voyage. The companies thus had a financial incentive as well as a legal obligation to complete the Passenger Lists responsibly.[4] Each American port tabulated the information from the Passenger Lists of vessels that arrived there and sent the results on to Washington, where they were aggregated. The results were reported in the *Annual Report of the United States Commissioner General of Immigration*.

McSweeney had already urged a revision of data collection the year be-fore in late 1897 or early 1898. But at that time the newly elected president, William McKinley, had just installed a new commissioner of immigration for the Port of New York, Thomas Fitchie, who wished to concentrate on other issues.[5] In June 1898 McSweeney again found an opportunity to raise the issue. He had asked Victor Safford, "who is capable and wholly disin-terested," to report on a minor argument among clerks at Ellis Island.[6] Some clerks had sharply questioned the accuracy of figures compiled by others. And "with his usual skill and thoroughness, he [Safford] has comprehen-sively treated the subject." Safford found that the real source of the dispute lay in ambiguities inherent in the bureau's classification system for immi-grants. In early June 1898, Safford submitted his report, a closely argued summary extending over several single-spaced typewritten pages.[7]

Safford found that the squabble had arisen because immigrant "nation-ality" had been misclassified. Especially troubling was the classification of nationality for immigrants who came from the multinational empires—Russia and Austro-Hungary in particular, but also the German and the Ottoman empires. Nationalities such as Russia, Russian Poland, Germany, German Pole, Bohemia, Other Austria, and Galicia were found on the Pas-senger Lists, and the terms were used inconsistently. Safford showed that there were several sources of error. Some clerks were simply sloppy or inat-tentive. More intractable was the challenge of recording thousands of pos-sible places of last residence. Thus town names "are usually misspelled" and "the change of a single letter may put a town in a different country." More-over, often the locally used names for towns "differ from the official desig-nation." Some regions were known by more than one name, but the precise boundaries of the region could depend on the name.

Yet Safford argued that all of these were secondary problems. The larger issue was conceptual, and it had to do with the ambiguity inherent in "na-tionality." He wrote, "The main cause of discrepancy [as to classification of nationality] is [due] . . . to different ideas as to what these statistics are intended to show. There is a confusion as to nationality, race and residence."

The confusion, in other words, was between two items (nationality and residence) found on the form and a third that Safford introduced, namely, race. Safford therefore recommended that the bureau clarify the terms already in use on the form and include a question about each individual's race as well. His discussion is worth close attention, because it illuminates the use of these terms and provides a cogent justification for the new classification scheme that would shortly follow; indeed, the justification in Safford's report is probably as full and clear as any that would appear over the years. As we shall see, his argument for race data also differed from those that others would offer later.

> Various classes differing widely from an industrial standpoint are coming to us from the Russian and Austrian Empires. The differences among them conform pretty closely to race and religion, although in most instances they can be made to conform to territorial districts.
>
> No one would think of combining Germany and Italy under one head in immigration statistics, and yet either the Russian or Austrian Empire includes even greater contrasts in race and language as well as from an industrial standpoint than Italy and Germany.

This was the fundamental issue: for the first time, large numbers of immigrants were coming from the multinational empires, especially Russia and Austro-Hungary. Yet all of the arrivals from such empires were being classified in terms of "nationality," which referred to *political status*, that is, to being a subject of the relevant empire. Moreover, many of the immigrating *peoples*—Jews, Poles, or Germans, for example—were distributed geographically across more than one of the European empires. "The Galician Hebrew is an Austrian, but in no material respect does he differ from the Hebrew from Russia or Germany [nor is] the Pole from Russia any different from the Pole from Austria or Germany."[8] Of course, this was not a totally new problem. Similar issues arose in connection with the Irish (or Scottish or Welsh) immigrants from the United Kingdom, or with French Canadians, although Safford did not mention the parallels.

In any case, by the 1890s the multiplicity of peoples arriving from one political entity had become a large problem for understanding the immigrations from central and eastern Europe. It was important, Safford argued, to state which people the immigrant from Russia or Austro-Hungary actually belonged to. "Contrasts in race and language" were as great among these peoples as they were among Germans and Italians. To this general argument Safford elaborated that the various peoples were quite distinct "from an industrial standpoint."

> During the past ten years there has been an exodus of Jews from Russia which rivals the one that Moses led out of Egypt. It constitutes an event in our history as well as in that of their own race. They have for the most part entered well defined fields of labor here and have given rise to special labor problems. The Immigration Bureau fails to give a clew to the size of this movement. They are lumped up [in the reported statistics] with the Poles, people of a distinct race and of different capacities who have gone into entirely different fields of industry. The word "Russia" is made to cover the most of them yet the true orthodox Russian has not yet made his appearance in our immigration. In the same way Austria sends us the Teuton, practically a German; the Bukowinan and others, true agriculturalists here as at home; the Magyar who has a recognized industrial status here; the Slovak who has another and the Galician Jew who is the same as his Russian [Jewish] brother.

Safford's conclusion, which follows immediately after these sentences, argues forcefully for a "racial" rather than a country-of-origin basis for understanding contemporary immigration—but entirely for economic reasons. Of all the people involved in justifying the List of Races over the coming decades, only Safford and McSweeney did so exclusively in economic terms. For them the key point was that geographic and industrial concentrations of immigrants were a result of language and group solidarity.

> This movement of immigration is not a senseless movement like the stampede of cattle but is in the main intelligent and fluctuates according to the supply and demand in the particular industrial field into which a certain class enters. The study of our labor conditions has been brought within the scope of the federal Government and economists even now look to us for certain data. If we fail to obtain information of economic value clearly within our power we can scarcely hope to escape being called to account for our neglect.

Safford made several recommendations. Some concerned the more mundane ambiguities he had noted in reviewing clerical errors. Thus, for example, clerical review could be improved and the boundaries of territories (e.g., Poland, Galicia) could be defined clearly to guide clerks. Also, the nationality question currently on the form had to be clarified: did it refer to "race, [country of] birth, political allegiance or [last permanent] residence." Finally, Safford urged adding a new question on race.

McSweeney added a cover letter to Safford's report and sent it on to his titular head at the Port of New York, Thomas Fitchie. McSweeney began by stressing an approaching deadline. Statistics of immigration were collected for each fiscal year, and the changeover to the next fiscal year was then but two weeks away. If they were going to improve data collection, they had to settle everything in the course of a fortnight—or wait a whole year.

McSweeney gave scant attention to the squabble that initially occasioned Safford's report or to Safford's suggestions for reducing clerical error. His interest was in Safford's larger conceptual point: the immigrants from each of the multinational empires differed greatly from each other, yet current statistics treated them only as arrivals from a single political entity. Mc-Sweeney attached a list of sixteen peoples of the Austro-Hungarian Empire, as well as an appendix with a much longer list of "races living in the Russian Empire" and a discussion of different Slavic peoples. "[These] peoples are entirely different from each other," he wrote, and "when they come to the United States [they] seek different avenues of employment and our statistics should insofar as possible, make the division on the lines of their industrial possibilities." By contrast, the categories of English immigrants from the United Kingdom, Canada, and elsewhere were overly detailed, "considering that we receive practically one sort of people. . . . For instance, what difference there can be in an alien from Manitoba and British Columbia passes my understanding."[9] McSweeney then called for an immediate general reexamination.

> My suggestion is that the matter be laid before the Commissioner-
> General with the recommendation that he appoint a committee of
> competent officials who shall make a report to him upon immigration
> statistics in full, defining the political and race divisions, not only
> according to the actual empire or political division but classifying them
> industrially. The Russian and Austrian Hebrew is a different industrial

potentiality from the Austrian Pole or Slav, and their classification can sometimes only be obtained by taking into consideration their race or religious affiliations.

Occupation statistics as given by us have also been of little value. Most of the Slavonic races are land workmen, but they are not skilled farmers, so that when they come here they are without occupation except for the most menial work and must necessarily accept any employment which comes their way. The mining fields have, therefore, held out to them the greatest promise on account of the unskilled character of the work and improved machinery has given them the advantage of working their way into certain classes of manufacturing enterprise, which they do with great eagerness.

Thus both Safford and McSweeney spoke of the races and peoples of the empires interchangeably, and both spoke of these as being more important than subjecthood in a particular empire. Neither argued that racial origin is important for its own sake, nor did either take up the question of whether racial differences are permanent characteristics or whether significant assimilation can occur within a generation or two. Rather, their rationale for collecting this sort of data was to examine economic concentration by race.

McSweeney's letter went out on June 18, but it had almost certainly been preceded by informal discussion with the commissioner-general of immigration in Washington, because the letter quickly reached him. The commissioner-general was Terrence V. Powderly, the former leader of the Knights of Labor. He had received his position as a reward for having helped McKinley in the 1896 presidential campaign. Thus Powderly had been rewarded for helping a Republican, McSweeney for helping a Democrat, but they shared a background in the labor movement. In any case, Powderly strongly supported McSweeney's proposals for change.

On June 22 Powderly appointed the review committee McSweeney had requested. Because the deadline for annual changes was approaching, the committee met in New York the very next day.[10] The committee consisted of McSweeney as chairman, Safford as secretary, and two other bureau officials: John Rodgers, the commissioner of immigration at Philadelphia, and Richard Campbell, an official in the Washington office under Powderly. At their meeting in New York on the 23, the committee in turn delegated to Safford and McSweeney the task of preparing the final report.

They managed to write the report (submitted on June 26) in three days. Safford and McSweeney then obtained the signatures of the other two committee members, and the final report reached Powderly on June 30.[11] A flurry of telegrams also prompted Safford to go to Washington so that he and Campbell could finish a supplemental form with new questions to be asked of arriving immigrants, in addition to those found on the Passenger List. And then Safford went to Boston to instruct agents there in the use of the new form in time for the new fiscal year—which began a few hours later.

Thus officially, the crucial impetus for change was Safford and McSweeney's report of June 26, which, not surprisingly, read rather like Safford's original report of June 6 and McSweeney's covering letter of June 18. But the Safford–McSweeney report of June 26 added some new features of interest. The authors "gratefully acknowledge . . . great assistance" from discussions with "some of the officials of the service whose former residence among the various foreign races we were trying to classify, . . . [gave them] consequent knowledge of the social, industrial and religious conditions which prevailed."[12]

Most crucially, they explained to the agents of the bureau why a concern with industrial organization leads to a classification by race and a reliance on language and religion.

> The object of such statistics is to show the kind of people that come to this country arranged . . . [to] furnish an approximately accurate means for estimating, from the known race characteristics of each order or class, its industrial and social value to this country.
>
> In some instances, such as that of the Hebrews, religion has been resorted to as a means of distinguishing race, but in general the mother tongue spoken is the criterion by which such classification has been made, since it constitutes the chief bond of social and domestic union which holds peoples together in all countries.[13]

This casual reference to the use of religion as a means of getting at the Hebrew race would come back to haunt the bureau.

In any case, they underscore that it is "race and language" that matters—far more than even the occupational background in the country of origin. The bureau had been collecting that information on premigration occupation, assuming that it would predict what line of work immigrants pursued in the new country. But, the authors argue, "this [assumption] is probably erroneous in four cases out of five, except for expert mechanics and some professions. We believe that the race or language of the peoples, together with the destinations by states, will furnish the nearest approach to tangible information [about what work the immigrants will take up]."[14] Race, then, is the covering "class," but it matters *because of* language. But then why not simply ascertain mother tongue and ignore race? No doubt they thought that a language-based prediction about where workers would concentrate could in some cases be refined by adding other characteristics (religion, province of birth, etc.).

In his testimony at the U.S. Industrial Commission Hearings in 1899, Safford said as much: "People that speak the same language and that have the same religious ties and that are bound to ally themselves together in this country, and whether they want to or not, be forced into the same occupations, were classified together. That was the main change." McSweeney added that they likewise gathered information on religion only in the service of predicting economic outcomes: "In some cases the mother tongue might give us an idea of the races, but sometimes the tongue would not do that, and then we had to ask what their religion was."[15]

Thus the creators of the List introduced multiple distinguishing characteristics (including what would become the hot-button characteristic, religious affiliation) to get at what they sought—rather than limiting themselves to language as a proxy. These characteristics, in turn, were all features of a kind of collectivity they called "race." Had they instead limited themselves to a single proxy, "language," then they might well have ended up discussing language categories rather than races. Of course, even if they had limited themselves to mother tongue, it would have been relatively easy for others later on to map the language data onto a racial classification, but a certain degree of distance between the government statistics on language and underlying races would have been preserved for those who wanted to insist on it. And it might have been possible too to avoid or at least minimize later protests that the underlying category could denote a religion in the case of the "Hebrew" category.

So the new questions were to be found in the supplemental form created to accompany the Passenger List. The supplemental form included the following new questions for each arriving immigrant—but no question calling for race: *color, nativity (country and province), mother tongue (language or dialect), subject of what country,* and *religion.*

All of these items—except color, to which we will return shortly—had been discussed in Safford's and McSweeney's memos as ways of refining the ambiguities in the "nationality" category of the Passenger List. The five questions seem to be directed at observable factors that distinguish among races. Perhaps, then, McSweeney and Safford understood that these five supplemental questions capture everything that distinguished the people of one race from those of another. Knowing these five features about an immigrant would be the same as knowing his or her race. Alternatively, Safford and McSweeney may have thought of these five factors as surface manifestations of an intangible, inner, deeper racial essence. Either way, the supplemental form was apparently a path to get at a race classification. In fact, the supplemental form used at the Port of New York, where a sizable majority of all immigrants arrived, may not have been used at other (much smaller) ports. At those places, the identification in terms of race may have been made directly, without reference to the extra questions.[16]

Whether or not they were aware of it, McSweeney's committee was almost certainly exceeding its legal authority. As we have seen, Congress preserved for itself the decision about which items of information were to be collected from arriving immigrants. Moreover, in asking about religion, the bureau exceeded its authority in an especially striking way. Struggles between Protestant nativists and Irish Catholic immigrants, often supported by clergy on both sides, had been severe in the middle decades of the nineteenth century, and flare-ups continued over the years. To inquire about the religion of the immigrant arrivals could not help but remind many Americans of such conflicts; thus the American state had claimed to be open to all faiths and the Roman Catholic Church had protested this claim as hypocrisy.[17] True, the religion question on the supplemental form was being explained as relevant especially for identifying *Jews,* not Catholic groups, but constitutional issues had occasionally arisen also in connection with the status of the Jewish religion in the United States over the course of a century. In any case, those involved in creating the List—not only McSweeney and Safford but also others from Commissioner Powderly on down—were obviously not afraid to include a religion question. Perhaps they did not anticipate protest at all. They were after all very rushed and may simply have missed this particular live wire. In any case, their interest was not in religious affiliation for its own sake but "as a means of distinguishing race," as the Safford–McSweeney report had explained.

By July 1, 1898, the supplemental form with its new questions had been printed and distributed. The most difficult deadline had been met, and a new experiment in federal record keeping had begun, albeit one as yet unknown to anyone outside the Bureau of Immigration. But now that the supplemental form was actually in use, the officials faced three additional tasks. First, they had to create a List of Races. Second, they had to provide their clerks with instructions so that they could fill in the supplemental form when questioning immigrant arrivals. And third, these same clerks, or others, then had to work with the answers given on the supplemental forms in order to classify the immigrant by race—that is, to choose a fitting category from the List of Races. Apparently, a single set of directions was issued to cover both tasks, namely, filling in the answers the immigrant gave to the five questions on the supplemental form and then finding the right category on the List of Races for that immigrant.

During the years 1898–1903, when the supplemental form was in use, the bureau never announced how the data were compiled, nor did it mention the existence of the supplemental form. Still, we know from the surviving correspondence that the committee members exchanged drafts of race classification schemes and of instructions for bureau clerks during July through September 1898. Drafts of the instructions are revealing.[18] First they cleared up the old ambiguity about "nationality." In the future, the term would refer to birthplace: "every alien should be credited to the country in which he was born regardless of later residence or political allegiance." Then, too, they define mother tongue as the "language, dialect or form of speech which the immigrant first learned from his parents as a child in his own home." The committee members note in this context that Yiddish is to be distinguished from German. Also, the emphasis on early usage in the home is important: any later assimilation was to be ignored—for example, Jews or Czechs who in adulthood might have taken up Russian or German, respectively. But of course some assimilation may have been already completed in the parents' generation; the effort to dig into origins did not extend to the ancient past. The instructions explained the usage of race.

> This is not intended to be an ethnological classification. It is not intended as a history of the immigrant's antecedents but as a clew to what will be his immediate future after he has landed. It is merely a grouping together as far as it seems practicable to do so of people who maintain recognized communities in various parts of this country where they settle, who have the same aptitudes or industrial capacities or who are found here identified with certain occupations. A guide to such differentiation is secured by the fact that for his own interest and self-protection an immigrant is bound to ally himself with people of his own language already here and will enter the pursuits in which these people have found they can succeed.

The instructions stress that the social rather than "ethnological" significance of race matters for immigration. For the short-term history of the List, the disclaimer is interesting because so many who took up the races in the List seemed to be using it with *some* sort of "ethnological" meaning in mind. For these users, if not for McSweeney and Safford, racial origins captured in the List would matter because such origins captured something about differences in the mental makeup of peoples that was transmitted across generations.

The reference to ethnology is important. Ethnology, in the late nineteenth century, was the study of characteristics that distinguished human subgroups around the world. The characteristics at issue were primarily physical, and the older influences that could explain how divisions among subgroups had emerged were likewise physical (particularly climate or terrain). Still, when subdivisions of more recent origin were discussed, these might have been cultural in nature, and they might have resulted from social, cultural, or political influences. The older the characteristics, the more likely that the reference was to physical distinctions and to the physical remains of prehistoric peoples.[19] The root of the discipline's name (*ethnos*) is from the Greek word for people. But the term "ethnology" should not be confused with our contemporary use of "ethnic group" and "ethnicity" (from the same root). We often use these terms explicitly or implicitly in contrast to race, with the latter implying a biological and the former a social or cultural focus. By contrast, ethnology did not rest on that distinction; moreover, it attended more to the physical than the sociocultural. Indeed, in the late nineteenth century, the common meaning of "ethnic," "ethnic group," "ethnical," "ethnical science," and "ethnologist" referred to that study of ethnology.

We also need to appreciate the disclaimer in the instructions' introductory sentence ("not intended to be"). This is the first of many similar disclaimers that we will encounter in connection with American federal statistics. The disclaimers typically introduce race and also (much later) ethnicity. Nearly always we will find that the disclaimer says how the terms should *not* be understood. But unlike nearly all of the later disclaimers, McSweeney and Safford also stated how the terms *should* be understood.

The instructions then provided a general classificatory rule.

Rule.
Whenever an immigrant does not clearly and unmistakably belong to an especially designated class or "Race," classify him with those of the same language or religion.

Generally, language would suffice; they had already explained that the addition of religion was used especially to distinguish Jews from others. But why was that useful for them? They knew that Yiddish was widely used among Jews. It is true that they may have wondered just *how* widely this was the case in the east. But to the extent that Jews spoke Russian or German or Polish rather than Yiddish, why not classify them with these other peoples? A similar point can be asked about the rule to define mother tongue as the language first spoken in the home. Thus the Czech who spoke German in Prague or Vienna was to be classified as Czech. The religion question in particular, but also the reliance on the language of earliest childhood, was meant to favor family origins over any later assimilation that might have occurred. But was it clear that this choice was the best one, given the rationale for the race question—that knowing race would help predict where immigrants would cluster in economic and geographical terms? Insofar as they thought about the degree to which groups underwent processes of assimilation within Europe itself, they seem to have opted for the choice to know about origins prior to such assimilation. Still, this choice carried them only as far back as the individual's birth. For example, whatever the Jewish origins their fathers had abandoned, Karl Marx would have been classified as German and Benjamin Disraeli as English under the instructions as to both religion and language.

What, then, of the color question: why was it included on a list created to handle the problem of distinguishing among European peoples from multinational empires? Notwithstanding the American obsession with skin color, the Passenger Lists had not included a color question. Presumably, the relatively small number of black immigrants and the 1882 Chinese Exclusion Act kept Congress from adding these questions to the Passenger Lists when Congress periodically revised the nineteenth-century immigration laws. The answer appears to be that McSweeney and Safford were indeed concerned with the Europeans from multinational empires, but the full committee that Powderly had charged with introducing the new data collection saw the worldwide nature of American immigration, even if it was almost entirely from Europe. The committee's June 26 report thus notes that it would eventually be necessary to confront the fact that the Chinese exclusion policy, which created "forbidden or undesirable classes," had not fully halted the arrival of Asian laborers. "Coolie labor" in the West Indies, Japan, or India will want to reach "the United States and once here, their low standards of living and willingness to work for almost nothing will be a constant menace to our workmen."[20]

Still another explanation for the color question was added later that summer in the instructions to clerks. The concern was African origin. And here the directions to coding clerks for the use of the color item seem entirely disconnected from the reasons given earlier for a race question: "The column of the manifest headed 'Color' is designed to secure racial distinctions which would not otherwise be apparent; and has special reference to the Negro race. All aliens clearly of Negro blood should be registered as 'black.'" In general, for color, "the five color designations of the races of mankind may be followed," that is, white, black, yellow, red, and brown. Only here is the meaning of race stated explicitly and exclusively in terms of physical characteristics and biological descent: color and blood. Thus the List indicates the many racial distinctions among Europeans. But the instruction goes on to clarify the purpose of the color question in terms of a broader sort of dividing line.

In sum, although the great majority of the racial categories on the List distinguished among Europeans, the "five color designations of the races" could not be ignored either—for at least two reasons. The first was the challenge of Asian "coolie labor" that might arrive from various lands. The second reason was the need to classify all arrivals "clearly of Negro blood" as black. This insistence to classify all those of African descent together will hardly seem surprising in the context of domestic racial distinctions, but no such distinction had been made on the earlier immigration questionnaires. In this context, it was a departure.

For classifying either Asian coolies or individuals with black blood, the color criterion for race trumped mother tongue or the other three answers on the supplemental form. Could this feature of the classification still be related to the economic explanation for the value of race data on immigrants? It seems likely that the color question and the instructions related to it did not in fact come from McSweeney and Safford, although there is no evidence that they protested the addition. They were probably reminded of broader national obsessions when they interacted with their fellow committee member Richard Campbell. He was a southern attorney then serving as assistant to the commissioner-general in Washington. Later, when he himself served as commissioner of naturalization, Campbell came to be known for his view that "off-color races [were] not only unfit but as well undesirable additions to the body politic."[21] It is possible that Safford and McSweeney accepted the use of the black-blood criterion as a realistic statement of how black immigrants would cluster in the light of residential and other forms of segregation. Nevertheless, they did not say so. Their silence, together with the presence of Campbell on the committee, suggests that the rule may not have been their preference.

The instructions to the coding clerks also refined the racial designation for the largest single immigrant group defined by country of origin, namely, Italians.

> Under the head of races, Italy is divided into Northern Italian and
> Southern Italian.
>
> Northern Italian includes the natives of the following "regioni":
> Tuscany, Emilia, Liguria, Venice, Lombardy, and Piedmont; also the
> people in other countries whose mother tongue is Italian.
>
> Southern Italian includes the natives of the remaining "regioni" of Italy
> and Sicily and Sardinia.

The idea that northern and southern Italians were of different races was
common at the time, but nonetheless it is worth pausing over its inclusion
here.[22] Like the argument about African blood, it did not appear in Safford or McSweeney's writing until they met in committee with Rodgers
and Campbell. But in the Italian case Safford and McSweeney might have
found the geographic divisions relevant to the industrial and labor distinctions that interested them. The northerners were much more likely to
have come from urban and industrial backgrounds and indeed to speak
different dialects that would make them somewhat likely to cluster as separate groups. Certainly this was the position McSweeney was to take
when he was challenged about some features of the List a year later.
During hearings of the 1899 Industrial Commission, he was asked about
the use of the use of religion and the Hebrew race category. He took the
opportunity of volunteering an explanation for the distinction among Italians as well. With Hebrews, religion helped in the identification; with Italians, it was region: "You will notice in this that we have differentiated as
between the Italians of the North and the South. We have not done this
because we wished to make any invidious distinctions or to throw any
aspersions on any race, but simply in order to get at these races industri-
ally as they come to this country."[23]

So began the List of Races. The crazy pace of preparation seemed preferable to losing a year of data collection. However, when viewed from the
perspective of many decades later, it is striking how much remained unchanged, or barely modified, for a half century. The use of the List was extended to other official contexts, and in time officials would defend it
against vehement criticism, not least as "the way the Bureau has worked
for some time."

Table 1. The List of Races and Peoples

African (black)
Armenian
Bohemian and Moravian
Bulgarian, Servian, and Montenegrin
Chinese
Croatian and Slovenian
Cuban
Dalmatian, Bosnian, and Herzegovinian
Dutch and Flemish
East Indian
English
Filipino
Finnish
French
German
Greek
Hebrew
Irish
Italian (north)
Italian (south)
Japanese
Korean
Lithuanian
Magyar
Mexican
Pacific Islander
Polish
Portuguese
Roumanian
Russian
Ruthenian (Russniak)
Scandinavian (Norwegians, Danes, and Swedes)
Scotch
Slovak
Spanish
Spanish-American
Syrian
Turkish
Welsh
West Indian
All other peoples

Source: U.S. Commissioner-General of Immigration, *Annual Report of the Commissioner-General of Immigration to the Secretary of Commerce and Labor for the Fiscal Year ended June 30, 1904* (Washington, DC: Government Printing Office, 1904), 20–21.

Presenting the New Classification Scheme to the Public

McSweeney and Safford's influence ended with the creation and implementation of the List. It was Terrence Powderly who wrote the initial texts that introduced the new classifications to the public; these were presented in the 1898 and 1899 *Annual Report of the United States Commissioner General of Immigration*.

Powderly's own views on immigrant races were more negative than those of Safford and McSweeney. And his race views tended to be justified by more than a concern with industrial concentrations of immigrants. Nearly a decade before his appointment as commissioner-general, Powderly had written in *The North American Review* (1888), "Whatever Know-Nothingism meant in former years, a man who advocates a restriction of immigration today is a patriot . . . [and not one whose opinions are based on] race hatred, prejudice or bigotry. . . . The population that came previous to 1860 was civilized and that which comes to-day is, in a great proportion semi-barbarous."

The large employers and steamship agents were bringing European surplus labor, men who would work for very low wages. In the end, Powderly argued, such laborers would undercut the American wage labor system. The economic argument is the strongest element in his essay. Similarly, he justified the Chinese Exclusion Act on economic grounds alone. The Chinese immigrant had been excluded "not because he did not behave himself, not because he was vicious or particularly bad, but because he interfered with the right of the American to earn his living." The new European immigrant was dangerous for the same reasons. And because he came without knowing English and with the intention of returning to Europe, he could not be expected to care about, let alone understand American republican institutions. The Knights of Labor sought to teach the worker in every land "that the right to enjoy life in the land of his birth is inherent in man." Powderly closed by arguing for the literacy requirement, a ban on premigration labor contracts, and a guarantee that arrivals came without a criminal record. Moreover, he believed that immigrants should be obliged to make a declaration of intent to immigrate three years before embarking. And upon arrival, he felt that they should make another declaration of their intent to become citizens.[24]

And so when it came time, at the end of the 1890s, for Powderly to introduce the List of Races in his *Reports,* we find a clear hint that the value of race data extends beyond industrial and geographic concentrations of immigrants: "With the beginning of the new fiscal year [July 1, 1898], there will be inaugurated a compilation of reports of immigration that will throw much additional light upon the subject . . . by race. . . . Such a distribution by race appears much more rational than the present one, which simply reports the countries whence the immigrants respectively come, and gives no clue to their characteristics and their resultant influence upon the community of which they are to become members."[25] And when he presented the first race data in the next annual *Report,* he elaborated on these themes. The multinational empires made classification by country of origin inadequate; consequently,

> in addition to showing the recent geographical or political origin of
> aliens who come to this country to settle, there is shown also the
> distinctive race to which they respectively belong, using the term "race" in
> its popular rather than in its strict ethnological sense; so that from an
> experience of the distinguishing occupations of each race, its moral,
> mental and physical characteristics, and their development under
> American institutions, a basis may be formed for estimating its effect. . . .
> From this aspect an Englishman does not lose his race characteristics by
> coming from South Africa, a German his by coming from France, or a
> Hebrew his though he come from any country on the globe.[26]

Powderly, too, like the committee that earlier wrote instructions to the coders, made the disclaimer that the race term was used in "its popular rather than in its strict ethnological sense." Nevertheless, he introduced a meaning that included "moral, mental and physical characteristics" that seem to go far beyond the interest in industrial characteristics that McSweeney and Safford had stressed.

Powderly and McSweeney presided over only the very first years of the List; the new president, Theodore Roosevelt, dismissed them both in 1901. Roosevelt cited inefficiency and, especially in McSweeney's case, hinted at corruption. Frank Sargent, yet another labor leader, replaced Powderly, but Roosevelt persuaded William Williams, an energetic patrician reformer with decidedly restrictionist sympathies, to run Ellis Island. He held the post for several years, and he would later be reappointed by President Taft (1909–1913).[27] The supplemental form survived its creators. Between July 1, 1899, and June 30, 1903, the form was in constant use, and the race classification of immigrants appeared in the *Annual Reports of the United States Commissioner-General of Immigration.*

The List of Races was not yet absolutely fixed. There were slight variations, mostly in connection with numerically marginal groups. Between 1899 and 1900, Albanian and Austrian were dropped as separate listings, and South American and Central American (two races in 1899) are replaced by Spanish American. Bulgarian, Servian, and Montenegran are aggregated into one group, and the Filipino group was added. Finally, while Magyar appears on the 1900 List, the year before both Magyar and Hungarian had been listed. In 1901 "Esquimaux," "Arabian," and "Swiss" make a brief appearance; in 1902 they are gone, as is "Hawaiian." Still more minor fluctuations betrayed other trivial uncertainties: Should groups be listed alphabetically, or should some marginal groups be listed at the end, and should similar groups be listed together? Should Korean be spelled with a K or a C?

Creative Ambiguities?

These shifts amounted to tinkering at the margins. A serious change concerned the title for the List: "Race or People" replaced "Race." Strangely, the reason for this modification was never explained in the *Reports,* nor has it been found in the archival record. Moreover, the *definition* of "people" and its relation to "race" was never given. In the 1899 *Report,* there was no mention whatever of "race or people." In the *Reports* of 1900 and 1901, some tables referred to "race or people," and others to "race" alone. Thus in 1899 Table V presented immigrants by "the countries whence they came and the races to which they belong," but in 1900 the same heading was phrased "the countries whence they came and the race or people to which they belong." And yet even in 1900, the discussion of that table in the *Report* refers only to "race." This is not a unique case; the choice to use "race" or "race or people" was often inconsistent within the same year for table titles, column headings, and discussion of the tables in the text. The title to Table VIII presented immigrant destinations in the United States by "race" for the first two years

(1899–1900) and by "race or people" thereafter. Yet in 1901, although the table's title had changed, the column heading for the groups remained as "race," and the text spoke simply of "races." Only from 1902 onward do both table title and column heading refer to "race or people." The discussion in the text would often refer only to "race" even many years later.[28] Finally, it appears that different parts of the report were handled by different offices at the bureau, or at any rate by different officials, so that the date at which one or another table shifts from "race" to "race or people" differs; columns in tables on immigrant health, for example, were still limited to "race" in 1903.[29]

What then was the significance of the shift from "race" to "race or people?" The most plausible explanation for the shift is a heightened terminological ambiguity. If someone disagreed that a given group—the Jews, for instance, or the Irish—constituted a race, he or she might accept the contention that the group formed a "people." It would be harder to criticize the List if its categories referred to either of two concepts rather than one only, particularly when both concepts remained undefined. All of this is conjecture, but a source written a few years later provides some supporting evidence. In December 1908, W. W. Husband, then secretary to the U.S. Immigration Commission, replied to an inquiry from one of the commission's members about the use of the List of Races and Peoples. "You will note that the words 'race or people' are used by the Commission. Let me explain that some . . . prefer the latter word and, as one suits the purpose quite as well as the other, both were included."[30]

The term "people" was occasionally used in ethnology at the time as well as more loosely. Thus Daniel G. Brinton, in his *Races and Peoples* (1890) discussed "Sub-Divisions of Races" (on the basis of geography, language, and government): "a *race* into its *branches*; a *branch* into its *stocks*; a *stock* into its *groups*, and these again into *tribes, peoples or nations*."[31] Nearly three decades later, in a letter to former President Theodore Roosevelt, the writer on immigrants and races, Madison Grant, used the term in a similar way. The Jews, Grant thought, were not an ancient, pure race with set physical features, but rather their characteristics were in the process of becoming permanently fixed. "I think we have here a people and not a race, that is a group of diverse origins with very marked and persistent secondary characteristics imposed on them through prolonged isolation."[32]

Thus usages for "people" might go beyond the common meaning of the term. These other usages nicely paralleled the common meaning of a group united by a common history of indeterminate length. Eventually the officials at the Bureau of Immigration entered into some contact with academic anthropologists, who might have suggested the additional term "people." Still, there is no direct evidence that bureau officials did in fact have the specific ethnological meaning in mind when they expanded the discussion from "race" to "race or people." And there is reason to suppose, as Husband's letter suggests, that the deeper motive for broadening the classification beyond the "race" term had to do with avoiding objections that could arise about classifying particular groups as races.

And yet, in the very years that the *presentation* of the List was being broadened beyond "race," the List finally received legal standing—but simply as a "race" item. In 1903, Congress issued a revision of the basic immigration laws. Among the little-noted changes in the new Immigration Act was the addition of "race" to the characteristics that were to be reported for each immigrant.[33] The modification went entirely unmentioned in the relevant congressional hearings and in the House and Senate discussions of the bill. Quite simply, part of the list of characteristics to be reported went from "nationality, residence" to "nationality, race, residence." With this change, Congress also threw the cloak of legality over the bureau's initiative in having collected race data over the five preceding years. The relatively few representatives and senators who were closely involved with immigration questions no doubt understood that in the context of the law, "race" referred to the List of Races—which by then was evolving into the List of Races and Peoples. These congressmen were, after all, already using the race data from the *Annual Reports* of 1899–1902 in their discussions.[34] The number of congressmen or bureaucrats who also understood that the act adjusted the legal status of the "race" item must have been very small indeed.

And so, beginning in 1903, Passenger List forms were printed with a new column. Over the next six decades that column on the forms was always headed "race or people," whereas all subsequent revisions of the Immigration Act continued to mandate a "race" (never "race or people") item. Whatever the immigrant "races"—nearly all European—meant to the legislators, no one seems to have found it valuable to make the terminology the same across bills and forms. It is true that precious few would have found the difference

consequential. And yet the bills before Congress were scrutinized by restrictionists and defenders of the immigrant as well as congressional aides
and immigration officials. It seems reasonable to conclude, as W. W. Husband had done in his 1908 letter, that using both terms with immigrants and
readers of reports seemed useful because some people liked one of these undefined terms, and some the other. But at the level of legislation the (undefined) "race" term was the one originally used, and the need never arose to
add the other, even for purposes of consistency with the forms. The forms,
after all, were seen by millions, and the uses of ambiguity were far greater
there. The list of items mandated for data collection in an obscure paragraph of a long bill was another matter altogether.

In any case, from 1903 on, "Race or People" appeared as an item on the
Passenger List form itself, while the supplemental form, with its five questions, was discontinued. The immigrant now answered the "Race or
People" question directly (rather than the five preliminary questions).
Prior to 1903, the decision about race seems to have been made by clerks
from the answers to the supplemental form's questions. It was after five
years of experience with the new system of self-reporting that W. W. Husband had written his abovementioned observation (in 1908) that some
immigrants preferred the term "race," whereas others preferred "people."

The Passenger List forms now included directions for filling out this item
at the bottom of the form. These directions would evolve in interesting ways
over the following decade, as we will observe later. In 1903 the instruction
read "Race or people—is to be determined by the stock from which they
sprang and the language they speak. List of races will be found on the
back of this sheet." "Race or People" was originally listed as one of two items
under a broader heading called "Nationality." The other item under that
heading was "Country." However, some reconceptualization was clearly in
progress, for after less than two years the form was changed slightly, and
"Race or People" was now listed under its own heading.[35] Thus the 1903 instructions now relied on only one of the five characteristics—language—
that had been listed on the supplemental form. But at the same time, a new
criterion had been added: "the stock from which they spring." "Stock" itself
was not defined.

Several innovations to the classification of races were undertaken at the
bureau in the years following the passage of the Immigration Act of 1903.

The instructions for answering the "Race or People" item on the Passenger List changed subtly, as did the presentation of the race data in the *Annual Report*. In 1906, an admonition was added:

> Column 9, (*Race or people*). . . . Special attention should be paid to the distinction between race and nationality, and manifests should be carefully revised by inspectors and registry clerks in this regard. For instance, "France" appearing on the manifest might not necessarily mean "French" by race or people, and similarly, "French" appearing on a manifest does not necessarily mean "France" by nationality. An alien who is Irish, German, or Hebrew by race might properly come under the heading of United Kingdom or any other country by nationality.

Nationality and race thus referred, respectively, to political membership and historical origins.

The instructions continued, "In this connection the following distinctions should be specially observed." The first four distinctions that followed involved the Cuban, West-Indian, and Spanish American races or peoples, and the "African (black)" race. The directions specifically exclude blacks from the three American categories. The fourth is defined as follows:

> AFRICAN (BLACK). "African (black)" refers to the African Negro, whether coming from Cuba, or other islands of the West Indies, North or South America, Europe, or Africa. Any alien whose appearance indicates an admixture of Negro blood should be classified under this heading.

Thus by 1906, the "color" instructions from the now-discarded supplemental form of 1898–1903 had reappeared explicitly in the instructions—the reference to "stock" apparently had been judged inadequate. Indeed, only one other distinction was noted for "special attention": northern versus southern Italians "and their descendants whether residing in Italy . . . or any other country." Most of the northern Italians "speak a Gallic dialect of the Italian language." Still, in the years to 1910, the instructions appear to indicate no fundamental change from those that McSweeney, Safford, and their colleagues had drawn up in 1898.

But if the instructions had become clearer in discussing color and stock, they skirted two threats to the intellectual constructions of race. First, how were persons of mixed origin to be classified? Surely there were more than a handful of such people among the European immigrants; what of their race or people? Yet only in connection with blacks and whites are persons of mixed origin discussed: drawing on a long American tradition, the instructions place any "admixture of Negro blood" in the "African" racial group. Other mixed origins are ignored.

Second, how are cultural change and assimilation to be incorporated into this scheme? The only hint that there may be a large issue lurking here is that the language and race are not perfectly coextensive. Language will usually be a good guide to racial origins, but apparently not perfectly so; if it were, there would be no need to mention stock. Indeed, if language were a perfect proxy for what was required, perhaps only mother tongue and not race need be ascertained. In practice, of course, the steamship officials completing the form would hardly have had the time or sensitivity to determine, for example, the race of a Jew or Czech who reported German as the mother tongue. In most cases, presumably, the official deferred to the immigrant's decision. In general, the proportion, if not the number, of immigrants with mixed origins or assimilated backgrounds may have been small. Only in connection with immigrants of African origins (most from the Caribbean) was there insistence about how mixture should be classified.

For a time there was also an effort to organize the race data in a manner ethnologists might find more meaningful. In particular, between 1904 and 1906, the forty or so "races and peoples" were classified under "grand divisions of race." These grand divisions should not be confused with "the five color races" that we encountered earlier. Here, the multiplicity of *European* "races" was being classified into broader and older racial types.

> More than 95 per cent of the immigration to this country comes from Europe. This European immigration may be separated by race into well-recognized divisions, which confirm more or less to geographical location. With the assistance of Prof. Otis T. Mason, Curator of Ethnology, National Museum, most of these races or peoples, or more properly subdivisions of race, coming from Europe have been groups into four grand divisions . . . Teutonic . . . Iberic . . . Celtic . . . Slavic.[36]

In this scheme, of the largest groups of immigrants, northern Italians were Celtic, southern Italians Iberic, and Hebrews were Slavic. This new scheme shows up in charts and summary tables, and it seems to be accepted for a few content areas of the *Report* (on populations of penal and charitable institutions, for example), but it is not included in the basic tables on immigrants by sex, age, country of origin, occupation, or destination. Still, the officials knew there was a science of racial classification; we have seen them repeatedly warn that their list was not built upon the science of ethnology. But now that the list was in operation, why not invite the ethnologists to offer suggestions, especially as to grouping (rather than altering) race categories?

But Otis Mason's organization of the categories into broader racial groupings made no practical difference, was used only in part of the reports, and was abandoned without comment after three years. Perhaps the only real impact of Mason's intervention was to reinforce in readers' minds the popular conception of a difference between the older and newer immigrants from northwestern and southeastern Europe, respectively. Thus even after the broader racial groupings had been abandoned, the 1908 *Report* informs the reader that "Until very recent times immigration was almost entirely from the Teutonic and Keltic countries … with a considerably greater proportion of the former. … However, now 66% of our immigration comes from the Slavic and Iberic countries."[37]

Whatever had led to the brief effort to sharpen the conceptual basis of the List, there was no particular bureaucratic gain to be had by relating its categories to Mason's broader groupings. Eventually, those who wished to generalize about immigration trends on the basis of *other* kinds of distinctions than Mason's would find it easy enough to aggregate the categories into broader groupings for themselves. Popular ways of doing so would be to distinguish between old and new or more and less desirable or (much later) Nordic and other immigrant groups.

CHAPTER 2

Immigration—Especially European— through the Lens of Race

WE CAN GET ONLY so far by analyzing the discussions of men like Safford and McSweeney if we want to understand the racial classification of immigrants. They had no reason to be fully explicit about the meaning of race in their work. And in any case, we have already encountered subtle differences in usage among the various federal officials involved in the List's early history. We can appreciate the usages better if we now step back from the history of the List to take in broader discussions of race, particularly as applied to immigration. Henry Cabot Lodge was among the most articulate and influential Americans to deal with race and immigration. In fact, he was the predominant U.S. senator to deal with the topic from the early 1890s until his death in 1924. Lodge's views on race had their idiosyncratic elements, but a great many themes important for him were shared by his contemporaries, even when they might disagree with his conclusions. Focusing on Lodge is therefore a useful way to introduce the key themes relevant to immigration and race.

Henry Cabot Lodge

Lodge was born in 1850 into the highest circle of the Boston Brahmins. He attended private schools and spent the Civil War years as a young teenager in a Republican anti-slavery home. He traveled in Europe for a year before entering Harvard, and for another before Harvard Law School, this time with his bride. In his last year as an undergraduate, he had been fascinated by a history course taught by Henry Adams, and so while doing the law degree, he also studied for a doctorate in history (among the very first Harvard bestowed), working under Adams on Anglo-Saxon law. Then he briefly taught history at Harvard and helped Adams edit the *North American Review*. But during these early years after finishing his studies, he also became active in politics (at Adams's suggestion).[1]

Lodge began his political career as part of a circle that regarded both major political parties with despair and contempt. President Grant's Republican Party was corrupt, and the Democrats were dominated by reactionary Southern interests on the one hand and Northern urban bosses on the other. Lodge became a leading young activist among those seeking a third way, and he had the brains, energy, connections, and economic security to stay the course. When the desire for creating a third party proved to be a pipe dream, Lodge campaigned as a Republican for the Massachusetts State House and entered it in 1878. By 1882 he was running for a seat in Congress; he won two election cycles later. Before that, he crossed an important line in 1884, when he had had to choose between supporting the Republican presidential candidate, whom he and many of his reform-oriented friends detested, and staying with an alternative candidate who would never win. By choosing the former path, he disgusted many of those former friends but also gained a lifelong reputation as a loyal and shrewd party member. He was, however, much more than a party hack; he did not shrink from public argument or fail to make principled claims for his positions. Lodge served as a congressman from 1886 to 1893, the year he entered the Senate. He remained in the upper house until his death in 1924.

Today, Lodge is remembered above all for his struggles with President Woodrow Wilson during and after World War I, and most especially over American participation in the League of Nations. However, Lodge also played a central role in the struggle for immigration restriction, particularly during the twenty-five years beginning in 1890. Our interest lies first in his concept of race and second in the way he marshaled racial classification for the analysis of immigration issues, especially European immigration. His explicit, articulate, and fulsome discussion provides a tour of the issues.

Lodge had been interested in the role race played in shaping character differences among peoples long before he championed immigration restriction policy. The race theme was already important to his doctoral research on Anglo-Saxons, if only as background. He published the dissertation research as a chapter in a volume of research by Henry Adams and three of his graduate students, *Essays in Anglo-Saxon Law.*[2] Each chapter in this volume painstakingly explored an aspect of law in the records of early England. And each was arranged to show that Anglo-Saxon law was similar to still-earlier laws in the parts of continental Europe from which the Anglo-Saxon groups had come—chiefly Denmark and Germany. The broader goal of such studies, as Adams wrote, was to follow "the slender thread of political and legal thought" back across two millennia to "the wide plains of northern Germany" where the popular assemblies "embraced every free man, rich or poor, and in theory at least allowed equal rights to all."[3] From these roots, via the Anglo-Saxons, came English Common law and English government, the British colonies of North America, and finally the liberties of the United States.

The authors believed in this loose way that racial traits lay behind the institutional development. Nevertheless, the belief was not required to shape the analysis; "race" is barely mentioned and all references to it can be read metaphorically. All that is necessary is a concept of institutional development over time. In a single paragraph, Adams mentions that there is no reason to try to follow institutional developments any further back in time than the authors do, namely, to origins in the Germanic tribes of early Europe. We know nothing of how "the Indo-European" people became distinct from others or whether the public assemblies could be traced any further back than the German branch of that people. "For all ordinary purposes of historical reasoning, the present division of Europe has existed from indefinite ages. The Germans have occupied the centre of Europe." And as to the law court in particular, he notes, "This popular assembly was the primitive law-court of the Germanic race."[4]

Lodge is nearly as terse on race in his own chapter. In England, "the purity of the race, the isolated condition of the country, and . . . tenacity of intellect" created a situation in which "the laws and institutions of the ancient German tribes flourished and waxed strong. . . . The great principles of Anglo-Saxon law, ever changing and assimilating, have survived in the noblest work of the race,—the English common law."[5] In a chapter of sixty-five pages, this is all he says about race. Adams very likely understood that their contribution neither required resolution of racial matters, nor could it add anything to such a resolution.

Two years later, however, in an anonymous book review, Lodge dealt with race and history much more directly than he had in the *Essays*. The Irish historian W. E. H. Lecky had chosen to arrange his *History of England in the 18th Century* in terms of the "permanent forces" of history rather than as a chronological narrative. Lodge applauded Lecky's idea since "these great social and political forces, when properly considered, . . . are what alone raise history from the level of annals to the rank of the sciences." Nevertheless, Lodge points out that Lecky ignores—or worse, dismisses—"a question which is one of the most important in the whole domain of history, that of differences of race."[6]

Lodge acknowledges that race alone does not explain what needs explaining, and that when racial arguments have been used crudely as "invectives against nations or classes," the arguments "are usually very shallow." Nevertheless, an historian who hopes to grasp "the causes which have made nations what they are," without considering "the fundamental cause of difference of race, is in danger of offering conclusions on very inadequate grounds." In the familiar contrast of England and Ireland, for example,

> War, conquest, and religious strife may leave lasting traces, but none of them singly, nor all together, have thus far succeeded in obliterating or creating great national characteristics. There are some qualities which are inherent in races from the time when they emerge into the light of history. One great cause of England's failure and Ireland's misfortunes is to be found in the fact that, to put it as civilly as possible, Irishmen are not Englishmen, and to this fact Mr. Lecky apparently attaches little or no weight.[7]

The second term Lodge uses is especially striking: no other factors "have thus far succeeded in obliterating *or creating* [emphasis added] great national characteristics." Such characteristics, it seems, developed *only* from differences "inherent in races from the time when they emerge into the light of history." To discuss these things honestly requires belittling some races in comparison to others, and thus he writes "to put it as civilly as possible,

Irishmen are not Englishmen." Is Lodge ranking races according to a single absolute scale? Or might he retort that each race has its distinctive strengths, with, for example, Celtic emotion balancing Anglo-Saxon stolidity? Either way, his claim that the Irish lacked the traits needed to avoid the tragedies of their history is a strong indictment.

Finally, were not the Scots, too, like the Irish, part of the Celtic race? Why then does Scottish history follow a pattern so much closer to English rather than Irish development? "The lowland Scotch, who made Scotland what she is, and saved her from the fate of Ireland, were of Teutonic blood."[8]

The Lecky review allows us to interpret with more confidence than we otherwise could Lodge's earlier stray comments on race in *Essays in Anglo-Saxon Law.* We already noted that the chapter is at least consistent with a strong role for race; it now appears likely that he believed in permanent differences among races when he wrote it. Are these differences in character preserved and transmitted through the physical (biological) in man? He does in fact speak of "Teutonic blood" in the Lecky review (albeit only once). And it is difficult to understand what outside the province of biology would yield differences that were as permanent as those he describes. But in the final analysis, it does not much matter how Lodge thought the transmission over many generations occurred. The permanence of group character and the paramount influence of group differences in character for social outcomes typically give arguments about race their power. How the racial transmission is preserved across generations matters much less in defining a theory as racial. Recall, finally, that Lodge is discussing this fixity of character differences across *European* races. Whatever he thought of character differences between Europeans and others, the race differences in character among Europeans themselves were very real indeed.

The Lecky review demonstrates that he strongly believed in virtually permanent character differences among races many years before he called for immigration restriction. Still, the Lecky review concerns differences between two peoples, two complete societies, each living in their in own territory. The case of immigration, by contrast, involves individuals who leave one society and join another. Comparing England to Ireland may make it easier to stress unbridgeable gulfs than thinking, for example, about Irish immigrants in Boston. In the context of immigration, eventual assimilation into the mainstream of the host culture might appear likely. Moreover, Lodge would also need to consider the physical mixture of biological legacies that occurs with intermarriage, for example, between the descendants of Celts and Anglo-Saxons in Boston. For both reasons, Lodge could still have been open to positions on immigration that leave room for greater accommodation of peoples over time than the comments of the Lecky review might at first suggest.

The last of Lodge's relevant early statements was also published anonymously, this time in the *Atlantic Monthly* only a few months after the Lecky review. In this piece, his concern is a republic that rests on universal suffrage when large numbers of voters are ignorant. Can freedom survive such a situation? It is true that "no other people ever displayed political talents of so high an order as that derived from the Anglo-Saxon stock." And no other political system "has produced on the whole so great an amount of human happiness and well-being" as found in America. But widespread ignorance among the electorate can bring down past successes.

> Everyone concedes, that the safety of our system rests upon education. . . .
> No doubt if education reached every man in the community, or even a
> very large majority of men, all would be well. But it does not. There is a
> dangerous amount of ignorance on the part of those who hold sovereign
> power in the United States. Education can remedy it, and may ultimately
> do so, but a long time must elapse before this state of affairs can be
> brought about. Meanwhile, this ignorance is lowering the tone of public
> life and the character of our public men, and threatens the safety of our
> whole *system*.[9]

That Lodge, a self-conscious heir to Massachusetts Whig reformers, would be a believer in the value of education is no surprise. The more novel point is that education may not be enough to ensure a wise electorate (even if it may have been enough to do so in the early republic). Later in the article, he proposed preserving the universal franchise but limiting its effect. For example, voters could be restricted to deciding only on their representatives rather than on every issue that comes up. And longer terms for representatives could restrict bad decisions, because annual terms tended to favor whims of brief staying power. But our interest lies in his analysis of the *sources* of voter ignorance. Among these are urbanization, industrialization, and related social changes that made it harder for the schools to reach everyone. Other sources of voter ignorance have a racial dimension: "We have received and undertaken to absorb an almost unlimited immigration of adult foreigners, largely illiterate, of the lowest class and of other races. We have added at one stroke four millions and more of ignorant negroes to our voting population in the South."[10]

Lodge unquestionably believed education could do some good, but its reach had limits. One limit was age: typically adults will not go to school to reduce their ignorance, whether black or white, native or foreign born. But clearly the threat of an unreliable electorate was especially great among "foreigners, largely illiterate, of the lowest class and of other races" and "ignorant negroes." On the one hand there were the principles of self-government that only an intelligent electorate could be expected to uphold and on the other was the inclusion into the electorate of large groups that did not qualify as intelligent, at least in the present generation, and perhaps beyond that. One partial solution was education; another was to tinker with electoral processes without erasing the principle of self-government. In all this Lodge gave articulate expression to anxieties about the vote during the late 1870s, and to solutions proposed, which have been ably described by historian Alexander Keyssar.[11] A dozen years later, having given up his academic post and his editorial work for Congress, Lodge would return to similar considerations as a reason for imposing a literacy restriction on immigrants.

During his first two terms in Congress, Lodge concerned himself with a variety of other matters: civil service reform, the tariff, copyright law, and the affairs of the national Republican Party. Then, in 1890, he championed an election reform bill—"The 1890 Force Bill" ("The Lodge Bill")—that engaged intense passions and gave him national attention. This measure would have required federal enforcement of voting rights in elections for federal office. Big-city urban political machines in the North would have been affected had the bill passed. But clearly the most important target of the bill was the near-total restrictions in the South on black suffrage. The bill did eventually pass in the House but died in the Senate.

A loyal Republican Party man like Lodge had plenty of self-interested reasons for promoting his election bill. In particular, exclusion of blacks from the Southern polls meant far fewer votes in that region for the party of Lincoln. But when it came to determining the number of congressional representatives from each state, the disfranchised blacks did count, equally with whites. Together, these arrangements weakened Republican prospects on all national issues. Yet Lodge surely had reasons to believe in the justness and constitutional importance of his bill.[12] Whatever he may have thought about the long-term potential of African Americans as citizens, their right to vote had to be protected. Any contradictions we might perceive between his notion of permanent race differences and protecting the black franchise were contradictions he believed had been built into the American historical record.

> The Negroes in the United States did not come here by any will or action of their own. They did not seek to force themselves upon us as the Chinese, whom we have excluded, tried to do. They were brought here by force under circumstances of hideous cruelty. They were held in bondage and ignorance.... [Now, with slavery destroyed,] [w]e have clothed them with the attributes of American citizenship. We have put in their hands the emblem of American sovereignty. Whether wisely or unwisely done is of no consequence now; it has been done and it is irrevocable.... No people can afford to write anything into their Constitution and not sustain it.[13]

Moreover, he contemptuously dismissed the Southern claim that black ignorance was a justification for disfranchisement. "It is a mere pretense to talk about the 'rule of an inferior race,' of 'organized barbarism.'" Only a small proportion of the seats in the national government would be determined by the black vote. Further, states were free to bar ignorant citizens from voting.

> The qualifications of a voter is left to the States. If any State thinks that any class of citizens is unfit to vote through ignorance, it can disqualify them from voting.... It has but to put an educational qualification into its constitution. But the disqualification ... cannot recognize color, and that is the reason that legal methods have never been tried [in the South].[14]

And again, a few weeks later, when a Southerner wrote to make the argument about black ignorance, Lodge replied,

Nothing in this bill or any other prevents a state from excluding ignorance from the suffrage. Massachusetts has an educational test. South Carolina can do the same, but will not because she wishes to exclude black ignorance and let white ignorance vote.[15]

Lodge's contempt for the pretense that Negro ignorance made Southern disfranchisement necessary was all the greater because he knew very well that illiteracy among native-born *whites* had always been far higher in the South than in any other region of the United States. By contrast, illiteracy among the native born in Massachusetts was negligible. How intensely he felt about all this is brought home in a confrontation that peaked with a speech he made to the House on January 13, 1891. He was replying to a snide reference to him as "The Oscar Wilde of American Statesmanship." The phrase, Lodge observed, was a euphemism for "effeminate." That "accusation ... is a view which is naturally taken of a higher civilization by a lower one. It is the view which would naturally be taken of the civilization of the public school by the civilization of the shotgun." He concluded by reminding the House which civilization had won the Civil War.[16]

At the same time, when Lodge wrote to his correspondent in South Carolina that "Massachusetts has an educational test," he was referring to a law that had been passed by the "Know-Nothing" nativist state governments of the late 1850s to suppress the new Irish immigrants from voting. Keyssar describes how the same legislature had also imposed a two-year waiting period before newly naturalized citizens could vote (and it nearly succeeded in imposing a much longer waiting period). While the waiting period for naturalized voters was abolished by the Radical Republicans during the Civil War, the education test remained in effect and was renewed with only minor modification in 1892.[17] Thus Lodge's thought reflected something of the legacy of Know-Nothing nativism as well as that of Radical Republicanism. Clearly, Lodge would have vigorously rejected any similarity between the restriction of the franchise in 1850s Massachusetts and 1890s South Carolina. It was perfectly reasonable for Massachusetts to deny the franchise to *all* illiterates, who overwhelmingly were Irish immigrants; it was quite another matter for South Carolina to deny the franchise to ignorant blacks, but not whites. Moreover, as already mentioned, Lodge readily admitted a fear of ignorant voters no matter what their origins. Still, in the face of Lodge's righteous reply to the his correspondent from South Carolina, it is worth appreciating that the literacy restriction was an easy way for nativists in the Massachusetts legislatures of the 1850s and after to deal with distrust of Irish voters, given virtually universal literacy among the native born.[18]

The dangers of an ignorant electorate, education's role in human progress, race differences in character and the uncertainties of racial assimilation, the need to respect constitutional protections for Southern freedmen, and mechanisms for restricting without destroying principles of self-government—Lodge was thinking about all of these at the end of 1890. The first session of the 51st Congress, during which he fought for the election bill, ended on October 1, with the bill stalled in the Senate. Two months after that, on the first day of the Congress's second session, Lodge submitted his first bill for immigration restriction. His bill seems to have been the first in the history of Congress to call for a literacy requirement.[19] Like the black franchise, the political participation of immigrants from alien races raised big problems. And like the schooling of the freedman and his children, schooling of immigrant children was essential. "The [immigrant] children who come here, of course, have the advantage of the public schools. . . . It is possible to educate them and to bring them up and make them American citizens very easily."[20] Broader assimilatory processes would be at work too.[21]

If education could help assimilate the children of immigrants, immigration restriction could do still more. Just as it was wise and just to bar illiterate citizens from the franchise, federal legislation could bar illiterate foreigners from the United States. Viewed in this way, the issues Lodge worked on at the time had considerable coherence and consistency, especially the support for the black franchise in the Force Bill fight and the literacy requirement for immigration restriction.[22] Indeed, during the fight for the Force Bill, he seems to have also been gathering the data for an article on "The Distribution of Ability in the United States" that related accomplishments to old-stock origins. The article was published in September 1891, when Lodge was already fully associated with the bill to restrict immigration by literacy.[23]

Although Lodge was the first in Congress to propose restricting immigration by literacy, others had been suggesting the idea in print for some years. The shifting composition of the immigration stream was becoming a familiar topic by the late 1880s. And its relation to unrest among the poor, especially labor unrest, did not go unnoticed. Then, in 1888, the American Economics Association offered a prize for the best proposal for immigration restriction, and Edward Bemis won with a proposal for a literacy requirement.[24] Lodge, of course, was no economist, but it is unlikely that he missed Bemis's new proposal; indeed, it appeared in print that same year (March 1888) in *The Andover Review*—a journal subtitled "*A Religious and Theological Monthly.*" There Bemis observed that a literacy requirement "has hardly been considered as yet. In fact, this may be for aught I know, the first public advocacy of it."[25]

By the end of 1890 Lodge had no doubt immigration needed some form of restriction. The immigration situation involved many dangers that could be phrased without reference to race, and Lodge never ignored those. On some occasions he stressed *only* the nonracial aspects of the issue. Fast, safe, and relatively cheap steamships had made immigration much easier than it had once been. And for their part, the steamship companies unscrupulously encouraged anyone to become an immigrant. No longer was there a self-selection by sturdy stock. An especially grim consequence was the rise of undesirable types: criminals, the insane, or feeble-minded, and violent far-left revolutionary elements.

But the gravest practical problem was the threat to American wages. Low-wage unskilled immigrant workers would drive down wages throughout the American working class. That wage decline would be more than a humanitarian catastrophe; the ensuing social inequality would threaten meaningful popular sovereignty. The desperately poor could not educate themselves or their children and could not therefore be safe holders of the franchise. "I am utterly opposed to a system which is continually dragging down the wages of American labor by the introduction of the cheapest, lowest, and most ignorant labor of other countries," Lodge wrote.[26]

Other spokesmen were to give this broad argument about immigration and wage levels a racial twist. Thus Francis Walker, former director of the U.S. census and president of MIT, developed a theory of "race suicide" (which was a great concern of Theodore Roosevelt as well): declining wages would not influence foreign workers who were used to terrible poverty. But the old-stock American workers would curtail fertility in order to preserve a decent standard of living for themselves and their children. The result would be their inexorable demographic decline.[27]

The unskilled immigrants also tended to settle in the great cities. There, Lodge stressed, they created slums, poverty, crime, and disease. All these ills became a drain on the public coffers. Finally, cheap transatlantic transport meant that workers might come to the United States for a season or two and then return with savings to Europe. These "birds of passage" were not going to be future citizens; as short-term migrants in low-skilled work, they were mostly young and ignorant adult men, who created disorder.[28]

By the end of 1890, then, Lodge had begun speaking of the many justifications for immigration restriction that could be explained without reference to racial concepts. At the same time, his very first remarks in favor of restriction in the House (in February 1891) show that he was also well on the way to analyzing the immigration issue through the lens of race.

> The immigration of people of those races which contributed to the settlement and development of the United States is declining in comparison with that of races far removed in thought and speech and blood from the men who made this country what it is. . . . We now have before us race problems that are sufficient to tax to the utmost the fortunate conditions with which nature has blessed us and the highest wisdom to which our public men are capable. I do not, for one, desire to see these race problems multiplied or complicated. I do not want to see the quality of American citizenship decline beneath the effects of unrestricted immigration.[29]

This emphasis on race differences in human character was entirely consistent with his earliest writings in the 1870s, as we have seen. The literacy restriction might still prove to be the best means to restrict immigration because the association between illiteracy and immigrant racial origin was strong. But the argument that literacy would effectively sift immigrant racial origins relied less on intrinsic connections among illiteracy, ignorance, and threats to self-government and more on the coincident prevalence of illiteracy among new immigrant races. In this respect, Lodge's proposed literacy requirement for immigration was reminiscent of the literacy requirement for voting that mid-nineteenth-century Massachusetts elites had imposed and that operated against Irish immigrants.

Lodge made his most important statement about the racial implications of immigration as chairman of the Senate Immigration Committee (March 16, 1896). The occasion was the presentation to the Senate of the bill for the literacy requirement that his committee had approved. Eventually, this bill would pass both houses of Congress. President Cleveland vetoed the bill, and while the House overrode the veto, the restrictionists in the Senate failed to marshal the votes to override. In sum, Lodge gave the 1896 speech from an important perch about a popular cause, and he no doubt wanted to make his case as fully and clearly as possible. And the speech did draw attention. The *New York Times* gave it extensive coverage, and a few days later Theodore Roosevelt wrote to Lodge, "That was an A-1 speech of yours on immigration."[30] Lodge would later have it reprinted in collections of his writings.

The first third of this speech reviewed the arguments for restriction that had nothing to do with race (i.e., the arguments just summarized). Also, he explained his preference for the literacy requirement as the means for restriction. He sometimes argued that the literacy requirement was preferable to a head tax because it did not rely on economic differences among immigrants: "This is a fair test, based on intelligence, and not money."[31] He must have understood that access to education in Europe was related to economic well-being, and that therefore literacy did in fact rest in part on "money." He never seems to have addressed this objection; perhaps he would have defended his position by noting that literacy might rest in part, but a head tax rested entirely on money. In any case, in the 1896 Senate speech, he did not bother to justify the literacy requirement as a "fair test" but turned immediately to the impact that the requirement would have.

> It will bear most heavily upon the Italians, Russians, Poles, Hungarians, Greeks, and Asiatics, and very lightly, or not at all, upon English-speaking emigrants, or Germans, Scandinavians, and French. In other words, the races most affected by the illiteracy test are those whose emigration to this country has begun within the last twenty years and swelled rapidly to enormous proportions, races with which the English-speaking people have never hitherto assimilated, and who are most alien to the great body of the people of the United States.

The remainder of this long speech—fully two-thirds of the whole—deals exclusively with the significance of racial differences to the immigration issue. Lodge justified the focus this way.

> The injury of unrestricted immigration to American wages and American standards of living is sufficiently plain and is bad enough, but the danger which this immigration threatens to the quality of our citizenship is far worse. . . . To determine this question we must look into the history of our race.[32]

Lodge first introduced the concept of "historical races" as opposed to "a race of original purity."

> There is no such thing as a race of original purity according to the divisions of ethnical science. In considering the practical problems of the present time we can deal only with artificial races,—that is, races like the English-speaking people, the French, or the Germans,—who have been developed as races by the operation during a long period of time of climatic influences, wars, migrations, conquests, and industrial development. To the philologist and the ethnologist it is of great importance to determine the ethnical divisions of mankind in the earliest historic times. To the scientific modern historian, to the student of social phenomena, and to the statesman alike, the early ethnic divisions are of little consequence; but the sharply marked race divisions which have been gradually developed by the conditions and events of the last thousand years are absolutely vital. It is by these conditions and events that the races or nations which to-day govern the world have been produced, and it is their characteristics which it is important for us to understand.[33]

In the Lecky review Lodge had emphasized the theme of racial permanence: the extent to which races have remained unchanged through historical time. In the 1896 speech he focused on the mixing of ancient racial qualities that occurs when different peoples have been thrown together by invasions or other migrations. His views may have changed somewhat in the dozen years between the two statements. Indeed, his views may have shifted somewhat during the course of the year preceding the speech. During that year he absorbed the work of Gustave Le Bon, which he discussed at length later in the speech. But the conceptions of racial evolution with which he was concerned were sufficiently vague—particularly as to time frame—to accommodate shifts in emphasis. Thus we may well ask, when did racial traits related to social and mental life become fixed? One answer would pertain to the "races of original purity"—the subject of ethnical science (and of philology, since Lodge was somewhat out of date in continuing to base race on language divisions). For such ancient races, the answer would be very far back indeed—long before any written record. But those races have long since blended and were of no interest to him anyway. It was, rather, "artificial" or "historical" races that concerned him; for these races, the formative time frame is very much shorter—historical rather than prehistoric or zoological.[34] The historical period had not yet been long enough, nor peoples of different character sufficiently isolated from each other to permit fixed characteristics to emerge among most peoples of the world, but such fixity of character had nonetheless already developed in a few cases, notably among the English. Lodge spoke of permanence without specifying exactly how fixed the characteristics are or how long a past is required to create permanence. This ambiguity will appear again later in the speech. In any case, where migrations and conquest involved people of similar early origins, and when these events ceased far enough back in historical time, modern historical races were most fixed in character. And note too that these historical races conform to a considerable extent with modern nations—"the races or nations which to-day govern the world."

These were Lodge's answers to two questions that were always at least implicit in racial analysis: the temporal connection between races in the prehistoric world and races today, and the spatial connection between peoples who might best be considered of one race but who were divided today among political states, languages, or religions.

"How, then, has the English-speaking race, which to-day controls so large a part of the earth's surface, been formed?"[35] His answer was hardly new; it called attention to the same racial processes that lay behind the evolution of laws and institutions that he and Adams had studied in *Essays in Anglo-Saxon Law*. Celts had prevailed on the Island of Great Britain in pre-Roman times. The Romans came, conquered, and eventually weakened. Then began the important part of the narrative. Teutonic tribes gained a foothold and eventually control of most of the island; these tribes became the Saxons. Another Germanic wave, this time from Denmark, followed later. Finally, in 1066 came the Normans, but these "were not Frenchmen. As Carlyle says, they were only Saxons who spoke French"; their own ancestors had emerged "out of the Germanic forests."[36] In sum, the post-Roman invaders, the Saxons, Danes, and Normans, "were all one people. They had different names and spoke differing dialects, but their blood and their characteristics were the same. And so this Germanic people of one blood, coming through various channels, lived in England." Moreover, they succeeded in "assimilating more or less and absorbing to a greater or less degree their neighbors of the northern and western Celtic fringe."[37] Notice that the tale involves narratives of three past eras. Most recent, if still pre-English, is the melding in Great Britain of three waves of invading Germanic peoples (Saxon, Dane, Norman). Further back in time, there had been Germanic people of north-central Europe living in ways described briefly in Tacitus. But even these were not the "races of original purity" in which the ethnologist is interested. How had the German branch separated from earlier "Indo-European" people, and did the former already maintain public assemblies and other seeds of liberty? We do not and need not know. As we have seen, Adams had dismissed the question, "For all ordinary purposes of historical reasoning, the present division of Europe has existed from indefinite ages. The Germans have occupied the centre of Europe." And so, too, in Lodge's speech: ancient German tribes were not the Anglo-Saxon people of his own time, but neither were they the "races of original purity."

The key point about English (and American) history for Lodge is that these not-too-diverse Germanic invasions ceased with the Normans more than nine centuries ago. Since then, "these people [in Great Britain] were welded together and had made a new speech and a new race, with strong and well-defined qualities, both mental and moral." By Shakespeare's time, this process was complete, with a culture of "individual conscience" and "intelligence its handmaid. . . . The making of the English people was complete, and . . . they were entering upon their career of world conquest."[38] Lodge had learned the importance of the Germanic origins insights from Anglo-Saxon studies. He melded it to Le Bon's claim that most modern peoples ("nations," "historical races") had not enjoyed centuries without racial mixing. And so the fixity of mental characteristics among the English was virtually unique, at least among the world's powerful peoples. He wrote, "Most of the historic races of Europe are still in process of formation. The English alone represent a race almost entirely fixed."[39]

What constitutes the fixed nature of the English? Again, Lodge could draw on Le Bon ("a disinterested witness of another race and another language"): among the English, a dominating, conquering ethos melded with qualities of self-control and stern morality that would be productive of stable governmental institutions. "[Great] will power . . . unconquerable energy, a very great initiative, an absolute empire over self, a sentiment of independence pushed even to excessive unsociability, a puissant activity, very keen religious sentiments, a very fixed morality, a very clear idea of duty."[40]

It was from this origin that the settlers of Virginia and New England had come. At about the same time, the Dutch settled the New York area and the Swedes the Delaware: "Both, be it remembered, were of the same original race stock as the English settlers." Later came the Scotch Irish, the Germans, and the French Huguenots. "It will be observed that, with the exception of the Huguenot French, who formed but a small percentage of the total population, the people of the thirteen colonies were all of the same original race stocks." And finally, during the nineteenth century "down to 1875, there have been three large migrations to this country in addition to the always steady stream from Great Britain"—that of the Irish, German, and Scandinavians. The latter two were clearly of Teutonic stock in the thinking of the day.

But how was Lodge to deal with the giant wave of mid-century Irish immigrants? The people who fled the Irish famine and those who had followed since, after all, had been a desperately impoverished rural folk, vastly different from the New England Yankees (not least in their Catholicism). Their arrival had been traumatic for the older stock as well as for the Irish immigrants themselves, and mid-century nativism had been the result. Lodge knew this history very well and had in fact lived through it in his childhood. Recall too how Lodge had earlier used the difference between Irish and English character in the Lecky review, stressing "as civilly as possible" the race differences between them. Now however, their connections appear in much rosier terms: "The Irish, although of a different race stock originally, have been closely associated with the English-speaking people for nearly a thousand years. They speak the same language, and during that long period the two races have lived side by side, and to some extent intermarried."[41]

Surely Lodge was treating the realities of the Irish immigration selectively to make his point—and to avoid offending the many Irish-American voters of Massachusetts. Still, he would probably have retorted that however traumatic the coming of the Irish may have seemed at midcentury, from the vantage point of 1896, the accommodation of children and grandchildren of the Irish famine was becoming a fact of life. Moreover, he meant to show that the present threat of new peoples was much greater than that of the Irish had been. The peoples now arriving—"Russians, Hungarians, Poles, Bohemians, Italians, Greeks, and Asiatics"—were "never hitherto assimilated or brought in contact [with older-stock Americans]."

Thus Lodge claimed that Europeans who migrated to the thirteen colonies and later to the United States had come—prior to his own time—either from the British fixed race or from related Germanic racial origins: "It being admitted, therefore, that a historic race of fixed type has been developed, it remains to consider what this means, what a race is, and what a change would portend."[42]

> That which identifies a race and sets it apart from others is not to be found merely or ultimately in its physical appearance, its institutions, its laws, its literature, or even its language. These are in the last analysis only the expression or the evidence of race. . . . You can take a Hindoo and give him the highest education the world can afford. He has a keen intelligence. He will absorb the learning of Oxford, he will acquire the manners and habits of England, he will sit in the British Parliament, but you cannot make him an Englishman. Yet he, like his conqueror, is of the great Indo-European family. But it has taken six thousand years and more to create the differences which exist between them. You cannot efface those differences thus made, by education in a single life, because they do not rest upon the intellect. What, then, is the matter of race which separates the Englishman from the Hindoo and the American from the Indian? It is something deeper and more fundamental than anything which concerns the intellect. We all know it instinctively,

although it is so impalpable that we can scarcely define it, and yet is so deeply marked that even the physiological differences between the Negro, the Mongol, and the Caucasian are not more persistent or more obvious.[43]

There are several remarkable features about Lodge's reliance on the contrast between "Hindoo" and Englishman. The first is the decision to contrast the English not with one of the European immigrant peoples now immigrating in large numbers—but with that Hindoo. After all, Lodge had described the groups upon whom the literacy restriction would fall heavily as "Italians, Russians, Poles, Hungarians, Greeks, and Asiatics." Why not compare the English to the gigantic numbers of arriving Italians, Russians, Poles, Hungarians, or Greeks? And for that matter, if a comparison to Asians was in order, why to Hindoos in particular? A relatively small number of Asian immigrants were arriving in the period of the speech (about 30,000 since 1890), but among these, the number of Hindoo arrivals had never even reached sixty over the course of a year.[44] Part of the reason Lodge chose the Hindoo example can be found in his twin observations that "you cannot make him an Englishman. Yet he, like his conqueror, is of the great Indo-European family." The Hindoo, then, is a very special kind of Asian. He is part of the broad "family" of Indo-European, or Caucasian people; from these (according to the theories that were then common) had also descended white Europeans. On the one hand, had Lodge chosen a more distant "Asiatic," he would have been open to the criticism that the differences about which he was anxious only distinguish Asian from European and that restriction need not be imposed on Europeans. On the other hand, had Lodge chosen one of the European groups—Italians, Russians, Poles, Hungarian, or Greeks—with which to contrast the Englishman, he would have had a harder time making the case that formal schooling and informal cultural processes could not, even over two or three generations, bring the assimilation of these new peoples to older-stock Americans. These European immigrants were closer phenotypically and geographically to the Teutonic peoples than they were to the Hindoo, and while few were Protestants, most were Christian, and the rest (Jews) part of the monotheistic origins of Western civilization. In fact, three of the groups—Greeks, Italians, and Jews—were famously known as founders of that civilization (as opponents of immigration restriction never tired of pointing out). By choosing the Hindoo, then, Lodge was having it both ways: he was taking the most extreme example he could find among the immigrating peoples that would still allow him to claim a common racial substratum, at least at the very broadest level. Of course, to claim that commonality was to delve much further back into racial history than Lodge's "historical races" of modern history, further than Henry Adams had thought possible for any historical study. And hence the sense of his last observations, that the differences between Hindoo and Englishman, "is so deeply marked that even the physiological differences between the Negro, the Mongol, and the Caucasian are not more persistent or more obvious." The Hindoo and Englishman are both Caucasians, but the differences between them are nevertheless as great as the physiological differences among the color races, the categories of which include the most distant races in the world.

The second remarkable feature about the passage about Hindoo and Englishman is that "it has taken six thousand years and more to create the differences . . . between them. You cannot efface those differences . . . by education in a single life." Here again, note that appeals to racial difference operate across a dizzying range of time frames. In the present instance, Lodge stresses a difference that developed not over the nine centuries of European life (as did the creation of the English people), but across six millenniums. Still, after that forceful emphasis on such a long development, Lodge seems surprisingly cautious in concluding only that the outcome cannot be effaced by education "in a single life." Can we conclude, for instance, that the differences might be effaced over the course of the Oxford Hindoo's *son's* lifetime? Or his *grandson's*? Lodge never addressed this question. He was concerned about the near-term and concerned to emphasize deep-seated race differences. Indeed, he sounds much like a romantic describing mysterious natural forces.

> When we speak of a race . . . we mean the moral and intellectual characters, which in their association make the soul of a race. . . . The men of
> each race possess an indestructible stock of ideas, traditions, sentiments,
> modes of thought, an unconscious inheritance from their ancestors,
> upon which argument has no effect. . . . These are the qualities which

determine their social efficiency as a people, which make one race rise and another fall, . . . about which we cannot argue, but in which we blindly believe.[45]

Yet he sounds less like a romantic appealing to the mysterious when he bases the difference in biology.

> There is only one way in which you can lower those qualities or weaken those characteristics, and that is by breeding them out. If a lower race mixes with a higher in sufficient numbers, history teaches us that the lower race will prevail. The lower race will absorb the higher, not the higher the lower, when the two strains approach equality in numbers. In other words, there is a limit to the capacity of any race for assimilating and elevating an inferior race; and when you begin to pour in in unlimited numbers people of alien or lower races of less social efficiency and less moral force, you are running the most frightful risk that a people can run.[46]

The intangibles of race can be lost by "breeding them out"; even the racial fixedness of English origins cannot survive too much of that. There are limits to the "capacity of any race for assimilating and elevating an inferior race." But here too, it is important to notice that the formulations do not quite address the key questions of long-term assimilative capacity. Lodge acknowledges the capacity to assimilate and elevate inferior races, but it is a question of magnitudes, of proportions of new versus old stock. The most striking point is that Lodge seems to acknowledge that very generous infusions of other races can in fact be absorbed before the limits to successful assimilation are reached. The problem seems to be "when the two strains approach equality in numbers." Presumably he would have hurried to explain that equality of numbers in the great eastern cities alone would have been enough to threaten the unity of the republic.

In sum, Lodge recognized that formal education and informal assimilation of the dominant culture can do some good, even if they do not transform the core of racial difference "in a single life." Whether they can effect such a transformation in the course of two or three lifetimes, without the added influence of intermarriage ("breeding"), Lodge did not say—but would probably have denied. He had noted that some intermarriage was already occurring among the descendants of the Irish famine and the Yankees. Such an interbreeding could be terribly dangerous if the races are radically different or if the proportions of the inferior race approach those of the absorbing superior one. But such a formulation leaves some room for successful absorption if policy manages the magnitudes.

These issues rarely receive such explicit attention in the context of federal debates. And to anticipate, later racial restrictionists had far less hope for successful assimilation than Lodge acknowledged. In particular, Madison Grant and his associates after World War I believed that the interbreeding of superior and inferior races led quite uniformly to lower-level offspring.[47] Thus every individual of inferior stock was a danger to the republic, and a danger especially in the long run when social assimilation would lead to interbreeding.

Against this background, we can understand why Lodge came up with a form of restriction (the literacy requirement) that would only trim rather than cut off immigration from the alien races, and why he was so dedicated to an educational test as the mechanism for restrictionist policy. We can, in other words, understand Lodge's position without claiming that he acted simply as a cynical politician seeking to get what he could for his party. The literacy requirement would cut off the very lowest of the inferior races. Then processes of formal education, informal acculturation, and eventual intermarriage could operate upon arrivals more successfully than they would have without restriction.

Of course, dwelling on intermarriage, even in the long term, between old-stock Americans and Magyars, Jews, or Italians may well have been distasteful to him as well as to many of his Senate colleagues. Where, then, did the specter of emotionally acceptable interbreeding end? Did it end with the educated descendants of the Irish famine? With descendants of "Italians, Russians, Poles, Hungarians, Greeks"—the European immigrants whose numbers the literacy bill would trim? Presumably, he could not contemplate it for the Hindoo, that Caucasian Asiatic, and still less for other Asian peoples (for example, the Japanese) or with the descendants of the African freedman. Lodge does not take up such a question, but it must have hovered over his contemplation of racial interbreeding over the long term, and the use of the Hindoo example may have made this contemplation less acceptable than a European example would have been.

In the end, Lodge warned that the literacy bill might not be enough. "I trust," he said, "that . . . the unerring instinct of the race will shut the danger out, as it closed the door upon the coming of the Chinese."[48] But the Chinese had been excluded, not restricted. And Lodge's concluding statement broadly hints that restriction may again prove inadequate: "The time has certainly come, if not to stop, at least to check, to sift, and to restrict those immigrants. . . . If we do not close [the gates], we should at least . . . challenge those who would pass through."[49]

The 1896 literacy bill eventually passed the House by a vote of 217–102 (with 36 abstentions), and the Senate by a closer vote: 34–25 (31 abstentions). When President Cleveland vetoed the bill, the House voted to override the veto by 197–123 (37 abstentions); but the Senate failed to act, and the bill died.[50] A decade later, Lodge nearly succeeded again. But in the end the Speaker of the House managed to substitute a study commission, the U.S. Immigration Commission (1907–1911), for the literacy restriction. Lodge became an influential member of that commission, and he helped ensure that it too would eventually recommend the literacy restriction. The bill would pass both Houses twice more (1913 and 1915), only to be vetoed successfully both times.

Congress finally succeeded in overriding a fourth presidential veto in 1917. Soon after, Lodge resigned his seat on the Senate's Immigration Committee. Surely, he must have felt that he had accomplished what he had set out to do there. In any case, he was then the ranking minority member of the Senate Foreign Relations Committee, and the United States was on the verge of war. In 1918, the Republicans recaptured the Senate, and Lodge became chairman of that committee, soon leading the struggle against Wilson's leadership. Lodge also had a brief but important role in supporting the 1924 Second Quota Act, and we will encounter his thinking again in Part II.

Racial Theories of Immigration: Dominant Themes Exemplified in Lodge's Arguments

Anglo-Saxons were a Teutonic people, and the Teutonic peoples had Indo-European origins. These historical claims had a long lineage. One strand of research was linguistic. By the mid-eighteenth century it had demonstrated connections across Indo-European languages from India to the Atlantic. And this finding stimulated early speculation about a possible ancient race, one speaking a form of the "Indo-European" language and conquering all across that vast space. Moreover, the continuum of languages suggested that other cultural expressions might line up in similar ways—in family arrangements, primitive legal systems, and the arts. Surely, extensive institutional similarities could be found for particular subdivisions of the Indo-European family; this was the point of the Anglo-Saxon studies that Lodge had undertaken with Adams. And as Lodge stressed in the 1896 Senate speech, distinctive cultural forms over such a long period expressed particular traits of group character. It was a long way from these historical studies of language and culture to careful studies of biology, but the cultural studies certainly encouraged speculation about mental traits of ancient races transmitted in the blood. For American race theories, and their relevance to immigration policy, the distant Indo-European themes were generally muted or ignored; what mattered was Anglo-Saxon character emerging out of Teutonic origins.[51]

By the time of Lodge's speech, more rigorous writers were actually criticizing speculations about ancient races, the evidence for which was based solely on language and other cultural expressions. Cultural diffusion across human groups could explain as much as a theory stressing a common biological legacy, and such diffusion could have occurred by migration and conquest.

But a parallel eighteenth- and nineteenth-century research tradition could still provide a link between ancient races and modern temperaments. This was the study of *physical* remains—skeletons and especially skulls. Such research could establish the locations of different types of remains. Those, in turn, could be linked to present-day physical characteristics found in the region. Then it would not be unreasonable to search for cultural continuities that might be part of a biologically transmitted legacy.

Another theme behind the racial thinking concerned the origins of racial diversity. In earlier nineteenth-century writings, one hypothesis had posited multiple creations. But eventually diversity of races seemed more credibly explained in terms of human interaction with diverse environments. Before Darwin, such interaction was generally explained by Lamarck's argument that acquired traits could be inherited. Darwin's insights contributed a third explanation for human diversity: a dynamic of natural selection through which those with advantageous attributes in a particular environment would be more likely to survive, multiply, and dominate. Lamarck's and Darwin's theories could each explain what needed explaining without the other, but they could also coexist in one theory.[52] And some variant of one of these two theories, or of both together, was nearly always present in the background, if not the foreground, of racial thought by Lodge's time.

And it is worth stressing this distinction between "background" and "foreground" because most of those who discussed how cultural features might be carried "in the blood" did not stop to elaborate how they thought human cultural diversity related to racial origins. Another aspect of race thinking tended to make the relations of race and cultural diversity dramatically looser still. As Elazar Barkan observes, the time scale along which Lamarckian processes and natural selection operated in racial arguments could be decidedly ambiguous—a zoological or a historical scale might be invoked, or even the assumption that change might occur within a decidedly *short* historical period (a few generations, for example).[53]

The combination of Lamarckianism or natural selection (or both) with the vague specification of time frame in turn had great implications for understanding the distinction between biological and sociocultural transmission. Typically racial theorists did not state explicitly whether *specific* cultural characteristics were carried biologically or through socialization. Even Lodge—and notwithstanding his emphasis on the futility of trying to make a Hindoo into an Englishman—is not explicit on the role of each kind of transmission when it comes to a particular group cultural trait at one moment in time. The crucial point was that such group characteristics could have, and typically did have, a biological basis. A characteristic first learned through socialization might, over time (and the time scale was left vague), be on its way to becoming part of a biologically transmitted character (whether by Lamarck's or Darwin's mechanisms or by both). There was, of course, an analytic distinction to be made between environmental and biological explanations for a particular group characteristic. But knowing empirically how to locate the analytic line of division between these sources of human cultural difference was impossible and not so important. It was impossible given the state of knowledge, and it was not so important because the line was constantly shifting, whether through Lamarckian or Darwinian processes or through both.

We know that those who spoke in terms of races in the late nineteenth and early twentieth centuries typically believed in Lamarckian and Darwinian processes, and we know that most of them spoke loosely about the line between social and biological transmission of group mental traits. We do *not* find a self-conscious explanation that because of these two processes it was usually pointless to specify whether social or biological processes were the crucial ones operating for a *particular trait* of a group at a particular moment in time. The assumption that one or both of these two processes might be operating, coupled with a sloppiness about the time scales in which they operated, made it possible, indeed natural, to believe that a given trait first acquired through socialization could over generations become a trait transmitted biologically, without self-conscious elaboration. By contrast, our own generation is finely attuned to the catastrophic potentials of any confusion between explanations resting on social and biological transmission processes. Of course, some writers faulted the assumptions about this loose interplay even at the turn of the century. But, as Elazar Barkan has emphasized, the major change in high and semipopular culture in regard to this loose confusion of the biological and social processes did not in fact emerge from scientific breakthroughs or from armchair analytical rigor; rather it was the reaction beginning in the mid-1930s to the uses of race theory in Germany.[54]

Rhetorical flourishes, often with political implications, increased the vagueness about heredity versus environment as explanations. The cavalier imprecision as to time frames provides a dramatic example. A confidential chat took place at the White House between President Theodore Roosevelt and James Ford Rhodes, who had published a history of the Reconstruction era that interested Roosevelt. They were discussing the sudden extension of the franchise to the freedman. Rhodes recalled, "[Roosevelt] was much struck . . . with my suggestion of what Lincoln [had he lived] would have done, how he would have worked up to the negro suffrage gradually, based on the negroes' winning intelligence and property. . . . The negroes, the President said, were 200,000 years behind (I suggested a million, an amendment which he accepted)."[55] A handicap of 200,000 (or was it a million?) years should not have been ignored: Lincoln would have "worked up to the negro suffrage gradually." But once again, over how long a period would the deficit be made up? Would Lincoln have "worked up" over years, decades, or generations? And yet, note too that even if not all of the deficit of 200,000 years was to be made up by this "gradual" action, the sense of the conversation is that much *could* have been made up—and made up in far less time than it took to create the differences.

One implication of all of this loose talk was especially important for social policy regarding immigration (or for that matter, for uplifting the freedman). The effects of undesirable races had both short- and long-term effects. The short-term effects might be directly related to poverty— dense concentrations of the immigrant poor and ensuing social problems related to crime, health, schooling, political corruption, and the like. But restrictionists could also relate the short-term effects to immutable racial features: the non-Anglo-Saxons would climb out of these limitations more slowly if at all (and not only because they had not come from a social context that did not require social or political self-reliance). Nevertheless, the long-term effects of undesirable personality characteristics related to race might be worse still, if they could not be socialized out or bred out through intermarriage. Which danger was worse—short or long term—did not need to be specified to argue for restriction.

Most discussions of race, popular and scholarly, also accepted an old assumption about the connection between skin color and racial divisions. White, black, and some others—typically red and / or yellow in the United States—were examples of the color groupings. Generally, the color divisions covered *multiple* races. Thus one spoke of the major racial divisions among humanity as marked by (related to) skin color. But *within* a major division might be found a continuum of races, smaller units of humanity that differed from each other in physical and mental features. And in American discussions of immigration, specific European races might be discussed as part of a white "family" of races or of a grand racial division. Yet the physical and mental differences across these white races were truly racial, transmitted in the same manner as differences between grand racial divisions.

In one variant of such thinking it followed that the differences among the white races, and between them and other races, meant that an objective scale of races from superior to inferior could be delineated, both within a grand division and between it and other grand divisions. A slightly weaker formulation was also possible: racial groupings, including both the many white races and the grand racial divisions, could be arranged in terms of suitability or desirability for certain human environments—most notably, in the degree to which they possessed the characteristics required for living in a republic with a universal franchise (or rather, a universal *male* franchise in this period). Specific European peoples—southern and eastern Europeans, for example—were white people, but racially undesirable white people. For Lodge and many others, southern and eastern Europeans differed from the desirable whites, namely, Anglo-Saxons (or Teutonic or Nordic peoples) by enough to cause disaster if immigration were left unregulated. Consequently, when less desirable European peoples arrived as immigrants, they were "white on arrival," rather than "becoming white" later—but at the same time they were racially undesirable white people. From a historical point of view, such undesirable white immigrants could accurately be said to have "become white" in the limited sense that the perception of the differences between themselves and the Anglo-Saxons declined over several generations; the circle of the desirable white races tended to expand to include peoples viewed earlier as undesirable white races, and indeed, eventually the concept of multiple white races itself declined in favor of a unified white race. Moreover, European immigrant working-class groups insisted on what united them to higher-status people of the society—namely, their whiteness—and distanced themselves from blacks. In this sense, too, they could be understood to be "working towards whiteness" or towards "becoming white" through the effort to weaken or remove the perception of race divisions among whites.[56]

But what made for differences between grand racial divisions as opposed to differences among races within a grand division? The most straightforward answer is that differences in crucial characteristics of mind and spirit were *further apart* from each other across grand racial divisions (color divisions) than among races within a single such division. This formulation, of course, is especially relevant to comparisons between the white (European) and nonwhite races.

Nevertheless, if this is the most straightforward answer, it is worth appreciating that this notion of "further apart" suggests metrics of difference along defined dimensions. Such conceptions are invoked, for example, to define differences between as opposed to within species. But was a desirable mental quality really more similar among all of the races within a grand division than among any pair of races across grand divisions?

Historian Oscar Handlin seems to have been delineating a similar set of issues when he wrote, in connection with the racial thought of the period, "In a world of biologically distinct species, the natives of Sicily were as distinct from those of Norway as either were from those of the Gold Coast." Contemporaries more often spoke of races than of species. But surely Handlin meant that when "race" was used to promote immigration restriction, contemporaries were thinking of a firmly fixed biological determinism that would apply to either level of classification, and in some cases, they did in fact discuss the differences relevant to immigration policy in terms of species. In any case, Handlin's formulation suggests that white races "were as distinct" from each other "as either were" from nonwhite races. The point is not historiographical: whether or not Handlin consistently held such a view or derived great conclusions from it need not concern us. We can use that sentence to challenge the straightforward view that the race differences between versus within grand divisions could be conceived in terms of "bigger versus smaller." Indeed, perhaps the difference in race differences really could not be conceptualized at all, or perhaps there was no difference between the two kinds of race differences. Perhaps they turned out to be the same upon closer inspection. In any case, it does seem worthwhile to focus more closely on how the discussions at the time handled these two kinds of race differences because they bear so directly on boundaries established by race in general and whiteness in particular.

At issue here is *not* how racial differences played out in domestic social history—in labor relations, residence, school segregation, or other forms of intergroup social tensions in America. Social historians do confirm that across generations in the North—to say nothing of the Jim Crow South—boundaries of color had a power and rigidity greater than any among white races. This was so for blacks everywhere and for East Asians and lower-class Mexican Americans where these groups were most concentrated.[57] But the focus here is narrower, namely, how the difference in race differences turned up in debates about immigration policy and worked its way into immigration law.

To jump ahead, a crucial part of the answer to our question will turn out to lie not in conceptualization but in rhetoric and context. Politicians consistently managed to avoid explicating how they connected the two kinds of race differences *by dealing with them in separate contexts*—about northwest versus southeast European races or white versus nonwhite (European versus non-European) races.

Nevertheless, some situations made it harder to ignore the distinction between the two kinds of race differences. We have seen that to no small extent Lodge bypassed the distinction between race differences among whites and between whites and others. Theodore Roosevelt found time for a much more pointed reflection in a confidential letter that he wrote during the Russo-Japanese War. Marking it "private and confidential," he commented,

> I am not much affected by the statement that the Japanese are of an
> utterly different race from ourselves and that the Russians are of the same
> race.... [T]here are some peoples of a very low standard from whom
> nothing can be expected ... [and] there are others, widely different one
> from the other, which, nevertheless, stand about on an equality.

Perhaps feeling that he could provide an example even more striking than his comparison of the Russians and Japanese, Roosevelt then compared "the modern Turks" to the Japanese. The former

> are just as much white people as the Balkan Christians, or as the Russians,
> and physiologically they do not differ any more from Danes, Englishmen,
> Swiss, or Italians, than the latter differ among themselves. But they are
> absolutely alien because of their creed, their culture, their historic associa-
> tions, and inherited governmental and social tendencies. Therefore, they
> are a curse to Europe.... The Turks are ethnically [i.e., in the terms of
> ethnological research] closer to us than the Japanese, but they are
> impossible members of our international society, while I think the Japs
> may be desirable additions.[58]

Roosevelt may have meant to distinguish here between the biological and social influences of racial histories. This interpretation is far from certain, especially if he regarded socialization as morphing eventually into biological transmission. But even if his intent was indeed to distinguish the role of biological and social influences, the crucial point for us is the relative ranking of the two groups he described. He ranked the Japanese high and the Turks and Russians low in terms of precisely those human qualities that made racial ranking so important to him. Clearly, in this letter he contradicted the dictum that all white races were further from all nonwhite races than either were from races in their respective families of "color races." Much more typical was the tendency (for Roosevelt as well as for so many others) simply to rank white races differently from each other; the distinctive and highly atypical features here were the extra steps of explicitly including a nonwhite race in the comparison and ranking it above some white ones.[59]

Later Directions in the Racial Theories of Immigration, and Dissenters

Some three years after Lodge's big speech on race and immigration, William Z. Ripley published a well-written synthesis of European race research.[60] Much of that research had not appeared in English before. Ripley had been trained as an economist and was especially interested in the influence of geography on human affairs. In order to better evaluate the environmental factor, he felt he needed to master the literature on the competing influence of heredity. Consequently, *Races of Europe: A Sociological Study* argued against loose racial explanations and for the careful evaluation of evidence for other competing explanations. Still, Ripley's approach took that competing explanation very seriously: mental traits did indeed vary in important ways across races, and this occurred through biological transmission. Consequently, his survey of evidence turned out to provide great support for the role of such racial transmission. Ripley's book was a standard text in college courses on physical anthropology for three decades.[61]

Classification of ancient races had to rest on physical traits such as hair and eye color, and shape of the skull. Ripley reinforced the view that the races could not be established by tracing contemporary languages back in time. And he dismissed the claims of nationalists that ancient races corresponded to contemporary nations. On the other hand, it was no simple matter to reach conclusions from the relevant physical evidence—ancient skeletal remains and physical types found in the Europe of his time. First, the ancient races of the continent had long since intermingled. Empirical study of physical evidence therefore required inferences about earlier forms. Second, even before the extensive intermingling, there must have been great physical variation among individuals of the same race. The very notion of the pure exemplar of an ancient race was thus an abstraction. Still, this kind of abstraction was common to much of scientific classification.

Ripley's book introduced many Americans to the notion that three major ancient races had prevailed in Europe: Nordic, Alpine, and Mediterranean. As the names implied, each of the races had been especially prevalent in a particular part of the continent. They were distinguished by physical remains alone, but the physical characteristics were also compared to those of inhabitants today. The conclusion was that while racial mixture had occurred everywhere, there did remain parts of Europe in which these racial types tended to be relatively pure and easily found to predominate in the local population. The Nordic in Scandinavia were an important case in point. All of this came with the authority of the latest methods and research projects.

But for all the emphasis on physical remains, once the ancient domains of the races had been established, one could conclude that each of these three basic European races had been associated with particular mental and spiritual characteristics, and the Nordic seemed decidedly most creative, forceful, and able to rule. In sum, despite the novel features of the new racial research, and the influence of Ripley's presentation, on the single most crucial issue his description of European races ran in much the same channel as the older Teutonic or Anglo-Saxon theories. This was especially true when it came to formulating a policy of immigration restriction. Specific groups needed to be restricted, and they were the same groups Lodge had been discussing without knowing the newer methods or research projects, and without mentioning Ripley's three basic European race groups.

Ripley's big book made him a very well-known authority. One result was that when he published some speculative additional reflections a decade later, people took careful notice. These articles tended to point policy in a new and more intolerant direction. Lodge and many of his generation believed that an advanced race could uplift a more backward one, at least so long as acceptable proportions of the two races were present. By contrast,

Ripley now suggested that racial comingling in people may follow the patterns of botanical interbreeding. That is, it might lead quite consistently to negative outcomes, to the disappearance of finer qualities, and to the dominance of more primitive ones. In terms of immigration policy, this hypothesis implied that the arrival of even small numbers of immigrants from backward races was a danger, for the biological processes Ripley was now highlighting seemed to guarantee that each such immigrant would have only a negative long-term impact on the American population through interbreeding.

Quantitative studies of race differences in social behavior of all kinds were also typical of the later period. Such studies were important well before Lodge's time, but they only gained in strength. European immigrant groups in the United States (as well as European societies) differed to some degree in crime rates, poverty, madness, fertility, urbanization, or creativity. Indeed, Ripley reported on numerous studies that measured these differences. Writers might—or might not—carefully indicate the range of possible explanations for the differences they had found. Either way, they were marshaling simple percentages or advanced statistics to show that groups differed on important social outcomes. Such differences were at least consistent with a notion that races differed in social and mental qualities as well as in physical characteristics.

Government studies of immigrants, such as the forty-one volume *Reports of the United States Immigration Commission* (1911), tended to strengthen the perception that such differences had been firmly established by objective methods. And when intelligence testing came to widespread notice by the early 1920s, many gave a racial explanation for the finding of large differences in IQ across groups.

After 1900, advances in biology and studies of heredity also contributed to a sense that racial explanations were grounded in scientific inquiry. Such inquiry was contrasted with historical speculation of the early nineteenth century, or reliance on hints from Indo-European linguistics and ancient cultures. The term "scientific racism," which has been used to characterize later racial thought, was in full bloom by the 1920s. How far back we should employ the term is less clear, not least because the definition of the term is not precise. Even in the earlier decades of the nineteenth century, the cultural studies (and especially the language studies among them) had been seen as "scientific" in that they rested on intensive study, rules of evidence, judicious review, and the like. It was even easier to make claims to science for the study of physical remains, by applying methods such as measuring skull shapes and sizes. Yet these studies had begun long before Darwin. A useful definition of the term "scientific racism" may be that it refers to the belief, often but not always stated, that scientific inquiry confirms an objective hierarchy of mental as well as physical qualities across biologically defined races—where science refers to social statistics as well as to findings of the natural sciences. This claim became strongest after 1900.

The eugenics movement, which developed in America shortly after 1900, urged public policies that would harness the insights of science to produce better-quality people—more of the finest, fewer of the worst. Eugenicists had a hand in some of the more chilling results of scientific pretensions in the first half of the twentieth century, such as the forced sterilization of the retarded, and (under the Nazis) even their destruction. But before these excesses and the reaction to them developed, the movement was widely supported, even by many with socially progressive and generally humane views.

For the most part, the subject of eugenics focused on differences found across families, not across entire peoples. And yet, a claim that immigration since the 1890s involved much less self-selection than it had in 1850 was grist for the eugenicists' mill. In their view, if the poorly endowed could not be kept out, then the human stock that would perpetuate the republic would decline. The argument did not need to characterize entire peoples as being poorly endowed. It was enough to note that social and economic life in various countries encouraged the poorly endowed in particular to immigrate to America. The countries of southern and eastern Europe were typically mentioned in this context. But eugenics could also be joined to racial rather than family differences. If scientific inquiry was demonstrating an objective ranking of relevant abilities across immigrant races, surely this finding was relevant to immigration policy.

All of these developments in racial thinking were familiar to a group of patricians in New York City who met regularly around 1908 to discuss important themes of the day. During that year, they invited Ripley to speak to them on race. Among these patricians was Madison Grant, who devoted himself to race questions over the next few years and published his own big book, *The Passing of the Great Race*, in 1916. The book relied heavily on the material Ripley had summarized in 1899. But whereas Ripley summarized an evolving discipline, Grant's simplified findings, presented as certainties, reached much more strident conclusions as to policy. Ripley had claimed to be exploring the racial past of Europe (with barely a word on the United States in his book). By contrast, Grant announced that he wrote in order to protect the racial future of the United States from disaster. He proposed legislating eugenic policies, most simply (albeit not exclusively) through immigration restriction. His book was reprinted after the war, and its influence was greatest in the early 1920s. In contrast to Lodge, who thought it best to restrict immigration from southern and eastern Europe to numbers that could be successfully assimilated culturally and biologically, Grant viewed every southern and eastern European immigrant as a purely negative addition and a promise of future degeneration through race mixing.

One of the glories of John Higham's history of American nativism, *Strangers in the Land* (1955), was its tightly argued narrative of the evolution of American ideas about immigrant races that culminated with Grant: "The man who put the pieces together was Madison Grant.... This finally was racism." However, Higham's analysis may leave the impression that the most widespread view of race and immigration, at least by the end of the period, was in fact Grant's. Actually, Higham was careful to distinguish the progression of views that led to Grant's formulations from the question of Grant's influence on the 1920s. Likewise, Higham spoke of that progression in ways that should alert us to the general direction at least as much as to the endpoint: "The old Anglo-Saxon tradition had finally emerged in at least one mind as a systematic, comprehensive world view." Chapter 7 will try to contribute to the assessment of older and newer views about Anglo-Saxons and race in the thinking and actions of the congressional actors who passed the severe and racially structured immigration restrictions of 1921–1924.[62]

Before leaving our discussion of Madison Grant, however, it is worth a closer look at how he dealt with the difference in race differences among whites and between whites and others. Grant was among those who were most emphatic that the Nordic race was radically superior to the other two European races (Alpine and Mediterranean). Moreover, there is enough discussion in his book to have tightly linked the difference between Nordic and other races to whiteness, had he wished to do so. In his view, the two lesser races, Alpine and Mediterranean, amounted to "western extensions of Asiatic subspecies, and neither of them can be considered as exclusively European." They mixed with the Nordic, with the result that they have a relatively white skin color. "With the remaining race, the Nordic, however, the case is different. This is a purely European type, and has developed its physical characters and its civilization within the confines of that continent. It is, therefore, the Homo Europaeus, the white man par excellence."[63]

But Grant did *not* stress whiteness in discussing the difference between the desirable and undesirable *European* immigrants. Eye and hair color and skull shape were more reliable *physical* markers of the monumental mental and spiritual differences across the three European races. True, "In various combinations [they—that is, all three taken together] comprise the great bulk of white men all over the world." And yet, he immediately adds, "These races vary intellectually and morally just as they do physically. Moral, intellectual, and spiritual attributes are as persistent as physical characters, and are transmitted unchanged from generation to generation."[64]

Similarly, Grant was perfectly familiar with the term "Caucasian" as a way of speaking about those who were racially white: "These three European subspecies, are subdivisions of one of the primary groups or subgenera of the genus Homo which, taken together, we must call the Caucasian for lack of a better name." Others are Negroes and Mongols or mixtures.[65] Nevertheless, the biologically based and unchangeable differences *among* the Caucasians were so great as to easily justify his book, and both "Caucasian" and "white" were of only the most marginal interest in that context: "The term 'Caucasian race' has ceased to have any meaning except where it is used, in the United States, to contrast white populations with negroes or Indians, or, in the Old World, with Mongols. It is, however, a convenient term to include the three European subspecies when considered as divisions of one of the primary branches or subgenera of mankind."[66] And yet, on occasion Grant did in fact distinguish between *all three* European races and the indigenous people they encountered or the African slaves they brought to the New World. He was quite capable of keeping both levels of distinction in mind at one time; he did *not*, as so many politicians did, find it necessary to discuss each of the two kinds of racial distinctions in isolation from the other.

> In Argentine and south Brazil white blood of the various European races is pouring in so rapidly that a community preponderantly white, but of the Mediterranean type, may grow up. . . .
>
> Australia and New Zealand, where the natives have been exterminated by the whites, are developing into communities of pure Nordic blood, and will for that reason play a large part in the future history of the Pacific. The bitter opposition of the Australians and Californians to the admission of Chinese coolies and Japanese farmers is due primarily to a blind but absolutely justified determination to keep those lands as white man's countries.[67]

Grant's primary focus was on the differences among the three European, white races. He rarely stressed (as he did do in the passage quoted earlier) that the Nordic was the "most" white of all. His distinction among the *European* races was *not* centrally a matter of stressing degrees of whiteness. Both topics—race differences *among* Europeans and differences between them and others—were important to Grant. His attention to the latter topic emerges not only in stray passages of his own book, such as those just cited, but also in his long introduction to a book by his friend Lothrop Stoddard, *The Rising Tide of Color against White World-Supremacy*.[68] Grant wrote about the European races in particular because such a large part of his interest was in the American future and immigration restriction. Nonwhites were already generally excluded.

For Grant, in any case, it seems to have been enough to think of the difference in race differences as a taxonomic problem and leave it at that: white races *did* share something that made them more like each other than they were like those in other "primary branches or subgenera of mankind." If pressed on how to conceptualize the issue of different kinds of differences further, he would probably have impatiently dismissed the challenge as being no different than countless other taxonomic divisions in ethnology. Presumably he would have dismissed Handlin's notion of the equality of race differences among Norwegian, Sicilian, and natives of the Gold Coast the same way.

It was not possible to prove that group differences in mental characteristics were *not* inherited biologically; consequently, dissent rarely took the
form of outright rejection of that hypothesis. Rather, dissenters expressed
skepticism about the evidence *in favor* of various racial claims. Was it really
clear that Africans in the bush or other primitive peoples were less intelligent than contemporary Europeans, or did evidence tend to show
only that intellectual ability expressed itself differently in different cultures?
Why should the poverty and low educational level of blacks be ascribed
mostly to heredity when they had endured so many generations of slavery
and then of rigid discrimination? Just what was really known about the
effect of racial intermingling? Moreover, in the absence of better knowledge on all of these questions, could the race laws of the American South
be justified? Could restriction against specific immigrant peoples be justified? The writings of anthropologist Franz Boas were critical in formulating
all of these skeptical questions; his relevant early essays were collected in
The Mind of Primitive Man (1911). But some of those essays first appeared as far
back as the 1890s.

For all his originality and influence, Boas had not been the only such
skeptic. An interesting example can be seen in an exchange of letters between him and the Chicago sociologist W. I. Thomas in 1907. Thomas had
recently published an article arguing for the high quality of thought among
the "lower races."[69] Boas himself had addressed a similar theme in 1901.[70]
Thomas wrote to Boas (with whom he was already acquainted) that he had
heard through the academic grapevine that Boas, or Boas's colleagues,
"think I ought to have made large acknowledgements to you" in the 1907
paper. Thomas continued, "It would have been a pleasure to make acknowl-
edgement to you in connection with many things, but in representing the
view that differences in mind are environmental in origin, rather than in-
nate, I felt that I was simply expressing in my own way a view common now
to a school of thinkers. . . . [In such an acknowledgement] I should have referred not only to your paper but to Waitz, Bastian, Tarde, Baldwin and a
number of others."[71] Boas wrote back a few days later to say he was surprised to hear of the rumor about his or his friends' resentment; it was untrue. Moreover, he wrote, "It is so obvious, as you say, that the recognition
of the sameness of the human mind in different races is an idea that is in

the air, that it would be hardly justifiable for any of us to claim it as his own."[72] In the air some breathed, at any rate.

After 1900, the rediscovery of Mendel's laws of genetics slowly eroded the very notion that observed physical characteristics were inherited as a single package. The probability diminished that mental attributes were transmitted with great uniformity within a race group, let alone in a package with physically observable traits. But this revolution in thinking about heredity and race did not triumph within biology until well into the interwar years.[73] Still, Boas had already stressed in the first decade of the century that the variety of intelligence within every race seemed vastly greater than any differences that might—might—ever be demonstrated to exist between races.

CHAPTER 3

First Struggles over the List

Jewish Challenges and the Federal Defense, 1899–1903

WITH ONE CRITICAL EXCEPTION, there was no protest against the List as a whole or against any specific category. For some groups, the classification by race and country of birth were the same, so the List made no practical difference to them. Many other immigrants were members of "races" from the multinational empires. Typically, their category in the List was familiar: Czech, Pole, and so forth. Moreover, insofar as such immigrants thought of the multinational empires as oppressive and illegitimate rulers, they probably welcomed a classification that did not describe them only as German, Austrian, or Russian subjects. Some immigrants may have been puzzled to learn that the category to which they had been assigned was defined as a race. But probably most were either uninterested or knew the term was vague enough to convey multiple meanings. In addition, recall that early on the Bureau of Immigration had quietly appended "and Peoples" to the List's name. As W. W. Husband would note in 1908, some immigrants were more comfortable with one term, and some with the other.

The organizations of the American Jewish elite, however, intensely opposed the List from the moment it was introduced. They protested primarily (and at first exclusively) not the wisdom of a List of Races, but simply the inclusion of a *Hebrew* race category. This opposition was persistent and regular until 1910, and it also flared up from time to time during the years from 1910 to 1950. In addition to the organizational protests, numerous Jewish individuals wrote to federal officials, from the president on down, expressing dismay and annoyance. However, the secretary of commerce, who supervised the Bureau of Immigration, conducted an unpublicized internal review of the issues in response to a Jewish protest in 1903. That review produced a clear set of responses that the bureau used in subsequent years. This chapter first takes up the positions of Jewish groups and then examines the federal review of the relevant positions.

Sources of the Jewish Protest over the List

Jewish organizations and leaders differed among themselves over the Hebrew category. Some publicly condemned the behavior of others. These splits, in turn, reflected how participants conceived of their Jewish identity. Still, many Jewish opponents of the List were especially consequential both socially and politically. Known as the "German Jews," they represented the older, economically established, and more assimilated element among Jews in America.[1]

Only a tiny number of Jews had settled in colonial America; they numbered perhaps 2,000 at the time of the American Revolution. The first Jewish immigration of any size began during the early nineteenth century. These Jews came as part of the great nineteenth-century immigration from German lands, that is, from the many small states of central Europe. Later (until well after 1900), more came from the German Empire that had united those small states in 1871. The proportion of Jews among German immigrants comprised perhaps one-tenth of the whole. They spoke either German or the Jewish language, Yiddish, which itself was based on medieval German. As late as 1840, the German Jews in the United States probably numbered only 15,000, but by the Civil War the figure was ten times greater, and by 1900 these immigrants, their children, and grandchildren probably numbered about one-quarter million. They comprised the vast majority of American Jews until the late 1880s, by which time a far larger immigration of Jews from eastern Europe was underway.

Most of the immigrant-generation German Jews had begun in small trade, starting work as peddlers across one or another part of the country. Often these immigrants eventually found their way into the middle class of America's larger cities, and if they did not, then often their children did. Also, a nontrivial number of the German Jewish immigrants came from the middle classes of the cities and larger towns of central Europe. And a few came with, or developed ties to, the European Jewish banking families. This small but highly influential elite group among the first- and second-generation German Jews tended to concentrate in New York City.

Cultural as well as class background matters to this story. By the end of the eighteenth century, the European Enlightenment had seriously affected the outlook of German Jewry; during the nineteenth century, most embraced a reformed version of the Jewish religion. And the Reform movement (as it was called) became a major force among the German Jews that had immigrated to the United States. In the new land Reform Judaism tended toward even greater change. American Reform Jews rejected much in the religious tradition, and particularly in the legacy of ritual requirements. At the core of Reform was a claim to rationality and a focus on the universality of theological and ethical principles. Not coincidentally, this approach to Judaism also carried implications for the position of Jews in society. Nothing in Reform Judaism restricted modern Jews from being full members of the society, economy, and state in which they lived: Germans or, later, Americans of the Mosaic persuasion. Nor would an enlightened state restrict a Reform Jew's citizenship or participation. And by far the fullest expression of this kind of enlightened state could be found in the United States, with its First Amendment protections and its religious pluralism on the ground. Indeed, the legal equality the United States offered Jews was the most secure, more secure even than in the liberal west European states, to say nothing of the systematic anti-Semitism in states further east.

It followed that enlightened Jews in an enlightened state were no longer to be regarded as a nation in exile. There was no need to anticipate an ingathering of the Jews to a resurrected, ancient homeland at the end of historical time; rather, the Jews could, and indeed must, fulfill their moral mission in the diaspora. The emphasis here was on rejecting nationhood in favor or religion. Thus in 1885 a group of rabbis had issued a radical but influential statement of Reform principles known as the Pittsburgh Platform that dealt directly with nation and religion. "We recognize in the Mosaic legislation a system of training the Jewish people for its mission during its national life in Palestine, and today we accept as binding only its moral laws. . . . We consider ourselves no longer a nation, but a religious community, and therefore expect [no] return to Palestine." The Platform made no reference to race.[2] Questions of the Jews' racial status were nonetheless developing in this period, especially in European thought (among Jews as well as non-Jews).[3] But even a quarter century after the Pittsburgh Platform, when an important spokesman opposed the Hebrew category of the List of Races and Peoples, he could bring the debate back to matters of nationality and the Jews' place in an enlightened state. "A certain portion of the Jewish people claim that the Jews are a race, especially the Zionists, who cling to the idea of returning to Palestine and founding a Jewish state.... The reform element [believe that] ... we are citizens of the country in which we reside, and we have been fighting in every possible way against the idea of founding a Jewish state."[4]

Such people, indeed probably most American Jews, saw themselves as enjoying equality under the law and saw the guarantee of that equality in the constitutional separation of church and state. A practical corollary of that separation was that the state would relate to its citizens without regard to their religion—the state would be, as we might say today, "religion-blind." At the same time, the concept of race would reverberate, modestly or forcefully, in American Jewish self-image across the half century after 1885, and it would carry a variety of associations. One of its most important associations, whether supported or vigorously rejected, related back to nationality, the nation state, and political Zionism (which grew in importance during the late 1890s). A belief in inherent differences between Jews and the people among whom they dwelled could be marshalled to undercut the Reform elite's argument that only a different enlightened religion separated Jews from other citizens, even in the United States.

In any case, in 1898 Reform Judaism was the outlook of the great majority of elite American Jews. Their Jewish organizations were actively involved with the well-being of Jewish co-religionists throughout the world. In fact, this elite was rapidly evolving into the world's most energetic, articulate, and powerful agitator on behalf of the Jews' suffering under the oppressive regimes of eastern Europe.

The very first protest was directed at the supplemental form that McSweeney and Safford had introduced in 1898. Recall that the supplemental form included a direct question about the arriving immigrant's religion as an aid to distinguishing among races—and in fact its principal use was no doubt to distinguish Jews from other immigrants who came from the same region and spoke the same language. Soon after, the bureau agreed to drop the religion question but persisted in identifying a Hebrew race category. A few years later, the bureau expanded the title of "the List of Races" to "the List of Races and Peoples." By that time, it would have been possible to argue that the "Hebrew" category referred not to a "race" but to a "people"; yet there was no letup in the Jewish protest over the List following these changes. It was *not*, in other words, the stigma attached to race that drove the protests. True, we will see that later (especially around 1910) the Jewish protest also began to question the permissibility of collecting race data on Europeans at all.

We should appreciate the broader context within which the Jewish leaders' insistence on the separation of church and state was taking place.[5] Their arguments were by no means always presented with the maximum clarity or the same emphases. Nevertheless, the critical constitutional arguments were two. *First* that the constitutional separation ensured that the federal government had no right to inquire into the religious affiliation of individuals—for example, in the decennial census or in the screening of arriving immigrants. However, federal officials would soon enough learn to argue in response that the List of Races had no interest in religion, its purpose being the same for Hebrews as for others: to classify by race. Consequently, the Jewish protest came to stress a *second* claim, a corollary of the first: even if the government's purpose was not to inquire about religion, but rather about something else (such as race or people), it could not do so in the case of the "Hebrews." That particular category also delineated a religious group coterminous with that race or people, and so whatever the motive for the data collection, it had the effect of requiring Jews to identify by religion.

Such specific contentions about religious freedom and government intrusion did not rest on explicit formulations in the First Amendment, nor on later congressional acts or court interpretations. The relevant clause of the First Amendment simply states, "Congress shall make no law respecting an establishment of religion, or prohibiting the free exercise thereof." The Jewish leaders framed their arguments as praise of the First Amendment and then asserted that their two claims followed—first, that the amendment *meant* that the government could not ask about an individual American's religion, and second, that it could not ask about some other classification (race or people) when the relevant category of that other classification was coterminous with a religion. Indeed, such was the power of the principle of religious freedom that the *first* claim—that the government may not require individuals to state their religion—seems never to have been explicitly challenged by the government officials who defended the List across the decades. However, the still-broader second claim was in fact directly challenged in some of the discussions.

By no means were all Americans as comfortable with the notion of a complete church–state separation as were the leaders of this religious minority. True, there was a strong American tradition, expressed most influentially by Jefferson's and Madison's support of a high wall between church and state. Others understood it to refer principally to divisions among Protestants, or at most among Christians. Still others might have accepted that the First Amendment covered all faiths (and perhaps even atheism), but only in the limited meaning of the text: no establishment of a national church and the explicit right of all to practice their own faith. Indeed, in some periods of the nineteenth century, calls to return the nation's constitution to Christianity were strong. These calls were prevalent enough during the early nineteenth-century awakenings, for example, and again in the last third of the century when challenges from Darwin or biblical criticism shook beliefs and when social tensions (not least the immigration of new peoples) seemed to endanger law and order. During the latter period, several bills called for the government to formally embrace Christianity. And in 1892 a Supreme Court decision referred to the United States as "a Christian nation."[6]

In sum, on the one hand, when the Jewish leaders protested the enumeration of Hebrews on the principle of church–state separation, they were not making undisputed claims. On the other hand, the ideal that American religious affiliations were free from government scrutiny certainly made the Bureau of Immigration's direct question about religion on the supplemental form seem indefensible. After this question was removed, the broader issue of a Hebrew category on the List was less clear cut, if still a subject for debate. Jewish leaders found themselves described in terms of race or people. They tried on occasion to dispute that description by challenging the clarity of the "race" concept or by challenging whether Jews were regarded by experts as a race. These objections typically only amounted to unsuccessful distractions. Sometimes they were expressed clearly, often not. But even at their best, they did not directly address why a Hebrew category was legally impermissible, even if it was being wrongly applied by the government. To make the category impermissible, either all race categories had to be so (a claim some Jewish leaders eventually explored) or the Hebrew race category in particular could not be allowed because it *also* designated a religious group.

Did the Jewish leadership really believe this second claim? They very probably did believe that Jews were discriminated against on the basis of religion, whatever the terms that were used. The issue is not whether the Jews themselves sometimes used terms like "race feeling" to describe their ties to each other, nor indeed how many Jews of that era believed that most late-nineteenth-century Hebrews could trace their biological heredity to the ancient Israelites. However common or rare such patterns of thought might have been, they need not have contradicted claims of the era's Reform Jewish thought: that what defined the faith was enlightened, rationalist, universal principles held by citizens in an enlightened state. If the logic of the Jewish claim about the List involves a tenuous or misleading feature, it is not that claim. The tenuous element is found in the second part of the defense, based on the interpretation of the American constitution: Did church–state separation really make a category for "race or people" impermissible if that category's members also comprised a religious group?[7]

And yet, the Jewish elite's protest involved more than a disagreement over the interpretation of the First Amendment. It also concerned, quite simply, a resistance to being identified as American Jews in federal publications for any reason. Such resistance would seem to fit James C. Scott's description of groups who resist being legible to a state. In *Seeing Like a State*, Scott noted that a state needs to be able to know certain features of its population, particularly to be able to marshal needed resources. For example, it needs to classify people by the amounts of property, income, or wealth they have for purposes of taxation or by age and sex for military service. The characteristics of interest are themselves simplified and standardized to ignore complexities, and of course other kinds of characteristics are ignored altogether. In this way, defined features of a person are made *legible* to the state. But often enough, when confronting the likelihood that they will be placed in a new category of interest to the state, the people involved would rather remain *illegible*, as in the examples of taxation and military service. They may try to resist the creation of a new classification, or resist its efficient use.[8]

Through much of European Jewish history, governmental authorities created special legislation about Jews and it was often oppressive. Until the nineteenth century, such authorities typically related to the Jewish community as a whole: for example, it declared an amount of tax for which the community was responsible. Jewish identity could also be the basis for all Jews being expelled from an area, or for a quota limiting university enrollment. This history of distinctive treatment was not always negative, as when Jews were recruited for nonagricultural settlement in late medieval eastern Europe (or accepted among recruits from German lands), or when Jews were allowed to practice usury forbidden to Christians, or assigned to be tax collectors by local rulers. However, American Jewish leaders certainly would have been very sensitive to the negative potentials inherent in being made legible to the government.

Did the Jewish leadership really think that in the United States Jews could be taxed as a despised community? Probably not, but why allow a step in that direction? Who could say what might eventually occur? Recall the Supreme Court's 1892 reference to the United States as "a Christian country." However, more than a slippery slope into the unknown was at stake, particularly in connection with restriction of Jewish immigration. Was it reasonable to fear restriction limited to Jews? Probably not in the then-current world of constitutional protections. And yet, just such an outcome had rather recently befallen the Chinese with the 1882 Exclusion Act. And how carefully had "the Chinese" been defined in the Exclusion Act? As a color, race, nation, people, religion? In 1907 a similar outcome awaited the Japanese. Could another people defined by religion or peoplehood qualify as well? Such anxieties no doubt propelled one influential leader of American Jewish organizations to write to another in 1909, "In order not to offend the susceptibilities of the Japanese, the word Asiatic is getting to be commonly used in Government circles. It will not be a very far step to declare the Jews Asiatic presently."[9] During the debates on Chinese exclusion (and later on Japanese restriction), the rationales focused on many ways in which the targeted group differed too much from Americans to expect assimilation. The specific negative characteristics ascribed to Jews were different, but could point to a similar conclusion: Jews were seen as clannish, obsessed with money, working in occupations that were "unproductive"—their masses in petty trade (think especially: peddler) and petty usury, their wealthy in international banking. Moreover, the fear of immigration restriction was hardly limited to the analogy of the Chinese Exclusion Act. The exclusion or drastic reduction in the number of arrivals from all "new immigrant groups" was a present danger. The large numbers of eastern European Jews then arriving were often cited as an important and particularly undesirable part of these new groups. Counting these arrivals in a discrete category did not inspire the confidence of the German Jewish elite.

Finally, and probably most crucially, American Jewish leaders also feared legibility not only because the *state* would "see" them but because the *public* would. These fears are expressed from time to time in vague mentions of "fanning the flames of bigotry." Counts of Jews, especially if cross-tabulated with the litany of negatively viewed Jewish characteristics mentioned above, would be grist for the mill of the anti-Semite.

It thus seems very likely that their leaders thought it was "in the interest of the Jews" to resist legibility. What, then, should we make of the leaders' constitutional argument that the American state cannot "see" a religious group, must remain "blind" to religious identity? This line of argument was self-serving, protecting material and political interests. But an elective affinity between interests and ideals is not "merely" and need not be "primarily" a self-serving ideology or a cynical ploy. Both the way the Reform Jewish leaders saw their place in an enlightened world and the way they interpreted what was special about the United States seemed threatened by the Hebrew category in federal statistics, whatever the specific nature of the slippery slope they envisioned. In this sense the Jewish protest was a matter of self-image and ideals as well as a self-interested resistance to legibility.

The concept of legibility provides a useful metaphor for one central theme in the struggles between the most influential Jewish groups and the federal government in the early years of the century and on into its later years. In other cases, however, we will find ethno-racial advocacy groups insisting on becoming legible, or trying to increase what the state could already "see"—especially in the half century since the civil rights era—since they regarded legibility as a net gain.[10]

The Jewish Protests to the Bureau of Immigration, 1899 and 1903

The most important of the Jewish critics in the first encounters with the federal government was Simon Wolf. In 1899, Wolf was in his early sixties. He had been a boy of twelve when his family moved from Bavaria to Ohio. There he had begun his career in the family's commercial enterprises. In his mid-twenties he studied law and then moved to the nation's capital. He began to work his way into Republican Party circles, eventually winning federal appointments, including an ambassadorship and a judgeship. At the same time, he devoted himself to the major organizations of German Jewish laymen in America—the B'nai B'rith organization and the Board of Delegates of the Union of American Hebrew Congregations. As the chair of the board, he had as good a claim as anyone to speak on behalf of American Jews. By the late 1890s he had cultivated personal connections with government officials and party leaders for many years.[11]

By 1899, Wolf's career was nearing its end. In 1906, a New York-based group, comprised of younger American Jews (most of whom were from the German Jewish, Reform-oriented elite) would establish the American Jewish Committee. This body would take upon itself much the same mission Wolf had claimed for himself through the Board of Delegates. But the new leaders would be acting from a position of much greater prestige, wealth, and influence than Wolf could muster. Some were in the professions, especially in the law (including some judges), or as rabbis of elite congregations. Others were especially wealthy leaders of commerce and finance. Their national board was self-recruiting.

Not even the American Jewish Committee could really command Jewish organizational life without competition in the new century. No group of the German Jewish elite could do so in the face of a giant new Jewish immigration from the countries *east* of Germany that had begun in force during the early 1880s and continued at ever-higher rates until the First World War. Eastern Europe was the demographic heartland of the Jews in the nineteenth century. Eastern European Jews, numbering some eight million strong in 1900 (and that was after a million had emigrated), vastly outnumbered all the other Jewish populations in the world combined. By 1890, the number of the *eastern* European Jewish immigrants in the United States already equaled the total number of *other* Jews— whether immigrants or their descendants—living in the United States. A decade later, eastern European Jews already comprised the great majority of Jews in the United States. During the peak years of Jewish immigration between 1905 and 1908, the number of eastern European Jewish arrivals *in each single year* was comparable to the total number of German Jews who immigrated during the entire nineteenth century.

The eastern European Jewish arrivals regarded the Reform Judaism of the German American Jewish elite as a pale mockery of the Jewishness they understood. If the new arrivals came from a religious home, and most did, the religion they were familiar with (whatever their own level of belief and observance) was Jewish Orthodoxy, reverence for textual knowledge, and rituals that radically separated the Jews from others. Moreover, the great majority of these immigrants spoke Yiddish, and they had grown up among local Jewish majorities in small towns or in the Jewish neighborhoods of large eastern European cities.

Finally, and critically, this huge new wave of immigration included a much higher proportion of people who had been engaged in some form of manual work, especially in manufacturing, than had been the case among those Jewish immigrants who had left the German lands around midcentury. This occupational profile partly reflected that of Jews in the eastern European societies. It also it reflected self-selection: the manual laborers among the eastern European Jews were more likely to emigrate than those who had decent commercial opportunities there. Still, the eastern European Jewish immigrants arriving in the decades after 1880 did not lack all advantages. Compared to Italians and Slavs arriving in the same years, the Jews were typically employed more in skilled manual labor, and more of them reached self-employment and commercial pursuits during their lifetimes. Nevertheless, compared to the children of the earlier German Jewish immigrants, the later eastern European Jewish immigrant arrivals seemed distinctly working class.[12]

For all these reasons, these new Jewish immigrants, and their American-born children, saw a gulf between themselves and the German Jewish elite who often endeavored to speak for all Jews in America and defend Jewish immigrants. The eastern European Jews generally saw in their Jewishness some combination of language, peoplehood, race, nation, and a demanding traditional religion—rather than merely the universal ethics of American Reform Judaism. And if appreciable numbers of these eastern European Jews were socialists (rather than Orthodox), they were all the more likely to define their Jewishness in terms of language, peoplehood, race, or nationality. Indeed, among both poles of eastern European Jewish immigrant culture—the traditional Orthodox and atheist socialists—there was a certain contempt for what they saw as the craven assimilation of the German Jewish Reform elite.

These ethnic, class, and cultural divisions run through the history of the American Jewish immigration after 1880. It is not surprising, then, that these divisions also run through sensitivities to the issue of defining "Hebrews"—in government statistics and elsewhere. Were the Jews representative only of a religion, as Simon Wolf would have it? If not, how were the other aspects of Jewish identity to be classified by the government, especially given church–state separation in America?

In 1899 eastern European Jewish immigrants were hardly at home in mainstream American politics, and they lacked the governmental connections enjoyed by Wolf's Board of Delegates. Wolf really had a position from which to claim leadership, and truly extensive contacts as well; officials paid attention when he contacted them. In a 1910 speech, Secretary of Commerce and Labor Charles Nagel gently criticized the belligerence of a more militant Jewish critic by comparing him to Wolf: "Mr. Simon Wolf is in Washington and keeps a pretty close watch on us. If we ever miss him, we think the world is going to stop. I frequently inquire about eleven o'clock, 'Has Wolf been here?' . . . The way brother Wolf approaches us is calculated to get the best results, because he comes to us fairly, good-naturedly; and when he is defeated he recognizes our point of view."[13]

The Jewish protests against the List began well before the Bureau of Immigration published information based upon it. In July 1898, the bureau had just introduced the supplemental form that Safford and McSweeney had designed. Recall that the form included five new questions for all immigrant arrivals—including the religion question. From these new questions the List of Races would be compiled, and one such race was "Hebrew." Jewish immigrants arrived daily from eastern Europe; many, of course, had heard about Jewish freedom in the new land. They must have been surprised and troubled to be asked about their religion, and they would have reported the experience to more seasoned American Jews. In addition, representatives of American Jewish organizations aided arrivals at the port of entry, and they too would have known all about the supplemental form very soon after it was introduced.

About a year later, Powderly published the first year's results for the List of Races in the *Annual Report of the Commissioner-General of Immigration for 1899*. Buried deep in that report was a single column within a single table reporting the responses to the religion question; no other information on religion from the supplemental forms was ever published.[14] It is interesting that not a word of discussion accompanies the religion data, and the title of that table does not mention religion. But for those with eyes to see, the federal government was explicitly asking each new immigrant about his or her religion. Thus, although McSweeney and Safford had intended the religion question simply as one of several useful criteria for establishing the best race category for each arrival, Powderly nonetheless had reported the responses to the religion question itself.

We know that Commissioner-General of Immigration Terrence Powderly was already in correspondence with Wolf about the List as early as April 1899, and that by then he was objecting to the way the Jewish press had criticized the List earlier still. Powderly told Wolf that the press accounts had misunderstood his bureau's use of the List. He emphasized that no special attention to religion or to Jews was involved—the immigrant was "questioned as to birthplace, the religion he professes . . . and all are questioned alike." Moreover, the data were only to be used for understanding statistical trends; they did not follow any individual immigrant beyond the port of entry. He had anticipated some misunderstandings, "for there is nothing on which men are so sensitive as the question of religion." However, he denied that the religion question was a new departure because in the decennial census "every man and woman is questioned as to his religious belief; not so much the belief as the denomination."

In fact, there was no such question in the decennial census. Powderly was confusing the enumeration of population with a separate federal census of religious bodies. Each institution reported an estimate of total membership, among other characteristics. But this inquiry involved no report of individual names of congregants, and it was not administered to individuals.

Powderly also claimed to wonder why the Jews did not in fact welcome the chance to know more precisely the magnitude of the Jewish immigration flow and concluded, "I believe that when our method of gathering statistics is understood, the Jews of this country will be the first to approve the measure. It will enable them to ascertain each year how many of their race and coreligionists have arrived, and will tend to show that they are a power in the United States." Moreover, other Americans will rejoice that such an attractive group of immigrants is arriving. "Many of my associates in the industrial movements were Jews, and I cannot recall a day when the Jew . . . did not stand for law and order."[15] Three more paragraphs lauding the Jews followed.

Some months later, Wolf reported to the Board of Delegates on his interactions with officials about the data collection. The report captures his style of quiet, elite negotiation. He wrote, "Pending a solution of this important question the Jewish press of the country had indulged in a great deal of criticism pro and con, and showed in the main a great lack of patience, for I can give the assurance that nothing will be neglected as far as I can prevent it, and in this instance the delay [in negotiating] produced the most favorable results." Wolf had in fact convinced Powderly to hold discussions with Jewish leaders in New York; McSweeney also attended. "Lengthy discussions took place" at which the Jewish leaders "cheerfully admitted . . . that a great deal of valuable information from the scientific standpoint had been gathered by the Bureau, yet it was setting a bad and dangerous precedent to continue the practice of describing persons in terms of their faith, and that it was letting down the constitutional bars, and when once down, there would be no telling how far fanaticism would go."[16]

Wolf and Powderly in fact reached an agreement "to abandon hereafter statistics concerning the religious denominations of immigrants." On January 1, 1900, Powderly ended the use of the religion question found on the supplemental form.[17] Thus one leg of Safford and McSweeney's racial classification scheme was kicked away: if some races could be meaningfully distinguished only by religion, what was their status in the List now that religion was removed? However, Wolf later claimed that Powderly had made a much broader concession: to remove the Hebrew category from the list of races.[18] Clearly, the Bureau did not do so.

In any case, after 1898 the Jewish protests no longer focused on the direct enumeration of religion but rather on "Hebrews" being a category on the list. Still, that initial skirmish over the supplemental form's direct question on religion must have helped convince the Jewish organizations that the existence of a Hebrew category on the List was indeed tightly connected to state inquiries into the religious affiliations of individuals.

By the end of 1900 Wolf knew that the bureau had dropped the religious question but was still classifying Hebrew immigrants by race. In mid-1903, he lodged a new protest, now leveled against the Hebrew category, with the new commissioner-general of immigration Frank P. Sargent, who in turn referred the matter to his own superior, Secretary of Commerce and Labor George B. Cortelyou. Wolf summed up his position.

> I have never for a moment wavered from the opinion that, first, the Jew at present has no nationality other than that to which he has sworn allegiance, and to which he owes obedience; second, the Jew, as an immigrant should not be classified as belonging to a race, because he does not land as a Jew, but comes as a native of the country in which he was born; third, that if this question is to be treated from a scientific or ethnological standpoint, then all immigrants should be treated uniformly so as to give the benefit of the classification to the world at large; fourth, but that if the classification is religious then I most solemnly protest, as it is contrary to the spirit and genius of our institutions and the government is assuming functions that were never contemplated in the Constitution of the United States; the administrative functions are political, not religious.[19]

For Wolf, the issue must have seemed worth raising anew for two reasons. First, there was a new cast of characters in high federal offices—president, department secretary, commissioner-general of immigration. Second, after the Immigration Act of 1903, the race-or-people classification had been added to the Passenger Lists themselves (rather than derived, as before, from the supplemental inquiries of Safford and McSweeney). Consequently, urging the removal of the Hebrew category from that list must have seemed even more important than before.

Secretary Cortelyou took Wolf's arguments seriously and began an internal review of the List and its Hebrew category. Meanwhile, Wolf led a group from the Board of Delegates to meet federal officials (it was "unanimously agreed that Mr. Wolf should act as the sole spokesman of the party"). They met the president, the secretaries of state and commerce, the Speaker of the House, and the chairmen of the Senate and House committees on foreign affairs. The List of Races and Peoples was by no means the only item on the agenda, but it was one item.

That fall, Wolf also wrote to various Jewish authorities to ask them whether or not the Jews should be considered a race. He then forwarded the responses he received to Cortelyou.[20] Thus, on the one hand, Wolf maintained that the Hebrew category in the List of Races and Peoples designated members of a religion, and consequently the federal government had no right to use it. On the other hand, since he believed that Jewishness connoted, or should connote, a religious affiliation only, he hoped to convince the federal officials that identifying the Jews as a race was not scientifically credible, quite apart from any constitutional objections to the category. The opinions of these Jewish authorities made no difference to Cortelyou's federal review; the government officials had found their way during the internal review stimulated by Wolf's first letter back in July. Nevertheless, they did study the new materials, and an official summed up the conclusions in a long and emphatic internal memorandum, written this time with less sympathy and more undisguised pique.[21]

And yet the responses to Wolf's survey on the Hebrew race question are intriguing in their own right, and they illuminate how fully the issue was familiar in that circle by 1903. Ignoring the attorney's first rule of questioning, Wolf had asked his question without knowing what the answer would be. No doubt, to his exasperation, opinion varied widely. Wolf breezily dismissed those who said that the Jews were indeed a race: "While some of my correspondents differ on the question of race, it must not be forgotten that they are Zionists, who believe in the ultimate return of the Jews to Palestine."[22] Use of this argument to exclude opinion he himself had solicited was probably not a winning strategy.

The responses reveal first of all that the racial status of Jews was far from settled among Jewish authorities. The range of views turned on the prevalence of conversions to Judaism and intermarriages. Had they been common enough to rule out any meaningful claim to Jewish racial purity? Cyrus Adler told Wolf that anthropologists "are divided as to the exact meaning of the term 'race.' . . . [But if race means] an ethnical stock, a great division of mankind having in common certain distinguishing physical peculiarities appearing to be derived from a distinct primitive source, [then] . . . there is not the slightest doubt . . . [that] Jews intermingled with other peoples."[23]

Another commented, "Neither the shape of the skull or the color of the eyes and hair, show a uniform characteristic." Another thought he knew what all this was really about: "Fight the good fight! . . . This classification may not be intended as a piece of anti-Semitic chicanery, but it resembles it very closely. We may remember it some day at the polls."[24]

However, other serious scholars and communal authorities reached precisely the opposite conclusion about the history of intermingling. Reform rabbinic leader Kaufman Kohler believed that "ethnologically the Jews certainly represent a race since both their religion and their history kept them apart from the rest of the people of the country they inhabit."[25] The scholar Solomon Schechter, by then leading the new Conservative movement's Jewish Theological Seminary in New York City thought so too: "the Jews are a race . . . [by virtue of] their common origin and their common blood, which has received very little admixture."[26] Talmud scholar Marcus Jastrow believed that the Jew "does represent a race for anthropological and sociological purposes . . . [And if the bureau is recording among Russian emigrants, Slavs, Finns, Germans, etc.] then, of course, we can take no exception to the Russian Jew being taken as a Russian belonging to the Jewish race."[27] No doubt worst of all responses, in Wolf's eyes, came from a writer who told him first that "for all practical purposes the Jews are a race," and second that he welcomed the statistical reports of the commissioner of immigration, for without them "we should not get any authentic reports of Jewish immigration, which is so important to have."[28]

Still another writer raised the convert question. Mentioning the classic case of Benjamin Disraeli, he notes, "Lord Beaconsfield . . . would have said, 'Racially I am a Jew, religiously I am an Episcopalian, and politically I am an English citizen.'"[29] Another stated that he himself felt that the Jews could not be thought of as an ancient race given the range of intermarriages and conversions through the ages. Nevertheless, he observed (presciently), "if races must be classified, our case is well-nigh hopeless" because the author of the introduction to the *Jewish Encyclopedia* had himself written that the Jews *were* a race, "and many of our orators have so often discoursed on 'our race' that the State Department will have no trouble in finding warrant for its assumption."[30]

A number of Wolf's correspondents were mainly interested in the implications of the classification, rather than addressing Wolf's question directly. Leo N. Levi, President of B'nai B'rith, perceptively observed that "[The Department of State] will make endless trouble for itself [by ruling either way] . . . I think you should explain to the Department that one of the most vexing questions of controversy among Jews is the one which it has undertaken to settle. Leading Reform rabbis of this country utterly repudiate the race doctrine and assent that the Jews are simply a religious community. On the other hand, many others, and especially the Zionists, assent that, aside from religious considerations, the Jews constitute a race."[31]

Finally, Judge Mayer Sulzberger raised broader constitutional challenges—not only to the use of religion, but to the use of racial categories as well—or rather to racial categories beyond the color divisions.

> I am unaware of any authority conferred on the officials of the United States to inquire into the religious belief of any person. I am equally unaware of any use of the word "race" in our Constitution or laws except to designate marked physical diversity of color, such as the red or Indian race, the yellow or Mongolian, the black or African. Not one, I think, will contend that the Jews belong to any other than the group called Caucasian, which doubtless includes many varieties or sub-races. Into the distinctions between them I do not think there is any legal warrant or practical use, or even theoretical capacity to inquire. The test among them has been, not sub-race, but nationality. . . .
>
> [I]n the sense in which the word "race" is used in our legislation the Jews are not a race.[32]

Sulzberger's concern would resurface with greater force in 1909, when the newly established American Jewish Committee, with Sulzberger as its first head, entered the debates about the List of Races and Peoples. But in 1903, Wolf seems to have ignored Sulzberger's constitutional challenge to race inquiries. Perhaps Wolf believed that he had enough to do with the religion argument. Moreover, Sulzberger's constitutional challenge would have necessitated a much broader attack: challenging the use of the List of Races and Peoples for *any* European group rather than merely eliminating the Hebrew category.

The disunity among Wolf's Jewish authorities was enough to sink his cause, but there was more. Bureau officials must have positively gloated when they received a letter from Phillip Cowen, publisher of the *American Hebrew*, in November 1903. He wrote to tell them of his upcoming editorial *supporting* the collection of data on Hebrews and rejecting the claim that the data collection was inappropriate because of the "coincident religious distinction." Cowen added in a cover letter that he had been one of those who accompanied Wolf back in 1899 to the meeting of Jewish leaders with Powderly and McSweeney to discuss the direct religious question on the supplemental form. "Mr. Wolf then took the same position as he does today, but I do not believe that any of us agreed with him, and I should be very sorry to hear that you have cut out this column [i.e., 'Race or People' column in the Passenger List form]."[33]

The Internal Federal Review of the List and Its Hebrew Category, 1903

Confronted with the issues Wolf had raised in mid-1903, Cortelyou conducted an intriguing series of confidential inquiries, soliciting opinion widely within the federal government. Thus the protest by one group (the Jews) against the way the state classified it now led to an intense federal review of the classification scheme itself, with a new set of officials weighing the List's strengths and weaknesses (including, as we shall see, its particular use of the race term). In the end, these state actors concluded that the policy could be defended.

It was clear, first of all, that the new federal officials, from the secretary on down, had to be brought up to speed as to where the List came from; after all, when they took office, it had already been in place for several years. Cortelyou or Sargent requested an internal summary of what was known about the origins of the List of Races and Peoples. They also asked for opinions about the specific claims Wolf was making: Did the constitutional separation of church and state really make identification by race impermissible when race and religion had congruent boundaries? Also, was it in fact reasonable to classify the Jews as a race? And finally, how had the federal government defined Jews in the past? Besides immigration officials, others at Census, State, and perhaps the attorney general's office also participated in this review. All this internal activity occurred at the federal offices during July 1903, the month following Wolf's letter.

The officials' informational memo on the history of the List correctly attributed the classification scheme to work by Safford in 1898 and noted that the bureau had then included a direct inquiry about religion. A thoughtful reflection on the classification system followed:

> This list seems to be somewhat arbitrary in that in some cases it represents language, as for instance the people from Switzerland are called German, French or Italian according to the language they speak; in some cases it represents blood strain regardless of language, as African black or Chinese; and in some cases it represents locality regardless of language, as Servian, Montenegrin, Croatian, Slovenian and Dalmatian, who all speak the Serbo-Croatian language. On the whole, however, notwithstanding the fact that the list is a mixture, it very likely is about as comprehensive and practicable a list of races or peoples as could be devised.[34]

This was apparently the first evaluation of the list by later, and indeed higher-echelon, officials. The List might be inconsistent in relying on different criteria for different groups—language, territory, and blood strain. But it worked well as a practical instrument for classifying races or peoples. Interestingly, the authors did not question the utility of that classification. But this restraint no doubt reflected the fact that the 1903 Immigration Act had added "race" to the items of information to be collected on each immigrant (as we shall see another of the internal memos argue).

The next question was "whether the Hebrews should be shown separately and whether there is such a thing as a Hebrew race or a Hebrew people." The writer began: "Ordinarily, we think of the Hebrews as a clannish people, with certain tendencies for money getting that are thought to be racial characteristics."[35] Our author obviously did not consider this observation gratuitous, nor did any official involved in the review trouble to demur; and obviously neither Cortelyou nor anyone else thought it best to return the memo so these phrases might be removed. It seems safe to conclude, then, that none of the readers thought such rumination particularly inappropriate, at least for an internal document of the United States government.

The author now proceeds to *challenge* the racial premise as it relates to the Jews. He cites Professor Otis T. Mason, chief of the Division of Ethnology at the Smithsonian Institution: "[They] have the racial traits of the people among whom their lot has been cast. . . . [They have intermarried over generations and] there is a law in biology . . . that after there has been more of the foreign than of the native blood ingrafted into a people, they lose, physically and mentally, their native racial characteristics."[36] A biological basis for the diversity of mental characteristics across historical groups seems to be a given. Likewise, there is no doubt that the concept of race in this statement is one based in the biological transmission of physical and mental traits. However, when it comes to the Jews, neither physical nor mental traits are (any longer) distinct; their "blood" has been extensively mixed.

Now the author turned back to the narrower concerns at hand. Whatever may be said about the racial unity of the world's Jews, he noted that the Jewish immigration to the United States was coming from eastern Europe. And while their blood, too, has been intermingled with the local peoples,' they do exhibit an *other, nonracial* distinctiveness. Specifically, the eastern European Jews can be defined in terms of language and social characteristics.

> Those who speak Yiddish as their native tongue could well be classified as Hebrews. . . . [Furthermore] that the average Hebrew is different from other aliens is clearly shown [by the figures reported in the *Annual Reports*] . . . the Hebrew comes to stay, and brings with him his family, and his children, which are numerous; . . . he is usually poor and often afflicted with disease and goes to the shops and trades of the large cities. . . . [Consequently, whether or not the Hebrews are a race,] it can still be held that their characteristics are sufficiently distinctive to justify calling them a people.[37]

Here was an explicit appeal to the useful ambiguity that had been provided when the "List of Races" became the "List of Races and Peoples." Moreover, the memo writer noted that *failing* to classify the Jews separately would in-

volve losing distinctive information on some 11 percent of the aliens arriving annually; Hebrews would then senselessly be classified with
Slavic groups.

Cortelyou now sent this memorandum, as well as Wolf's initial letter,
to Census Director S. D. North for comment. As Commerce Secretary,
Cortelyou supervised both Census and Immigration, so he was in effect
soliciting opinion about a problem in one bureau he supervised from the
director of another. Moreover, Census too dealt with classifying the
population; perhaps the director then had some experience with the issues
Wolf raised. In addition, North was an expert on demography whereas
Sargent had been a labor leader before his federal appointment.

North reached a more guarded conclusion than that expressed in the
memorandum he had been asked to review. The Hebrew category referred
to Jews across the globe, and clearly no single language or locality characterized them all. Thus "the inclusion of Hebrew in this list must be necessarily under the second category, namely blood strain." His meaning was
probably not that inclusion was obviously justified but rather that a defense of inclusion would need to rest on a claim that Jews across the world
shared a distinctive blood strain (the claim Smithsonian ethnologist
Otis Mason had rejected). North's crucial contribution was to highlight
Wolf's constitutional point: "The question is so nice a one, and at the same
time so important, not only from Mr. Wolf's point of view but from a constitutional view, that I suggest it ought to be determined by the Attorney
General. . . . [Surely Jews did qualify as a people] but whether or not in
[listing Jews as a distinct group] unintentional discrimination is made
against the Hebrew, from the standpoint of religious faith is a proper matter
for legal determination as to the meaning of the word Hebrew."[38]

The census, he added, has not asked respondents any question on religion, "probably in accordance with the spirit" of the First Amendment. Indeed, *no one* involved in the internal review simply asserted the government's
right to ask about an individual's religion. Such a position presumably would
have been the most contentious way forward.

Of course, when Safford and McSweeney had created the List and its Hebrew category, classification rested not only on language, blood strain, and
locality, but also on religion. Without that fourth criterion, a Hebrew category could be restricted to the Jews of eastern Europe, defined by language

and locality. Or else it could refer to all of the world's Hebrews, defined by a common blood strain (if Mason could be proven wrong).

During the two weeks after North urged legal opinions, three more memos were written. One came from the State Department. "In the absence of any Court decision on the subject, it is important to know what is the precedent of the Executive branch." Most important has been the "our correspondence with foreign powers" concerning anti-Semitism in those countries. Those powers most often "regard the Jewish question as chiefly a race question." Still, "The Secretary of State in his correspondence has spoken of Jews as a race or has distinguished them by their faith; usually in the latter way." At the same time, "The State Department would not feel itself precluded from classifying Jews as a race . . . and there is nothing repugnant to" such classification "in the precedents."[39]

The second memo, probably from an attorney in the Bureau of Immigration, reviewed the legislative basis for the List of Races and Peoples. It stressed that whatever had been the legality of the initiative Safford, McSweeney, and Powderly had undertaken a few years earlier, the revised Immigration Act of March 3, 1903—passed a mere three months before the memo was written—established the legal basis for the List by adding "race" to the items of information required from immigrant arrivals. This memo also cited dictionary definitions of race to argue that the Hebrew category in particular was also legitimate: the Jews met the dictionary definition of "a people at least 'believed or presumed to belong to the same stock.'" Moreover, "The racial distinction is not less apparent because there is a coincident religious distinction." Finally, "the religious is not predominant," since if a Jew converts, "he is still called a Jew."[40]

Here was the explicit rejection of Wolf's central contention: the "coincident religious distinction" was simply irrelevant. Even if religion and race were congruent in the case of the Jews, this "coincident" outcome was no constitutional bar to the data collection on immigrant races and peoples. The third memo, probably by an assistant to Cortelyou, summed up the other two and concluded that Wolf's "request should . . . be denied."[41] Reviewing all this, North now agreed.[42] And so in the end, Cortelyou let the existing policy stand. Perhaps he considered whether Wolf's organization might mount a legal challenge. But if he did consider that possibility, he probably rejected it as unlikely on any ground, and certainly not on their second corollary to church–state separation (i.e., that the List's Hebrew category was unconstitutional because it involved a "coincident religious" enumeration of Jews). This elite, and Wolf in particular, eschewed direct confrontation with the federal government, preferring instead persuasion among friends.

After the 1903 internal review, the bureau had a file of arguments with which to refute periodic challenges to the Hebrew race category. The arguments rested on an awareness of the bureaucratic origin of the List of Races and Peoples, the diversity of factors that defined the categories on the List, and a reasonable understanding of expert opinions on the Jews (religion, people, or race). If the Hebrews were not a race (and this was not certain), they could certainly be considered a people. Finally, the Hebrew category should not be dropped just because a "coincident religious" enumeration of Jews occurred in the course of enumerating races and peoples for purposes of understanding immigration. The Hebrew category would probably not come before the courts, and even if it did, it would probably not be ruled a violation of the First Amendment. The Bureau of Immigration could remind those who objected to the Hebrew category that it was not defined by religion but by race or people.

CHAPTER 4

The United States Immigration Commission, 1907–1911

IN 1907 IT SEEMED THAT CONGRESS, as in 1896, was on the verge of passing Lodge's literacy bill. But once again, the bill did not pass, this time because Speaker Joe Cannon opposed the measure and managed to pressure enough representatives to reject the literacy restriction in favor of a definitive study of immigration, a measure designed (successfully) to postpone any additional restriction for several congressional sessions. And so was born the U.S. Immigration Commission, which worked with a large staff and a large budget for some four years and produced forty-one volumes of reports. The commission was to play an enormous role in the evolution of the List of Races and Peoples.

The act creating the commission provided for nine commissioners: three to be appointed by President Roosevelt, three more by the president of the Senate, and the last three by the Speaker of the House. Roosevelt and the Senate president both wanted to appoint restrictionists; Speaker Cannon, however, did not. Nevertheless, the law creating the commission had also stipulated that the congressional appointees were to include the chairmen of the House and Senate committees on immigration. And because the House committee chairman was a restrictionist, Speaker Cannon was left to make only two appointments that were skeptical of restriction. The chairman of the Immigration Commission was Vermont Senator William P. Dillingham (chairman of the Senate's Immigration Committee), and hence it came to be known also as the Dillingham Commission. The other consequential senator appointed was Henry Cabot Lodge. President Roosevelt's three appointments included his commissioner of labor, a California businessman with public service experience, and, crucially, Jeremiah W. Jenks, a professor of government at Cornell. Jenks was a veteran of other federal investigations and an expert on contemporary government. He did much to organize the Immigration Commission. Senator Dillingham's able aide for immigration matters, W. W. Husband, became its key administrator ("secretary").

The scope as well as the size of the *Reports of the United States Immigration Commission* (1911) were meant to make them the definitive inquiry. Twenty volumes concerned the role of immigrants in a wide range of industries; five more dealt with the children of immigrants in schools. Other volumes dealt with immigrants in cities, immigrants and poverty, immigrants and crime, immigrant women workers, immigrant occupations, and so on. Crucially, the first two volumes of the *Reports* provided a summary of the rest. But even these two volumes taken together exceeded 1,000 pages. And so the first fifty pages of Volume I were given over to a "Brief Statement of the Investigations." Unlike the rest of the volumes, the long and short summaries were both produced by the central staff of the Immigration Commission, presumably under the close supervision of Secretary Husband. Most readers probably did not proceed beyond the fifty-page summary. Whatever may be said of the many detailed reports, those summaries marshaled the evidence in a way that highlighted contemporary problems and that tended to make the case for restriction.

Near the beginning of the "Brief Statement," the reader learns that an "old" and a "new" European immigration may be distinguished. The old and new immigrations came, respectively, from northern and western versus southern and eastern Europe. "The old and new immigration differ in many essentials." The nature of these essentials may be appreciated from the description of the southern and eastern Europeans that follows:

> The new immigration has been largely a movement of unskilled laboring men who have come, in large part temporarily, from the less progressive and advanced countries of Europe. . . . They have almost entirely avoided agricultural pursuits, and in cities and industrial communities have congregated together in sections apart from native Americans and the

older immigrants to such an extent that assimilation has been slow as compared to that of the earlier non-English-speaking races.

The new immigration as a class is far less intelligent than the old, approximately one-third of all those over 14 years of age when admitted being illiterate. Racially they are for the most part essentially unlike the British, German, and other peoples who came during the period prior to 1880, and generally speaking they are actuated in coming by different ideals, for the old immigration came to be a part of the country, while the new, in a large measure, comes with the intention of profiting, in a pecuniary way, by the superior advantages of the new world and then returning to the old country.[1]

The Immigration Commission members actually did not spend much time relating research to policy. But at the end of four years' of work by the research staff, the commissioners made short work of finding the best policy going forward, and all but one recommended the literacy restriction. The country no longer needed such a high proportion of unskilled immigrants, and other trends in contemporary immigration created social and political problems. The commission concluded that the best method of restriction was indeed the literacy requirement. It also mentioned an alternative: assigning to each race an annual quota of immigrants, amounting to a certain percentage of the average of that race's arrivals during a given period of past years. Either form of restriction would considerably reduce the number of undesirable arrivals.

At the heart of the commission's work was the List of Races and Peoples. The commission's *Reports* presented all research in terms of the List. Literally thousands of tables classify immigrants and their children in terms of the List and then cross-tabulate the races and peoples with various other outcomes, including age, gender, industry, occupation, wage, literacy, length of residence in the United States, naturalization rates, and children's schooling. Many tables cross-classify immigrants in terms of two or more of these characteristics. Because the List showed many differences across its categories on these immigrant outcomes, it was easy to conclude that race or people was itself an *explanation* for observed differences.

Moreover, one volume of the *Reports, The Dictionary of Races and Peoples* (Volume 5), has become a classic example for historians of the racist and downright bizarre products of the era. Following a general introduction on race theorists, the *Dictionary* discusses each group in terms of its political and social history as well as its physical and mental qualities.

The commission used the List so extensively for at least two reasons. First, the Bureau of Immigration had been presenting its most illuminating data in terms of that classification scheme for nearly a decade. The commissioners therefore believed it to be very important that their new data collection should be comparable with what was already available. Second, commissioners generally agreed with the initial conclusion that Safford had come to long before: the older form of presenting immigrant data by country of origin was next to meaningless since so many different immigrant peoples, with very different attributes, were coming from Europe's multinational empires. Consequently, the intertwining histories of the List and commission exhibits the expansion of the racial classification system into a new and very prestigious context, notwithstanding its more humble origins among the Bureau of Immigration's mid-level officials. Moreover, the commission would soon exploit the same arguments about the List to urge that it be used to classify Americans' origins in the upcoming 1910 census.

In historical writing on immigration and the rise of restrictionist thinking, the Dillingham Commission has long held an important place. Most historians have stressed, as Oscar Handlin did as early as 1952, the extent to which the "social science" of the commission's summary volumes was deeply flawed and twisted the findings in the full reports so that they supported restriction. In this view the commission appears as a step forward in the formation of the restrictionist thinking that would peak with the legislation of 1917–1924, which ended mass European immigration and severely changed the country-of-origin distribution for later entrants. Robert Zeidel recently warned, however, against exaggerating the racial concerns of the commissioners or the bias shown in its full reports (whatever the nature of the summaries). Zeidel emphasized how much the progressive-era ideal of meaningful social research guided the commission's work. Moreover, he stressed that most commissioners were in fact not committed to the literacy bill (or to severe restriction generally) at the time they were appointed. In addition, Zeidel and Aristide Zolberg emphasized that a wide range of issues other than race—such as an excess of unskilled laborers among the immigrants—worried the commissioners and helped in determining the recommendation for restriction in general and for the literacy requirement in particular.[2]

Our focus will be on the connections between the Immigration Commission and the List. Those connections include the intellectual outlooks among the commission's senior research staff. This was a group that operated just below the level of the commissioners themselves. As a group, the senior research staff has received virtually no attention from historians over the century since the commission's time. The senior research staff held a wide range of outlooks about immigration and restriction. Among them were some very well-known figures, such as Franz Boas, and others less well known, such as Daniel K. Folkmar, author of *The Dictionary of Races and Peoples*. But even Boas's role in the commission's history raises new considerations when it is seen in the context of his interactions with other commission staff members—not least when they asked for his thoughts on draft entries for the *Dictionary* itself. Finally, a number of the senior research staff members moved to the Census Bureau on completion of the commission's work and carried out similar research work in connection with the 1910 census. By studying senior staff activity, rather than only the role of the commissioners, issues of the commission's anti-immigrant racial bias and its conduct of policy-oriented social research appear in new ways.

The commission's use of the List of Races and Peoples was actually much more extensive than it had been in the Bureau of Immigration. Whereas the Bureau counted only immigrant arrivals at their port of entry, the commission also studied immigrants long after they had arrived—for example, at work, in their neighborhoods, and in their choices of whether or not to apply for American citizenship. The commission also applied the categories of the list to the next generation: the native-born children of immigrants, who were American citizens by birth. And it was this two-generation use of the List that the commission would eventually recommend for adoption in the 1910 census. Admittedly, the commission did not envision preserving this classification for immigrant descendants beyond the second generation—at least not for European races. The commission's secretary, W. W. Husband, had numerous opportunities to explain the point. For example, in a letter to commission member W. Wheeler, he wrote, "Beyond the second generation the Commission made no reference to races except in the case of Orientals, negroes and American Indians."[3] The commission was not sacrificing anything by stopping at the second generation in recording European origins. Its interests were in the new immigration waves of southern and eastern European immigrants. These groups simply had not yet had time to produce a third generation by 1907 when the commission began its four-year career.

The Immigration Commission strengthened the authority of the state classification system captured in the List. Recall first the humble origins of the List as the brainchild of the mid-level officials at the Bureau of Immigration, Safford and McSweeney. As the role of these actors (a fairly low-level medical man and a former labor leader) suggests, the Bureau of Immigration was not a home to many officials who were professionally trained in population studies or other social sciences. By contrast, the commissioners were supposed to be a top-drawer group. Three of the nine—Lodge, Jenks, and another Roosevelt appointee—had serious academic credentials. Probably more significant still, the commission was authorized to produce the ultimate authoritative study, and its dozen or so senior researchers tended to have impressive credentials. The commission's heavy reliance on it enhanced the List's authority. The uses of the List now extended beyond the ports of entry into American social life across two generations. Moreover, the commission then urged the *further* extension of the List to the U.S. census.

The Commission Takes on a Divided Jewish Elite, 1909

After more than two years of work, the Immigration Commission called for comment from interested parties. About half came from Jewish organizations.[4] Moreover, at a hearing in December 1909, the ubiquitous Simon Wolf (now in his mid-seventies), and Julian Mack, an important member of the new American Jewish Committee's executive board, testified about the Hebrew category in the List of Races and Peoples. But they were up against Henry Cabot Lodge, who also thought he knew a thing or two about race.

Wolf began with a very few familiar phrases: "The point we make is this: A Jew coming from Russia is a Russian; from Roumania a Roumanian ... that Hebrew or Jewish is simply a religion." But Senator Lodge would have none of it.[5]

Senator Lodge. What if he comes from Poland?

Mr. Wolf. I suppose he is a Pole; or if he belongs—

Senator Lodge. "Poland" is a geographic expression [i.e., Poland was not a state in 1910]. ... Do you think that Poles ought to be classified as Prussians, Austrians, Russians, depending upon which part of Poland they come from?

Mr. Wolf. I do.

Senator Lodge. And the Irish as British.

Mr. Wolf. Yes, sir. ...

Senator Lodge. Do I understand you to deny that the Jews are a race? ... That I think is an important point. I have always supposed they were. I find [the point confirmed] in the preface of *The Jewish Encyclopedia* which is signed by Cyrus Adler. ... How would you classify Benjamin Disraeli? Was he a Jew? ... He was baptized. He then ceased to be a Jew?

Mr. Wolf. Yes; religiously he ceased to be a Jew.

Senator Lodge. Ah! Religiously. He was very proud of the fact that he was a Jew. ... Did the fact that he changed his religion alter his race? ... I have never supposed for one moment that the Jews who are put down in the immigration returns as such are classified according to religion.

Mr. Wolf. You classify them under the supposition as I understand—

Senator Lodge. On the supposition that it is a race ... as the Poles are a race, though they have no country and no nationality; as the Irish are a race although they have no nationality and no country. ... It is important, very important, to get the race classification as nearly as we can.

Mr. Wolf. Yes.

Lodge, who was long committed to particular views of race and history, was not the only one to challenge Wolf's insistence that Jews were only (or even primarily) a religious group. Later in the discussion another commissioner, William Wheeler, reflected, "I must say that I never understood the word Jew or the word Hebrew to describe a religion. I have running through my mind now half a dozen prominent Jewish families in San Francisco who attend Christian churches. But we know them all as Jews."[6] Lodge went on to elaborate on the difference between scientific races and historical races, which we have already observed in his Senate speech on race and restriction some fourteen years earlier. In the ancient, scientific races "the difference in the skulls and so on has all been retained"; whereas the historical races "have been formed gradually [in the historical era] as the English, the German in which there is a great mixture of blood but which are historically racial." And "the classification made by the Immigration Bureau is on the basis of historic races."

Julian Mack, representing the American Jewish Committee at the hearings, had apparently come to testify about other issues. But he seems to have been tempted beyond endurance to jump into this colloquy.

> *Mr. Mack.* Permit me to say a word. If Disraeli had come to this country after he had attained his fame he certainly would have said in answer to the question asked him at the port that he was an Englishman.
> *Senator Lodge.* He would have been classed racially as a Jew.

Eventually Lodge raised a further distinction:

> *Senator Lodge.* There are, I know, bodies of Jews who are not racially Jews at all. Doctor Adler refers to one tribe in Abyssinia [i.e., Jewish in faith]. If we had here an immigration of Abyssinians they would never be classified as Jews, no matter what their faith might be. . . . They would not be classified as Jews on account of their religion.

The Abyssinian Jews are Jews only "on account of their religion"; Disraeli was *not* a Jew only on account of his. Presumably, Lodge thought the Abyssinian Jews were later converts to Judaism who were not descended biologically from the ancient Hebrews. Perhaps, too, he was thinking of the fact that the Abyssinian Jews were black and meant to use this fact to hammer home the point that more united European Jews than religion. Would Wolf really be willing to insist that the Jews of Frankfurt were equally close to the Jews of Warsaw and Abyssinia? Finally, the example is forceful too because for Lodge it apparently involved a mass conversion that did not result in intermarriages with those who were racially Jewish.

In the end, Lodge added, "All ethnology is approximate." That imperfection is an opening wedge for Mack to raise another objection.

> *Mr. Mack.* I am afraid ethnology is not in a position at the present date to form the best basis. Ethnology has not advanced that far.
> *Senator Lodge.* You can go approximately that far.
> *Mr. Mack.* You can divide the world into five races.

Mack would accept divisions based on the five color races; these are the broadest categories of Lodge's "scientific races," ancient and still visible. But Lodge himself was comfortable with much more detailed subdivisions, at least among the white races, subdivisions that emerged in more recent times (the historical races).

Wolf then took up the argument that the classification scheme can lead to anti-Semitic feeling; Lodge was skeptical. Wolf responded, "My dear friend Senator Lodge, you of all men certainly do know that a great deal of it [anti-Jewish feeling] exists. I have come in contact with gentlemen from your own State . . . who voice that sentiment." Eventually Mack returned, almost inadvertently, to the division among Jews: "I do not recognize the Jewish race. There are Jews who do. I do not." Lodge pressed him on the point, in ways that would soon come back to haunt Mack.

> *Senator Lodge.* There is some division on this question?
> *Mr. Mack.* Yes. The newer element of Jews in this country who largely are not yet American citizens . . . claim there is a Jewish race—and they want to re-create it as a nation.
> *Senator Lodge.* Like the Poles?
> *Mr. Mack.* Yes . . . [But most Jews who are American citizens] certainly do not feel themselves racially Jews although they are proud of the achievements of all the men who have been born Jews.
> *Senator Lodge.* They are proud of their race and justly so.
> *Mr. Mack.* They are proud of their people.
> . . . .
> *Senator Lodge.* Is there an Irish nation? . . . An Irishman is classified as an Irishman no matter where he comes from.

Mr. Mack. No matter whether he believes in home rule or not.

Senator Lodge. No matter what country he comes from—whether
   Australia or Canada.

Mack was keen to introduce nationhood and peoplehood into the stark
religion–race contrast, but Lodge resisted. We cannot be certain of their
motivations, but Mack may have wanted to introduce concepts of nationhood and peoplehood to show how slippery and uncertain the List's race
classification was—that is, the race classification of Europeans. If so, it is
also striking that no one present—and certainly not Lodge—pointed out
that the full title of the List of Races and Peoples could have been interpreted
to mean that some categories should be conceived only as peoples, not as
races. Lodge in particular probably would have had little patience with the
distinction between race and people. The full argument presented in his
1896 speech suggests that Lodge would have viewed "peoplehood" as indistinguishable from "historical races," or at least on a continuum in which
peoples were on their way to becoming historical races. And the speech
made clear that in fully formed historical races, mental characteristics are
fixed through inheritance carried in the blood.

Finally, the commission chairman concluded discussion of the "Hebrew
race" issue.

The Chairman [Senator Dillingham]. It seems to me Mr. Wolf's contention
   would come to this: we would be compelled to go back of the whole
   question of race and take them by their political associations.

Senator Lodge. The classification, of course, would be worthless.

The Chairman. Yes.

These interchanges between Wolf, Mack, and Lodge received immediate and extensive attention in the Jewish press. A series of angry out-
bursts followed in the press and in correspondence both to the American
Jewish Committee and to the Immigration Commission itself. Now the
American Jewish Committee leadership was in a particularly awkward position. It had not authorized Mack to take any position on the List of Races
and Peoples.

Herbert Friedenwald, the American Jewish Committee secretary, had
also attended the Immigration Commission hearings, but he had remained

silent. Two days later, he reported to Mayer Sulzberger, president of the American Jewish Committee, that Wolf had not been "very convincing" and while Mack was more so, it had little effect on the commission, not least because "Senator Lodge asked particularly searching questions which were very difficult to answer." A week later Sulzberger was asking Friedenwald to query American Jewish Committee board members about the value of a meeting on immigration questions. Friedenwald would soon report that the board members did indeed want to meet, and not least because they were uncomfortable about what Wolf and Mack had said. One member of the executive committee itself, Rabbi Judah Magnes, held views that differed sharply from those presented at the hearing. Magnes, a young Reform rabbi, already stood at the head of New York's aristocratic Temple Emanuel. However, his interest in the living cultural (rather than only religious) expressions of the Jewish people had always been much broader than was typical of German Jewish Reform movement thinking. And Magnes's position was becoming ever-more distinct from the Reform movement's as the years passed. By the time of this episode, he had established the New York Kehillah, a city-wide organization meant to represent all Jews, of whatever religious orientation, including Reform, secular socialists, and the traditional Orthodox. He was also favorably disposed to Zionism as an expression of the culture of a people. Friedenwald reported that "Dr. Magnes is particularly up in arms" as a result of Mack's comments, but he was, for the moment, remaining silent.

Meanwhile, others were publicly condemning Wolf's and Mack's statements. A Zionist society in Baltimore wrote to the Dillingham Commission to *support* "the stand taken by you that the Jews are a strongly identified race and that the present method of classifying immigrants, Jewish immigrants included, is the only useful one."[7] Eventually, Magnes's organization, the New York City Kehillah, also mounted an official protest, urging the American Jewish Committee to disclaim "the statements made by Judge Mack to the fact that the Jews are not a race . . . believing that we are both a race and a nation."[8]

Meanwhile, Mack wrote to Friedenwald, expressing the hope that the American Jewish Committee would soon endorse his *denial* of a Jewish race.[9] Moreover, Mack enclosed a letter he had received from David Phillipson, a Reform leader who was very supportive of the line Mack had taken and troubled by the absence of a clear American Jewish Committee statement. Phillipson's private letter also expresses the exasperation of a mainstream Reform figure confronted with Magnes's comments: "I fear however that your efforts [to end the racial classification of Hebrews] will be hampered so long as the 'nationalist' nonsense continues to be advocated in pulpits as prominent as Emanuel of New York [i.e., Magnes's pulpit]; witness the recent address [from there] entitled 'Reform on a nationalist Basis.'" In any case, Friedenwald would soon write (no doubt with some relief), "at its meeting of December 28, 1909, the Executive Committee of the American Jewish Committee resolved that it is unwise to make any further attempt to have the classification 'Hebrews' altered as no good purpose can at this time be served by further agitation of the subject."[10]

By 1909 the increasing influence of the eastern European Jewish immigrants and their children combined with the generally divided opinions about the nature of Jewry—a Jewish race, cultural nationalism, and perhaps even political Zionism. The episode made it clear to the American Jewish Committee that it could not claim legitimacy to lead a protest on the themes bound up in the List's Hebrew category; even less could it expect to prevail against the Bureau of Immigration and the Immigration Commission in the context of such divisions.

Meanwhile, during the course of the year after the hearing, the United States Immigration Commission was moving toward the release of its forty-one volumes of *Reports*. The general introduction to those volumes, "Brief Statement of the Investigations of the Immigration Commission," by far the most read of its text, included a three-page section on the List of Races and Peoples as well as a specific explanation of the Hebrew category.[11] After all, commission *Reports* were classified in terms of the List. These three introductory pages thus provide, first of all, the basic explanation for the meaning of the List. For the sake of comparability with the data collected over a decade by the Bureau of Immigration, it was important to use the same list of races. But the explanation of what the List captured was more specific: "In this connection it may be explained that the Commission, like the bureau, uses the term 'race' in a broad sense, the distinction being largely a matter of language and geography, rather than one of color or physical characteristics such as determines the various more restricted racial classifications in use, the most common of which divides mankind into only five races." Note, however, that the value of race data for immigration policy was assumed to lie in the association with *other* characteristics.[12]

The "Brief Statement" noted that until the introduction of the race-or-people classification, practically all statistics had been recorded by the immigrant arrival's country of birth; this worked well for the earlier immigrations from northern and western Europe because "the country of birth as a usual thing also fairly established the racial status."[13] It was somewhat easier to make such claims, we might add, because "Ireland," then not an independent country, nevertheless had been listed as a country of birth. In any case, the "Brief Statement" implied that the purpose of the statistics had *always* been to capture "racial status" and that country of birth had sufficed for that purpose with the older immigrations.

Not so with the later immigrations, as twelve races were recorded among those born in Austro-Hungary and seven among those born in Russia. "In the case of both countries *the distinctions are even greater than those indicated merely by language* [italics added], for among the immigrants the Teutonic, Slavic, Semitic and even Mongolian races are all largely represented." In other words, language—while decidedly an imperfect marker of racial status—remains the best indicator available for it. By the time this text was written, the Census Bureau had added a mother-tongue question to capture racial origin. "By this amendment the result desired by the Commission will be essentially attained."[14]

Finally, the introductory section on "Racial Classification of Immigrants" confronted the Jewish protest directly. The only opposition to the List pertained to the Hebrew category and that on the grounds that the Jews "are not a distinct race in the ethnological sense and that the terms 'Hebrew' and 'Jewish' rightly refer to a religious sect and not to a race." Nevertheless, the text points out, in many cases Jewish authorities themselves had discussed the issue of a Jewish race or a Jewish people. Indeed, the commission text includes a striking example from the editors of the recently published *Jewish Encyclopedia*. Wolf's and Mack's testimonies at the hearing were also referenced in the text, but with the observation that the commission had also received correspondence from other Jewish groups that were critical of their testimony. The summary concludes, "the terms in question [Hebrew and Jew] are used interchangeably to designate a religion as well as a race or people, but the commission has employed them only in the latter sense." The unstated implication was the same as the one stated in back in the 1903 internal review that Cortelyou had conducted: constitutionally, the motive for federal action trumped inadvertent effects.[15]

The "Brief Statement of the Investigations of the Immigration Commission" was surely drafted over the course of 1910 and went to press shortly thereafter. In all likelihood, the person responsible for it—and probably the author of the entire introduction, or the coordinator of its authors—was W. W. Husband. Husband had articulated many of the same points in a letter he wrote to one of the commissioners, William Wheeler, about a year earlier, in December 1908. Wheeler had heard about the List and about the protests over the Hebrew category, and he had asked Husband for a clarification. In that context too Husband took pains to make the point that Jews were classified as a race and not as a religion (already at that time also citing the *Jewish Encyclopedia* as well as several other Jewish sources). Probably because of this exclusive focus, the letter differs in one striking respect from the later version in the introduction to the *Reports*. Husband does not even mention the fact that the List's racial classification is based on language. Instead, he insists that it is used in "an ethnological sense," that "race and not religion is intended."[16] The failure to even mention the language criterion for race in this context is worth bearing in mind not only because it underscores the difference between the meaning, or essential nature of race, and the criterion for marking it. We shall see this linguistic marker become increasingly important after 1910—as "mother tongue"—and even Husband, decades later, describing the whole meaning of the List of Races as a matter of language differences. So it is important to be clear about this difference between the marker and the meaning of race itself.

And yet, as we have already stressed, it is also true that in the usage of the Immigration Commission, the race of *Europeans* was tracked only over two American generations. After that, people were listed as American-born of American parentage—unless they were Asian, black, or American Indian, in which case race continued to be recorded regardless of generational status. By definition, this difference in the treatment of people past the second generation reflected a difference in the meaning of race for the two groups—at a minimum that the Europeans had a greater potential than nonwhites to assimilate into the American mainstream during those generations. Moreover, recall that the willingness to restrict the data on European racial origins to two generations also reflected the fact that the special target of the inquiry, the southern and eastern Europeans, did not yet extend back more than two American generations in 1910, so that nothing was lost by treating them differently than nonwhites in the counts. On the one hand, then, this feature of the Immigration Commission's work with race softened its impact for whites. At the same time, and somewhat contradictorily, the concept of race itself—marked in one case by language and in the other by color—meant something in the commission's *Reports* beyond either marker (language or color) in themselves, something that was important for immigration policy and the future of America.

The Commission's Research Staff, 1907–1911

Thus far, like most historical analyses of the Immigration Commission, ours has not probed below the level of the nine commissioners themselves. But the commission was a vast undertaking, involving many who designed studies and collected the evidence on local conditions. Moreover, while the commissioners were the ones who would sign the final report, people of surprisingly different viewpoints were recruited for responsible staff positions.

In 1908 Franz Boas, as professor of anthropology at Columbia University, was already an international authority. At that time, his most influential formulations were still found mostly in dispersed papers, but this would soon change. These papers concerned the primacy of cultural, compared to biological, influences in determining differences among peoples; likewise, they argued for a certain relativism in comparing cultures. Still, by 1908 Boas had been emphasizing for a decade that mental attributes observed in various races around the world seemed much more similar than had been generally believed. And in particular, beliefs about the mental inferiority of African Americans rested on weak evidence. Consequently, he had been directly condemning American racial discrimination for several years. In 1906, at the invitation of W. E. B. DuBois, Boas had delivered Atlanta University's commencement address.[17]

Boas interacted with the United States Immigration Commission in two ways, both of which were relevant to the interpretation of race by commission researchers. One connection is virtually unknown, and we will return to it later; the other was already well known at the time. It was the commission that supported and published his research, *Changes in Bodily Form of Descendants of Immigrants,* which would eventually become the thirty-eighth volume of its *Reports.* And Boas made sure that the study received plenty of attention in the press as well. To everyone's surprise (including his own), Boas had found that head size and shape changed over the course of a single generation in a new environment. These two features of bodily form had been thought to be highly stable; indeed, they were seen as measures that could be used to classify races across the ages. If these supposedly most stable physical features were in fact quite plastic, how much more must it be possible for *mental* characteristics to be influenced by environment?[18]

For several years, Boas had been interested in exploring racial stability and change among American blacks and immigrants. In fact, he had proposed a somewhat similar research project to another possible donor in the years just prior to his work for the Immigration Commission.[19] So when he entered into discussions about funding the study of immigrant bodily form with Jeremiah Jenks in 1908, he was proposing a research project that had intrigued him for some time. Exactly how and when Boas and Jenks first met is unclear, but by March 1908, they clearly had been in contact for a while, because Boas was pressing Jenks for a decision on funding. Jenks reported back regularly on the interest of the other commissioners and their requests for more information.[20]

For our purposes, this episode is an example of the commission's willingness to get involved with a prominent researcher, one whose iconoclastic views about racial difference had been in the published record for a decade. Admittedly, neither the commission nor Boas expected outcomes so dramatically suggestive of racial mutability. Nevertheless, working with Boas was no way to guarantee traditional findings about racial determinism or immigrant characteristics—even if the commissioners chose to ignore Boas's Jewish and immigrant origins. Yet they put a considerable sum at his disposal. Moreover, as historian Robert Zeidel has pointed out, when Boas requested additional funding from the commissioners, he made the direction of his findings to date crystal clear. The commissioners nonetheless agreed to the additional funding. Finally, there is no evidence that when the results came in, the commission ever considered burying the study. True, the summary volumes (over which Boas had no control) would eventually stress that the Boas project was an isolated study whose outcomes would need to be digested and confirmed. But Boas had said as much himself. In sum, the commissioners' funding and their tolerance for the results do indeed appear to indicate a certain degree of openness as to research findings on race and immigrants. Before we address the other connection between Boas and the Immigration Commission, we will examine some of the other senior researchers.

Emanuel Alexandrovich (E. A.) Goldenweiser was a rising star in economics in 1908 and much younger than Boas. Later, he would work briefly at the Census Bureau, where we will encounter him again, and then he moved to the Federal Reserve, where he served most of his career as chief economist. He also served a term as president of the American Economic Association. Goldenweiser had been born in Kiev in 1883 into the "secular, cosmopolitan Jewish" home of a well-known Russian jurist. The father felt his sons' futures would be blocked in the Russian Empire, and the family immigrated to New York City after Emanuel finished secondary school in Kiev. He enrolled at Columbia University, and eventually completed a doctorate in economics there. Because the subject of his graduate research was the Russian immigration to the United States, he was hired straight out of graduate school to head up the Immigration Commission's data collection project on "Immigrants in Cities." Emmanuel also had an older brother, Alexander Alexandrovich (A. A.), who would finish his own Columbia PhD in 1910—in anthropology under Boas. It is very likely, then, that E. A. Goldenweiser also knew something of Boas's work on race in general, and surely he knew of Boas's research for the Immigration Commission.[21]

Goldenweiser's background prior to 1909 hardly suggests that he would have interest in or respect for a simplistic racial ranking of immigrants or a concern for the putative threats immigrants posed to the republic. His writings over the next few years demonstrate a willingness to criticize those views explicitly in scholarly and semischolarly journals. In *The Survey* for January 1911, he published a summary of findings from the "Immigrants in

Cities" project he had led at the Immigration Commission. At just the same time, the commission's *Reports* were moving toward release. He clearly meant to have his own say, whatever Jenks, Husband, and the commissioners might be concluding.

> The Italian, the Hebrew and the Slav, according to popular belief, are poisoning the pure air of our otherwise well-regulated cities; and if not for them there would be no congestion, no filth, no poverty. . . .
>
> [In fact this] study strongly indicates that racial characteristics are entirely subordinate to environment and opportunity in determining the immigrant's mode of life . . . the more successful members leave for better surroundings, until finally the entire colony is absorbed in the melting pot of the American city.[22]

A year later, he published a path-breaking paper in the *American Journal of Sociology,* the first refutation of Francis Walker's famous argument that immigration causes "race suicide." Walker had argued that the poor immigrants drove down wages and the native worker responded by restricting fertility. Goldenweiser showed that the evidence for Walker's theory—that areas of high immigration and low native fertility were correlated—was spurious. Both were the product of urbanization and industrialization.[23]

Another senior consultant to the commission was Maurice Fishberg. Raised in Kamenetz-Podolsk, in the Russian Empire's Jewish Pale, he came to the United States at the age of eighteen. By 1908, he was a physician in New York, where he worked first in private practice and then as chief medical examiner for the United Hebrew Charities. He was best known by that time as an anthropologist of the Jews. Fishberg had been publishing on the topic for some time, and since 1903 his reports expressed increasing skepticism of the idea that the Jews could be considered a race. In his magnum opus, *The Jews: A Study of Race and Environment* (1911), he would argue that environment in European ghettos, rather than heredity, led to their so-called racial characteristics. Consequently, he predicted the rapid disappearance of these characteristics among American Jewish immigrants. He and Boas knew each other professionally in New York.

When the Immigration Commission decided to explore reasons for mass emigration from Europe, they naturally included an investigative trip to the Russian Pale of Settlement, where nearly all Russian Jews lived.

Fishberg was hired to accompany the commissioners as "confidential advisor or agent." At the very least, involving Fishberg suggests a desire to get the best information in the anthropology of the Jews, and a willingness or even a desire to get it from a Russian Jewish immigrant.[24]

The commission had also hired Roland P. Falkner to head its giant investigation of the children of immigrants in schools. Falkner, however, had resigned before the project was completed in order to become assistant director of the Census Bureau. From that desk he wrote in 1911 to congratulate author I. A. Hourwich upon the publication of an article critical of immigration restriction and added his own views of the Immigration Commission's policy recommendations.

> I have read [your article] with a greater pleasure in that it confirms and as it seems to me with unimpeachable testimony the views respecting immigration which I have had for a long time.
>
> . . . The vigorous language of the restrictionist, its apparent appeal to patriotic feelings in the preservation of American institutions has misled many who ought to have known better. It was a distinct disappointment to me personally that the Immigration Commission came to the conclusion that restriction was desirable. I cannot believe that a judicial weighing of the facts which were brought forward by them should incline opinion to such a view.[25]

The pronouncements by Goldenweiser and Falkner, as well as Boas's known views, make it difficult to make sense of a statement made by Jeremiah Jenks (in a lecture to the senior class at the Sheffield School at Yale). Jenks claimed—as evidence for restriction—that of all the more than one hundred agents of the commission whose views were known supported restriction by the time its work had been concluded.[26]

Of course, there were others among the commission's top research staff whose views were much closer to those of Lodge or Jenks. Joseph Hill, who would serve for many years as the Census Bureau's chief statistician, may have been one of these; certainly, he was also involved with eugenics societies.[27] His assistant, Julius H. Parmelee, also on loan from the Census Bureau to the Immigration Commission, likewise seems to have placed a good deal of weight on racial heritages (as we shall see in Chapter 6).

For our story, the commission's most important senior researcher who held such views was Daniel K. Folkmar, the author of the *Dictionary of Races and Peoples*. Folkmar, who turned fifty in 1910, had grown up in Wisconsin, attended a local college in his early twenties, and then studied briefly at both the University of Chicago and Harvard University. Later, he taught at two teacher-training institutes (known as normal schools) and eventually led one of them. Then, in the mid-1890s, he undertook advanced study at European centers, receiving a doctorate in anthropology. In 1900 he published a version of his doctoral study, *Lecons d'Anthropologie Philosophique: ses Applications a la Morale Positive*. Much of the value of the lessons, it turns out, concern the understanding of different racial characteristics for the policymaker. There is a good deal about primitive races in the global scheme of things, but there is also much about how racial differences among immigrants will affect America's future. Folkmar deals here with differences among Europeans as well as with the "color races."[28] An important passage, dealing with immigration, captures the flavor.

> For the study of emigration problems, the survival of the fittest is . . . crucial. The study of such questions shows us the close connection between anthropology and practical policy. . . . The legislator cannot govern wisely the races under his dominion without knowing the qualities and limits of the powers of races and nations and the influence that climate or the environment have upon them. . . . Babington [author of *Fallacies of Race Theories as Applied to National Characteristics*, 1895] is right to combat the tendency to always be thinking about race. . . . But Babington goes too far in denying the existence of race and attributing all the phenomena of life to the environment. He says, for example "Differences of present condition (between English and Irish) are sufficiently accounted for by long-continued differences of environment. . . ." Yet what he calls "long-continued differences of environment" cannot be related to individual particularities unless one takes into account heredity, and such variations in the course of succeeding generations that amount to what evolutionists call the origins of a new race.[29]

Thus survival of the fittest, and possibly Lamarckian mechanisms, explains how environment creates new races over "succeeding generations." These races, such as the English and the Irish, in turn differ in character. All this, moreover, is background to legislating immigration policy.

After completing his European studies, Folkmar served as anthropologist and lieutenant governor in the Philippine Civil Service, where he served from 1903 through 1907, and produced an *Album of Philippine Types* (1904). He then joined the staff of the Immigration Commission as anthropologist. It is likely that during his Philippine service, Folkmar had met Jeremiah Jenks, who was then on a federal study commission dealing with the Philippines and would soon be appointed as an Immigration Commission member. After two years with the commission, Folkmar moved to the Census Bureau, and then for a time during World War I he moved to the War Department, where he studied soldiers' characteristics in connection with intelligence tests.

There is no evidence that Folkmar's views about the centrality of racially stable attributes changed appreciably from the time of his doctoral dissertation to the writing of the *Dictionary* a decade later. In 1909, he testified before the Senate's Census Committee with W. W. Husband about the advantages of adding the race-or-people question to the census enumeration. He argued, "The inquiry into the racial elements of America is the inquiry which will disclose the crucial elements of weakness and of strength in the nation—of far greater moment in the long run than a census of manufactures and of wealth. It will give us the first true picture of the American race of the future, and its necessary place in the world's civilization."[30]

The *Dictionary of Races and Peoples* was originally intended to guide Immigration Commission workers, but it soon enough became clear that the *Dictionary* would not appear in time to be useful in that way. Instead, the *Dictionary* was to stand as the commission's summation of knowledge about each race or people. In part the work rested on disciplines we would think of today as history, economics, sociology, and anthropology, but it also relied on evidence of the much more distant past from ethnology and archeology. It also included a generous sprinkling of ethno-racial stereotyping and generalizations about national character. The *Dictionary* has been reviled and mocked at least since Oscar Handlin gave it a special place in his devastating criticism of the commission's *Reports* in the early 1950s. Yet, when the *Dictionary* had first appeared, the *New York Times* ran a respectful full-page story about the interesting discussions it contained. And the circle of people around the Smithsonian's physical anthropologist Ales Hrdlicka in Washington continued to speak of it with respect a decade later.[31] In any case, *The Dictionary*, approached in terms of its relation to the evolving usages of the List of Races and Peoples, repays attentive consideration.

The *Dictionary* regularly stressed differences in the mental attributes among peoples. In contrast to his writing in the doctoral dissertation, in the *Dictionary* Folkmar almost never mentions how these differences had come about—in particular whether socialization or biological transmission was the more critical. Yet it is hard to imagine that he did not think biology played a great role, given the formulations in his dissertation (and assistance from his prominent eugenicist wife, Elnora). Recall that he thought of cultural tendencies as becoming part of a race's physical inheritance over time. Consequently we may suspect that it was pointless to determine the precise role of heredity and environment (physical or social) because the effects of the latter eventually became part of the former.

Nevertheless, Folkmar did touch on the issue in his introduction to the *Dictionary*. In discussing the basis for the classifications in the List of Races and Peoples, he notes that in the first instance they reflect the "chief divisions, or basic races of mankind" that are "familiarly called, the white, black, yellow, brown and red races." This "primary classification" rests directly "upon physical or somatological grounds," even if there is rather less agreement than in the past even on the boundaries among these chief divisions. The crucial point for the *Dictionary*, given that the overwhelming majority of immigrants were coming from Europe, is its procedure for distinguishing races *within* the major white race category.

> The subdivisions of these [basic races] into a multitude of smaller "races" or peoples is made largely upon a linguistic basis. The practical arguments for adopting such a classification are unanswerable It is not merely because it is most convenient to call a man English, Irish, or German according to the language spoken by him or by his ancestors in the old home; this is also the classification that has the sanction of law in immigration statistics and in the censuses of foreign countries. In no other way can figures be found that are comparable as to population, immigration, and distribution of immigrants.[32]

The *criterion* for the grand racial divisions was color and for the relevant racial subdivisions it was language. These were both observable proxies for more basic commonalities of mental characteristics that characterize the various races. Still, according to the *Dictionary,* the present basis for best classifying these races may be improved in the future: "It may be that neither the ethnical nor the linguistic school has reached the ultimate word, but that a more natural and acceptable classification of peoples will be based in the future upon continuity of descent among the members of a race or of a stock, whether such genetic relationship be established by somatological, linguistic, sociological or historical evidence, or by all combined." Language is not of interest because people who speak the same language settle together in America (as Safford and McSweeney had argued); it is a way of gaining access to the same realities that "the ethnical . . . school" (the school that studies ethnology) seeks in the ancient past. Both are ultimately keys to what is passed on by the "continuity of descent," the "genetic relationship."

Moreover, languages change, and so can racial membership. But the best linguistic proxy will illuminate fairly old membership.

> In some European censuses race is determined by the mother tongue of the individual, in others it is determined by "language of converse" or "customary language." It is evident that an Irish family that has lived for generations in England would be called Irish by the first test, English by the second. But how long a residence in England will entitle an Irishman, or a Scotchman, or a French Huguenot, or one of Norman French Stock, to be called English if the mother tongue is the test? Evidently this phrase must be interpreted to mean the ancestral or racial language in dealing with a stock which has kept itself quite pure in descent. . . . In the narrow sense, the race of an immigrant is determined by ancestral language, as above indicated. The historical limit which determines the transition from one race into another as thus defined varies with different races.[33]

For McSweeney and Safford, the older language criterion would have been pointless. For them, race was useful only because groups were tied together by the language they spoke. There was nothing to be gained by knowing what language their forbearers had spoken. For Folkmar, the evidence of ancestral language is an approach to the "continuity of descent," to the "genetic relationship." In sum, racial traits are long-lasting, racial boundaries are captured by ancestral language, and a people's mental characteristics may evolve over long time periods into biologically hereditary realities. But at the same time, assimilation may transform both an individual's language and even one's racial membership itself. These formulations seek to capture complex processes in which semipermanent hereditary mental qualities are recognized as subject to a degree of gradual modification.

By contrast, Boas had been moving away from such views over the same period of years since the completion of Folkmar's doctoral dissertation. By 1908 both men were working with the Immigration Commission, albeit in very different capacities. Late that year, Boas gave an address at the annual meeting of the American Anthropological Association (of which he was vice president) entitled, "Race Problems of America." He was concerned with "The development of the American nation through amalgamation of diverse European nationalities." Boas criticized some of the fears of restrictionists that the process of racial melding in America would be so different than it had been in the European past. For the most part, however, he stressed the paucity of data about changes in physical "type" across generations in new environments: "The whole problem of the effects of race intermixture upon the various characteristic traits of human types is entirely unsolved." This, of course, had been the subject of his own ruminations for several years, and was tied to his research supported by the Immigration Commission.[34]

At the same time, data were needed on all aspects of racial intermarriage—including the social. The very question of intermarriage rates was critical, Boas thought, but it was not treated in the census data: "We do not know the influence of racial cohesion. Obviously, this is one of the fundamental points that ought to be known to gain a clear insight into the effect of recent immigration . . . I may therefore express the hope that this question may be included in the census to be organized next year."[35] Similarly, some months earlier, Boas had written to Jenks, "The further I get along in my work the more important becomes the question of intermarriages, which you told me is being investigated on the basis of the Census Reports by your Commission." He even suggested, apparently without success, that everyone

involved get together to discuss the issue.[36] Husband independently contacted Boas to request a copy of the "Race Problems in America" paper
because Folkmar had reported that it called for "taking the United States
census by race" and that "this has been a matter of discussion here for some
time."[37] Boas did send the paper, but Husband did not pursue the issue
further, probably realizing that Boas had only mentioned "taking the . . .
census by race" in a single vague sentence.

Nine months later still (late September 1909), Husband turned to Boas
with another request. This time he wanted Boas to comment on Folkmar's
early work on the *Dictionary*.

> I think I have mentioned to you casually the work of Dr. Daniel Folkmar,
> who is preparing a "Dictionary of Races" to be included in the report of
> the Immigration Commission. . . . It seems to me . . . that is will be an
> addition of value to the report, but of course, we wish to exert every
> effort possible to make it as correct and authoritative as may be possible.
> The enclosed introduction was rather hastily drawn, having been
> prepared by Dr. Folkmar early in the work. I am also enclosing articles
> on the Hebrew, Ruthenian and Polish races. The article on the Hebrew
> race represents some of Dr. Folkmar's earlier work in this regard, and, as
> you will note, is much briefer. . . . I think this will give you a pretty clear
> idea of what we have in mind, and I want to ask your opinion relative to
> it. In the first place I would like to know whether you think the plan is a
> good one, and if so, whether you would approve in general of the way it
> is being carried out . . . [and] how can we best satisfy ourselves as to its
> accuracy and scientific value from an ethnological standpoint. I know, of
> course, there is considerable disagreement as to various racial classifi-
> cations, etc. . . . [Still,] how can we make it the best thing possible in
> this line[?] . . . Dr. Folkmar is anxious to submit this work to some
> authorities on the subject, and because of that, I suggested that I would
> write to you.[38]

There is no reason to doubt that both Folkmar and Husband wanted
serious readings of the work. But it may also be that Husband was unsure
how Folkmar's views were regarded among anthropologists dominant
in the field. Might Folkmar prove a political embarrassment? Getting a
reading from someone as different from Folkmar as Boas might yield

insights. In any case, from a historical perspective, we are dealing here with a surprising cast. At the Immigration Commission we have Folkmar, author of the notorious *Dictionary,* and his supervisor, Husband, a major figure at the commission, and later a key player in the creation of the National Origins Quota Laws. These two are soliciting advice from the central actor in the reorientation of anthropology from the study of race to the study of culture. What would Boas do with the invitation to comment on drafts of *Dictionary* articles?

Boas never offered his own opinion directly. Instead, he wrote, "I took the liberty to submit the manuscript to Dr. Simkovitch [a Columbia colleague], whom I asked to look over the remarks on the Ruthenians. I send you his reply. I have submitted the section on the Hebrews to Dr. Fishberg, whose reply I will send when it comes."[39]

We have neither Simkovitch's nor Fishberg's "peer review," but it is clear that the former was thoroughly negative (although we do not know why). Husband comments,

> Although Dr. Sinkhovitch's [sic] letter is one of condemnation rather than criticism, still I am exceedingly glad to have it. As I wrote you, the matter is one concerning which I have no knowledge. . . . Notwithstanding Dr. Sinkhovitch's condemnation, I still think that good results will be obtained.
>
> Of course I will lay the letter before Dr. Folkmar in order that he may profit by such criticism as Dr. Sinkhovitch has made, because of course the Commission would not authorize the publication of inaccurate and unscientific material upon this or any other subject. I am glad you submitted the section on Hebrews to Dr. Fishberg. Dr. Folkmar has told me that he consulted Dr. Fishberg to a considerable extent in writing the article. . . .
>
> There will be a meeting of the Commission in New York on October 19th and if you have time I would be very glad if I could see you for a little while to talk over this particular piece of work and perhaps others.[40]

It is surely striking that Folkmar had already "consulted Dr. Fishberg to a considerable extent"—that Folkmar had reached out on his own to the authority that Boas thought best. Recall that the commission also had engaged Fishberg as a consultant on the Jewish immigration. Whatever we think of the *Dictionary,* we should not view it as the product of an ignorant man or of one wrapped in a cocoon of cultural insensitivity and academic boorishness. Folkmar sought help from the likes of Fishberg and Boas, and he received some feedback.

A few days later, Boas was also able to forward Fishberg's comments. Husband replied that it "is gratifying because it appeals to me as really interested criticism. I will be glad of the privilege of talking the matter over with you and Prof. Jenks if he can remain in New York."[41] It appears that they did get together for a talk, but we have no record of what was said. It is not out of the question that Husband used the New York meeting to be sure Boas was still "on board," and that the celebrated scholar was not so upset with what he had read that he would denounce the *Dictionary.* Husband and Jenks would have taken very seriously any advice Boas might have wished to give about the *Dictionary.* Boas, in other words, could well have affected the text and perhaps the decision to publish it at all should he have wanted to be more involved. Two years later, Boas's skepticism about the role of biological determinism in cultural differences would dominate his influential collected essays, *The Mind of Primitive Man.*

However, all indications are that Boas was reticent in communicating with Husband on the subject of the *Dictionary.* Perhaps he simply felt he had said all he could in the essays already published, including the one Husband had requested earlier. However, it is also possible that he felt the *Dictionary* entries could be read from various anthropological perspectives without bringing down the contempt it does today. Also, the data from his own project for the Immigration Commission were still preliminary. This study would be by far the most directly relevant to the *Dictionary* and the commission of all studies in *The Mind of Primitive Man.* Then, too, he may have had little respect for most activities of the commission and for most of the commissioners. And he may have thought it both hopeless and distasteful to try to debate with them, especially since Husband had read his cautions in the address "Race Problems in America," which he had sent them nine months earlier. This range of considerations could all apply as well to Fishberg's constructive tone about Folkmar's article on the Jews. For both, but especially for Boas, there was also the matter of commission funding (recall that Fishberg had been a commission adviser on the trip to the Russian Pale). Boas had his own large project, funded entirely by the commission, to consider; indeed, he sought *more* funding. He may not have wanted to endanger that future research support—particularly if he indeed did not respect the funders or thought his own very relevant research the best reply he could make.

By placing its categories at the heart of their work, the commission surely enhanced the authority of the List of Races and Peoples. The Bureau of Immigration was never regarded as a particularly professionalized and high-caliber operation; it was more of a plumb for former labor leaders who supported a particular president: McSweeney, Powderly, and Sargent, for example. That the bureau had developed the List was no particular recommendation for the classification. By contrast, the Immigration Commission was meant to include an intellectually and professionally high-caliber membership, with the aim to produce the definitive study of its subject. The commission not only made the List central to its studies. It also greatly extended the substantive reach of the List, from the immigrants arriving at the port of entry to the later lives of immigrants and of their children as well. This extension also implied that the classification scheme could legitimately be extended to American citizens.

Exactly what the Immigration Commission thought it was studying under the topic of "race or people" is another matter. We have followed what it said in the introduction to the *Reports,* in Folkmar's *Dictionary,* and in the range of views of its senior research staff. Folkmar came closest to making explicit statements about the role of biological transmission in perpetuating mental differences among groups. Others said less, and some of the staff clearly believed less. As for the commissioners themselves, they were most represented by the recommendations, and perhaps too by the text of the fifty-page summary. The diversity of views among the commission's research staff provides some additional grist for historian Robert Zeidel's contention that the commission undertook serious policy research—open-minded at least at the level of forming questions, selecting research staff, gathering data, and writing detailed reports. Nevertheless, the broad range of research it supported must be understood quite separately from the political agendas of the commissioners.

Zeidel seems to agree with Handlin that the rewrites for the summary volumes of the *Reports* did indeed channel findings in a restrictionist direction.[42] He also provides an excellent discussion of the process by which the commissioners met throughout, and the nature of the crucial last meetings at which they hastily decided on their recommendations. The commissioners did indeed welcome, or at least accept, studies from the pens of widely divergent writers. Still, the range of these researchers' views and the quality of their work are not the only relevant issues. Certainly the Immigration Commission came into being as House Speaker Joe Cannon's stalling mechanism against the literacy bill, not as an effort to seek truth. And its commissioners expressed a belief in favor of restriction to which most were predisposed (and in several cases strongly committed) at the outset.

The commissioners were not copies of Madison Grant, and their recommendations were not those of the 1924 Quotas Act. Nevertheless, most of the commissioners had spoken for *some* form of immigration restriction before they had been appointed. We have examined Lodge's views at length. Burnett held more extreme racial views than did Lodge. Dillingham and his assistant, W. W. Husband, first proposed and later revived the solutions that became the Quota Acts of the 1920s. Jeremiah Jenks held to a form of racial determinism, he worried about a social danger that might result from the mixing of discordant stocks, and he believed that it was best to think about groups of immigrants in terms of the shared traits that he thought prevailed in distinct populations.[43]

The nine members of the Immigration Commission did tolerate a diversity of views among the top level of their research staff. Some of their research was solid and arrived at insights that worked to undercut restrictionist views. But it does not follow that the research findings convinced most commissioners of anything central to their political message—however often they may have proclaimed that they were waiting for the facts to come in. The discovery of such a heterogeneous and talented staff, the range of materials the staff could amass, and the opinions they could develop—and in some cases publish independently—are indeed a testament to the degree of pluralism and sensitivity that federal research could produce in the early years of the century. However, the process could sustain that diversity without threatening the voice and opinions of the commissioners.

CHAPTER 5

Urging the List on the U.S. Census Bureau, 1908–1910

FROM DECEMBER 1908 TO APRIL 1910, the United States Immigration Commission repeatedly urged that the List of Races and Peoples be incorporated into the U.S. census. Had the commission been successful, the census would have presented Americans with a view of various European origins as distinct races. Such a presentation, in turn, might have had profound and lasting effects. Yet it was opposed only by Jewish organizations, and initially even their opposition had had nothing to do with racialization. Even later, when Jewish organizations did criticize the constitutionality of the race usage for divisions among Europeans, this argument was of only secondary importance to their case.

In fact, other groups who became involved—Slavic leaders and organizations of social service and policy—did so to *support* use of the List in the census. And in the end, Census Bureau officials found a distinctive solution. Although this episode involved an important turning point for federal bureaucracies and concerned organizations, it left only the smallest trace in the institutional memory.

Early Skirmish, January 1909

The struggle over extending the List to the census began in the last days of 1908. Senator Dillingham, chairman of the Immigration Commission, had asked that the Senate Committee on the Census support the extension. The

Senate committee agreed, and the proposal first entered the *Congressional Record* (and indeed the written record in any form) when the Senate committee's chairman, Chester I. Long, made the proposal as one of a series of amendments to the 1910 Census Bill. Long moved that the Senate support "a committee amendment . . . to insert the word 'race'" into the list of items to be canvassed. Whether Long understood this to be a significant step is impossible to say; but given the off-hand way it was treated, he probably did not think so. Surely the senators did not. They passed the measure without discussion, by a voice vote.[1]

A "color or race" question already existed in the census. So there was some ambiguity involved in the wording of the resolution to add "race." Still, the existing census question had never subdivided the white race (except insofar as mulattoes were often classified separately). Whatever the ambiguity of the actual wording, Senator Long made it clear that its purpose was to accommodate the Immigration Commission's desire to gather consistent data on the dynamics of immigration over time and generation.

And the matter might have been left this way; the Senate Census Committee would have delegated to census officials the task of working out the details of a new question on "race." That new question would have affected primarily (or exclusively) the population of European origin. That population would have been described in terms of the several dozen white races on the List of Races and Peoples.

Of course, it is revealing too that once again there was no need to add the words "or people"; "race" was enough. The latter term might placate some respondents during enumerations, but generally the relevant comparisons across groups were understood as being about race.

Detailing European races would have involved a further complication that was left unspoken in the Senate motion: How many generations of Europeans was the category meant to capture? A hint is found in the Census Bureau's nativity questions: birthplace and parental birthplace were recorded, but third- and later-generation descendants of European immigrants appeared there as "native born of native parentage," and under "color or race" as white. Very likely, the high rate of intermarriage among the European-origin population would have led the Census Bureau to apply the same procedure to a detailing of European "races": it would have designated them only across two generations.

In this case too, the German Jewish Reform elite challenged the action through the American Jewish Committee, established in 1906. In fact, this challenge actually occurred nearly a full year before the publicized debate concerning the Hebrew category among Wolf, Mack, and Lodge at the Immigration Commission's public hearing (discussed in Chapter 4).

Including a race-or-people question on the census would have raised the prevalence and centrality of the List to a new height. The Bureau of Immigration used the List to classify immigrant arrivals. The Immigration Commission used it to classify the immigrants (including long-term residents in the United States, many of whom were U.S. citizens) and the native-born children of immigrants. The census too could be expected to use the List to survey foreign-born residents and their children. But the census covered the entire population whereas the commission's surveys dealt with selected samples (e.g., immigrants in a particular industry found in certain cities). So at a minimum, with the extension of the List to the census every first- and second-generation American would have been classified in terms of the List. Moreover, the census would be repeated every decade, and once an item was added, there was a reasonable chance it might be kept in future enumerations. Finally, whatever the authority of the Immigration Commission was in the political culture, that of the census was surely greater. The census attracted more attention, and it was referred to consistently for many purposes; it was also regarded as an objective, "scientific," apolitical document. Thus if the List of Races or Peoples were to be introduced into the census, it could be expected to have a substantial impact. It could be expected to influence the way the public defined American groups.

The American Jewish Committee leadership took note of Senator Long's amendment to insert the new "race" item into the upcoming census. Two days after the Senate voice vote on the Long amendment, American Jewish Committee President Mayer Sulzberger sent a handwritten note from Philadelphia to the American Jewish Committee secretary in New York, Doctor Herbert Friedenwald:

Dear Doctor,
The House Census Bill . . . was amended to include the ascertainment of "race." . . . Please call at once a conference of our New York members to

consider whether our policy is to do anything. . . . This is *urgent* [under-lined twice]. Whatever is to be done must be done quickly.[2]

At about the same time, Cyrus Adler (a member of the American Jewish Committee's executive committee) was contacting a legal authority in Washington to clarify "the use of the word 'race' in federal law."[3] The energetic Friedenwald reported the next day. His reply provides a glimpse of an ethnic lobby at work in the early twentieth century.

> I discovered this morning that the House had appointed a conference
> Committee of which Crumpacker of Indiana is Chairman. I conferred
> with Dr. Adler by telephone and telegraphed to Mr. Newberger of
> Indianapolis and to Senator [Simon] Guggenheim [Republican of
> Colorado]. I telephoned to our Washington man [attorney Fulton M.
> Brylawski] and instructed him to see Senator Guggenheim and Mr. Gold-
> fogle [Congressman from New York] and others, and also told him what
> to say. I telegraphed to our advisory member Dr. Rosenau in Wash-
> ington and also wrote him the enclosed letter which has also been sent
> to Senator Guggenheim and Mr. Goldfogle. Mr. [Louis] Marshall
> [attorney and a member of the Executive Committee] telegraphed to
> Mr. Goldfogle and to Senator Carter [Republican of Montana]. I also
> telegraphed to Mr. Newman to protest to Senator McEnery [of Louisiana]
> who is the ranking member of the Democrats of the Senate Committee.
> Have you communicated with Senator Penrose [Republican of Pennsyl-
> vania]? If not, it might be advisable.[4]

Friedenwald's cable to Guggenheim that day read: "Amendment to Census Bill adopted by Senate Friday introduces new features requiring American Citizens to state race to Census taker. Our Committee much opposed."[5] Later in the day, he elaborated the American Jewish Committee's position in a letter to the senator. Since anthropologists did not agree as to the meaning of the term "race," he argued,

> the schedules are bound to follow the practice of the Immigration
> Bureau, which in turn is being followed by the United States Immigra-
> tion Commission. Their schedule of races is a purely arbitrary one and
> will not be supported by any modern anthropologists. Besides, what
> can they do if a Jew answers that he belongs to the Caucasian race? And

what value will there be in statistics collected upon so involved a subject by ignorant census taker[s]?

Moreover, for the Jews, this involves a religious element, for almost everyone who says he is a member of the Jewish race professes the Jewish religion. American citizens are American citizens, and as such their racial and religious affiliations are nobody's business. There is no understanding of the meaning of the word "race" which justifies the investigation which it is proposed the Census Bureau shall undertake. So far as citizenship of the United States is concerned, we know only the great divisions of the human family—white, black, American Indian and others. [Otherwise, we will] land ourselves in justifying discrimination against certain classes of citizens, which will result in a destruction of the American idea of the equality of all citizens.

For these reasons, we are opposed to the investigations it is proposed the Census Bureau shall make into the "race" of American citizens, and trust that you will use your influence against the amendment.[6]

Friedenwald's arguments were somewhat more general than those Wolf had made during the preceding decade. He does not even mention the question of whether the Jews in particular are indeed a race (the subject on which Wolf elicited opinion). Rather, the argument here is much more concerned with the dangers of extending the use of the race criterion to subdivisions among the Europeans. First, a subjective response may well be quite useless—"what can they do if a Jew answers that he belongs to the Caucasian race?" Second, "what value will there be in statistics collected upon so involved a subject by ignorant census taker[s]?" There is also a constitutional argument: "So far as citizenship of the United States is concerned, we know only the great divisions of the human family,—white, black, American Indian and others." Extending federal recognition of race lines between Europeans "will result in a destruction of the American idea of the equality of all citizens." The American Jewish Committee as an organization had now adopted the position Mayer Sulzberger had pointed out to Wolf when the latter had written back in 1903. In addition, Fridenwald does mention, if briefly, the older argument that the congruence of religion and race in the Hebrew category would violate constitutional religious protections.

But note that he seems to have no problem accepting federal recognition of the "great divisions of the human family,—white, black, American Indian and other." The most generous interpretation of these lines is that Friedenwald's point here was the same that Sulzberger had stated in 1903: that there is precedence in constitutional law for racial divisions between whites and others. And the most generous interpretation, in turn, of Sulzberger's position is that he referred solely to the record of precedents, not to their ethical standing or even their constitutional consistency. A less generous interpretation would ask why Friedenwald and Sulzberger did not challenge the federal precedent, perhaps on the basis of the Civil War constitutional amendments. But such a challenge would have been difficult to mount; for example, the Chinese Exclusion Act effectively excluded a group on racial origins and it had been passed and renewed long after the Civil War amendments had become part of the Constitution. Still, Friedenwald and Sulzberger might at least have made clear that they *regretted* the constitutional recognition of the color races, but they did not say so. In their turn, they might have retorted that they were not interested in tilting at windmills; moreover Sulzberger, as a judge, may have felt it inappropriate to declare regrets about features of the constitutional record. In any event, for the first time, the basis of the Jewish organizations' protests against the List of Races and Peoples emphasized the inherent constitutional dangers of extending the race criterion to immigrants and their children, rather than merely protesting the Hebrew category.

The fate of the Senate bill to include the "race" item in the 1910 census now turned on Colorado Senator Simon Guggenheim's actions. His German Jewish family had become immensely wealthy from mining in Colorado. Simon Guggenheim is best remembered for the fellowship program he established and for the quality and quantity of liquor at his Washington parties.[7] To this list we should add his role in keeping the race-or-people classification out of the 1910 census during the early months of 1909. As a member of the Senate committee on the census, he first contacted Long to oppose the measure in January of that year.[8] As he later explained, "There is a Jewish society in New York which called my attention to this. It is headquarters for the Jewish people practically throughout the United States, composed of the very best citizens in the United States, and I did not see fit at the time to believe that this committee wanted to give offense to that society by inserting that word [i.e., "race"]. There is no justification for it, as we see it."[9]

On the morning of Friday, January 15, 1909, the House-Senate Census Bill Conference Committee held a hearing to reconcile their two versions of the bill—including the amendment on race found in the Senate version but not the House version. The senators agreed to drop the race question. Friedenwald received telegrams later that morning from both Illinois Congressman Sabath and New York Congressman Goldfogle: "The word 'race' in Census bill stricken out by conferees." The full Senate supported the conferees' version five days later.[10]

Thus the whole process had taken no more than twelve days from beginning to end and consisted of the following steps: first the Senate voice vote to include the new race question, then a day later the American Jewish Committee's objection, later the House-Senate conference on the measure, and finally the Senate floor vote to accept the conference decision. The proposed new race question had passed the Senate without discussion and been defeated in committee behind closed doors. Consequently, no one except the participants involved paid the episode the slightest attention. Not surprisingly, it has been entirely ignored in intellectual and political histories of race, immigration, and the census. Nevertheless, it does appear that but for the lobbying of the American Jewish Committee, the List of Races and Peoples would have been included in the 1910 census. It had already passed the Senate, and no other group seemed interested in stopping it in the House. And once on the census, it might have stayed there for some time.

The day after the Senate accepted the version of the Census Bill without the new race question, Friedenwald sat down to write to W. W. Husband, adding some fresh themes.

> Though I am personally of the opinion that groups of individuals have marked racial traits, . . . I believe that the Immigration Commission is treading on dangerous ground in making investigations of this character. . . . In view therefore of the involved nature of the investigations along racial lines which the Immigration Commission is undertaking, and the dangers that may arise in creating race questions in this country as a result of these investigations, I venture to express the hope

that the Immigration Commission will reconsider its determination to collect these statistics in this way. Whether rightly or wrongly, the great majority of American citizens who happen to be of the Jewish faith object seriously to stating that they are other than American citizens.[11]

The new element in this letter is Friedenwald's personal belief that "groups have marked racial traits." But that belief was not meant to contradict three others: first, science had not adequately specified finer divisions than those for the color races; second, American law had no business dealing with such finer divisions; and third, distinguishing American Jews as such would disturb most of them.

The Second Round, April 1909

Three months later, the Immigration Commission again attempted to have their race question added to the census. This time, on April 6, 1909, W. W. Husband testified before the Senate Census Committee "to make a brief statement on an amendment which the Commission desires."[12] He brought with him Daniel K. Folkmar, who was then working on his *Dictionary*.

Husband's opening statement set out the familiar argument for the race question, namely, that many different peoples were arriving from Europe's multinational empires. Hence "the racial status of the present-day immigrants from southern and eastern Europe cannot be determined by the country of birth." The Bureau of Immigration and the Immigration Commission used the List of Races and Peoples to report the range of racial categories; if the U.S. census would adopt this procedure too, much more would be known "as to the stability, progress, distribution, occupation, and other interesting data relative to these recent immigrants."[13] Once more, Husband referred to the List as a racial classification only—not as a list of "races or peoples."

With the advent of the new congressional term, progressive Republican Senator Robert La Follete Sr. had taken over as chairman of the committee. His Republican colleague from Colorado, Simon Guggenheim, was still a member. Of course, membership on the committee implied no particular expertise on issues of race and immigration. Even the most conscientious of the committee members dealt with a great many other matters that affected the census—addition and deletion of other census questions, patronage versus quality in choosing census takers, the rights of card-reading-machine manufacturers, the degree to which the census director was responsible to the commerce secretary, and so on. Nevertheless, if the committee's half dozen U.S. senators were not scholars of ethnology, they were all knowledgeable and sophisticated Americans who did have some special reasons to be aware of demographic and ethnic issues. Consequently, we are lucky to have the verbatim transcript of the Census Committee's discussions for the day Husband and Folkmar came calling.

Once again, the Jewish protest about the Hebrew category dominated much of the discussion. But this time the German Jewish elite were not testifying as respectful witnesses; an irate Senator Guggenheim represented their position. Quite apart from the topic of the Hebrew category, the Senate hearing led to a fascinating discussion of issues of race among Husband, Folkmar, and several senators.

First, the senators were uncertain about the meaning of the term. In particular, several wondered whether it was being confused with nationality.

Senator Carter. How do you distinguish between nationality and race in your classification? What do you mean by the word "race?"

Mr. Husband. The Commission has been following the practices of the Bureau of Immigration since 1899. . . .

Senator Carter. What general classification of races do you recognize?

Mr. Husband. It is not the racial classification by color that is commonly known. . . .

Senator Carter. You refer to the Poles as a race; they are not a race at all, as I understand the word "race." It is a nationality. Would you refer to the Irish as a race? They are not a race; they are part of a race."

. . . .

Senator Carter. [In Immigration Commission work] you treat the Irish as a race and the Poles as a race, and so forth.

Mr. Husband. Yes, sir.

Senator Carter. There seems to be a confusion of nationality and race.

Senator Cummins. Nationality would strike you as better than race?

Mr. Husband. Everything is taken by nationality also.[14]

The interchange captures revealing misunderstandings. Carter asked how the commission used the term "race." Husband thought the senator did not realize that the term could be extended beyond the "color races." But Carter focused elsewhere: Should distinctions among European groups be classified as "nationality" or "race"? Once again, Husband mistook Carter's point, this time because the two men were referring to different usages of nationality. Husband meant citizenship, that is, political membership in a state. But Carter's sole examples, the Poles and Irish, show that he had an altogether different meaning of nationality in mind because neither a Polish nor an Irish state existed in 1909.

Other senators asked Husband how this racial classification would operate for specific European groups.

Senator Shively. Suppose the nativity of the individual to be Austria. Suppose that he were of Polish origin. Is there anything in the classification you make now that discloses that fact—that he is Polish?

Mr. Husband. Yes.... His nativity is Austrian.... [But] I think ... there is no such thing as an Austrian race.

Senator Shively. Then he is a German?

Mr. Husband. He is a German or some other race—a Pole or Bohemian or Moravian [or some other race].[15] Even the five great racial divisions are a subject for debate.

Senator Guggenheim. There are five races. The negro belongs to the African race, for example.

Senator Cummins. Yours is the broad definition of race?

Senator Guggenheim. Yes....

Senator McCumber. Suppose you include in this "race," in its broadest sense, as the Caucasian and Mongolian races, as we know them, and then in addition you simply get the nationality, would not that answer every purpose? ... We would like to know how many black people, and how many yellow people there are, anyhow. We ought to have the color statistics in that way ...

Mr. North [director of the census who was also at the hearing]. There are five classifications, white, black, Chinese, Japanese and Indians.

Senator Cummins. These are not colors. Under the head of colors what would you put down? What would a Chinaman be?

Mr. North. He would be put down as a Chinaman.

Senator Shively. With reference to the Malays, for instance, you do not
tabulate them as brown?

Mr. Husband. No, sir; we tabulate them by country of birth.

Senator Bailey. It looks to me like it [the race classification proposed]
would not be much better than a geography. If you are going to give
the race—still it would seem to be an incongruous thing to take the
Irishman in his country and call it a race instead of a nationality, and
then take the Hebrew for his religion. They are not even a nationality
except of the nationality where they are born. Senator Guggenheim
is an American. Another Hebrew gentleman might be born in
Germany. Of course, by races they would be Caucasians. . . .

Senator Carter. Well, if we should develop a general racial subdivision
known to ethnology [i.e., "Caucasians, Semitics . . . Aryans . . . and so
on"] instead of the principalities, kingdoms and States to which you
refer . . . [that] would be of practically no value. . . .

Mr. Husband. No it would add nothing.[16]

Chinese counted as a race, but not Malays. And as Bailey summarized,
geography, nationality, and religion all seemed to serve as criteria for establishing race. It is intriguing that Census Director North, who had participated
actively in Cortelyou's 1903 review (discussed in Chapter 3), happened to
be present at this hearing as well—when the criteria for race implied by
List categories again came up for discussion. Yet North limited his contribution now to simply listing the categories of the race question included
in the most recent census (1900). North offered that information because
Senator McCumber had spoken of the value of "color statistics" on "black
people and . . . yellow people." But for his pains, Senator Cummins dismisses the census race categories, saying, "These are not colors. Under the
head of colors what would you put down? What would a Chinaman be?"
And North's answer, of course, ignored color: "He would be put down as a
Chinaman." The senators did not pursue the puzzles in North's statements
on color and the Chinese; they had problems enough with Husband's proposal on racial classification.

These interactions also suggest that the List of Races and Peoples was
not well known, even among well-placed members of the American elite

outside a very narrow circle concerned with immigration flows. The List was entering its second decade of use at the time of the hearing, but it is clear that the senators were having trouble following its logic, and they offered no sign that they had ever encountered it before.

Husband himself was confused about the origin of the List: "[This is the] race classification which was agreed upon, I believe by the Bureau of Ethnology of the Smithsonian Institution; at least, I understand someone connected with the Smithsonian Institution worked out the classification of races."[17] In fact, as we have seen, Safford and McSweeney provided the List; half a dozen years on, the Smithsonian's Otis Mason had grouped the forty races into a few "grand divisions." But that contribution had in fact been dropped a few years later still. Somehow, an official as close to the issues, as highly placed, and as able as W. W. Husband had absorbed a more comforting narrative, one in which the List had a scientific pedigree.

In any case, the senators were skeptical that the classification system was really a settled matter. Even if two other federal agencies used the List, did it have a place in the census? Moreover, could census enumerators be expected to make the relevant ethnological determinations?

> *Senator Cummins.* We will first have to agree to a definition of what is a race [before we can classify].
>
> *Mr. Husband.* It is contended by some that the classification . . . is not a scientific classification. . . .
>
> *Senator Bailey.* Why should we have to commit an error because the Bureau [of Immigration] did?
>
> *Mr. Husband.* That would not be necessary. . . . There should be a very careful classification of races made before the census is taken.
>
> *Senator Cummins.* After all it would depend upon the judgment of the man who made the census, because there are a dozen ways of classifying races recognized by ethnology. . . .
>
> *Senator Bailey.* The trouble is they want us to conform our bill to what they are doing in another place.[18]

Then another familiar issue loomed: How far through the generations should the new racial classification be maintained? Here we pick up also one of Senator Guggenheim's grievances, for he contended that "Americans" would be classified as "Hebrews." "I was born in Philadelphia. Under this census bill they put me down as a Hebrew, not as an American." La Follette then raised another interesting objection to enumerating native-born Americans of European origin.

> *The Chairman.* I can see there would be extreme difficulty if that question is asked of everybody. . . . Conditions are such that a great many people could not really state where they belonged. . . . But if it you limited it strictly to immigrants, that difficulty would be avoided.[19]

La Follette thus raised the challenges posed by extensive intermarriage among the late-generation descendants of immigrants and of the limits of family memory. A related matter is subjective versus objective understanding of people's origins.

> *Mr. Husband.* [Some people mentioned races not included in the Bureau's List,] but still the persons interviewed insisted they were of that race and objected to being classified as anything else.
>
> *Senator Guggenheim.* They may be wrong.
>
> *Mr. Husband.* They may be wrong, yes.
>
> *Senator Guggenheim.* They are wrong.
>
> *Senator Cummins.* Do you classify the Spanish and Italian people as of different races?
>
> *Mr. Husband.* Yes.
>
> *Senator Guggenheim.* As what would you classify a Spaniard?
>
> *Mr. Husband.* We have classified them as Spaniards.
>
> *Senator Guggenheim.* Suppose they were Jews who came from Spain, would they be classified as Jews or Spaniards?
>
> *Mr. Husband.* That would depend a good deal on what the man claimed to be.
>
> *Senator Guggenheim.* I don't think that has anything to do with it. It is purely a question of what is right.[20]

Much of this hearing's time, and surely most of the passion it generated, was taken up with the familiar Jewish protest that Guggenheim had raised numerous times. Indeed, many of the ruminations on other matters were suggested to senators as they listened to Guggenheim's efforts to defeat Husband's mission. Guggenheim first jumped in after Senator Carter had managed to ask only two questions.

Senator Guggenheim. This whole question was threshed out in . . . [an earlier hearing], Mr. Chairman. . . . Personally, I object to it not because I am a Hebrew but I object to it because it is not in place. . . . Take a man of the Jewish religion from Russia; is he a Jew or a Russian?

The Chairman. I can see broad ethnological reasons why some time it would be important to know from what blood and race the man came.

Senator Guggenheim. Why not ask his religion?

Senator McCumber. The Jews are not a race, of course. They do not belong to a race merely because they are Jews; there is no such thing as I understand it, as a Jewish race.

Senator Guggenheim. They are to be classified as a race under the proposed classification. . . .

The Chairman. I just do not get your objection to this, Senator Guggenheim. What objection can one have to having the race to which they belong correctly entered?

Senator Guggenheim. Because it is not correct when stated in that way; the Jews are not a race. . . . They belong to the country from which they came just as much as other people who have come. . . .

The Chairman. Then if they are not a race they would not be classed. They would be classed simply as foreign-born citizens under whatever race that country was classified. . . .

Senator Guggenheim. If that word "race" goes into this bill a few coming here from Russia will not be classified as Russians but as Jews.[21]

At several points Husband tried to compromise: not only could the census authorities give up the racial classification of the second generation, but they could reexamine the List itself, and in particular they might choose to drop the Hebrews (as the committee chairman had suggested). But Guggenheim clearly doubted that any compromise could be trusted ("if that word 'race' goes into this bill").

The transcript shows how concepts of race, people, nationality, geographic origin, political allegiance, and religion were all floating in the intellectual stew. The Jewish issue, of course, was a key impetus to the senators' ruminations. Indeed, some of the senators had been on the same committee during the preceding congressional session (when the issue had been aired the first time in the January House-Senate committee conference), so they may have been familiar with the Jewish organizations' arguments. In fact, they may have understood that this amendment was no more likely to pass now than before; they might as well gain some points for collegiality with Guggenheim by helping to frustrate it.

But such an interpretation of the transcript would be incomplete at best. It is clear from La Follette's remarks, for example, that he tried to follow Guggenheim's argument ("I just do not get your objection to this, Senator Guggenheim"). The key constitutional argument of the Jewish protest— that enumeration of a religious group was impermissible even if the purpose was to count race—was complex and new to many, and it was not expressed particularly well by Guggenheim. In any case, it is clear that the senators were concerned about more than the Hebrew category. They would have needed assurances about a number of other issues before supporting an amendment to accept the List in the upcoming census.

In particular, the senators were decidedly uncomfortable about the definition of race and they wondered how, with definitional problems, the census could incorporate the List. The senators were not dealing with the question *already* on the census, "color or race" (for which, in any case, they could substitute the notion of skin color). It is important to grasp, as evidence about the understanding of the race term at the time, that these intelligent men did *not* treat race as though it could be used loosely for any human collectivity, nor did they find it simple to interpret Husband's proposal to adopt the List in terms of a common understanding that a later generation would call ethnicity. Rather they were troubled that the race term Husband was proposing had debated meanings in ethnology. Moreover, *beyond* those ethnological meanings the categories of the List seemed to confuse at a minimum race with nationality and perhaps with religion and color as well.

Ethnic and Other Counter Pressures

In the end, nothing came of Husband's visit to the Senate Census Committee. And so, during the first three months of 1909, the Immigration Commission had made two unsuccessful attempts to have the race question placed on the 1910 census schedule, with both attempts foiled by the American Jewish Committee and Senator Guggenheim. But the matter did not stay quiet. A variety of interested individuals and organizations were well aware that *some* sort of classification beyond country of birth would be necessary if the huge numbers from Europe's multinational empires were to be meaningfully classified.

First of all, many southern and eastern European immigrants, particularly Slavs, were disgusted at being listed only by country of birth and therefore only as members of one of the multinational empires that were oppressing diverse peoples. To appreciate the extent of the problem, consider the following categories of the List of Races and Peoples: Armenian; Bohemian and Moravian; Croatian and Slovenian; Dalmatian, Bosnian, and Herzegovinian; Finn; Hebrew; Lithuanian; Pole; Ruthenian; and Slovak, as well as Austrian, German, Magyar, and Russian. Defined by country of birth, immigrants from virtually all of these groups were classified only as Austrian (or possibly Hungarian), German, or Russian.

Consequently, by late 1909 the Census Bureau was being pressed to add more information on origins—and not only by the powerful members of the Immigration Commission. On March 7, 1910, the *New York Times* noted under the headline, "Want Each Race Counted" that "State Senator John D. Prince, who is a professor of Languages at Columbia and Prof. M. I. Pupin of that University have inaugurated a movement" to press the census to include "peoples and nationalities not recorded separately. They point out that Slovaks, Croats, Slovenians, Roumanians and other races should be classified as such, and not as Hungarians. . . ." Moreover, "President A. S. Ambrose of the National Slavonic Society has called a meeting in Pittsburgh today . . . to prevail upon President Taft to take action."[22] A petition with several thousand signatures reached Congress.

Not only ethnic leaders were getting involved now. The Charity Organization Society of the City of New York had been corresponding from May to August 1909 with Census Bureau officials, urging that they make detailed tabulations of a few local areas in the city. Kate Claghorn, who was well known as a scholar and activist on immigrant issues, wrote to the bureau on behalf of a special census committee (which also included Charles S. Bernheimer, author of an important early study of Russian Jewish immigrants): "It is of little value for us to know that there are so many thousands of Poles in Buffalo and so many thousand Poles in New York City unless we also know that the Poles in Buffalo are Catholic Poles, so called, and the Poles in New York are Polish Jews. The two are as different as Italians and Germans, in their race characteristics and [so too are] the problems that arise with these different peoples."[23] Census Director Dana Durand now had to contend with such views as well as the commission's demands to use the List in the 1910 census. But above all, Durand had to find a path between Jewish protest and Slavic advocacy for that measure.

~

CHAPTER 6

The Census Bureau Goes Its Own Way

Race, Nationality, and Mother Tongue, 1910–1916

NATION AND NATIONALITY CARRIED multiple meanings at the turn of the twentieth century. Some meanings concerned a political state; others did not. Moreover, the meaning of these terms differed across the European languages. We can best appreciate these differences by considering at the outset two thoughtful discussions in major reference works of the period.

The Meanings of Nationality

The fabled eleventh edition of the *Encyclopedia Britannica* (1910) was the first edition of the encyclopedia that included an entry for the term "nationality."

> *Nationality.* A somewhat vague term, used strictly in international law . . .
> for the status of membership in a nation or state . . . and in a more
> extended sense in political discussion to denote an aggregation of
> persons claiming to represent a racial, territorial or some other bond of
> unity, though not necessarily recognized as an independent political
> entity. In this latter sense the word has often been applied to such people
> as the Irish, the Armenians and the Czechs. A "nationality" in this
> connection represents a common feeling and an organized claim rather
> than distinct attributes which can be comprised in a strict definition.[1]

Thus there were two meanings for nationality: first, citizenship (or subjecthood), and second, peoplehood. The latter, "more extended" meaning refers to a group that perceives a bond among themselves, yet the group is "not necessarily recognized as an independent political entity."

The last sentence in the *Britannica* entry blurs an otherwise sharp dichotomy of meanings; thus nationality as peoplehood carries with it not merely a "common feeling" but also "an organized claim." But if an "organized" claim is a "political" one—a claim upon other powers to recognize greater political independence for the particular nationality—then the "more extended meaning" points back toward political nationalism, or at least toward the inseparability of peoplehood and politics. Indeed, by 1911 when nationality was used in the second sense, that political claim was common. Nevertheless, an "organized" claim did *not* necessarily mean a "political" one; for example, members of a people could declare that they feel a certain commonality based on some combination of religion, language, territory, biological origin, and the like. The stress placed on each of these elements would differ from one nationality to another. The claim would be "organized" in the sense that activists were studying and praising the specific characteristics of the nationality—through its history, folklore, arts, and social conditions. Typically—but not always and certainly not immediately—the work of such activists lead sooner or later to political demands. And these demands, of course, served as a further stimulus to the praise and study of inherent characteristics of the nationality.

The *Oxford English Dictionary* of the same era provided examples for this second usage of "nationality" (as peoplehood) extending back to the 1830s. By the early 1860s, John Stuart Mill and Lord Acton were using the term in *Britannica's* second sense. Mill argued that to ensure free institutions "the boundaries of government should coincide in the main with those of nationality," or else a sovereign might exploit divide-and-rule tactics. Meanwhile, Acton argued just to the contrary, that "the presence of different nations under the same sovereignty . . . provides against . . . servility" by "balancing interests" and "multiplying associations."[2]

The *Britannica* entry should be enough to alert us that English speakers of the period could misunderstand which usage a speaker had in mind when mentioning nationality—peoplehood or citizenship. And this is precisely the sort of confusion that Victor Safford had mentioned when he first detailed the weaknesses of the Bureau of Immigration's old data collection system in his memo to Edward McSweeney: it left ambiguous whether the "nationality" item was calling for political membership or peoplehood.

In fact, these ambiguities went beyond the English-language usage and were occasionally discussed in European sources. French usage also generally referred to political membership when nationality was discussed; German and eastern European usage referred principally to peoplehood. These differences across language were by no means unknown. They were discussed, for example, in the entry for *Nation* and *Nationalitat* in *Meyers Grosses Konversations-Lexikon* (1908). Like the *Britannica*, it was an authoritative encyclopedic dictionary in a major European language. *Nation* is defined as "a part of the human race related by descent, custom and language," and *Nationalitat* as "membership in this part."

> The word *Nation* [is used] only in this sense, the word *Volk* in this sense as well as to designate the members of a particular state. One can speak both of German *Volk* and German *Nation*, by contrast of an Austrian *Volk*, but not of Austrian *Nation*. It is also noteworthy that in English and French usage the term *Nation* is precisely reversed, signifying the *Volk* of the state (the political nationality), hence nationality signifies citizenship [*Staatsangehörigkeit*]; while *Nation* in the German sense of the word, [refers to] the primitive *Volk* (the natural nationality), commonly referred to by the words *Peuple* (French) and *People* (English). The concept of *Nation* lies in the consciousness of common descent and belonging: national feeling [*Nationalgefühl*].[3]

In sum, the juxtaposition of these reference works suggests that by the turn of the twentieth century, the term *Volk* combines both of *Britannica's* meanings for nationality (and perhaps more), but the term *Nationalitat* conveys approximately the meaning of *Britannica's* second meaning, namely, nationality as peoplehood. In English (and French) the most precise (and perhaps most common) meaning for nationality was citizenship, while a "vaguer" meaning signified peoplehood. But in German (as well as in European languages prevalent east of Germany), the term *Nationalitat* routinely signified *only* the second English meaning.

The *Meyers* entry also notes that consciousness of national differences is common, and that members of each nation routinely take pride in their own group's accomplishments. As a result, national hatreds sometimes arise and a high valuation on national self-preservation is universal, as is a resistance to the domination of any other nation over one's own. For the same reason, each nation seeks to preserve its national peculiarities, or national character, especially through its national language and its use in a national literature. The easiest way a nation can achieve all of this is if it comprises the largest population element of a state, without other large national elements in the same state. These conditions will also provide a natural basis of stability for that state (a version of Mill's argument). But history knows many other connections between nation and state: the oppression of one nation by another within one state (e.g., Poles in the Russian Empire), the merger of the members of old nations into a unified political order (e.g., the Roman Empire of antiquity and modern France), and the equality of multiple nations within one state (e.g., Switzerland). Moreover, the cynical exploitation of national feeling has often helped rulers in states divided by nationalities. But while all these circumstances are possible, the nineteenth century also witnessed the successful realization of the first outcome: a political state in which one nation is demographically dominant (e.g., Italy and Germany). A second nineteenth-century pattern was that of the Austro-Hungarian Empire, within which a degree of national autonomy existed. This striving for national freedom "has even been put forward, almost as a political principle, that each *Nation* could claim it as its right to form a particular state of its own (nationality principle [*Nationalitätsprinzip*])." However, this notion, too, has been exploited by cynical political leaders and balanced by other principles and realities because not every *Nation* finds itself historically able to create such a state.

Behind all of these modes of realizing the connection between nationality and states, we should also appreciate how commonly issues of nationality—in *Britannica's* second sense (as peoplehood)—do in fact end up in the political realm, even if *Nation* means, at its simplest meaning in *Meyers,* "membership in a part of the human race related by descent, custom and language." These features of the term will matter when immigrants are referred to in America as members of nations or nationalities, that is, united by descent, but in a way that "an organized claim" often drives the group into demands for political autonomy or independence.

We need not survey the intellectual and political history of European nationalism to support the observation that the term nationality will carry an explosive ambiguity about political implications into the American milieu. But a brief glance at some relevant strands of nineteenth-century thought will help situate the meaning of the *Britannica* and especially the *Meyers* entries.

In the late eighteenth century, the German philosopher J. G. Herder gave special force to the claim that each nation (in the nonpolitical sense of each "people") experienced reality in a distinctive way. Each therefore had a contribution to make to human development, and that contribution would be most authentically captured in its national language. This linkage of nationality and language in turn became a crucial part of the definition of national boundaries, both demographic and territorial. Admittedly, linguistic assimilation could occur (and was occurring), either naturally or by compulsion, but the ancient linguistic differences provided an authentic reflection of ancient nationalities.[4]

Generally, at least until the later years of the eighteenth century, Herder's legacy was rather too vague on these national differences to take a clear-cut position on the role of biological and social transmission of these national differences. But within a few decades, the role of biology in this process of transmission was at least mentioned and often emphasized. Moreover, during much of the nineteenth century many observers thought that the boundaries of both race *and* nationality were best marked by the boundaries of language use. For nationality the emphasis on language went back at least to Herder's formulations. In the case of race, the connection to language arose with the discovery of historical links among widely disparate modern languages in the eighteenth century. Admittedly, arguments about an Indo-European language and people were very different from Herder's interest in languages as reflections of national distinctiveness. Nevertheless, they did share the notion that boundaries of both ancient races and authentic nationalities were marked by language use.

However, by the end of the nineteenth century the role of language in demarcating race in particular had become problematic. Recall that William Z. Ripley's synthesis of current research and speculation, *Races of Eu-*

rope (1899), summarized the new understanding of language as well. In most of Europe, race had not existed in unmixed form since the prehistoric ages. Since then, many other factors of environment and eventually of social history brought people together and influenced their physical and intellectual development. Consequently, Ripley stressed, the ancient racial stratum must be considered independent of both language and nationality. Indeed, present-day boundaries of race, nationality, and language usually differed. As to nationality, Ripley rarely distinguished between *Britannica's* first and second usages—between citizenship and peoplehood. But he stressed that the boundaries for *either* could well differ from the boundaries of a particular language. And his key point was that language and nationality were very unlikely to have a revealing connection to the distribution of ancient, pure races. Both language and nationality are entirely distinct from race in some cases and at least partially so in every case.[5] Still, for Ripley, "ethnic factors," that is, ethnological (physical) factors of common origin (whether of a single race or not) typically did play *some* role in creating nationalities.

Another strand in the discussion concerning nationality and language is far less well known today, especially to English-language readers. During the third quarter of the nineteenth century, European census officials explored ways to capture nationality in their enumerations. Not surprisingly, this effort was especially great in the multinational empires and strongest of all in Austria-Hungary. That empire encompassed a large number of peoples, their political strength was significant, and census-taking was well established. By contrast, although the Russian Empire also encompassed many peoples, those peoples faced autocratic oppression, and the first full census of the Russian Empire did not occur until 1897.

A regular forum for the discussion of censuses and definitions of terms emerged when the statistician Adolph Quetelet successfully created the International Statistical Congress for government statisticians in 1853. It would meet every few years thereafter. From the first congress, nationality statistics were listed as a desideratum for the population reports. But just how to capture nationality in census enumerations challenged the participants through the 1870s.[6]

Early discussions recognized that nationality was a complex and subtle phenomenon. How, then, could the census-takers operationalize the concept for purposes of enumeration? Even after decades of discussion, influential Austro-Hungarian authorities would write that nationality was a "feeling, analogous to religious denomination . . . on which belonging, region of origin, race-character and everything that depends on it acts, and which, in order to reveal itself, uses language as its tool, just as religion uses dogmas and ceremonies." More specifically nationality was "ethnographic affiliation," and it "consists of a number of objective factors, such as common origins and historical development, common residence and shared cultural development, expressed above all in religion and language."[7]

But which of these "objective factors" could be enumerated in government statistics? How could a language question serve as an adequate proxy when no single factor (including language) could define all nationalities? Yet most of the characteristics of nationality *other* than language (and area of residence)—"common origins and historical development" and "shared cultural development"—were hardly "objective" in the sense an enumerator needed.

The statisticians at these conferences also rejected another alternative: to simply ask the respondents to report their nationality. Self-consciousness of nationality was a developing phenomenon, especially in a society that was only semiliterate. The statisticians did not want to capture the perception that ignorant and often illiterate individuals would report "a sum of truths, half-truths, of things that would be misunderstood, that were lies and totally thoughtless."[8] Demographers, in other words, seemed to agree that respondents could be part of a nationality even if they were unaware of being so.

At the same time that the congresses were calling for study of the nationality issue, they also were also listing "langue parlee" as a valuable item to be included in the modern censuses, not at first as a proxy for nationality but simply for its own sake. Eventually, however, language was embraced as the proxy for nationality, at least from Germany eastward. The German demographer Richard Boeckh turned against the earlier fulsome definition of nationality based on a list of factors producing "ethnographic affiliation." He urged his colleagues to reconcile themselves to simply ascertaining each individual's "vernacular." It was, he argued, the closest they would get to an enumeration of nationality. In 1872, the Eighth International Statistical Congress accepted his argument that only by this means could "the boundaries of nationalities be recorded."[9]

This position radically restricted the range of definitional problems, but it did not end them entirely. Which "language" would serve as a proxy for nationality—the *mother tongue* first learned in childhood, the *current home vernacular* of an adult, or the *current vernacular in public contexts?* Some individuals might have given three different answers to these three specifications, as a result of assimilation, conquest, and national policies. Many would have given two. Obviously, the choice of which meaning for language the census-takers would select depended on which temporal reality they sought to illuminate. Moreover, the results of these enumerations could sway political consciousness and demands in parts of Europe. So short-range political considerations were waiting in the wings to influence the choice of which language would be a proxy for nationality.

The 1872 congress had hoped to move beyond this ambiguity. It commissioned three experts to offer position papers at the next congress (several years off) on how to formulate the relevant language question. But these papers were not taken up at the following congress, perhaps because no resolution was expected. And so the congresses had defined language as the way to trace "boundaries of nationalities," but in the end they left to each country the choice of what specific question about language should be asked.

Still another issue was whether responses to the language question were to be reported simply as such, or would they be explicitly presented as nationality counts? Thus reports might list languages, or they might list nationalities, or they might list a variant of the latter, such as "nationality—by spoken language." But rigorous statisticians could not long countenance the first approach; at a minimum, the counts had to mention in some way that the criterion for the nationality numbers had been language. All of these issues would show up in the American context as well.

Finally, when the 1872 congress resolved that language would be a proxy for "nationality" in the German sense, they agreed that censuses could also include a direct question on "nationality" in its primary English-language sense, namely, as citizenship or subjecthood.

In the decade before World War I, the problem of multiple nations existing within a state and demanding greater political autonomy was growing in Europe, but this was not the big issue for the United States, where issues of peoplehood showed up in connection with oppressed color races or in connection with immigration. African Americans of the period, primarily in the Jim Crow South, lacked the power to make compelling demands for political autonomy, even if they had wanted to. Immigrants typically were not oriented to making such demands. In fact, it was quite the reverse: discussions by both immigrant leaders and American native-born elites were intensely concerned with absorbing immigrants on the basis of political equality. Indeed, for native-born elites, it was precisely this issue that was threatening. If immigrant character and ability were inadequate, the arrivals should be restricted.

Competing Usages: The Bureaus of Census and Immigration Part Ways

As we have been tracing American discussions related to the List of Races and Peoples, most of the references have been to race but not to nationality. And, of course, in the American context "nationality" typically referenced political membership. Still nationality, in the sense of peoplehood occasionally surfaced self-consciously as a term used to define the immigrant groups. And when nationality did surface in this way, it came up not infrequently with an awareness that something different from race was referred to. We have already observed a particularly striking instance of this at the hearings of the Senate Committee on the Census:

> *Senator Carter.* How do you distinguish between nationality and race in your classification? What do you mean by the word "race?" . . . You refer to the Poles as a race; they are not a race at all as I understand the word "race"; it is a nationality. Would you refer to the Irish as a race? . . . There seems to be a confusion of nationality and race. . . .
> *Mr. Husband.* Everything is taken by nationality also.

Senator Carter had in mind the peoplehood meaning of nationality—that is why he focuses on the examples of Poles and Irish, as neither had a state of their own at that time. Husband, however, misunderstood this and replied in terms of political membership.

We can now return to the dilemma that Census Director Durand faced early in 1910. Should he bow to the resistance of Jewish groups or to Slavic and other groups in favor of bringing the List of Races and Peoples into the 1910 census? Durand eventually chose to replace race with nationality and used mother tongue as a proxy for nationality. The Census Bureau later published its results exclusively in terms of mother tongue. How the bureau and its director reached that decision, and how we come to know about the decision-making process, is itself a strange tale.

It is strange as well that Daniel Folkmar had not suggested this path earlier. Folkmar knew all about the European census's use of language questions to obtain nationality counts. In fact, when he had accompanied Husband to the Senate Census Committee hearing in April 1909, he actually suggested to the senators that they could exploit mother tongue as a proxy. But he suggested it be a proxy for race, not nationality. In fact, throughout the next few years in internal and public contexts, Folkmar held tenaciously to the term race in classifying European groups, even as many around him shifted toward nationality or simply spoke of mother-tongue data. His loyalty to the nomenclature of race was rooted in his insistence that biological heredity was an important component in the formation and persistence of distinctive traits in groups. In any case, we will observe him again trying to reconcile his usage of race with the increasing usage, at least at the Census Bureau, of other terms.

At the Senate committee hearing that Folkmar attended with Husband, he suggested the language proxy—urging it as the European usage.

> It might be well to preface my very brief remarks by defining what we mean by race. I think I can do that best by taking one of the European Censuses—the census of Servia, for instance—and reading the list they have. The point is that race is according to language and not color. Here is the Servian list: Servian, Albanian, Bulgarian, Greek, English, Hebrew, Armenian, Magyar, German, Polish, Romanian, Russian, Slavic, Slovenian, Italian, Turkish, French, Croatian, Bohemian, Romanian-Macedonian, Gypsy, other. . . .

[Several conclusions follow from these considerations]

1. [The U.S. should do] what many countries in Europe and the Americas are doing. . . . Especially the larger countries, such as Austria, and Hungary and Russia . . . form a brilliant example of what can be done in the census of races.

2. The Russian government has nearly seventy races in its division, while we, as you know, according to the Immigration Bureau, have only about forty. . . .

6. The present use of "Nationality" rather than race in such topics as the above are often misleading. [Half the Russians by nationality in immigrant statistics are Jews]. . . .

9. The practicability of a census by races [involves asking a single question]. . . . The question is simply "what is your mother tongue, or that of your ancestry in Europe?"[10]

In this testimony Folkmar cleared up one confusion about enumerating races: he was not concerned here with the color races. Yet at the same time he passed on the opportunity to introduce the nationality nomenclature because he wanted a language question that would produce a "census of races." It is especially striking that the European countries that he cited as models had in fact adopted the nationality nomenclature. For example, Folkmar told the senators that "the Russian government has nearly seventy races" in its usage. The Russian Census, however, did *not* present material in terms of race but rather discussed "nationality—by language."[11] Presumably, Folkmar knew all of this but felt that explaining it would simply raise useless complexities: he wanted to retain the race usage for ancient origins. And so, too, in his sixth point he insisted on preserving only the *political* meaning for nationality (*Britannica*'s first usage).

Finally, Folkmar offered advice on how to handle the Jewish protest. Most Jews "speak the 'Judisch-Deutsch' [Yiddish] as it is called. That is a dialect of the German language. . . . They would be counted . . . with Germans if we wished to interpret it that way." Again, this was a strange formulation. On the one hand, Folkmar anticipated how the Gordon knot would eventually be cut: mother tongue would not identify *all* Jews (as race would). Some Jews had been brought up on Russian, German, or English. Still, Yiddish mother tongue would certainly have identified *most* Jews in 1910. However, Folkmar did not guide the committee down that path. Rather, he fudged the anticipated question: When Jews report Yiddish, would they be classified into a separate Yiddish category or with German? If the latter, the data would have failed to identify the second largest immigrant group of the decade: Jews would be classified among the German immigrants, confusing the data on both groups. And yet Folkmar did come close to proposing the nationality-by-mother-tongue solution.

We should recall that he offered this suggestion in the presence of an angry Senator Guggenheim and after the other senators had also been expressing skepticism on a variety of points. Perhaps even if Folkmar had not confused the issue by retaining the race terminology and merging German and Yiddish, the senators would still not have listened sympathetically. In any case, at the April 1909 hearing, the opportunity to solve the problem by effectively substituting mother tongue for race was not taken. Instead, as we have seen, the dilemma worked its way to Durand over the course of the following months. It did so through I. A. Hourwich.

I. A. HOURWICH'S INTERVENTIONS ON RACE AND NATIONALITY, 1909–1910

I. A. Hourwich was one of those improbable characters whose life touched social and intellectual spheres that we think of as quite separate. Within a seven-year period, he was at work in the Washington federal bureaucracy, a candidate for the Russian Duma, a writer of half a dozen articles published in the most prestigious journals of American social science, a socialist labor leader at the center of a bitter and important clash, an attorney, a congressional candidate for the Bull Moose Party, and the author of a monumental and influential study of American immigration.[12] He knew Lenin and Louis Brandeis, the director of the U.S. Census Bureau and radical Yiddish socialists. In our story, he played a surprisingly important, if brief, role, so it will be helpful to know something more about him before following his approach to the issues of race and nationality.[13]

Hourwich was born in Vilna, into a middle-class, culturally modernizing Jewish family. Sent to Russian schools, he eventually graduated from the local gymnasium. Indeed, although he was raised in an intellectual center of the Russian Jewish Pale, by upbringing he was more a Russian than a Yiddish intellectual. He went on to the University of St. Petersburg, but at the age of nineteen he was arrested for membership in a revolutionary group and in 1881 sent to Siberia, where he remained for five years. Like some other revolutionary intellectuals, he managed to use the time for a study of local conditions. In Hourwich's case, it was a study of the peasant migration into Siberia, published soon after his release. After Siberia, he managed to spend a year studying Russian law and passed the examinations to practice. Nevertheless, by 1890 he had fled Russia for New York. And so, at about age thirty, he was interacting with the American immigrant labor movement, in which the Yiddish sector was much larger than the Russian. Having earlier studied in Russian, he now had to work on his written Yiddish to reach Jewish working-class immigrants. Eventually, he wrote extensively for various socialist journals in both Russian and Yiddish.

During this period of the early 1890s, Hourwich passed the American bar and earned a PhD in economics from Columbia University with a dissertation on "The Economics of the Russian Village." In general, he wrote from a loose, revisionist-Marxist perspective. He envisioned worker progress, particularly for the United States, through rather than against the institutions of the established political order. For a time, he taught statistics at the University of Chicago. Strangely enough, he met Daniel Folkmar during that time and even helped him with the statistics on one of Folkmar's early papers.[14] But Hourwich was soon dismissed from the university, apparently for his socialist views. He had a law practice in New York for a while and contributed throughout to the left press in Yiddish and Russian.

The big shift, for our purposes, came around 1900 when he moved to Washington, DC, to take a position as a translator and then statistician in government offices and also to work at the Census Bureau for much of the decade as an expert on mining. During this crucial decade, he continued his Yiddish and Russian journalistic writing, but he did so under pseudonyms. He also began publishing in the American scholarly journals, first in 1904 and then again between 1910 and 1913—three papers in the *Journal of Political Economy*, others in *Proceedings of the American Political Science Association*, *The American Economic Review*, *Political Science Quarterly*, and *The Amer-*

ican Journal of Sociology. Hourwich's hiatus from writing for scholarly publications after 1904 coincides with his return to Russia during the 1905 Revolution to run for the Russian Duma. He was nearly seated there. Apparently he took a leave from his job in the federal bureaucracy for this adventure, and when hopes were disappointed in Russia, he returned to his desk in Washington.

And so, in November 1909, when he enters our story, Hourwich was turning fifty and working once more at that Washington desk. He believed that good data on the Jewish immigration was critical for policy and social work, and he was appalled that the Senate Census Committee had tabled the Immigration Commission's proposal for a question based on the List of Races and Peoples. In his view, the Senate committee's decision came about because the assimilated Jewish Senator Guggenheim had irately objected, and the other senators on the committee cared little about the issue.

We have an unusual glimpse of Hourwich's perspective because a few years later, in 1915, he wrote an account of the relevant events for the New York Jewish press in both English and Yiddish. The two versions were clearly meant for different audiences, with the English for a more assimilated group that would even include some of the German Jewish Reform elite. The Yiddish version was for more recent eastern European Jewish arrivals. The difference in nuance is revealing. The English version reads:

> The race composition of the United States has within recent years
> become paramount in the minds of American sociologists. . . . This plan
> [to enumerate "races" in the 1910 census] encountered the opposition of
> Senator Guggenheim of Colorado. . . . He thought that the inquiry in
> relation to the Jews would be equivalent to an inquisition into the
> religious affiliations of a portion of the population of the United States,
> and it was beyond the sphere of our government to enter into such an
> inquiry. Senatorial courtesy led other members of the Committee on the
> Census to yield to Senator Guggenheim.[15]

The Yiddish version has it:

> Against this [enumerating Jews], the high and mighty American
> German Jewish elite [*Amerikaner Yahudim*—a common term of derision]
> protested strongly that this would stimulate anti-Semitic tendencies. . . .

There is no doubt that the classification by nationalities [*nationali-taten*] is the result of race hatred [*raasen-has*] against the immigrants which has increased greatly in the recent period. . . . [It is] directed not against the Jews alone, but against the Italians, Poles and other Slavic nationalities. . . .

[At the 1910 Senate Census Committee hearings, the nationality question encountered] sharp questions from the Jewish Senator Guggenheim. . . . Well [*Nu*], when a Jewish Senator says no one should ask Jews whether they are Jewish, obviously the gentile senators, out of deference to their colleague, will not insist on the question: it is no great concern [*grosse dayge*] whether one will have statistics about Jews or not; and the question was eliminated.[16]

Hourwich consistently defines the immigrant groups as nationalities, not races. And yet when it comes to defining the sentiment *against* immigrants, he has "no doubt that the classification by nationalities is the result of race hatred." It may be that there was no convenient term available to him for hatred of nationalities, and therefore he speaks of the hatred of races. But it is more likely that he meant to emphasize that even if the new groups were better understood as nationalities than as races, the *anti*-immigrant faction thought of the immigrant groups as races and leveled against them a racial hatred.

In any case, he wanted to reverse the outcome of the Senate Census Committee hearing. His best chance seemed to be to influence the outlook of the American Jewish Committee (AJC). He therefore reached out to a member of that AJC board whom he no doubt considered to be most sympathetic to his views. This was Judah L. Magnes.

Magnes's biography does not quite match Hourwich's for improbable combinations of experiences, but he, too, was an unusual figure. Born and raised in the San Francisco Bay area, Magnes become an American Reform rabbi after studying at the movement's Cincinnati seminary. From there he moved on to Berlin for further Jewish studies. While based in Berlin, he made trips to the traditional Jewish communities farther east in German Poland and in Galicia (the Austro-Hungarian province of Poland). The nature of Jewish life in eastern Europe fascinated Magnes, grounded as it was in a dense cultural base, and not merely in tenets of American Reform Judaism. When he returned to the United States, he supported a kind of cultural nationalism for Jews in general and became greatly interested in the new eastern European Jewish immigrants, who embodied what he saw as a vibrant, dense culture—a national culture.

Magnes was a gifted speaker and a shining light of Reform Judaism, and at an early age he was appointed rabbi at the prestigious Temple Emanuel in New York City. He also joined the executive board of the AJC. At the same time, he founded and led the New York Jewish Kehillah (1909), an effort to create a communal organization for all New York Jews (over a million in number)—Orthodox and Reform, secular, socialist and Zionist, bankers and garment workers, German second generation and Russian immigrant. The organization could claim a commonality only through a sense of a common Jewish cultural base, or through membership in a Jewish people. This orientation eventually led Magnes too far afield for his Reform Jewish congregation, and he resigned his prestigious position at Emanuel in 1910. Later still (after he crosses our stage), he would become active in American pacifist circles protesting involvement in World War I. In the mid-1920s he moved to Palestine to become the founding rector of the Hebrew University, a position he held until his death in 1948. In Palestine, he would emerge as a major supporter of a single, bi-nationalist Arab and Jewish state—and thus as a thorn in the side of the Jewish national movement's political elite there.[17]

Hourwich and Magnes probably knew each other personally by 1909, through the efforts to found the Kehillah. But even if they had never met, Hourwich would have known of Magnes's views on Jewish cultural revival and Jewish nationalism. It was surely because of these views that Hourwich thought Magnes would be the best conduit to the AJC. Hourwich told Magnes that "statistics as to the Jews of the United States is a desideratum and that we Jews need have no fear as to the deductions that will be drawn from them"; he urged that the executive board of the AJC reconsider its opposition to the census race question. And he was defining the issue as "the inclusion of nationality as distinct from place of birth in the new census."[18]

Magnes replied that the AJC now accepted that the Bureau of *Immigration* could legitimately classify newly arriving immigrants by race or people; it could be argued, he said, that collecting as much information as possible about arrivals was desirable and acceptable. The census, however, was another matter. That enumeration distinguished primarily between citizens and noncitizens and did so for purposes of apportionment of population. Furthermore, it was contrary to the spirit of American institutions to have any governmental inquiry made into the race or the religious beliefs of its citizens.

Magnes's reply did not develop this last point, but it seems clear that he was repeating the position Friedenwald had expressed earlier in 1909 (discussed in Chapter 5). Collecting race data on American citizens was in itself impermissible—or at least (in Friedenwald's formulation) this was the case when the data extended beyond broad color differences.

Thus Magnes explained that the AJC's position seemed to be in conflict with Hourwich's. However, Magnes also urged him to explain his own view further. Hourwich replied that there existed a Jewish nationality, based in part on racial origins, and it could be discussed without a primary focus on religion. He compared the situation of the Jews to that of the Armenians, who were also a people (nationality) with a distinctive church coterminous with its nationality.

Magnes agreed with much of this, but he disagreed with some points, especially on the practical political implications Hourwich drew.

> I am in complete agreement with you as to the existence of what might generally be called a Jewish nationality, based in part upon Jewish race. I do not however, agree with you that the word "Hebrew" or "Jew," no matter if used as you use it in the racial sense, has no religious implications for the ordinary man, be he Jew or non-Jew. . . . [And] it would seem to me to be contrary to the "spirit of American institutions" to have such an inquisition made by the census; . . . there is not as yet, fortunately—so it would seem to me—any evidence of an inquisition into the religious affiliations of the citizens of this land. The European example of such an inquisition into a man's religious connections may, I think, serve as a warning to us of the dangers involved in this. If it were not for this point, I should agree with your apprehension that we are allowing a chance for gathering statistics in this country to slip by.[19]

Still, Magnes again asked Hourwich for more, this time for the text he would like to see in a census bill. No doubt Magnes thought it best to have the wording of a sympathetic expert on hand in case the issue came up again.

Even Magnes, the AJC leader most sensitive to cultural nationalism, was on the other side of the divide from Hourwich here. Hourwich would write, at least by 1914, of "race hatred" against the new immigrants. But it did not stop him from supporting the new data collection. In November 1909, Magnes was concerned with the dangers of religious hatred against Jewish immigrants in particular. He did in fact see the envisioned data collection as a potential stimulus to anti-Semitism. He must have understood that race-based hatred against immigrants, and even against Jews in particular, was growing on both continents. But it did not follow for Magnes that religious hatred was not a real issue, too, and the data collection might contribute to religious hatred. Hourwich's November 1909 effort to influence the AJC through Magnes failed.

But Hourwich had another opportunity to intervene in the questions of race, nationality, and the census a few months later. It proved much more direct, influential, and successful. This opportunity occurred only two weeks before the 1910 census enumeration was to begin, after the Slavic petition calling for a race question had been presented to Congress. The House and Senate census committees as well as Census Bureau Director Durand now had to face the conflicting demands about including a question based on the List of Races and Peoples in the enumeration. We know what happened next from one source only, namely, Hourwich's own 1914 accounts in the aforementioned Jewish press.

> The House and Senate Committees on the Census called for an opinion from the Director of the Census. Dr. Durand called a conference of the census experts to discuss the question. The present writer was among those who were asked to attend the conference. The question was a highly delicate one. On the one hand, the Poles and Bohemians insisted on being treated as distinct races. On the other hand, however, the question of race had been tabooed by Congress. The present writer suggested an inquiry relating to "the mother tongue" of the foreign born and the immigrant parents of the first native-born generation. The inclusion of Yiddish among the mother tongues of the foreign stock would not raise any religious questions. There was still some doubt as to

whether the question would cover the whole Jewish race. The writer referred to the results of the Russian Census of 1897 which showed that 98 percent of the Jews of the Empire reported Yiddish as their mother tongue. The writer's suggestion was approved and "mother tongue" was included among the Census inquiries on population.[20]

Assuming his account is accurate, Hourwich had been able to save the day through familiarity with the central-European usage of nationality and with European censuses' use of mother tongue as the proxy for nationality. And so it was that the mother-tongue question first entered the American census as an alternative to classifying European immigrant peoples as races.

There was at least one other person working at census at the time who was well aware of the European usages: Folkmar. As we have seen, he had tried to bring the use of mother tongue as a proxy to the attention of the senators at the Census Committee hearing on the "race" item. It is possible that Folkmar, too, was at Durand's meeting described by Hourwich. However, as we have seen, Folkmar was too wrapped up in his own concerns about race terminology to make an effective case for mother tongue as a proxy for nationality. Still, another reason Folkmar had failed at the Senate Committee hearing while Hourwich later succeeded at Durand's meeting was surely that, in the interim, the issue had taken on the character of a minor crisis.

Hourwich's account does not deal directly with the collapse of the Jewish protest. He seems to suggest that race was taboo, but nationality and mother tongue were not. Why not? First, the AJC may have realized that they could not fight the Census Bureau once Durand had made up his mind. The fight would be too public, and it would pit the Jewish opposition against a well-publicized Slavic effort as well as against Jewish nationalist groups, social workers like Kate Claghorn, and the Census Bureau itself. Following the reaction they had encountered after the U.S. Immigration Commission hearings only a few months before (in December 1909), the AJC board members were surely in no mood to open another campaign about this issue. And second, their impermissibility argument based on church–state separation rested on the congruence of race and religion for Hebrews. But the congruence between Yiddish mother tongue and religion categories was less complete—conceptually and practically. Indeed, it was particularly irrelevant to the second-generation German Jewish Reform elite.

DURAND PROPOSES "NATIONALITY OR MOTHER TONGUE" TO CONGRESS

Durand now wrote to the House and Senate Census Committee chairmen— just three weeks before the enumeration was to begin. He urged Congress to mandate a new question for the 1910 census: nationality captured by mother tongue. Durand's letter represents a crucial turning point in the effort to classify immigrants in American federal statistics. With that letter, the Census Bureau turned away from the notion that relevant sub-divisions of Europeans should be described as races. It offered a new conception and terminology, based on nationality. Moreover, the only operational measure of nationality was mother tongue. Consequently, it was far from clear from Durand's letter that nationality itself would come to occupy an important place in discussions of the data. And in fact, na-tionality, like race, was soon abandoned in Census Bureau discussions of the mother-tongue data. It would be mother tongue that came to sup-plement birthplace information. Nevertheless, Durand's letter succeeded by replacing racial categories for Europeans (for "whites") with nation-ality categories.

Durand wrote the identical letter to both House and Senate chairmen, requesting authorization to include the new question.

> This amendment provides for adding . . . a question with regard to "nationality or mother tongue" [of the foreign-born population]. . . . It is a well-known fact that in several of the leading foreign countries, notably in Russia, Austria and Turkey, the population is far from being homoge-neous, but is made up of a number of decidedly distinct nationalities, sometimes referred to as races.[21]

The usual term, he now implied, was not race at all but nationality—in the sense of *Britannica's* second meaning of peoplehood. His last phrase implied as well that race is the *less appropriate* term: "distinct nationalities sometimes referred to as races."

The next sentence clarified what a nationality was and offered some clarification about its relationship to race.

> The differences in racial characteristics, language, and habits of life, as between these different sections of the population are often very marked, and unless they are recognized in enumerating the population from these countries the census will fail to disclose facts which are of much importance from the practical as well as the scientific standpoint. In considering legislation relating to immigration particularly, information with regard to nationality of the foreign-born population is of great importance.

Durand—like Ripley, Hourwich, Magnes, and others—had no need to deny that nationality differences may be founded in part on "racial characteristics." But much else contributed to making a nationality. That was the first point. The second began with what seems a platitude—information on nationality would be useful "from the practical and scientific standpoint." But the next sentence was much more pointed: nationality information would be important "for considering legislation relating to immigration particularly." This formulation was very close to the Immigration Commission's mandate, and to their reason for requesting the inclusion of race data on Europeans in the first place. In the context of congressional debate during those years, the most obvious kind of "legislation" would deal with restriction; data on immigrant nationalities would enlighten that discussion.

Durand closed by noting that "Aside from the scientific value of a report on nationality, it appears that the members of some of the nationalities" insist that information on nationality be added to that on country of birth; that is, "the various Slavic nationalities coming from Austria-Hungary . . . appear almost unanimously" to support collection of the additional information "so that they will not be supposed to be Austrians or Hungarians." Indeed, he mentioned a danger that without the nationality question, these groups might not fully cooperate with the census-takers. Durand's letter tactfully avoided mention of the position taken by the Jewish groups as to the List and the Hebrew category.

The rest of the letter concerned the practicalities of the last-minute addition. The millions of census forms had already been printed and distributed to enumerators. Supplemental instructions would be written and enumerators would follow them by recording mother-tongue data in the column originally intended only for birthplace. The punch card technology would accommodate the change. Yet this technical section of Durand's letter did not discuss how nationality would be operationalized.

In a letter of six paragraphs, Durand mentioned the term "nationality" nine times and "mother tongue" only once—the latter when first mentioning his proposal "to add a question with regard to 'nationality or mother tongue.'" Perhaps he was thinking of European usage, in which "nationality" was proxied by "mother tongue." Perhaps he worded the proposal for the new census item in the broadest possible way, leaving the actual wording of the new question for the coming days. Whatever the explanation, Durand's text was strangely vague in describing that question. Once again, as with Safford and McSweeney in 1898, a real innovation was being introduced on a madcap schedule. And Durand's discussion of mother tongue as proxy for nationality may have fallen victim to the haste.

When Congress took up Durand's letter, their discussions of all of the relevant terms—race, nationality, mother tongue, and even parental mother tongue—were looser still. Congressmen were quite willing to add the new question to the census, but they did offer some suggestions of their own. And they followed Durand's lead in studiously avoiding mention of Jewish groups' opposition to the inclusion of Hebrew in the earlier race question.

> *Mr. Crumpacker.* There are countries in Europe . . . where political
> division is not a correct designation or a true criterion of the
> question of nationality or race, or racial distinction. [Examples
> include] Russia, Austria and Turkey . . . the Kingdom of Great
> Britain. . . . Those people feel a just attachment to mother country . . .
> and this great body of adopted citizens have petitioned Congress to
> make the classification. . . . A large delegation . . . visited this city last
> week. . . .
>
> *Mr. Sabath [who proposed the act in the House].* . . . Its main purpose is to
> preserve in the census statistics the various nationalities . . . from
> Austria-Hungary and Russia. A great many thousands . . . would
> [otherwise] lose their identity with respect to their nationalities in
> the enumeration.[22]

Sabath had been among the congressmen working with the AJC against the race amendment back in January 1909. Now, in April 1910, everyone was lining up in favor of mother tongue.

If any in Congress wanted to retain the race terminology, as Folkmar probably did, they did not speak to the point. But they could console themselves that the operative use of the new question would still tell them what they wanted to know. The reaction of Henry Cabot Lodge is revealing. He had not been consulted on the hurried submission of the Durand letter.

> *Mr. Lodge.* Mr. President, that seems to me a very important bill . . . I
> want to have an opportunity to look at it. . . .
> [A few minutes later, with discussion still in progress:] I have had an
> opportunity to examine [the bill] . . . I see no objection.[23]

Lodge, we have seen, had strong views about race differences in the mental attributes of immigrant peoples. We can hardly be surprised to learn that he considered Durand's request "a very important bill." Having read it over he no doubt felt it a very welcome change in the situation, and realized that he could learn most of what he wanted to know from the data the new question would provide.

Congress made some interesting modifications to Durand's proposal. The relevant House committee expanded the question, so that it would cover *two* generations of language usage. Thus enumerators were instructed "whenever a person gives a foreign country as the birthplace of himself or either of his parents, before writing down that country ask for the mother tongue" of that foreign-born person. By contrast, mother tongue was *not* asked of any American-born individual—even when it *was* asked for his or her foreign-born parent(s).[24] Congress quickly approved the addition of a "nationality or mother tongue" question.

Then a strange thing happened. Nationality, like race, virtually disappeared from the Census Bureau discussions of European immigrant peoples and their descendants. The enumeration concerned mother tongue only. This shift, while extreme, must have seemed sensible enough, since the European census enumerations, too, had typically asked only about language. The 1920 census would preserve the mother-tongue questions as well as the crucial decisions about presentation.

MOTHER TONGUE OR BLOOD? THE BUREAU OF IMMIGRATION, 1910

The Bureau of Immigration had been printing brief instructions at the bottom of the Passenger Lists to help shipping line personnel fill out the race-or-people question (Chapter 1). Since 1903 the relevant line of instruction had read, "'Race or people'—is to be determined by the stock from which they sprang and the language they speak." But around the middle of 1910, Passenger List forms appeared with an elaboration after that sentence: "The original stock or blood shall be the basis of the classification independent of language. The mother tongue is to be used only to assist in determining the original stock." This elaboration was now placed at the head of the List of Races and Peoples, whereas the elaboration it replaced had appeared as a footnote to the List. And so, at the very time the Bureau of the Census turned to "Nationality or Mother Tongue," the Bureau of Immigration finally and self-consciously made the biological meaning of race explicit for Europeans as well as non-Europeans.

It is tempting to conclude that the Bureau of Immigration was reacting to the Census Bureau's decision in March 1910 to replace European racial distinctions with "nationality or mother tongue." The Bureau of Immigration, it might appear, was reaffirming its own usage in reaction to the direction taken by another branch of government.[25] Nevertheless, there is a simpler, if no less surprising, explanation for the appearance of the new Passenger List instructions: they were a defensive reaction to the Jewish criticisms of the List's Hebrew category. In July 1910, F. H. Larned, the assistant commissioner-general of immigration, explained yet again the matter of the Hebrew category in the List of Races and Peoples in response to a query from a congressman: "There is no intention to record Hebrews in accordance with their religion. The language or mother tongue is to be used only as a means of determining the stock or blood . . . entirely independent of his religion or language." Some months later, in 1911, another letter of explanation expanded upon the same wording. This time, Benjamin Cable, the acting secretary of commerce and labor, wrote, and he did so at the request of the White House, in answer to a query that had been put to President Taft. Cable's letter cited, "the well-known standard work of William Z. Ripley, entitled 'The Races of Europe.'" Ripley was quoted on the difference between political and racial boundaries, and on the Jews in particular: "social ostracism" based upon "difference of belief" has kept the Jews "truer of a single racial standard perhaps than any other people of Europe."[26]

Thus, during 1910–1911, the Bureau of Immigration was again defending its use of the Hebrew category as a racial rather than religious term. Of course, the bureau's argument did not answer the Jewish protest's claim that the Hebrew category violated church–state separation even if the motive for creating the category was unrelated to religion (since religion and race were congruent for Hebrews). But the relevant federal officials rarely if ever explicitly confronted this argument in public; in essence, they ignored it in the public arena. In private, Cortelyou's review (1903) had concluded that the argument had no constitutional weight. Nevertheless, the more clearly, explicitly, and convincingly officials at the Bureau of Immigration (and the U.S. Immigration Commission) stated that they were collecting data on a Hebrew race and not on religion, the better they could rebuff that part of the Jewish protest they apparently took seriously—that they should not gather data on an individual's religion. It must have seemed a small step to add the general point to the List's instructions.

The discussion had come a long way from the first explanations of Safford and McSweeney in 1898. The Bureau of Immigration may have seen the new sentences discussing stock and blood as a minor clarification. But it was the bureau's most explicit explanation of what race meant. This new instruction remained for decades. Ironically, the need for the Bureau of Immigration to be explicit that Hebrews were a race and that race meant blood came as a reaction to Jewish groups' protests against identifying Jews by religion. To the extent that these groups were also concerned not to have Jews classified in federal statistics at all—and, of course, to the extent that they argued that any classification of them amounted to classification by religion—they lost. And in that loss, they had pushed the Bureau of Immigration to defend itself by arguing that the basis of the races in the List was found in the blood.

No less ironic was that the Bureau of Immigration took this course at just the same time that the Census Bureau chose to shift discussions from European races to nationalities, eventually avoiding both in favor of mother tongues only. Census, too, chose this new course because of the

Jewish protest. Insofar as Yiddish mother tongue proxied for a Hebrew religion or race category, the result here also was a loss for the Jewish protests. In this case, at least each side could argue that the proxy was imperfect and hence could be accepted, or at least tolerated.

Interpreting Mother-Tongue Data at the Census Bureau, 1910–1913

By late 1910, the U.S. Immigration Commission was winding down. Jeremiah Jenks returned to Cornell. He and another researcher at the Immigration Commission, William Jett Lauck, soon authored *The Immigration Problem*, a restrictionist text that drew heavily on the commission *Reports* and came to be widely used in college and university courses. Meanwhile, I. A. Hourwich, supported fully by funding from the American Jewish Committee (arranged with the mediation of J. L. Magnes), wrote *Immigration and Labor*, which came to be known as the authoritative critique of the Immigration Commission's conclusions. A fundamental point in Hourwich's book was that the commission had attributed far too many of the differences among immigrant groups—in rates of poverty, crime, fertility, and unskilled employment, for example—to racial origins while ignoring other features of settlement patterns, such as length of residence in the United States. Both of these texts were revised and reprinted repeatedly through to the end of the 1920s as developments in immigration and restriction policy required new editions.

Also, in late 1910, the Census Bureau was gearing up to write the reports that would be based on that year's enumeration. The bureau needed expert analysts and found some of them among the group that was just then completing its work at the U.S. Immigration Commission. Roland Falkner had left the commission earlier than most in order to become the Census Bureau's assistant director; Joseph Hill, the chief statistician at Census, and his assistant, Parmelee, both on loan to the commission, now also returned to the bureau. And finally, A. E. Goldenweiser and Daniel Folkmar—two men of very different outlooks—came to Census to work together on the "Mother Tongue" chapter of the census report (in 1914, they also co-authored another Census Bureau report, this one on Japanese immigration). Finally, all of these people interacted with I. A. Hourwich at Census.

Folkmar was put in charge of the new unit that would handle the mother-tongue data, propose the tables to be constructed, and write the relevant interpretive chapter. Thus the author of the *Dictionary of Races and Peoples* came to be in charge of the mother-tongue data, the measure that Census Director Durand had described as the proxy for nationality. But as Folkmar had told the Senate Census Committee, it could also be thought of as the proxy for the categories of the List. Folkmar must have seemed to be the sensible choice, at least in the sense that his expertise about the different peoples described in his *Dictionary* was directly relevant to the groupings that the mother-tongue question was meant to capture. At the same time, Folkmar did not have a free hand; given the structure of the Census Bureau, no one in charge of a chapter was working independently. All of the big decisions—including the tables to be constructed (and the consequent work with the punch cards), as well as the amount of space allotted to each issue—were discussed in committees and reviewed by the chief statistician and the director.

The question that faced Census Bureau officials was now what to draw from the new data. Most of the relevant staff at the bureau apparently thought that mother-tongue tables were needed only for the populations of the multinational empires; for other immigrants and their children, countries of birth would be adequate. By contrast, Folkmar wanted tables based on each reasonably large mother-tongue group. He also urged that all speakers of the group should be included: French speakers in Belgium and Switzerland must be added to those of France, for example. Only in this way, he argued, would mother-tongue counts be complete. Finally and most revealingly, all sorts of items should be cross-tabulated by mother tongue—occupation, place of residence, fertility, intermarriage, and so on. As usual, Folkmar argued for all this in terms of races: "The only safe course which I see is to follow a consistent classification of races by mother tongue throughout the subjects in which this is practicable. This is what all European censuses taken by races or mother tongues have done."[27]

Other Census staff members were less sure how much space to allocate for these matters—particularly if the material would also have to be broken down by generation (immigrants vs. their American-born children) and by single vs. mixed parentage. The disagreement between Folkmar and others emerged at an early stage of the planning when it was necessary to decide on how to set up the IBM punch card readers for tabulations.

Apparently Folkmar was brought into these discussions at the last minute. He had been working on another topic at the Census Bureau, and perhaps his supervision of mother-tongue issues was only just beginning as the other project ended. In any event, he felt shut out of earlier decisions in which "others" (probably including Chief Statistician Joseph Hill and A. E. Goldenweiser) had argued for restricted mother-tongue tabulations. Folkmar appealed to Hill and also to Census Director Durand for a review. In this connection, he made the point that many topics—especially intermarriage—could be better served in terms of mother tongue (reflecting, as he argued it did, "race") than in terms of birthplace. But for the sake of continuity he felt both should be tabulated at present. Folkmar suggested that Durand read his April 1909 Senate Census Committee testimony, as well as the *Dictionary*. And he detailed the significance of the choice between place of birth and mother tongue: "I believe that, in time, the classification by mother tongue or 'nationality' will replace that by country of birth. I base my belief on the study of foreign censuses, and upon the experience of our own Bureau of Immigration.... Race is a more fundamental factor in social life and in America's future than is country of birth. If either is to be dropped, let it be the latter."[28]

In an additional memo he pleaded for exact and mutually exclusive terminology—which he interpreted as a return to his usage of race and to a strictly citizenship-based meaning of nationality. He wrote, "The term 'Russian,' for example, should not be used for both the *race* (Great Russian) and the geographical group or *nationality* in the stricter sense (those born in Russia). Yet the terms 'Russian race' and 'Russian nationality' might be used if race and nationality are defined in the senses just indicated. Whatever the terminology, let it be clear, concise, and capable of exact definition."[29] Far from following Hourwich and Durand's path of avoiding race and discussing "nationality or mother tongue," Folkmar held out for a return to the race term and restriction of nationality to the citizenship (or nativity) meaning. And he stressed that "Race is a more fundamental factor in social life and in America's future than is country of birth"—not only, it would seem in the case of immigrants from the multinational empires. Still, apparently he recognized that there would be a need for compromise on terms.

Folkmar probably freighted race with a more explicit insistence on biological inheritance than Hourwich or Durand gave to nationality (as peoplehood). Indeed, the Census discussions about how to present the mother-tongue data were proceeding while Folkmar was still involved in shepherding his *Dictionary* through the publication process. And because he had discussed the importance of racial differences in the *Dictionary* (as discussed in Chapter 4), he must have felt a need to defend his formulations in the new context as well. Durand had just argued for the mother-tongue question in other terms and very likely had no interest whatsoever in belaboring its connection to race.

Like Folkmar, J. H. Parmelee was also interested in the new census question. He had earlier suggested that the bureau explore regional origins in Italy, since the racial origins of the northern and southerners were so different. And in an internal memo that surveyed "American Census Practice Regarding Population of Foreign Stock," Parmelee was enthusiastic about the new beginning in 1910: "The addition of the mother-tongue inquiry . . . opens a wide field . . . for a piece of careful, scientific work in the field of anthropology—and study of foreign race and nationality under the census microscope."[30]

But most officials did not agree, including the decision makers Hill, Durand, and Falkner, as well as well as Hourwich and Goldenweiser (if either of these last was consulted). Ultimately, there was a competition for space; only a fixed number of tables could be published. Durand, himself an economist by training, was probably more influenced by Falkner, Hourwich, and Goldenweiser—fellow economists all—than by the ethnological outlook of Folkmar and Parmelee.

Ironically, almost *no* cross-tabulations of other variables by mother tongue were published because of budget overruns at the bureau.[31] And finally, we should not leave the bureau discussions of mother tongue without recording two other ironies of the mother-tongue story. Joseph Hill's copious files reveal several discussions about missing data. A fair number of Russian-born immigrants had no mother tongue recorded. It was obvious from their names that many of these people were Jews. Should the bureau staff simply go ahead and fill in Yiddish for mother tongue?

Here was quite a twist: mother tongue had been adopted in the first place to avoid the appearance of identifying Jews directly. Yet when the mother-tongue question had been left unanswered, identifying Jews by their names helped the bureau fill in the item.[32] Although the staff did not record noting this particular irony, in preparing for the 1920 census Joseph Hill recorded another. Back in 1910, he said, the mother-tongue question had been forced on the Census Bureau to produce a race count. But looking back from 1920, in the aftermath of the dissolution of the multinational empires that followed the Great War, "only with the aid of the 1910 and projected 1920 mother-tongue data can we ensure continuity of the counts across the decades for immigrants from those parts."[33]

The staff at Census had to provide interpretive introductions for the chapters on "Country of Birth of the Foreign Born" and "Mother Tongue." The former lurched between old and new terms. It noted that not all immigrants from a given country of birth were of one people: "On account of the variety of races represented among the immigrants from certain foreign countries, the Bureau of the Census has avoided the use of such terms as 'Germans,' 'Russians,' 'Austrians,' etc.... Confusion would arise from identifying country of birth with race or nationality. Persons born in Germany, for example, are not all Germans, but include Poles, Hebrews, and others.... [34]

By contrast, the introduction to the "Mother Tongue" chapter is more careful. The census publication lists Folkmar as the sole author of the "Mother Tongue" chapter; however from the evidence of his other writings (and from the internal correspondence available to us), it is clear that the sparse nature of the discussion was not his idea. Indeed, these sources suggest that Goldenweiser may have been responsible for some of the wording, and in particular avoidance of the old race terminology. Moreover, in the same month that the census publication appeared, the *Publications of the American Statistical Association* published an issue devoted to the 1910 census. This was an authoritative and semiofficial event. Of the four papers, Durand wrote one and Hill another. A third paper was devoted to the mother-tongue question—and Goldenweiser rather than Folkmar authored it. Moreover, this journal article closely paralleled the 1910 census *Population* volume's chapter on "Mother Tongue." Both publications avoided "race" terminology in favor of "ethnic stock." Indeed, the only notable difference between Goldenweiser's paper and the chapter in the *Population* volume is that the paper provides somewhat more space to evaluating the quality of the Yiddish data.[35]

Perhaps most revealing of things to come, both the introduction to the Census Bureau's "Mother Tongue" chapter and the article on the subject in *Publications of the American Statistical Association* avoided mention of race and nationality—the concepts for which mother tongue might be a proxy. Instead, the chapter includes a subsection, "Mother tongue in relation to ethnic stock," but neither ethnic nor stock is defined. "Ethnic" would have been familiar not in our current sense but rather as referring to groups studied in ethnology. However, the precise role for biological heredity in connection with ethnic stock is not discussed. "Stock" after all could reference biological connections (as we have seen in the instructions for completing the race-or-people item on the Immigration Bureau's Passenger Lists). But at Census, "stock" was primarily familiar in connection with the immigrant generation and their American-born second generation, as in the "foreign stock." It was a biological connection, surely, but not one extending over uncounted generations as the "race" term was.

In any case, Goldenweiser's purpose was to evaluate how well mother tongue could in fact serve as a proxy for the familiar divisions of "ethnic stock." There were only two important cases where congruence was imperfect.

In most cases the returns for mother tongue may be taken as indicative of ethnic stock. The principal exception to this rule appears in the case of persons reported as English and Celtic, this group including four ethnically distinct peoples, namely, the English, the Irish, the Scotch, and the Welsh. In the case of these people country of origin statistics come much nearer showing ethnic composition than do mother tongue statistics. . . .

While English and Celtic as a mother tongue covers more than one group of people, the opposite is true of Yiddish, which is the mother tongue of only part of the Hebrews, the others being returned as speaking Polish, Russian, German, etc. A comparison of the returns for mother tongue made by persons born in Russia, Austria, and Germany, however, with the returns on "race" given for immigrants in the reports of the Commissioner General of Immigration, indicates that the census returns on Yiddish-speaking people gave a fairly complete enumeration of the foreign-born Hebrews in the United States.[36]

Goldenweiser's only use of the term "race" is in quotation marks, and it refers to work of another agency, the Bureau of Immigration's use of the List. But, as to the practical question, he concludes that Hebrew race and Yiddish mother-tongue immigrants are of roughly the same number.

Daniel Folkmar and Franz Boas Debate Race, Nationality, and Mother Tongue, 1915

Beginning around 1910, Daniel Folkmar wrote several defenses of his usage of the race term. These tended to argue for limiting usage of the nationality term to the citizenship meaning. Even in the *Dictionary*, we find some self-conscious elaboration: "A distinction [is] to be made between race and nationality. . . . The English nationality includes all native and naturalized citizens of England. It therefore included members of other races besides the Englishman in the ethnical sense. . . . Physically as well as linguistically, the English are a very composite product. . . . Tall, long-headed and generally blond."[37]

In February 1911, he finally had the page proofs of the *Dictionary* in hand, and he had by this time moved to the Census Bureau, where he would take up the presentation of the mother-tongue data. All this surely stimulated reflection and reaction to the use of nationality around him. In a talk to the Anthropological Society of Washington, Folkmar laid out his argument, but we have, alas, only a tantalizing synopsis. The audience would have been sympathetic to his larger concerns with biological heredity, as the Washington branch of the society included a considerable number of physical anthropologists.

> Dr Daniel Folkmar presented a paper on *Some Questions Arising in the First Census of European Races* in the United States. . . . The main part of the discourse was . . . occupied by a defense of the terminology, or nomenclature, adopted in the schedules of the census and in the dictionary [i.e., *Dictionary of Races and Peoples*], viz., "race" to designate the linguistic divisions of the immigrants, and "nationality" for the country of birth.

The speaker admitted that in anthropology and biology the term race is applied to physical traits, but maintained that with the census it was not strictly a scientific question but a practical one, to designate and distinguish given groups of peoples who come to the shores of this country. The use of the term "race" seemed to him justified to designate linguistic groups, inasmuch as it points out something essential, that which descends by heredity.

The paper as well as the dictionary, which the author laid before the society, was discussed at some length by Drs. Hrdlicka, Michelson and Hough and by Mr. Diesurud.[38]

The juxtaposition of two clauses here is remarkable. On the one hand, "The speaker admitted that in anthropology and biology the term race is applied to physical traits," but he defends the use of the term in the practical contexts of census immigration studies in connection with "linguistic groups, inasmuch as it points out something essential, that which descends by heredity." Folkmar therefore concluded that the essential something ought to be referred to as race. Language points to that essential element.

Meanwhile, during these same years Franz Boas had been moving toward a rejection of biology as the carrier of mental characteristics. In a 1915 paper entitled, appropriately enough, "Race and Nationality," he wrote,

> This notion [racial purity] prevails among ourselves with equal force, for we shake our heads gravely over the ominous influx of "inferior" races from eastern Europe. Inferior by heredity? No. Socially different? Yes, on account of the environment in which they have lived and therefore different from ourselves and not easily subject to change provided they are allowed to cluster together indefinitely. Equally strong is our fear of mongrelization of the American people by intermixtures between the Northwest European and other European types.... Careful inquiry has failed completely to reveal any inferiority of mixed European types.[39]

And then Folkmar and Boas found themselves face-to-face in a discussion of race and the new census mother-tongue data. They were together on a panel of the Anthropology section at the Second Pan American Scientific Congress, held in Washington at the end of 1915.[40] Indeed, Folkmar's paper, "The United States Census of Immigrant Stocks," immediately followed Boas's, "Modern Populations of America." Folkmar's paper apparently was more empirical and less self-conscious about terms than the paper he had delivered to the Washington Anthropological Society four years earlier. Still, Folkmar mentioned the "mother tongue census or enumeration of the European races or ethnical stocks that have emigrated to this country." And he observed that the United States was now following European and the other North American countries in a "more or less careful attempt to enumerate races on the basis of mother tongue." Likewise, the U.S. Bureau of Immigration had, since 1898, been classifying immigrants "by race or ethnical nationality as well as by political nationality or citizenship."[41] As a result, it would be possible for the first time "to determine the proportion of English and German blood in the entire population [i.e., of whatever generational standing], making a fair division of persons of mixed blood."[42] Budget appropriations are awaited to finish the job of classifying

> each immigrant stock or mother tongue as regards its social characteristics, its illiteracy, and its marital condition, or even the sex of the children of foreign-born parents . . . I see in such a tabulation the possibility of a more exact science of ethnology, which might be called ethnometry or statistical ethnology.[43]

Already, he added, it was clear that the German element was larger than the English, and that following them, in order, were the Italian, Polish, and Yiddish. Eventually, it would be possible to estimate, for example, the proportion "Celto-Teutonic."

Folkmar concludes by noting that the "American race of the future" will be

> a true composite of European races, a genuine product of the "melting pot," a new race in a statistical sense. . . . While distinctively the intellectual child of old England, it is already not English, not German, not Irish, or Scandinavian, not French, Spanish or Italian but American.[44]

This concluding flourish might have made Israel Zangwill, author of *The Melting Pot*, proud.[45] But it is a sign of the complexity of the time that it was a throw-away line coming from a member of a Washington eugenics association. In what sense is the pedigree of an "intellectual child of old England" "already not English"? The anticipated new science of "ethnometry or statistical ethnology" will be able, he asserted, to trace the proportions of various bloods in this new "melted" American race. We should also recall that in earlier years (in his dissertation and at the Senate Census Committee hearing), he had stressed how that evidence would be essential for the policymaker, too. This was not his theme in the 1915 address, but there is no reason to think he would have rejected this extension of his remarks.

Finally, Folkmar was careful to emphasize that mother tongue was defined in this census as "the language of customary speech in the homes of the immigrants before immigration, and not the language of their ancestors which in some cases is entirely different." Once again (as in the *Dictionary*), he was warning that an ethnological purist would prefer the language of ancestors as it provides a better guide to descent.

In the course of his concluding remarks, Folkmar also referred to "Anglo-American," "Saxon-American," and "Spanish-American." All of this was a bit much for Boas.

> *Mr. Boas.* Mr. Chairman, as a rule I am not given to discussion of
> terminologies, but I think it is generally understood that the word
> "race" implies descent. In the terminology of the census we find the
> compounds "German-American," "Dutch-English" and so on, used,
> and I cannot but express my regret at the use of this term by the last
> census which is bound certainly in the public conception, to create
> very great confusion, because it expresses the idea or conveys the
> idea that people who happen to speak their mother tongue are of
> descent from that race combined with the American. I think it would
> be very desirable if the census were to say that what is meant by that
> word is merely mother tongue or native tongue.[46]

Thus Boas stressed the extent to which we *cannot* derive racial descent from mother-tongue data. Folkmar now had to underscore that the bureau avoided the term "race," and that he had not used it in the title of his talk. Nevertheless, he could not quite drop his own belief that "race" was a useful term. Indeed, the (mis)understanding that Boas laments is, more or less, just what Folkmar seems to suggests consumers of the public statistics *should* derive from the mother-tongue data.

Mr. Folkmar. May I just say a word of explanation as to the position of the United States, and I may say of European countries as well as to the term "race"? The United States census does not use the term race officially in this connection. It uses the term which is expressed in the heading of this paper, i.e., "stocks."

As to the word "race," Dr. Boas is entirely right, of course, from an anthropological point of view, but not from a statistical point of view, from the point of view of the census, taken as expressed through decades of European censuses where the word "race" or "nacionalidad" is used uniformly in a dozen countries. This has been discussed by very competent men. I read a paper reviewing some of their discussion before the Anthropological Society of Washington in the course of this census work, and I think the position was maintained that the word "race" was used for convenience in census taking in default of a better. There are four or five distinct definitions recognized for the word race in Webster's and other dictionaries. We even speak of the Caucasian race, and of the subdivisions of this as national races. Of course the word "nacionalidad" or "nationality" is used in two senses, ethnologically and politically, and is used, for instance, in the census of Austria-Hungary, and in that of Servia in the sense I have employed it in this paper.[47]

Folkmar acknowledged here the confusions he had been helping to perpetuate. The enumerations in various other countries had *not* in fact typically spoken of races but of nationality in the sense of peoplehood. But note that Folkmar does not speak of peoplehood but of "ethnical" (vs. "political") nationality. Ethnical factors were not necessarily limited to those physically transmitted across generations, but they always included and generally stressed such physical sources.

The mention of Serbia is especially striking because five years before at the Senate Census Committee hearing, he had used the same example—but had called it a census of races. But he seems throughout to have taken it upon himself to justify the usage of the Bureau of Immigration and the U.S. Immigration Commission. These choices were consistent with the mission explicit in his earlier pronouncements. Policy could be critically enhanced by awareness of racial characteristics of the population. He had told the senators that such awareness was more important than economic indicators. If the usage at the Census Bureau restricted what he could say in the bureau's name, he nevertheless struggled not to abandon his own understandings that something "essential" having to do with "descent through heredity" was captured through the mother-tongue question.

Meanings of Nationality: Another Context, 1916

Misunderstandings arising from the dual meanings of "nationality" showed up again in a quite different context, but one that involved some of the same American figures we have already met. Once again, the incident concerned Jewish issues. This time, however, the debate was not about federal statistics but limited to various American Jewish organizations. They were seeking a way to help the Jewish minorities of east-central Europe from military and civilian attacks during World War I.

The American Jewish Committee (AJC) was a self-recruiting elite group that eschewed publicity. Many of the most illustrious and able German Jewish leaders in America, as well as their wealthiest philanthropist (Jacob Schiff), were at its helm. So the committee consistently enjoyed a good deal of influence. But the AJC also stirred opposition; the eastern European Jewish immigrant generation (and some other notable Jewish leaders who took their part) resented the committee for its self-anointed, elitist, and secretive behavior. During World War I these resentments boiled over into active opposition.

This was a tense time for American Jewish leaders. The battlegrounds of the war's eastern front were in the region that included the world's greatest concentrations of Jews. And these were the same places from which the vast majority of America's Jewish immigrants had come. In the wake of the war's devastation, unrest produced murderous attacks on Jews there on an unprecedented scale. At the same time, there was a widespread recognition that the terms of political life in those regions would change after the war. Jewish communities in the west—in the United States, the United Kingdom, and elsewhere—organized to press for Jewish rights in these areas.

Within this charged political and cultural context, the attack on the AJC as elitist, distant, and illegitimate gained force among the eastern European

Jewish population in the United States. By 1915 the large Jewish immigration from eastern Europe had been in progress for thirty-five years. Some two million of these immigrants and their children felt ever-more able to navigate the American political and cultural terrains, even if most of them still worked with their hands or engaged in small-scale commerce. Furthermore, they resented being told that the AJC would quietly handle their concerns—without them. They condemned that elitism as particularly inappropriate to Jewish life in a free and democratic America. This resentment was, in sum, the reflection of an ethnic and social class division among American Jews.

The key discussion about protecting Jews in eastern-central Europe (especially in the anticipated postwar regimes) took the form of supporting "the national rights of minorities." There were many such minorities in the region who had suffered under the old empires. And no matter how borders would be drawn after the war, many people would remain national minorities in the new states that would be created. Consequently "the rights of national minorities" was an issue that the victors would have to take up after the war.[48]

But the German Jewish elite in America, and the AJC in particular, had tried to define Jewishness solely in terms of religion. How could it pivot to lead, or even support, a fight for Jewish *national* rights? Moreover, by 1916 the Zionist movement was also a significant reality, posing a related challenge to the AJC's definition of Jewish identity. Indeed, American Zionism had gone decidedly mainstream since the appointment, a few months earlier (June 1916), of its American leader, Louis Brandeis, to the U.S. Supreme Court. In this context, discussion of "Jewish national rights" called to mind not only protection of Jewish communities in eastern-central Europe but also agitation for a Jewish national territory. And indeed, the British would issue the Balfour Declaration supporting a Jewish "national home in Palestine" in late 1917, less than two years after the events discussed in this section. Formulations such as those of Simon Wolf about how "Hebrew" referred only to a religious affiliation (Chapter 3) were somewhat less prevalent by 1916 than they had been in 1900; nevertheless, recalling them helps one appreciate how unwilling the eastern European Jews in America were to entrust leadership on any discussion of "national rights" to the AJC's German Jewish Reform elite.

In this context, calls for a new organization to represent American Jews gained immense popularity. It would be no *committee,* but rather a *congress,* made up of Jewish representatives from all organizations and communities. And like the American national congress, it would function in the open. By 1916 its organizing committee claimed to represent close to a million individuals.[49]

However, when discussions took place among competing Jewish groups, and particularly between the AJC and the organizing committee for the American Jewish Congress, everything connected with Jewish nationality emerged as a stumbling block. We need not follow most of the tortuous negotiations that finally led in 1918 to the creation of the American Jewish Congress. But because Jewish nationality figured so centrally in the debates of what the congress would be, misunderstandings over the term "nationality," and self-conscious efforts to resolve the misunderstandings, are directly relevant to our theme. And once again, we have verbatim transcripts.

During the summer of 1916, representatives of two clusters of Jewish groups met to try to work things out. These were the organizing committee for an American Jewish Congress, the more nationalist group in the deliberations, and the Conference of National Jewish Organizations. The latter comprised half a dozen organizations that had joined forces because they were uncomfortable with the nationalism of the organizing committee. Included were strange bedfellows such as the American Jewish Committee (well-to-do, primarily German, English-speaking) and the National [Jewish] Workingman's Committee (Yiddish-speaking, proletariat, socialist-oriented). The meeting captured the self-conscious awareness, at least among some thoughtful group leaders, about the different usages of the term "nationality" in Europe and the United States. All of the speakers cited here were from the less-nationalistic Conference of National Jewish Organizations (except one so indicated).

> *Judge [Julian W.] Mack.* Some men . . . object to the implications involved in the word "national." They desire for the Jews in countries where group rights are recognized, group rights for the Jewish people [too]. . . . [However, they] believe that the use of the word "nationality" implies that American Jews endorse nationalism as expressed in the Zionist Movement. . . .

Dr. [Samuel] Shulman. To the American Christian this [the principle of "National Rights"] would imply that the Jews here consider themselves a Nation and desire even here to secure national rights. That would be dangerous. . . .

Dr. [Frank] Rosenblatt. The National Workingman's Committee wanted the words "National Rights" used, but the representatives of the American Jewish Committee were afraid that it would be impossible to present the matter to Government officials who are not acquainted with the European use of the word "national."

[Summary of the recording secretary]. It was admitted that in Europe the word "national" is used in a legal sense to cover a well-known situation that exists in many countries.

Dr Rosenblatt. Further, we do not want to raise the question, "Are the Jews a nation?" That is why the word "peoples" was used.

. . . .

Mr. [Joseph G.] Grossberg [from the more nationalistic organizing committee]. The fear of "Zionphobia" is greatly exaggerated. If the word "National" is generally used in Europe, it would be childish for us to use another term. . . .

Judge Mack. The word "Nation" in English, and the word *"Nation"* in German have quite different meanings. This is what I have been trying to explain at Zionist meetings for some time.[50]

Judge Mack's awareness was anything but universal; still, discerning observers, with a knowledge of Europe, could draw on it.

I. A. Hourwich, who claims to have made the critical 1910 intervention at the Census Bureau, was also deeply involved in the efforts to create the American Jewish Congress. He was in fact a member of the (more nationalist) organizing committee and attended these same meetings. And so, appropriately enough for our tale, he once again found occasion to observe that the European concept of nationality could help reconcile the irreconcilable. Commenting on the negotiations between the two groups of Jewish organizations just quoted, Hourwich observed that the difficulty over national rights "lay in the paucity of the English language which had no word comparable to the German word 'Nationalitat.'"[51]

Struggles over the List: Concluding Thoughts on Part I

A long tradition in European thought conceptualized group origin and community in terms of nationality, in the sense of peoplehood. Like race, nationality might be discussed vaguely enough to encompass the biological transmission of group physical and mental characteristics. Similarly, a nationality might be based in part on the common racial origin of all or most of its members. There was in fact no bright line distinguishing race from nationality on the issue of biological transmission for the mental qualities of groups. And yet surely that transmission was generally more central to discussions of race.

The European statisticians seem to have had little to do with race counts in their nineteenth-century censuses. Indeed, David Kertzer and Dominique Arel observe that "the biological idea of race . . . was entirely discarded from pre–World War I censuses in Europe. . . . The entire [European] census practice [was] of rejecting race as a category."[52] By contrast, censuses in the Americas had often been sensitive to "color" groups, and this had been true for all of the U.S. enumerations. By 1900 the name of the question on the U.S. census had evolved from "color" to "color or race." Nevertheless, extending that practice to differences among European-descent groups in 1910, as the Immigration Commission was urging, would have been a significant step further, and in the light of Kerzer and Arel's observation, all the more so. Mara Loveman has stressed that many countries' census agencies closely watched the behavior of others as to classification schemes. And yet, she observes, in the United States the Census Bureau may have been atypically unconcerned with international practice.[53] Three features of the 1910 episode at Census seem to support that caveat: first, the initial drive for a race question that would distinguish among Europeans; second, the pressure against such a question did not have its source in "rejecting race as a category" (as Kertzer and Arel put it), but in Jewish protests over the connection of race and religion and the Slavic counterprotest; and third, Hourwich's presentation of European census practices regarding nationality and mother tongue for Durand.

An interesting feature of that standoff is the apparent silence of the Jews and the Slavs about each other's positions and interests. It is possible that both sides thought that public criticism of the other was gratuitous and counterproductive. In any event, Census officials were faced with contradictory and competing pressures, but not, apparently, with statements that explicitly attacked each other.

Paul Schor thoughtfully discussed early ethno-racial mobilization on census issues, noting that the 1910 Slavic organizing included substantial elements of "mobilization for pure prestige." In such cases, "groups mobilized to demand that government agencies should take account of their existence in a different way, in a context where no material advantage was at stake."[54] By contrast, Simon Wolf and the American Jewish Committee's goal was always to *avoid* being counted explicitly as Jews. For the Jews, the constitutional principles at stake were real, but the leaders of these organizations *also* clearly believed that the violation of those principles would negatively affect their "interests," both legal and material.

And yet, the more ethno-national perspective of the eastern European Jews was different. As Schor notes, once the Census Bureau had adopted the mother-tongue alternative, articles in the Yiddish press encouraged Jews to proudly declare themselves. For example, one paper advised, "[Do] not deny that you are Jews. This information goes only to the government and cannot be used against you by any anti-Semitic groups. . . . This is one opportunity for Jews to be proud of themselves. The insertion of this question into the census was a victory for the recognition of the existence of national minority groups."[55]

Note that the paper reassured readers by distinguishing between a threat from anti-Semites rather than from the government; as noted earlier, this is an unusual variant of the resistance to legibility. Moreover, the message of pride and the "recognition of national minority rights" come together. Schor's key point is to distinguish mobilizations defined principally by goals of prestige rather than of material interest. He sensibly calls for a nuanced understanding of reasons for group mobilization against census categories, reasons that go beyond a simple claim for material advancement. But, as Schor also notes, political advantages might accompany a mobilization that was *mostly* but not entirely about prestige.[56] This was the case here: even the concerns of the Slavic and Yiddish press in 1910 were not "purely" for prestige. We may want to designate motives for rights and power as different from "material" interests, and we should especially note that prestige loomed large in the 1910 case, but in the end that mobilization cannot be "purely" about prestige. Perhaps for this reason Schor titled his paper with a question mark: "Mobilizing for Pure Prestige?"

The Slavic groups and the Jewish nationalists' reaction to legibility was to take a stand *in favor* of specific classification and against what amounted to illegibility (as undifferentiated subjects of a multinational empire). *This* use of the legibility metaphor closely tracks Schor's discussion of mobilizing for recognition even if recognition would not have direct material advantages. He describes various stands in favor of recognition and distinguishes among them in terms of the degree to which the group's material advantage stimulated each.

The compromise on the classification system lasted for many decades at Census. By contrast, at the very same moment, the Bureau of Immigration moved to strengthen its explicit reliance on the hereditary qualities of race—"stock or blood." The two federal agencies were considering almost identical extensions of racialization and responded in very different ways. That two state institutions could act in these opposite ways shows a certain freedom of action for federal data collection at a substate level. Paul Starr distinguished between countries with or without a central statistical office, with the United States being in the latter category.[57] Other things being equal, countries with such an office would be more likely to coordinate classifications and meanings across agencies. In time, such independent action at two bureaus of the executive branch would become less likely. We will encounter (in Chapter 10) a case in point in the early 1950s, when a relatively new agency, the Office of Statistical Standards (OSS), was charged with approving any new classifications. Such coordination and review amounted to a step in the direction of a central statistical office. But note, too, that the divergent 1910 outcomes were also conditioned by the degree of importance of the issue to the higher-level officials in the executive branch, in this case very low. Had the protests over the race classification mattered more to the president or his top staff, the resolution would have been handled in a more centralized way (or perhaps revised in the direction of uniformity when the divergence in procedures was discovered). Such an outcome would not have been inconceivable, for example, if the ethnic politics of the situation had become more public.

Finally, recall that it was not the choice of nationality over race, so important in 1910, that mattered over the long run. Very soon after embracing nationality over race, the Census Bureau forgot all about the covering conception of nationality and focused only on mother tongue. Also, precious little was done to unearth older origins through parental mother tongue. And finally, partly for unrelated budgetary reasons, it turned out that few socially important variables were cross-tabulated with mother tongue. Note also that in all of this, Durand, Hill, Goldenweiser, and Hourwich seemed to align on one side, with Folkmar, the physical anthropologist with strong commitments to the importance of biological transmission of group traits, on the other. Hill's case is worth another look: he was from an old Protestant family, educated at Exeter and Harvard. And when it came to the eugenics movement, Hill and Folkmar were both supporters.[58] But at Census, Hill seems to have had much more sympathy for the opinions of the Russian Jew Goldenweiser than for Folkmar's. In particular, Hill, Durand, and Goldenweiser all showed restraint in limiting the amount of mother-tongue data on grounds of common sense and space in publications. Moreover, it was Goldenweiser who was chosen to join Hill and Durand as author of the paper on mother-tongue data when the American Statistical Association devoted an issue of its *Publication* to the 1910 census.

Does the 1910 census episode also have a historical importance in its own right, beyond what it illuminates about the concepts in use at the time and the forces supporting or opposing them? Did the outcome matter for the history of race, immigration, and federal statistics? The whole episode captured a decidedly minor place in public attention even at the time, with little awareness in institutional memories and none in historical writing. Moreover, the episode did not involve a clear-cut confrontation in which the racialization of white immigrants was consciously rejected. And yet the events of 1910 did indeed mark a turning point. The Census Bureau never came closer to racializing subgroups of whites; turning instead to mother tongue, it moved in another direction.

It is often pointed out that the racialization of European immigrant groups was never institutionalized in federal law or classifications. This observation is meant to support the larger point that the racialization of nonwhites differed in its scope and severity from that of the southern and eastern European immigrants even at its height.[59] Both the observation and the larger point it supports are basically accurate, albeit with one important caveat. They are true for American law insofar as it governs behavior domestically, within the United States. But the claim is decidedly false when it is applied to the federal laws passed in 1921–1924 to restrict immigration into the country, and these laws remained in effect for four decades. We will take up this feature of immigration restriction policy in Part II.

For the moment, however, our concern is with the legal framework and the other institutions that govern behavior *within* the republic and the fact that these did not racialize differences among Europeans. Precisely here the little episode at Census in 1910 takes on a particular interest. It shows how close Congress and federal officials actually did come to introducing such a race-based classification to distinguish among white people, and how unselfconsciously it was done. It was the Census Bureau's *pivot away* from such a racialization in federal classification of whites that was exceptional at the time.

That pivot may have involved little self-consciousness about "racializing Europeans" at the time or institutional memory of the episode later. During the following years, especially 1910–1924 when the debate over immigration restriction grew ever-more intense, the Census Bureau would produce counts cross-tabulated by immigrant country of birth and mother tongue. And restrictionists who believed that undesirable traits were passed through the blood could and did regard mother tongue as a useful proxy for direct data on European immigrant races. Indeed, had these racialists *not* found the mother-tongue data useful, the pressures on the Census Bureau to include some other form of the List of Races in later enumerations would probably have resurfaced during those years.

But if what happened at Census in 1910—pivoting away from the race term itself—was an exception to the trend of the times, and it was not an *inconsequential* exception. Census data could be an authoritative mirror that the federal government held up to its population. Thought to be largely above the political fray and guided more by scientific expertise than most governmental agencies, the Census Bureau had produced a long string of authoritative reports dating back to the foundation of the republic. This was the agency that would *not* be providing data on European immigrants in terms of racial categories. If others chose to use mother tongue as a proxy for clusters of hereditary mental traits carried in the blood, they were free to do so, but the burden of justifying that position fell upon them; they could not rely on the census taking such a position for granted in its classification scheme.

The choice to introduce a new census question is the result of dynamics in social and cultural history. But once a census question has been adopted, it also shapes later social and cultural developments. The decade and a half following 1910 was the high-water mark for the trends known as scientific racism. Had Census used racial terminology to distinguish among Americans of European origin, such trends of the late 1910s and early 1920s might have been stronger still. Nor should the survival of census questions be underestimated. The kind of terminology that might have developed for Europeans in the census was already in place for Asians in 1910, with two separate race categories for the Chinese and Japanese. Those census categories have remained in place for 110 years (see Chapter 11). In fact, they have long survived racialization of Asians in American immigration law.

Daniel Folkmar's intellectual struggles can be read with profit in the light of this counterfactual. At the Senate subcommittee on the census; in work on the *Dictionary*, the mother-tongue question, and his address that same year to his colleagues at the Anthropological Society of Washington; and in his debate with Boas some years later, Folkmar tried to link blood, mother tongue, race, and nationality as tightly as he could. Had the census stayed with the race term in 1910, Folkmar's road forward would have been notably smoother.

A poignant interchange about the stakes in the struggles over the List of Races and Peoples has survived in a 1927 exchange of letters between W. W. Husband and Max Kohler. This correspondence took place nearly twenty years after the debate at the Immigration Commission hearings, and three years after the passage of the Second Quota Act that permanently restricted southern and eastern Europeans to tiny numbers of arrivals. W. W. Husband, whom we encountered as secretary to the Immigration Commission, had moved on by 1927 to serve as commissioner of immigration and then assistant secretary of labor. Max Kohler was a member of the American Jewish Committee board and for decades an assertive attorney for immigrant rights cases, especially those dealing with Jews or Asians. Appropriately enough, he was the son of Kaufman Kohler, one of the leading German-born Reform rabbis in America. Max Kohler wrote Husband in 1927 to report that he had, at long last, changed his mind about the Hebrew category on the List of Races and Peoples, and he now disagreed with the position of "our mutual friend, the late Simon Wolf."[60] Kohler had come to believe that because Jews reported themselves under country of origin by their former citizenship, this was enough to answer Wolf's appeal to the principle that "A Jew from Russia is a Russian." Moreover, Kohler had also finally come to reject the claim that a count of Jews by race amounted to a constitutionally forbidden count by religion (given the near-perfect congruence of Jewish religion and "race"). Husband answered a few days later to say, "I do not need to tell you that I read this with real interest." And he added,

> I think it was always apparent that neither the Bureau of Immigration nor the Immigration Commission . . . ever had any thought or interest in the religious beliefs or connections of any immigrants. The classification of races or peoples was little more than a classification of mother tongue groups, and as such I have always thought that it served a valuable purpose not only as a government statistical record but that it also afforded information of real value to the various immigrant groups themselves.[61]

Recall that the correspondents were looking back at the Immigration Commission's work across a period that encompassed not only the Quota Acts of 1921–1924 but also the inclusion of the mother-tongue question in two successive decennial censuses. However, Husband had also discussed the nature of race in the List at least twice about twenty years earlier. First, in the December 1908 letter to William Wheeler (a member of the Immigration Commission), he had pointed out that race is used in "an ethnological sense," without even mentioning language.[62] And then in the 1911 introduction to the Immigration Commission *Reports,* he (its probable author or coauthor) explained that the commission "uses the term 'race' in a broad sense, the distinction being largely a matter of language and geography." Still, a few lines further on, he had noted that among the races of the Austro-Hungarian or Russian Empires, "the [race] distinctions are even greater than those indicated merely by language."[63] Thus when he described the List in 1927 as "little more than a classification of mother tongue groups," he seems to have drifted away from more ethnologically based core meanings of race, meanings for which mother tongue might proxy but did not fully capture.

As Daniel Folkmar had put it in his address to the Washington Anthropological Society in 1911, "the term 'race' seemed to him justified to designate linguistic groups, inasmuch as it points out something essential, that which descends by heredity."[64] This was the connection Husband had decoupled in his 1927 letter to Kohler.

Husband's statements were more than Kohler had meant to sign onto. He quickly replied, "I greatly appreciate your frank treatment of the question.... I will be equally frank in answering." Yes, Kohler said, the Hebrew category was acceptable at the Bureau of Immigration, and "it is practically a designation of 'language.'" Nevertheless, he did not trust the motives of the commissioners toward Jews, nor that of Ellis Island officials of those years. And "Since then, 'Ku Klux Klanism,' 'Nordic theories,' 'Fordism,' and the growth of relative racial evolutions has greatly aggravated this situation."

But Kohler's critical argument concerned the real meaning of the Immigration Commission's work for immigrants generally. He wrote, "I think the action of the Commission, in conducting all its investigations in terms of race, was most deplorable and greatly injured the position of millions of residents of our country, and was a great blow at true American ideals.... It led logically to Quota Laws, based on racial distinctions and preferences, which I abhor, while conceding that the War required new methods of restricting immigration."[65]

Thus it was possible to concede a great deal—that the List did not violate church–state separation, that the Hebrew category was "practically a designation of 'language,'" and even that "the War required new methods of restricting immigration." Yet conceding all this, Kohler could still argue that the commission's use of the List had been "most deplorable" and "a great blow to American ideals." Furthermore, this use of the List had "led logically to Quota Laws, based on racial distinctions and preferences" that shared so much with "'Ku Klux Klanism,' 'Nordic theories,' 'Fordism,' and the growth of relative racial evolutions" that had become especially popular in the two decades since the commission.

Finally, recall that the 1910 shift at Census pertained only to the terminology applied to *Europeans*. There had never been any thought to avoiding enumeration of "the major racial divisions," "the color races." Historians stress that in the following decades the race line drawn between whites and nonwhites would retain its strength, while divisions among white races would disappear.[66] The 1910 episode at Census was a step in that conceptual development as well, since it blocked the use of race to distinguish among whites in the enumeration—while at the same time relying on race to separate white from nonwhite. Nevertheless, these generalizations cover only the *census* history. As the next chapter will show, racialization of European (white) subgroups did come to be institutionalized in federal *immigration law* through the 1921 and 1924 Quota Acts—and remained so for more than four decades.

PART TWO

Institutionalizing Race Distinctions in American Immigration Law

CHAPTER 7

~

The Second Quota Act, 1924

THE NATIONAL ORIGINS ACT OF 1924, which remained the law of the land for four decades, had three principal effects. First, it drastically reduced the total number of European immigrants admitted to the United States each year; never again would their number be left unregulated. Second, it established a severe distinction between what its authors considered the desirable and undesirable white races, thus ensuring that there would be virtually no change in the actual flow from north and west but a radical reduction from southern and eastern Europe. Third, it recodified all of the total exclusions that were already in place against Asian immigrants and replaced the somewhat less thoroughgoing restrictions against the Japanese with a full exclusion.

In a word, then, the 1924 act made a drastic practical difference in the magnitude of American immigration at the expense of the huge flow of southern and eastern Europeans. Despite the completion of Asian exclusion, the act cut the number of Asian arrivals by far less than that of Europeans. Most Asians, after all, had been excluded earlier. Nevertheless, the animus in completing the Asian exclusion was not lost on the proud and nationalistic Japanese public opinion.

The act institutionalized two kinds of racial distinctions: those *among* white races and those *between* white and nonwhite races. When arguing for reductions in the numbers coming from southern and eastern Europe, restrictionists emphasized the distinctions among white races, while ignoring those between white and nonwhite races. When supporting East Asian exclusion, restrictionists emphasized distinctions between white and nonwhite races while ignoring those among white races. Moreover, in trying to hold back the legislation against European immigration, the *anti*-restrictionists condemned racial theories as vicious myths, but most of them were silent about, or only tersely supportive when it came to excluding Asians. All of this must be understood as part of one narrative to make sense of racialization in the struggle for the 1924 act.

This chapter focuses especially on the distinctions among the European races, but it sets these squarely in the context of a duality of race distinctions so that one can appreciate how they could operate together. Chapter 8 considers three additional features of the immigration debates of the 1920s, all of which focus especially on the distinction between white and nonwhite races.

The National Origins Act of 1924 did not speak directly of racial distinctions at all; instead, it introduced the terminology of "national origins." But contemporaries explicitly used this new term as a proxy for what had previously been termed "the various European races." And the term's resonances are with us still; it would be remembered across the next generation and would reappear as early as the 1940s in state and then federal civil rights legislation banning discrimination on the basis of race, color, creed, or national origin.

"National origins" meant something between the *Encyclopedia Britannica*'s two recognized meanings of nationality—as peoplehood and as citizenship. In the 1924 act, national origin was formally defined as country of birth even as legislators explicitly embraced it as the best available proxy for race.

Observers at the time and historians since then have stressed the extent to which the racial appeals of the 1921, and especially the 1924 debates over restriction, were influenced by "scientific racism" of the sort set out by Madison Grant and Harry Laughlin. Nevertheless, the older racial thought of Lodge's 1896 speech persisted and would have sufficed to show the "need" for legislation like that proposed in 1921–1924. It presented legislators with subdivisions of humanity that were virtually identical to those made by the scientific racists. We should therefore ask: Are Grant and Laughlin best seen as influential, or simply as welcome allies in Congress?

Recall that the 1917 restrictionist legislation passed the literacy requirement Lodge had wanted. It also excluded from immigration people living in the Asiatic Barred Zone, defined to include most of the Asian mainland south of the Russian Empire as well as the Asian islands south of Japan and Korea—except territory under U.S. control (notably the Philippines). The Chinese Exclusion Act, of course, had long prohibited the largest source of one-time Asian immigration, and the Gentlemen's Agreement already greatly reduced Japanese immigration. Few immigrants had come from other places in the zone, but the restriction was meant to systematize exclusion and to make a statement. The two prongs of the 1917 act—demanding literacy and excluding Asians—can be considered as the most severe of the prewar restrictions or as the first of the more severe restrictions influenced by the nationalism and social controls of the World War I and postwar era.[1] The efforts at social control of immigration in the 1920s included more than passage of the 1921 and 1924 Quota Acts, notably the curbing of immigrant radicalism. Still, both approaches acknowledge that the 1921 and 1924 acts advanced well beyond the severity of the literacy bill.

But beyond the broad cultural stimulus of the war era, a concrete reason for the success of the harsh restrictions at that time had to do with the character of the House Committee on Immigration and its new chairman, Representative Albert Johnson of Washington State. Johnson held this role throughout the 1920s. Under his leadership, the committee became the dynamo energizing ever-more restrictive bills. His outlook, however, predated the war and never fundamentally changed.

The Postwar Leader of Congressional Restriction—Before and After He Met the New Racial Theorists

Johnson started out as a newsman working in a number of cities, and eventually he settled down as the publisher of a minor newspaper in Washington State. Angered by the labor protests of the Industrial Workers of the World (IWW), he became deeply concerned about radical labor. At the same time, he became a vehement opponent of the Japanese and other "unassimilable" immigrants.[2] In 1912 he ran a successful campaign for Congress based on these concerns. From the time he first arrived in Congress, he worked unceasingly for immigration restriction. Indeed, during his first year, Johnson proposed a complete ban on immigration—a decidedly extreme position at the time. In 1914 he stressed that the mechanism for restriction "is not so important as that the step be taken—anything that will restrict [will do]."[3] With that principle in mind, he supported the literacy bill to exclude those who could not read. But he also made it clear that he wanted stronger legislation. First, he thought it would be preferable for the literacy bill to also exclude those who could not write. He also urged consideration of another restrictive measure the Immigration Commission had suggested: a quota limiting annual immigration from any given country to a percentage of the number of foreign-born residents from that country already living in the United States. Congress would eventually turn to the quotas in the early 1920s. But passionate debate was swirling around the bill to restrict those who could not read, and Johnson's calls for still-stronger legislation went unheeded in 1914 and for some years more.[4]

By the 66th Congress that began in March 1919, Johnson's length of tenure and his party's reclaimed House majority gave him the chairmanship of the House Immigration Committee. From that seat, he shepherded the crucial Quota Acts of 1921 and 1924 through succeeding Congresses and continued to press for still-further restrictions during the second half of the decade. Even before Johnson took over, the House committee had held hearings on a temporary halt to immigration. While the committee was prepared to recommend such an action at the war's end, the committee members judged that there was not yet adequate support for it, since the numbers of arriving immigrants had not yet returned to frightening magnitudes. The committee instead concentrated on other matters, such as deporting radicals.

By the summer of 1920, large-scale immigration was resuming, and at just the same time, the economy was turning downward. This, the committee members judged, was the auspicious moment; accordingly, they introduced a bill calling for a two-year halt to all immigration because of an "emergency." Specifically, they stressed conditions in postwar Europe and especially in east-central Europe. Destruction there was said to have produced chaos, mass unemployment, and starvation—as well as a rise of Bolshevism. An ensuing immigration wave was already underway, and it might soon exceed prewar levels. Immigrant ghettos would grow again in American cities, and they would become self-sustaining, rather than emptying out. From such ghettos would come all the attendant problems of crime, health concerns, and failed assimilation (particularly of groups that were hard to assimilate in the best of times). The solution? First, Congress must impose a temporary ban on all immigration. During the respite, it could develop a reasonable long-term policy. In the absence of great demand for more American workers, these arguments encountered little opposition from employers.[5]

There was certainly widespread sentiment in Congress for new restriction measures. Most congressmen seem to have viewed the 1917 literacy requirement as too porous a filter to use on postwar realities. Ironically, the literacy solution had been a subject of political struggle for twenty years, but once enacted, it was barely mentioned during the postwar debates.

And yet, many in Congress were far less sure than the majority of Johnson's committee that a total ban on immigration was needed or acceptable. Especially important was the skeptical attitude of the Senate Immigration Committee chaired by Rhode Island Senator Le Baron Colt. Moreover, by the time the Senate got around to the House bill, the economic conditions had shifted again: now there was some improvement, and the demand for workers was again an important consideration. Many senators (not least Colt himself) were sensitive to employer concerns and to foreign-born voters. Sensing an emergency no longer as dramatic as before, the senators were uncomfortable supporting a two-year total ban. After all, the country had never adopted such a policy in the past. As a compromise with the House, Senator Dillingham (chairman of the old U.S. Immigration Commission, 1907–1911) now introduced a version of the commission's old quota plan. The Senate settled on that solution, and the House eventually signed on (after stiffening the terms somewhat). This was the First Quota Act (1921).

The Quota Acts of 1921 and 1924 were a triumph for racial theory and racial classification. The first half-dozen years after the war saw the high point for Nordic theory in general, the writings of Madison Grant in particular, and also for the application of eugenics to immigration issues. This last was especially important in the work of Harry Laughlin, superintendent of the Eugenics Record Office at the Cold Spring Harbor Laboratory on Long Island.

Johnson apparently came to know Grant and Laughlin during the course of the year preceding April 1920 when Laughlin first testified (on "Biological Aspects of the Melting Pot") before Johnson's committee.[6] The next day, the committee appointed Laughlin as its "Eugenics Expert" and encouraged him to carry out further research on immigration. Late in 1922, after the First Quota Act, Laughlin testified again, this time to summarize the long report, "Analysis of the Metal and Dross in America's Modern Melting Pot," that he had produced for them. By 1923, Albert Johnson was serving as president of the Cold Spring Harbor Eugenics Research Association.

Laughlin provided reams of evidence on differences in group rates for many illnesses as well as for crimes. He drew the policy conclusion that some groups needed to be restricted much more than others for the sake of the future of America. Specifically, Laughlin argued that defective families should not be admitted as immigrants because biology was determinative. Moreover, the data showed that such families were more concentrated among the southern and eastern European immigrants than among other Americans.[7]

Thus there is no question that Johnson and his committee were in touch with Grant and supportive of Laughlin by 1922–1923. But does this connection mean that Grant and Laughlin greatly influenced the directions of Johnson's legislation, and thereby the nature of the Quota Acts? That contention, stated or implied in most histories of those laws, needs closer scrutiny.

This is especially true for the First Quota Act. In the first place, older racial formulations persisted in Congress throughout the period 1919–1924, particularly variants of Anglo-Saxonism prevalent for more than a half century. And these older racial formulations could lead restrictionists to the same policy outcomes as those put forth in the writings of Grant and Laughlin—namely, restriction of new immigrant peoples. There is, in fact, no evidence that specific legislative options emerged from the newer racial theories in particular. Recall, too, that Johnson's committee had proposed the most draconian policies even before he became involved with Nordic or eugenic theories, or with Grant or Laughlin. Johnson himself had supported a quota option the first year he arrived in the House. And by 1918–1919, many House bills had called for a complete halt to immigration for a period of one to four years; indeed, the committee had favorably reported on a bill for a halt of four years in March 1919.[8] Committee members had eventually determined not to bring the bill to a floor vote at that time, but by 1921 they thought the same bill had a better chance, and they did bring it to a vote. This chronology has nothing to do with the committee's discovery of Grant and Laughlin in the intervening period, or the fact that they had made the latter their eugenics expert. It was simply due to the political exigencies of the moment. Neither Johnson nor his committee's majority shaped new policies or were energized to act in new ways as a result of their eventual closeness to Grant and Laughlin.

What of the House membership more broadly? Might they have been decisively influenced by the new theories prevalent between 1919 and 1920? Here the documentary evidence is mixed. In the record of debate, there was simply no mention of Grant or Laughlin in the House debates on the First Quota Act (December 9–13, 1920). Likewise, there was almost no mention of Nordic races—not from supporters or from opponents of restriction.[9] And yet, on December 13, 1920, the House voted 296–42 for a bill suspending immigration to the United States for fourteen months. The suspension never became law because the Senate substituted a quota bill for the House bill on suspension. However, the relevant point here is that without notable mention of the newer racial ideology, the House still voted for suspension by a seven to one ratio.

At the same time, there are other sorts of evidence of what political leaders were saying or thinking at the time. Perhaps the most striking concerns Calvin Coolidge, who had just been elected vice president. Coolidge wrote a piece, "Whose Country Is This?," in the widely read journal *Good Housekeeping* in February 1921—that is, a mere two months after the House vote. In this brief article he wrote, "There are racial considerations too grave to be brushed aside for any sentimental reasons. Biological laws tell us that certain divergent people will not mix or blend. The Nordics propagate themselves successfully. With other races, the outcome shows deterioration on both sides."[10]

The Coolidge statement surely suggests some diffusion of Grant's Nordic theory among political leaders at about the time of the first House vote, notwithstanding the lack of mention of it in Congress. And yet, given the minimal mention in Congress *and* its overwhelmingly lopsided vote to suspend immigration, can we really attribute the suspension vote to the influence of the new ideological influences? Even if we posit that some members who were not restrictionists a year or two earlier were swayed by the same sort of material that Coolidge had articulated so clearly, can we seriously believe that this was true of many in the House— while they nevertheless refused to mention Grant, Laughlin, or Nordics? Indeed, one would need to explain not only why there was so complete a refusal to mention these new names in the House but also why that refusal did not extend to the vice president.

Finally, whatever the degree of awareness congressmen had about the new racial thinking, how important was such awareness in determining their vote? Were Grant's views simply one more reason to oppose a non-Anglo-Saxon immigration? Or did awareness of these views really sway many in Congress to vote for restriction? Can that awareness, in other words, really explain why the First Quota Act came in 1921, and not, for example, during the years since 1914? For the leaders who were pushing for restriction—those on Johnson's committee—it seems safe to repeat that the new views were welcome but not determinative.

By the time of the Second Quota Act, Johnson's personal connections to Grant and Laughlin, the latter's detailed report as "eugenic expert," and the many attacks on Grant, Laughlin, and Nordic theory by the anti-restrictionists are all in evidence. And outside Congress, we have observers and, later, historians widely documenting that the crucial moment for the popularity of new formulations relevant to restriction occurred between 1923 and 1925.[11]

Complicating the historical record is the fact that Johnson and his like-minded colleagues in the House and Senate were not trying to win an academic debate; if they thought they had a better chance to win the vote without discussing various themes, they avoided such discussion. This strategy explains why the lion's share of attention to Grant, Laughlin, and the new racial theories during the Second Quota Act debate came from *opponents* of the theories. In addition, on several occasions Johnson explicitly distanced himself from any reliance on these ideas. In one exchange during 1924, Congressman Gallivan of Massachusetts ridiculed the importance of "the light-haired, long-headed race," and later Congressman Jacobstein of New York bitterly criticized the reliance on Nordic theory. Johnson replied,

We are not responsible for the outside public classification, or even for the classification of the Commissioner-General of Immigration [i.e., the List of Races and Peoples]. So far as we are concerned, we do not care whether they are round heads, longheads, or bone heads. We are going to cut down the number that come here.[12]

In another 1924 exchange, Congressman Mooney of Ohio exploded,

How rapidly a falsehood will spread.... Suddenly a new word made its way into the English language—Nordic," "Nordic," "Nordic"—everywhere you turned. There is not a fifth-rate extension lecturer but does not speak of it with scientific exactness. Newspaper editorials, magazine articles, know exactly what the word means, what it implies.... But suppose, for the sake of argument, there is such a race as the "Nordic." Has its superiority been established? Has the superiority of any race been established? It is a thing of common knowledge among ethnologists and anthropologists that this talk of racial superiority is largely verbiage.[13]

Johnson asks him to yield for a moment.

Mr. Johnson of Washington. I would very much like to say on behalf of the committee that through the strenuous times of the hearings this committee undertook not to discuss the Nordic proposition or racial matters.

Mr. Mooney. I have tried to make that clear, that it is propaganda. There is no doubt in my mind as to the fairness of the committee, and I am only speaking of the propagandist.[14]

Finally, in his committee hearings Johnson tended to turn discussion away from direct angry or excited condemnations of Grant and Nordics. A dramatic instance occurred when Gedalia Bublick, the outspoken editor of the *Jewish Daily News*, a Yiddish paper in New York City with English sections and a circulation of 60,000, testified.

Mr. Bublick. This bill that is before us is a bill of discrimination based on race prejudice.... We citizens of America who are from stocks which are not Nordic feel that this bill is a discrimination ... against our position in American life.... It is just in the same spirit as the laws of the Russian Czars....

> *The Chairman [Johnson].* Now let me ask you a question. . . . Those
> various countries over there in Central Europe . . . don't those
> various little countries in Central Europe always seem to be in
> trouble?

A few moments later, Bublick recovers and cites a notorious passage from
Madison Grant: "'These immigrants adopt the language of the Americans,
they wear his clothes, they steal his name, and they are beginning to take
his women, but they seldom take his religion or understand his ideals.'"

> *The Chairman.* Now, why do these people change their names? Why did
> this man with some "sky" to his name try to change it by some order
> of court, to "Cabot?"[15]

Thus at the time of the Second Quota Act we also find only cautious mention of Nordic theory, or of Grant's and Laughlin's policy conclusions among
Johnson's committee members. Nor can we learn much about the actual
impact of these influences from the fact that the militant *anti*-restrictionists,
including the few minority voices on Johnson's committee, castigate these
theories and bemoan their influence. These opponents used whatever
means they could against the large majority supporting more restrictionist
legislation. That the anti-restrictionists were eager to accuse the majority of
believing repugnant pseudoscientific ideas is not good evidence that those
ideas had led the majority to vote for new restrictions. So too, great majorities voted for the *First* Quota Act when there is no evidence of Nordics, or Laughlin and Grant in the debate. We can reasonably conclude
that large majorities would have voted to make the quota principle permanent in the *Second* Quota Act even without the growing popularity of
Grant and Laughlin.

The nature of the contacts between Johnson and Grant or Laughlin are
good evidence that these men's ideas were welcomed by the committee—
but not that these men greatly influenced results. Above all, whatever
weight we give to the newer "scientific" racial theories at the time of the 1924
debate, we should appreciate the intellectual continuities between the terms
of this act and *earlier* conceptions and classifications that led legislators to
the same policies. This caution applies to Johnson's committee, Congress
generally, and the wider political culture.

Thus a series of features linked Lodge's restrictionism of the 1890s to Johnson's, and even to Grant's and Laughlin's in the 1920s. These features included the immigrant groups deemed undesirable, the basis of their undesirability in a cluster of traits described in terms that had not varied appreciably, the emphasis on "race" as the critical source of these traits, and the meaning of race as rooted, at least in part, in biological transmission.

Grant's biological determinism went further than Lodge's, especially in stressing that every additional undesirable immigrant weakened the republic in the long run because biological transmission could not be influenced by processes of assimilation and group melding. Lodge had a certain degree of faith in the possibilities of assimilation so long as the number of undesirable immigrants did not become too great for processes of assimilation to operate. Johnson may or may not have followed Grant rather than Lodge on this point. But he made it clear that the niceties of race theory, like the specifics of the restriction measures, mattered less than the basic principle of holding down the number of undesirable immigrants— actually placing him closer to Lodge than to Grant in this respect.

"National Origins" as Proxy for European Races

What remains, however, is a need to examine the terminology and conceptual basis of the 1924 Quota Act, especially the term "national origins." At first sight, this term might seem to suggest a turning away from racial classification in favor of a classification related to nationality. But, in fact, there were key moments during the congressional debate over the bill—precisely the moments when the national origins criterion was explained—that clarified how national origin was to be considered as the best practical proxy for European races.

The meaning of nationality as peoplehood rather than citizenship became somewhat more widespread during the decade prior to 1924, not least through conflicts over national aspirations in central and eastern Europe. We encounter it in references to "nationalities" and to "race and nationality" among social scientists and intellectuals, whether in connection with affairs in central Europe or with American immigrants and their children. Nevertheless, nationality as peoplehood never came to dominate American discussion enough to drive out classification of European peoples in terms of race. In the debates over the Second Quota Act, this reliance on race was on display, even as the explicit terms in the law referred to "national origins," defined not as peoplehood but as birth in particular European states. Yet national origins also served as a proxy for racial differences among Europeans (whites).

The First Quota Act (1921) had already based the quotas on "nationality," with "nationality" defined in the act to mean country of birth. In that measure, Congress had capped annual immigration at 3 percent of the foreign born counted in the 1910 census. This cap was imposed on each nationality separately. Use of the 1910 rather than 1920 census for counts of the foreign born tended to weight the quotas more heavily in favor of immigrants from northern and western rather than southern and eastern Europe. After all, there had been a giant infusion of southern and eastern Europeans between 1910 and 1920. Also, fewer of the immigrants who had arrived earlier had died by 1910 than by 1920. The 1921 act also preserved the exclusions of East Asians already in effect on the Chinese and all people from the Asiatic Barred Zone, while the Gentleman's Agreement continued to restrict Japanese immigration.

There was no need for the quota formula to invoke the controversial List of Races and Peoples or indeed *any* data collected by the Bureau of Immigration. Census Bureau data on countries of birth provided an authoritative count. The country-of-birth criterion may seem a crude way to classify European races, but it was well suited to the need. All the undesirable European races could be covered by referencing the states of southern and eastern Europe.

The congressional impetus for further restriction after 1921 came again from the circle of legislators around Albert Johnson. Everyone knew the votes were there to make a law like the First Quota Act permanent. The restrictionists used their advantage to try to achieve still fewer "undesirable" Europeans. The cap itself could easily have been reduced with no fundamental change in the method of calculation. Thus instead of a quota allowing immigrants to number 3 percent of the foreign born from each country already residing in the United States, some lower percentage could have been adopted in 1924—for example, 2 percent or 1 percent. But restrictionists wanted to do more than reduce the cap: they wanted to further reduce the proportion of immigrants from southern and eastern

Europe in particular. To put it differently, they did not want an even tighter cap to work against immigrants from northern and western Europe. Johnson's committee first proposed to reach their goal by basing the quota on the counts of foreign-born Americans in the 1890 rather than 1920 census (that is, before arrivals from southern and eastern Europe became prevalent).

But the restrictionists had overreached. The arbitrary reliance on the 1890 criterion enraged immigrant groups and disgusted others as well; it seemed blatantly discriminatory and insulting. This anger may well have increased criticisms of another committee initiative, the support for Harry Laughlin's reports. So, too, the anger probably increased the criticism of the broader Nordic race talk in the public culture noted earlier. Jewish and Italian leaders in particular—journalists from the immigrant press, congressmen from immigrant districts, petitioners from immigrant organizations, and so on—were vociferous in decrying the discriminatory nature of the 1890 criterion. Their outcry also stimulated like-minded objections from liberal journals, and from others who had not been thought of principally as spokesmen for the immigrants. Congressmen from these camps account for the great majority of the references to Laughlin, Grant, and Nordics in the 1924 congressional debates.[16] We have already encountered examples in the preceding section—the speeches of Congressmen Gallivan and Mooney and the testimony of Gedalia Bublick before Johnson's committee. In general, Congressmen Sabath, LaGuardia, Dickstein, Jacobstein, Celler, and a half-dozen others made long and forceful orations. And on April 2, 1924, Senator Le Baron Colt of Rhode Island, chairman of the Senate Immigration Committee, bitterly condemned the new restrictionist behavior as institutionalizing racial prejudice.

Do you wonder that the 6,000,000 people from southern and eastern Europe [currently living in the United States] claim that this is a gross discrimination against them? The effect of going back to the census of 1890 is just the same as if under the present quota law you admitted 1 per cent from southern and eastern Europe and 5 per cent from northern and western Europe....

Are we, for the first time in our history, going to raise, so far as Europe and the white race is concerned, this question of racial

antagonism and racial prejudice, which has wrecked more than half of
Europe? . . . Ah, but raise that question that they are undesirable and you
sow the seeds of discontent and bitterness, not only among the
6,000,000 but among 18,000,000 if we include the children of these
6,000,000, for they feel this discrimination just as keenly. . . .

Why, if we go on with the present quota law . . . [the number of the
foreign born] will gradually lessen every year so that in the course of a
decade even the Nordics will be pleased with the result.[17]

Such accusations did not stop the House from passing Johnson's version of the bill a few days later—with country quotas based on the 1890
criterion.

Nevertheless, these outcries did stimulate other restrictionist legislators to find a different basis for the quota. The key player now was Senator
David Reed of Pennsylvania, who assumed the management of the restriction bill in the Senate. He took over this task from Senator Colt who
was in poor health and was in any case unsympathetic to demands for
further restriction.[18] The day after Colt's speech, Reed introduced what
became the new quota principle. The quota, Reed argued, should reflect
the origins of *all* Americans, native as well as foreign born (rather than the
origins of the foreign born only). By *all* Americans Reed actually meant
all white Americans. Thus, determine the proportion of ancestors of the
white population that had come from each of the European countries.
These proportions were the "national origins" of the American [white]
people. Annual immigration would be limited by a cap, and under that
cap each European country would be allocated the same proportion of
immigrants as its proportion of the national origins so calculated.[19]

Because the great majority of all white Americans were native-born descendants of pre-1890 arrivals, the national origins criterion for the quota
guaranteed that southern and eastern Europeans would get a very low allocation in the quota—about as low as they would have received by using
the 1890 count of the foreign born. And yet, Reed stressed, the desired result would be obtained without the perceived discrimination inherent in
exploiting the 1890 census year. Quite the contrary, Reed insisted: it was
the original quota principle of the 1921 law that was unfair. By failing to

consider native-born Americans, that law had worked "a great discrimination in favor of southern and eastern Europe."[20]

Reed omitted Asian Americans from this computation of "national origins of our whole population" as they were "aliens ineligible for naturalization" under the 1790 statute limiting naturalization to "free white persons." And what of African Americans? After the Civil War, Congress had modified the 1790 clause so that thenceforth people of African origin were in fact *eligible* for naturalization. Yet Reed's national origin counts also disregarded descendants of involuntary migrants—of slaves—"as they themselves would wish to be disregarded, the negro population of the country, because they do not want, and we do not want to allow great immigration from Africa. That is self-evident to us."[21] These decisions on Asian and African origins could be written into the law without mentioning Asia or Africa or Orientals or Negros explicitly. Instead, the law appealed only to "universal" principles: it omitted from the national origin counts those ancestors who were ineligible for naturalization and those who had come involuntarily.

Determining the national origins of American whites was, however, no simple matter. A refined count would have required, for example, information on the origins of early arrivals, but they were not recorded by country of birth before the early nineteenth century. And it would have required knowing a great deal about immigrant descendants by origin—fertility and intermarriage patterns in particular. No such evidence was in fact available. Reed acknowledged not only that no count could be precise, but also that even relatively crude estimates would take several years for census demographers to calculate. For the meantime, he proposed using a temporary quota based on the 1890 counts.

Reed's proposals were eventually accepted. It might seem that the National Origins Act involved race only in its exclusion of Asian and African Americans from the quotas. But the debates show how fully the rationale for the national origins criterion was also based explicitly on distinctions among European (white) races. The point can be obscured not only by the terminology of national origins, but also by the fact that one major part of the debate on the 1924 law did indeed focus on the difference between the Japanese and European immigrations. Also, a third, albeit much more marginal, part of the debate concerned the difference between the *Mexican* and European immigrations.

For almost two decades, immigration from Japan had been controlled by the Gentlemen's Agreement that severely restricted laborers from migrating. For many western congressmen the highest priority was to create a firm and unambiguous basis in law for Japanese exclusion, as there had been against the Chinese since 1882, and against most of the rest of East Asians since the creation of the Asiatic Barred Zone in 1917. The Gentlemen's Agreement, by contrast, appeared vague and potentially impermanent. However, while congressmen representing western states pressed to bar the Japanese as well, the State Department warned that such a move would be unwise as an act of foreign policy. The Japanese public intensely and angrily followed the American debates, and Japan's representatives presented official communiques about it to the State Department and to Congress. The Japanese immigration took up a vastly greater part of the debate over the 1924 act than the number of Japanese comprised among all immigrants. Members of Congress from the West Coast emphasized the chasm between the "white" and "yellow" races. And they stressed that the Japanese would never become a docile, servile race in America, as they believed was true of the Chinese. Moreover, Southern congressmen drew out similarities between Asian–white relations on the Pacific Coast and black–white relations in the South.

Consequently, rhetoric about races in the 1924 debates often involved multiple kinds of comparisons. On the one hand, there was a comparison of white and nonwhite races; on the other, there was the comparison of desirable and undesirable *white* races. One difference between the two congressional debates was that no one was defending Japanese immigration nor questioning the principle of racial exclusion; unlike the southern and eastern Europeans, no one in Congress spoke for a meaningful number of Japanese immigrants. Only the standoff with the Japanese state was really subject to discussion.

In this context, the most ferocious defenders of southern and eastern European immigration explicitly stated support for Japanese exclusion. For example, Representatives Sabath and Dickstein, the anti-restrictionist minority on Johnson's committee, authored a minority report opposing further cuts in southern and eastern European immigration. However, the minority report was silent on the majority's recommendation to exclude the Japanese. During the floor debates, Sabbath and Dickstein explicitly asserted their support for Japanese exclusion—albeit in single-sentence statements that seem to betray discomfort.

What were these opponents of [European] restriction thinking in supporting Japanese exclusion? The range of plausible views is wide, and there is no reason that the balance of motivations was the same for all the relevant congressmen. Perhaps a few of these congressmen actually believed that racial biology between nonwhite and white minds really mattered. Perhaps they believed, as historian Gary Gerstle has put it, that "a campaign against the Japanese could benefit immigrants from southern and eastern Europe [because it] . . . magically fused all Europeans"—enhancing the connection of the new immigrant groups with desirable old-stock whites (in this cause at least).[22] Perhaps these congressmen acted only from a realistic sense that the drive for Asian exclusion could neither be halted nor limited, and they should not expend their minimal political capital on the cause; this calculation might have operated in the same direction as the first but might have had little to do with "becoming white." Or perhaps they honestly believed that, given the way Asian immigrants were treated in American life, it was best to prohibit additional arrivals for the sake of American social peace. Congressman Meyer Jacobstein (from Rochester, New York) expressed such a view briefly, but he still spoke more loquaciously about the issue than Sabath or Dickstein. Excluding the Chinese and Japanese was *not* "unfair," he said, despite his passionate speech that the quota bill on Europeans was outrageous for a country governed by the principle that all men are created equal. He explained,

> I would not go to a country where I did not have an equal status with other people in that country, and I say this in justice to those foreigners [potential Chinese or Japanese immigrants], I am not thinking only of America. I am thinking of those who come here because if we do not assimilate them they can not help us. It is bad for them and bad for us. . . .

Jacobstein might seem at best hypocritical—wouldn't social peace, as restrictionists gleefully asked, be enhanced still further by suspending southern and eastern European immigration? He flew at that argument too.

I would rather suspend [immigration from Europe for a period] ... if it were necessary than to pass a law that sets loose prejudice, antiracial and anti-American feelings. . . . But it is not necessary. . . . [It is untrue that] the flow is too great, that we cannot assimilate them [i.e., European immigrants], and that this is a menace.[23]

In the final analysis, however, the larger point is not about motive but context: the congressional debate about *restricting* European immigration on the basis of race went on in the context of a second debate about the details of *excluding* the Japanese and in the latter debate all whites were taken as a group. And second, there is no avoiding the bizarre tableau in which few if any congressmen who argued against European restriction failed to accept Asian exclusion.[24]

The discussion of Mexican immigration raised slightly different nuances. The defenders of the southern and eastern Europeans argued that it was hypocritical to worry about how different such people were from older-stock Americans when at the same time Mexican immigration was to remain unregulated because big farmers in the Southwest wanted it so. In this case, no one had to say that they supported restrictions on Mexicans. Nevertheless, the anti-(European) restrictionists certainly did not go out of the way to argue that Mexicans were the equal of the white population or even that Mexicans were no more different from Anglo-Saxons than were southern and eastern Europeans.

In sum, discussions of the Mexicans as well as of the Japanese kept the white–nonwhite race distinction front and center in 1924—on the very days that comparisons between the Anglo-Saxons and southern and eastern Europeans were *also* front and center. These latter Europeans were unmistakably white; at the same time, they were described as racially different from Anglo-Saxons. Senator Colt's argument (quoted earlier) against a discriminatory law provides an apt example: "Are we, for the first time in our history, going to raise, *so far as Europe and the white race is concerned* [italics added], this question of racial antagonism and racial prejudice, which has wrecked more than half of Europe?" Colt, of course, was *opposed* to Reed's bill, and indeed to any further restrictions on European immigration. By attending to several byways in the debates on the bill, we can learn how those who supported the proposed restrictions thought about national origins.

When Reed tried to introduce the concept of national origins, Colt hectored him with numerous questions, perhaps partly in pique over his own declining role. But Colt also meant to show senators that Reed's neat solution was not giving them exactly what they thought they were getting—because determining the national origins of American whites (even if these could be accurately computed) was not the same as determining their racial origins.

> *Mr. Colt.* May I ask the Senator from Pennsylvania whether [the estimates of origins that he is citing] are based upon races or upon nationals?
>
> *Mr. Reed of Pennsylvania.* They are based entirely on nationals. It is not practicable to separate people according to races. . . .
>
> *Mr. Colt.* May I ask the Senator if it is not a fact that in making the computation upon national grounds we can not distinguish in any way or separate the races?
>
> *Mr. Reed of Pennsylvania.* I think we do distinguish broadly—when we distinguish them according to nationality.

Since the requisite racial data are missing, birthplace data will be used in their stead. Colt continued to argue that the proxies were imperfect and hard to construct anyway. He then made the mistake of citing an extreme example.

> *Mr. Colt.* May I cite this example? The quota from Turkey is about 2,500. Of that 2,500 only 158 were Turks. There were 417 Hebrews, 658 Armenians, 631 Syrians, 179 Greeks, and these figures do not include various other races; and if you take the nationals from Czechoslovakia or Yugoslavia or Poland, you find that you then have a number of different races. Therefore, if you are coming to racial stock and not national stock, which is entirely distinct, these figures, based upon nationals and not based upon racials, throw little if any light upon the different racial stocks.

Now Henry Cabot Lodge intervened. He had resigned from the Senate Immigration Committee in 1917 after the passage of the literacy restriction; in the years after he had chaired the Senate Foreign Relations Committee. Now, in April 1924, he was a few months before a sudden death. His thirty years in the Senate, his long association with immigration restriction, and a background in historical study gave Lodge's intervention special weight.

> *Mr. Lodge.* Of course, there are some countries, like Turkey and Asia Minor, where there is a great admixture of races. . . . There are other countries where the race is almost exactly represented by the nationals, like the Scandinavian countries. I have made some researches myself on this subject, and as a rule the nation pretty well represents the race, as, for instance, England or France or Italy or Poland; but Turkey is a very peculiar place. . . . Therefore, Turkey is no guide whatever.
>
> *Mr. Colt.* May I ask the Senator from Massachusetts whether . . . the United Kingdom does not include the Irish, the Welsh, the Scotch, and the English; and will he say that there is no racial distinction between the Irish and the English or between the Scotch and the English?
>
> *Mr. Lodge.* Oh, of course, Mr. President, there is a racial distinction between the Irish and the English. Everyone knows that . . . I am speaking generally of the thing. . . . "United Kingdom" convey[s] a very good idea of what the immigration is . . . but when you get down to these places where the races are mixed and have been mixed for thousands of years, it is not a fair example of the rest of the countries of Europe. You can get immigrants of a different race from many countries, from Germany or any country; but the bulk of them are German and of German origin. . . . As far as . . . the races created by history, it comes pretty near to being exact—for all practical purposes sufficiently exact.[25]

The great majority of individuals in a given country were of one historical race; consequently, national origins could indeed proxy for racial origins. At this point, various senators probed just how imperfect the proxy would be.

> *Mr. Walsh of Montana.* Is it not a fact, however, that a large percentage of the inhabitants of northern Italy are Teutonic in origin?
>
> *Mr. Lodge.* True; Lombardy is almost altogether Teutonic. . . . But speaking generally, for purposes of statistics, what we are doing here

in taking the nationals comes very near what we desire to get at, which is the national distribution. We have had no racial distribution in the statistics that I know of. . . .

Mr. Harreld [of Oklahoma]. . . . If we based the quotas on races, because of the distribution of the Hebrew race over all the world . . . would [this method] result in having a great many more Jewish immigrants to this country than those of any other race? . . .

Mr. Lodge. No. The Jewish people have always objected to any racial distinction. We had a long hearing about that in the Immigration Committee some years ago. They wish to be classified according to the countries from which they come, and they objected at that time to being classified according to their race, or what people believed to be their race. It cannot be accurate ethnically to classify immigrants by nations, but it is sufficiently accurate for the statistics we need in legislating.

Mr. Reed of Pennsylvania. Mr. President, of course we cannot legislate for the admission of people by races. . . . As a matter of common-sense legislation, however, we have to treat the people in what is now known as Italy as one group, because they have made themselves one group by constant intermixture, so that they are a well-defined, separate nationality. . . . If we once got into a study of the ethnology involved in this question we could not pass an immigration law in the next 50 years, because we would not ever be satisfied with the product.[26]

The next day Lodge won Reed's undying gratitude when he fervently supported a new quota based on Reed's notion of the national origins of all white Americans. Yet it is striking that he did so within the terms of the older racial language—without reference to the ideas of Madison Grant on one side or central European usages of nationality on the other.

The quota under the amendment . . . would rest on the distribution of races . . . at the present moment. It will take some time to make the calculations, but they certainly can be made. I have examined with care the computations so far made and am convinced that it is possible to ascertain the division of races in this country with sufficient correctness. If such a basis is adopted, there can be no question then of discrimination, because it will treat all races alike on the basis of their actual proportion of the existing population. I think it is of very great importance to adopt this amendment for that precise purpose.[27]

A few days later, the senators returned to these connections between race and nationality when Reed again offered a summary of his proposal for basing the quota on the national origins of the entire white population.

> *Mr. Pepper [of Pennsylvania].* [If] one were to imagine all the immigrants from other countries in a given year congregated on board a single vessel, the ... racial stocks on board, would be in microcosm the United States of America in its racial distribution. Is that correct?
>
> *Mr. Reed of Pennsylvania.* That is exactly correct. . . .

But Senator Sterling of South Dakota raised a new suggestion.

> *Mr. Sterling.* . . . The question in my mind is whether we do not confuse now this question of racial group with nationality. . . . The racial distribution to which [Mr. Pepper] referred after all means nationality, as so many would come from Germany, for example, rather than Germans. Is not that the idea?. . . .
>
> *Mr. Reed of Pennsylvania.* The Senator is exactly right. We have to base it on nationality, because racial distinctions are impossible.
>
> *Mr. Sterling.* That is what I thought. But in certain countries is not the racial group quite distinct. Or, to put it in another way, is there not a plain, commonly recognized distinction between racial groups, so that the number that might come from any particular country could be apportioned among the several racial groups?
>
> *Mr. Reed of Pennsylvania.* That would be a further refinement to this that we might someday adopt, but I do not think it is practicable to adopt it now.
>
> *Mr. Sterling.* Would it not be practicable with reference, for example, to the three countries, Russia, Rumania, and Poland?
>
> *Mr. Reed of Pennsylvania.* It might be.[28]

Russia, Rumania, and Poland were the three countries sending the largest number of Jews, and Sterling sought to reduce Jewish arrivals below the level Reed's method would define by using racial quotas within national quotas. Reed acknowledged that someday such a procedure might be regarded as a refinement of his own proposal. The interchange demonstrates again that the ultimate goal is thought of in racial terms.

Reed probably expected that the kind of refinement that Sterling had in mind would never come into being; by acknowledging Sterling's logic to be a refinement of his own goals, he may have simply been treating his colleague politely. But within the week, Sterling introduced an amendment to include the refinement in the 1924 law.[29] Sterling's amendment proposed,

> When it shall appear that the people of any nation are composed of commonly recognized and well-defined distinct racial groups [the quota for that nation] shall then be apportioned to the several racial groups in the ratio that the number in each group bears to the entire population of such nation. . . . Immigrants belonging to any racial group shall not be admitted in excess of the number so apportioned.

The amendment went nowhere, but the colloquy it stimulated between Sterling and Reed is illuminating.

> *Mr. Sterling.* By way of illustration, I might give an example of what present conditions are and what they permit. Four Jews [immigrated from Poland in July–August 1921] for every Pole. The quota for Poland was exhausted in December, 1921, and the Poles, it is said, were mourning bitterly because they had not been given a square deal, nor had they, for the population of Poland is something like 17,000,000 Poles and 3,000,000 Jews. This illustrates, Mr. President, the reason and the justice of applying this principle of apportionment of the quota mirroring the well-defined and well-recognized, racial groups. Take another illustration: [of 2014 Rumanians arriving in July–August 1921] 1,411 were Jews. . . . The Jews in Rumania are in the minority. Russia is another example. Mr. President, where, as I understand, there are 51 Slavs to 1 Jew. It is to permit the other racial groups in the several nations to have their just and fair apportionment of the quota among them that this amendment is submitted. . . .
>
> *Mr. Reed of Pennsylvania.* My only apprehension is that it is unworkable. . . . I do not believe it is humanly possible for any consul of the United States to take a Polish emigrant and analyze his race and find

out to which of the racial groups he ought to be assigned. . . . [He may have Jewish, Czech, and Slavic origins] and no consul would have the ability or the means at his disposal to make the necessary research. My objection does not lie to the idea of the Senator from South Dakota. I think his idea would be fine if it could be worked out. But the moment you come to apply it to any particular emigrant you would find yourself up against a hopeless enigma.[30]

The senators, Reed was explaining, must be satisfied with the proxy of national for racial origins. Moreover, a key to determining the components of a population—this time the European rather than American population—is that the work can be done only at the aggregate level, in terms of "numerical equivalents."

This discussion is intriguing because Sterling's proposal—and Reed's support for it in principle—actually appeals to an entirely different logic than the one Reed had been using to justify the national origins principle. Reed had argued for national origins as a way to ensure that the immigrant profile would replicate the already-existing American profile. Sterling was arguing that "fairness" meant taking race into account when possible as well as nationality. Specifically, Sterling wanted to admit the people of a single country in accord with their racial distribution *in that country*. But Sterling's "refinement" would actually have violated Reed's principle of mirroring the origins of the *American* white population. No doubt Sterling's violation of Reed's basic principle would have eventually been noticed had the amendment not been so quickly shot down as impractical. Still, the exercise showed an overeager effort to find one more supposedly nondiscriminatory arrangement by which to achieve discriminatory goals.

Reed's proposal for the national origin quotas eventually passed the Senate. The House eventually agreed to it as well, scraping its earlier bill based on the 1890 counts of the foreign born for the country quotas. Colt, bitterly opposed to the end, observed, "America has now adopted an immigration policy based, so far as Europe is concerned, upon the exclusion of certain races. . . . Tell the world, tell these millions of people here that they are undesirable and that America is going to change her policy toward Europe from one of nationalism to one of racialism.—Oh, go back to Germany and look at her history of racialism."[31]

For his part, Congressman Albert Johnson had worried that Reed's alternative method might unravel the deal for severe restriction. After all, the national origins system could not be put in place for several years, because researchers working with the Census Bureau had to work out the numbers. Indeed, Johnson (not unlike Senator Colt) also worried that it might prove impossible to ever come up with acceptable numbers.[32] In the end, the researchers did offer their national origin counts, but it took them five years and the relevant quotas were not introduced until 1929. Resting on those 1929 quotas, the 1924 National Origins Act, which came to be known also as the Johnson-Reed Act, remained the law of the land until 1965. Reviewing the triumph on the House floor, Johnson concluded, "The United States is undertaking to regulate and control the great problem of the comingling of races. Our hope is in a homogeneous Nation."[33]

The Impact of the National Origins Act: Race, Law, and Demography

Examining the *demographic* effects of the 1921 and 1924 acts reveals the impact of these conceptions of human difference (see Table 2). During the five years before World War I, immigration averaged about one million annually. Of these, 87 percent came from Europe (2.6 percent from Asia, 3.5 percent from Latin America, and 6.6 percent from Canada). Among the Europeans, 723,000 immigrants came from southern and eastern Europe, and 183,000 from northwestern Europe. During the first five years under the National Origins Act of 1924, the total magnitude of European immigration was cut by 83 percent, leaving 36,000 from southern and eastern Europe, and 122,000 from northern and western Europe. This amounted to a decline of 95 percent in the arrivals from southern and eastern Europe compared to 33 percent from northern and western Europe.

But notice that much of the decline came from the imposition of a *cap on total European immigration* that drastically reduced the flow (each national origin being limited to 3 percent of their estimated prevalence in the population). Overall, the operation of the new legislation cut European immigration by 83 percent from what it had been before—from 905,000 to 158,000 each year. Put another way, Congress could have achieved an 83 percent decline in European immigration *simply by capping annual immigration* at this number (that is, 158,000)—without bothering about ethno-racial quotas by country. Indeed, when Johnson and his committee supported bills to temporarily halt all immigration, they showed their willingness to consider such solutions. Had that policy prevailed, the results for southern and eastern Europeans would have been similar. The outcomes would be as follows: a total ban, 100 percent kept out; national origin quotas, 95 percent; a simple cap, 83 percent. The numerical similarity in outcomes reflects the overwhelming predominance of immigrants from southern and eastern Europe among all European arrivals in the years before the two Quota Acts (1921 and 1924). Given that predominance, any action leveled at all Europeans fell mostly on those from the southern and eastern areas of the continent.

The key reason the policymakers did *not* adopt a race-blind cap was that it would have reduced *desired* arrivals from northwestern Europe by the same harsh proportion as the *undesired* from the other end of the continent. Instead of a reduction of 83 percent or 100 percent from northern and western Europe, the 1924 act reduced their proportion by only a third (183,000 to 122,000). This was the achievement of the claim that the racial composition of the European immigration should reflect the racial profile of all past European arrivals. If that embrace was hard for some in Congress, we should realize that it was an act of symbolic politics that was welcome to others. In many constituencies across all regions of the United States, it was a welcome vote, and it passed by large majorities. While the literacy requirement bills had been vetoed four times by three presidents during the two decades before the war, neither the First nor Second Quota Acts faced a veto.

The List of Races may not have been created to capture the division between Anglo-Saxons and southern or eastern Europeans, but it did capture it. At the time the bill for the *First* Quota Act was conceived and debated (1921), neither popular discussion nor congressional debate showed much reliance on the specific character of Madison Grant's racial outlook rather than that of Lodge. There is no reason to doubt that *Second* Quota Act (the National Origins Act of 1924) could have easily carried with the same array of congressional and popular opinion. Grant and Laughlin were welcome allies by 1924, but not the necessary or sufficient cause for the 1924 act. At the same time, the conception of national origins should not be confused with either conception of nationality (as citizenship or as peoplehood). It was explicitly linked to race at crucial moments of the debates.

The 1924 act initiated a federal law by which specific white races were deterred far more from entering the country than were those of Anglo-Saxon (or Teutonic, or Nordic) stock for forty years. Discrimination among white races was not a feature of domestic American law—even if the Immigration Commission's proposal that the 1910 census classify Americans by categories of the List would have made a tentative beginning in that direction. Nevertheless, discrimination of this kind was decidedly institutionalized in American immigration law. We rightly consider the period's exclusion of Asian races to be institutionalized racial behavior at the federal level; nor do we consider the Asian exclusions in this way only because such institutionalization was paralleled by domestic social laws and behaviors. It is true that the restrictions against undesired Europeans were less complete than were the exclusions against Asians. On the other hand, when one considers the low quotas that the 1924 act assigned, the difference between restriction and exclusion was not so great; the 1925 quota for Italians was 6,203. Furthermore, when one considers the number of immigrant arrivals prior to the Quota Acts, the impact of "restriction"

Table 2. Impact of the National Origins Act of 1924: European Immigrant Arrivals

Average annual immigration for five-year period	Immigrant arrivals (000s)		
	Northern and Western Europe	Southern and Eastern Europe	Europe total
A. ACTUAL			
1910–1914	183	723	905
1925–1929	122	36	158
Proportion declined, 1910–1914 to 1925–1929	0.33	0.95	0.83
B. HYPOTHETICAL: Decline expected from "race blind" cap on arrivals			
1925–1929	32	126	158
Proportion decline, 1910–1914 to 1925–1929	0.83	0.83	0.83

Note: Total immigration from all countries declined (in 000s) from 1,035 to 304. Non-Europeans included in 1910–1914 (1925–1929): Asia 26 (4), Latin America 35 (57), Canada 66 (84), other 2 (1).

Source: Susan B. Carter et al., eds., *Historical Statistics of the United States* Millennial Edition, (Cambridge: Cambridge University Press, 2006), Table C-89. See also William S. Bernard, "Immigration: History of U.S. Policy," in *Harvard Encyclopedia of American Ethnic Groups*, ed. Stephan Thernstrom (Cambridge, MA: Harvard University Press, 1980), Table 1.

was gigantic; in the last year before the war (1914), 283,738 Italians had arrived. The 1925 quota cut 98 percent of Italians from that prewar number.

At the same time, it is striking how even the ardent non-restrictionists could support or acquiesce in the *other* form of racial discrimination—that between European and Asian. This behavior deserves careful attention before it can be meaningfully understood. It stands at the very heart of the debate because African and Asian Americans were simply excluded from the calculation of American national origins. The concept of a greater distance between color races than among races of one color family is one meaningful way to grasp the whole, but the tension deserves more analysis as an intellectual construct.

CHAPTER 8

~

Immigration Law for White Races and Others

Three Episodes

DURING THE DEBATES OVER the National Origins Act of 1924 members of Congress spoke of racial differences among whites (Europeans) and racial differences between whites and nonwhites as if these were separate subjects. They virtually never compared these two kinds of differences. Here we take up three more minor episodes of the late 1910s and the 1920s in which there was explicit recognition of what we might call this difference in racial differences. Reformer Sidney Gulick urged a policy of immigration restriction that would apply a common principle to all immigrant races; the Supreme Court compared Asian and European immigrants when considering the appeals of the former for citizenship; and after decades in the House, Albert Johnson suddenly chose to become involved with congressional oversight of the census just as he came to focus more sharply on how Mexican immigration was distinct and as the upcoming 1930 census acquired a "Mexican race" category.

Sidney Gulick Argues for an "Ethnic Group" Quota, 1914–1921

Sidney Gulick grew up in a California missionary family. After a graduating from Dartmouth, he, too, entered the ministry and spent much of his life in Japan, learning the language well and eventually teaching in a Japanese university. When he returned to the United States in 1913, it was with a good sense of how Asian and especially Japanese opinion saw American immigration policy.

Gulick supported restriction, and indeed he thought that only a small immigration from Japan was desirable. He also agreed with the goal of greatly reducing immigration from southern and eastern Europe. But he pressed for a policy that would accomplish these goals without legislating special restrictions on the Japanese, and therefore without pointlessly insulting them. The solution, he believed, was to avoid explicitly singling out *any* country's immigrants. He argued that all of the specifically anti-Asian measures—the Chinese Exclusion Act, the Gentlemen's Agreement, and the Asiatic Barred Zone (introduced in 1917) should be discarded.

Instead, he thought a variant of the quota idea could handle all strands of immigration policy. He offered two major refinements to the quota ideas that were being discussed at the time. During the period of discussion prior to the passage of the First Quota Act (1919), Gulick proposed first that the quota should be applied to all immigrants, not just Europeans, in a uniform way; and second, he proposed that the actual calculation should rest on a different kind of count than Congress was considering.

He first introduced his ideas on restriction before 1914, and returned to them when he testified at congressional hearings on the 1917 literacy bill and then again during the run up to the First Quota Act in 1920–1921. He was taken seriously in Washington, and his own plan had been sufficiently close to Dillingham's, for the senator and W. W. Husband to welcome Gulick's intervention.

The Japanese question was not getting the virulent attention in the 1920–1921 struggles that it would in 1924. Consequently, Gulick's insistence on including Asian groups prior to the passage of the First Quota Act did not seem altogether implausible, and Gulick's plan had a backer in Senator Sterling of South Dakota. Thus, for a time there were two quota bills before the Senate's Immigration Committee. Still, in the end Dillingham decided to drop the equal treatment of Asians from his own bill in order to gain more support.

When Gulick first presented his plan in 1914, its quotas were determined by "the number of aliens of any race," and race in turn was defined by "single mother tongue group." Thus he seems to have been building on the compromises over the 1910 census and the discussion of races as "designated" by mother tongue in the introduction to the Immigration Commission's *Reports* (1911; see Part I). Each country's allocation under the cap would be based on the number of foreign born currently in the United States *proven to have already assimilated.*

> Those born abroad who have, however, been here long enough to learn our language and our political life and to accept our ideals are the ones to exert wholesome influence on newcomers from their own native people. They constitute the natural channel by which the newcomers enter our life. The larger the number of naturalized citizens from any particular foreign people, the larger the number whom we can safely admit from that people.[1]

And he elaborates why the relevant category is "the single mother tongue group."

> An English Jew, though completely assimilated, would be of no particular aid in assimilating a Polish Jew. The central principle is the power of those already assimilated from a particular foreign group to serve as an assimilating agency for the later comers from that group. For this they must have belonged, in the not distant past, to the same social group and must still have ability to speak the same language. . . . The names and boundaries of such groups might be left either to the Bureau of Immigration or to the Department of Ethnology [of the Smithsonian].[2]

Gulick thus rests his proposal for a nondiscriminatory quota on an understanding of the sources of cohesion among immigrants. Indeed, in seeing the basis of cohesion in language, he was remarkably close to the explanations that Safford and McSweeney offered when first presenting the List of Races.

But at the hearing Gulick was asked, "Is there not a fundamental difference between the Asiatic and the Caucasian so that assimilation is impossible and intermarriage intolerable?" He made a critical distinction between the social and the biological: "Sociologically speaking Asiatics are as assimilable as any people." However, there was a proviso about interracial marriage. He testified, "The results of inter-marriage have not been sufficiently investigated to enable us to speak with certainty. . . . A commission on the problem of Race Assimilation should be established [composed of] . . . biologists, psychologists and sociologists. . . . If it is found that race inter-marriage is harmful . . . a national law should be enacted."[3] Gulick's thinking is remarkable for his refusal to treat Asian differently from European immigrants and for his thoughtfulness on what will encourage assimilation. And yet his concern about intermarriage is an important reminder of how a thoughtful observer, with a deep knowledge of Japanese language and society, remained uncertain about racial mingling.

Recall that not so many years before Gulick's testimony, Franz Boas had also expressed uncertainty about the nature of intergroup marriage. Both men insisted on carving out as much room as possible for social and cultural equality while still acknowledging that a democracy in which modern life has brought multiple races into contact might—might—need to take biological differences into account. Moreover, in his discussions, Boas had not restricted attention to intermarriage across the color line, and it appears that the same was true for Gulick's testimony in 1914. Gulick's questioner probably did have in mind intermarriage across the color line. But in his reply, Gulick nowhere made that distinction.

However, if this aspect of his thought reminds us of his distance from our own times, it is his insistence on the social that demonstrates how far his own formulations were from much congressional and popular discussion.

> This distinction between social and biological heredity and inheritance
> is of the highest importance in considering the problem of Race
> Assimilation. Civilization, mental habits of every kind, moral and
> religious ideas and ideals, with all the practices to which they lead, are
> matters of social, not of biological heredity and its processes. These are
> the factors which make a man to be the man he is. They form his mind,
> furnish the categories of his thinking, provide the motives and standards
> of his conduct, and in a word, determine a man's race, sociologically
> speaking. . . . These things can be imparted to individuals of any race
> when they are young and plastic. . . . The social assimilation of races,
> then, can proceed independently of their intermarriage. . . . Young
> Japanese and Chinese are as assimilable as are Italians or Russians.[4]

The substance of Gulick's proposals remained constant over the better part of the decade during which he urged them.[5] Yet his terminology did change in an interesting way, and that change seems to have been related to his evolving sense of the complexity of immigrant life. In 1920, when he revised his earlier proposals for a quota law, he no longer wrote of "a single mother tongue group." The new term he used was the "ethnic group." Moreover, he no longer cavalierly delegated group definition to the Bureau of Immigration or the Smithsonian. Instead, he envisioned a committee including the cabinet secretaries of labor, commerce, agriculture, and interior who would work out all of the details, including a classification scheme for ethnic groups. Also, he no longer assumed that group cohesion and assimilation could be understood only in terms of mother tongue. The board would define and interpret the use of the ethnic group term, "taking into account questions of race, mother tongue affiliation, nationality and such other relationships as tend to constitute group unity." Gulick, in short, meant to draw on nationality and mother tongue, the two categories that Census Director Durand had learned could replace the use of race in 1910 immigration questions—as well as on race itself. Gulick's adoption of the "ethnic group" term occasioned an intriguing colloquy during the 1921 Senate Immigration Committee Hearings, when W. W. Husband was testifying on the Senate's alternatives to the House bill calling for a total ban on immigration.

> *Mr. Husband.* There are two bills before the committee which propose to limit immigration to a percentage of immigrants already in the United States. First, Senator Sterling's bill [i.e., Gulick's proposal] which would fix the limit on the basis of ethnic groups. Second, Senator Dillingham's bill [i.e., Husband's own proposal] which would fix the limit on the basis of nationality. Either plan, I believe, would accomplish the result suggested [although the Dillingham bill would be easier to administer]. . . .
>
> *The Chairman [Senator Colt of Rhode Island].* Let me interrupt you a moment Mr. Husband. What is the distinction between "nationality" and "ethnic group."
>
> *Mr. Husband.* The "nationality" is the political status of an immigrant. The "ethnic group" is his race.
>
> *The Chairman.* Thank you.[6]

Nationality is indeed used here in the typical Anglo-American sense, which we discussed in Chapter 6. And whatever Gulick's refinements, Husband understood that there was an alternative to grouping immigrants in terms of country of origin (which is what "political status" meant in the vast majority of cases). It was to group them as he had learned to do at the U.S. Immigration Commission a decade earlier, by "race." In this interaction, there is no reason to think "race" meant only the biological transmission of group characteristics, nor that "ethnic group" excluded the idea of such transmission. But race was the term most people used and thought they understood.

Gulick proposed a quota that would apply in the same way to all immigrant origins and that rested on "proven assimilation" since the assimilated would influence the new arrivals. This principle allowed him to challenge the need for treating Asian immigrants differently from European immigrants. To introduce this approach did not oblige him to articulate the degree of difference among European races or between them and others. He could in fact bypass all questions about the realities of race differences. On social grounds alone, he could claim that his criterion of successful assimilation would severely restrict the Japanese as well as the southern and eastern Europeans. Still, he did take seriously the biological uncertainties about racial mixtures, or at least he left room for such concerns. Presumably he meant the mixture of any races, not merely Asian–white mixtures. Research might turn up a need for legal prohibition of such mixtures.

The Supreme Court on European versus Nonwhite Races, ### 1922–1923

In November 1922 and February 1923 the Supreme Court ruled on two cases involving the right of Asians to naturalize. At issue was a clause in a 1790 naturalization law that restricted eligibility to "free white persons." After the Civil War, this wording was expanded to also allow people of African descent to naturalize, and it explicitly confirmed that former slaves were citizens. Nevertheless, congressmen of the 1870s rejected the suggestion to drop the clause altogether. Keeping the clause meant that Asians immigrants could not become citizens. And so matters stood at the time of the 1922–1923 cases.

The first case concerned Takao Ozawa, a Japanese-born, longtime resident whom all sides agreed was a thoroughly assimilated and accomplished individual. He had completed study at an American high school and several years of university study at Berkeley. He spoke English at home and was a member of an American church. His children had also been educated in American schools. Ozawa pointed out that a 1906 reform of the naturalization law had not reaffirmed the 1790 restriction; consequently, he argued, the latter was no longer in force. Moreover, the 1790 clause had been meant to apply, he argued, only to the nonwhite groups that had concerned the founders—American Indians and African slaves.

However, the Supreme Court ruled that the 1906 reforms were meant to function *within* the limitation of the "free white persons" clause, and had the intention been otherwise, the 1906 legislation would have explicitly stated that it was meant to overturn a statute in place for more than a century. And while the 1790 restrictions may have been passed to deal with the immediate challenge of Indians and Africans, the wording also included other nonwhites.

The harder questions posed by *Ozawa* pertained to the definition of "white." But even the harder questions could not have seemed so very hard to the Court. The opinion was assigned to George Sutherland, the most junior member of the court. He had been appointed in early September, the case was heard in mid-October, and the unanimous opinion came down in mid-November. The Court agreed with a long line of precedents in lower courts that had argued that "white" in the statute was not meant to describe the color of an individual applicant but referred to membership in a race. And the definition of the white race in turn did not rest on ethnological science. Rather, courts had generally interpreted "'white person' . . . to indicate only a person of what is popularly known as the Caucasian race. . . . With [this] conclusion . . . we see no reason to differ. Moreover, that conclusion has become so well established . . . that we should not at this late day feel at liberty to disturb it." The opinion warned that reliance on the *popular* meaning of Caucasian "simplifies the problem, although it does not entirely dispose of it," because "border line cases" would no doubt continue to arise. Nevertheless, for Ozawa the implications were clear: he "is of a race which is not Caucasian."[7]

Three months later (January 1923), the Court also ruled against Bhagat Singh Thind. This immigrant had argued that as a high-cast Punjabi Hindu he was of Caucasian, or (according to similar classifications) Aryan origin. Since ethnology recognized one or both of these to be the origins of the white race, Thind claimed the right to naturalize. Again, the case was assigned to Sutherland and quickly decided unanimously against Thind. The new opinion added to *Ozawa* in noting that ethnological discoveries about prehistoric racial origins of Caucasians were irrelevant: "[The] popular, as distinguished from [the] scientific application [of the term 'Caucasian'] is of appreciably narrower scope.... [The] racial test ... must be applied to a group of living persons now possessing in common the requisite characteristics, not to groups of persons who are supposed to be or really are descended from some remote, common ancestor ... but who ... have ceased altogether to resemble one another.[8]

In an original and influential treatment of these two cases, legal scholar Ian Haney Lopez argued that the Court implicitly reversed its reasoning between the two cases; it seems to have applied a definition from *ethnological science* in *Ozawa* while rejecting it in favor of the *common understanding* of "white race" in *Thind*. However, legal historian Mark S. Weiner suggests an alternative interpretation, namely, that *Ozawa*, too, had not relied on ethnological science but used "Caucasian" only as "popularly known." The justices therefore thought of *Thind* as simply clarifying that the reliance on "Caucasian as popularly known" also ruled out an appeal to the science of ancient origins in order to understand what the term "Caucasian" meant. That term too was to be based on popular usage.[9] Weiner finds additional support for his interpretation in some features of Sutherland's broader approach to adjudication (e.g., it rested on natural law, and therefore the justice could not have subordinated it to empirical findings in ethnology). But even ignoring this point, the two opinions can easily enough be read as Weiner suggests. Moreover, two other considerations also support the consistency of *Ozawa* and *Thind*. First, the decision was unanimous and other justices, including Brandeis (who had a very different approach from Sutherland to basic principles of adjudication), concurred. Had the two decisions by the Court's most junior member really contradicted each other, other justices might well have suggested a revision. Second, the narrow time frame in which the two cases came up and were decided strongly suggests that all the justices (and certainly Sutherland) would have known at the time they ruled on *Ozawa* that they would immediately have to face a claim resting on ethnological science in

Thind. Could they really have ruled in the first case without considering the implications for the second?

But it is less the consistency of the Court's approach in these two naturalization cases of 1922–1923 that is relevant here than the consistencies and contrasts between the Court's approach and that of the legislative branch behavior in dealing with the two Quota Acts of 1921 and 1924. The Court heard and ruled on both *Ozawa* and *Thind* midway between the congressional debates on the First and Second Quota Acts (1921 and 1924). And although congressmen occasionally expressed some awareness of the decisions upholding the ban on Asian naturalization, the judicial and legislative dramas seem to have had little or no direct impact on each other.

And yet the Supreme Court ruling and the 1924 quota legislation both rest on the understanding of racial difference. One obvious similarity is the Court's insistence that the rulings involved no claim about racial *superiority,* only about racial *difference. Ozawa:* "Of course there is not implied—either in the legislation or in our interpretation of it—any suggestion of individual unworthiness or racial inferiority. These considerations are in no manner involved."[10] *Thind:* "It is very far from our thought to suggest the slightest question of racial superiority or inferiority. What we suggest is merely racial difference."[11]

These formulations are identical to a stock expression that was common in the House and Senate rhetoric during the 1924 debates on restriction. Our first reaction might be to dismiss the rhetoric of congressmen as a nearly transparent lie that covers bigotry—even as we accord considerable respect to the pronouncements of the elevated jurists. It was not merely Sutherland, but also Brandeis, Holmes, and Taft who were among those who signed this opinion. But surely such a distinction is too simple. In the first place, some of those jurists had been politicians. These notably included the chief justice (former president Taft) and the decision's author, Sutherland. Indeed, years before Sutherland joined the Court, he had been elected to Congress, and at that time he stated that one important priority for him would be the extension of the Chinese Exclusion Act: "We already have one race problem in the South with the negroes, and to open our doors to the unrestricted immigration of Mongolians would be to invite another and more serious race problem in the West."[12] Such rhetoric was hardly rare; the point is that the argument was not strictly inconsistent with Justice Sutherland's opinions two decades later.

That rhetoric might have been entirely genuine in some cases, but surely the claims were a matter of self-delusion for other writers and speakers, and an altogether cynical lie for still others. We usually cannot, and need not, resolve the ambiguity. But the evidence of this case helps one appreciate that the branch of government from which the pronouncement came and the politician's greater need to consider low motives are inadequate foundations for historical interpretation.

The most interesting contrast is in the approach of Court and Congress to the two kinds of racial distinctions: among Europeans and between them and others. A seemingly tangential section of the *Thind* decision compared the American experience with Asian and European immigrants. First, that section reviews the history of growing distinctions *among white people* since the time the naturalization policy was first passed in 1790.

> The immigration of [the framers' time] was almost exclusively from the British Isles and Northwestern Europe. . . . It was these immigrants— bone of their bone and flesh of their flesh—and their kind whom they must have had affirmatively in mind. The succeeding years brought immigrants from Eastern, Southern and Middle Europe, among them the Slavs and the dark-eyed, swarthy people of Alpine and Mediterranean stock, and these were received as unquestionably akin to those already here and readily amalgamated with them. It was the descendants of these, and other immigrants of like origin, who constituted the white population of the country when § 2169, reenacting the naturalization test of 1790, was adopted; and there is no reason to doubt, with like intent and meaning.[13]

The wording is remarkable for insisting that *all* Europeans were considered white—including (by the time the statute was reenacted) the new immigrants from "Eastern, Southern and Middle Europe, among them Slavs and the dark-eyed swarthy people of Alpine and Mediterranean stock." This phrasing could hardly fail to call to mind the tripartite division of European races (Nordic, Alpine, and Mediterranean) on which Ripley and Madison Grant had based so much. Likewise, both Quota Acts distinguished among immigrants from different parts of Europe, while the Court emphasized that despite these distinctions all Europeans "were received as unquestionably akin . . . and readily amalgamated."

A second passage from this section of *Thind* places more emphasis on the social realities of the Court's own time, and stresses at greater length that all Europeans are easily assimilable.

> It is a matter of familiar observation and knowledge that the physical group characteristics of the Hindus render them readily distinguishable from the various groups of persons in this country commonly recognized as white. The children of English, French, German, Italian, Scandinavian, and other Europe parentage, quickly merge into the mass of our population and lose the distinctive hallmarks of their European origin. On the other hand, it cannot be doubted that the children born in this country of Hindu parents would retain indefinitely the clear evidence of their ancestry. . . . [This difference in "physical group characteristics"] is of such character and extent that the great body of our people instinctively recognize it and reject the thought of assimilation.[14]

"The children" of all European immigrants "quickly merge into the mass of our population and lose the distinctive hallmarks of their European origin." Here again is a striking assertion about assimilation at a time that so many congressmen were justifying the Quota Acts precisely on the grounds that this statement was false—that some Europeans were very difficult to assimilate and that unless their numbers were radically curtailed, the republic would be in danger.

Is it possible that the Court meant to send a message to Congress or to the electorate more broadly, a message that the quotas on Europeans were unreasonable? This hypothesis is unlikely, not least because assertions that went so far beyond the specifics of the case would never have received the justices' unanimous support. A much simpler interpretation is that the wording is a variant of the phenomenon that we already observed in the congressional debate itself. Apparently, the Court meant to stress that even in the face of legislation distinguishing between Nordic, Alpine, and Mediterranean immigrants, these differences were minor when compared to American perceptions of difference between white and nonwhite races.

But if this was the case, the Court was making its point about the importance of white–nonwhite divisions by using the very terms and rhetoric that restrictionists in Congress and the press were using to limit white immigration by race: Nordic / Alpine / Mediterranean, swarthy, Italian. By contrast, when congressmen spoke of excluding Asian immigrants, they did so by contrasting them to an undifferentiated category of whites. Sutherland's opinion is thus notably more confrontational: it explicitly calls attention to divisions among whites and then dismisses these as vastly less important than the division between Asians and whites in the American experience of assimilation. That he meant to do any more than that—that he meant to mock the arguments about undesired Europeans—seems unlikely, and more unlikely still that the other justices would have allowed him to do so. That Sutherland had some personal experience in the Western-state resistance to Asian immigration may have made him more willing to speak explicitly about this difference in race differences. But even if so, his Eastern-bred colleagues on the Court all voted for the opinion. In *Thind*, two racial usages usually kept discrete operated together. Yet that is all that happened here: there was an unusual recognition of the two usages, but not an elaboration or critique.

More Restriction Needed: Taking on the Mexican Race, to 1930

John Higham ends his classic history of nativism, race, and immigration restriction in 1924, with the passage of the National Origins Act. The great political energy to restrict immigration, he argued, had ended with the passage of the act, as did a century of large-scale European immigration. Nevertheless, the House Immigration Committee actually continued its energetic efforts under Albert Johnson through the 1920s and into the first year of the Great Depression. If Johnson's committee had no great additional restrictionist victory, it was not for want of trying. Moreover, as more recent historians have made clear, Higham's focus almost exclusively on the movements against *European* immigrations did little to link or compare those movements to restrict non-Europeans. When the historical perspective on restriction is expanded, Johnson's efforts of the later 1920s fit seamlessly with his earlier concerns about undesirable arrivals. He turned after 1924 to migrations across the Rio Grande. He had tried to confront those in the early 1920s too, but had failed. Now he attempted to complete that work.[15]

Johnson and his committee would also have reduced European quotas further after 1924. But the gigantic reductions of the 1924 quotas meant that any additional action could not generate much interest. The same was true for East Asian immigration, since the Asian Barred Zone had excluded all but the Japanese since 1917, and the 1924 Act extended the exclusion to that last group.[16] But Western Hemisphere immigration, especially across the Mexican–U.S. border, was another matter. This "back door" migration stream had been left untouched in the 1924 struggles, and so Johnson's committee sought to generate interest in closing the back door during the half-dozen years that followed the National Origins Act. Over the years, his committee held several hearings on immigration from south of the border.

The social and racial arguments against this immigration are familiar from the earlier debates about the undesirable Europeans and Asians. In social terms, Mexicans were unskilled workers and uneducated migrants who were not needed and threatened to lower wages for American workers; moreover, their poverty was bound to cause social problems in the American Southwest. In racial terms, this group would prove unassimilable. Unlike the Anglo-Saxons, Mexicans had no experience of self-government and lacked other virtues of the old American racial stock. In addition, the Mexican people were of mixed white and nonwhite origins— descended partly from the Spanish arrivals in the New World, but mostly from the native peoples of the region. Indeed, the committee heard several influential witnesses on this last point, not least of whom was the eugenicist Harry Laughlin.

The House Immigration Committee's emphasis on Mexican multiraciality served two purposes. First, nonwhite origins in themselves were undesirable and mixtures of white and nonwhite were as well. Moreover, the constitutional prerequisites for naturalization could be marshaled to keep undesirable people out. Under the 1790 naturalization statute and its successors, the native peoples of Mexico (who were neither white nor African) could not naturalize. And under the terms of the 1924 National Origins Act, those who could not be naturalized were barred from immigration as well. Accordingly, the restrictionists hoped that if the *whiteness* of the Mexican immigrants could be challenged, so too could their immigration, perhaps even without a major new legislative struggle.

But other factors weakened this strategy. Above all, the Treaty of Guadalupe Hidalgo, which ended the U.S.-Mexican War, had guaranteed full citizenship to Mexicans living in the lands the United States acquired. Moreover, a half-century later, a U.S. Federal District Court in Texas had reaffirmed the point, applying it to a Mexican immigrant rather than only to Mexican residents of the conquered area at the time of the treaty (*In re Rodriguez*, 1897). Indeed, the federal court ruling had explicitly stated that the whiteness issue was irrelevant in the case of the Mexicans: "Whatever may be the status of the applicant [Rodriguez] viewed solely from the standpoint of the ethnologist, he is embraced within the spirit and intent of our laws upon naturalization." When first turning to the Mexicans, Albert Johnson and his colleagues in the House may not have known about the 1897 case. Alternatively, they may have felt that there was room for adjustment. In particular, they thought that by bringing attention to the mixed Spanish and American Indian origins of the Mexican population the whiteness issue might be reopened, for some or all Mexicans.

Against this background, consider now the U.S. Census Bureau revision to the race question introduced for the 1930 census. The census listed a new race category: Mexican. The instructions explained the addition:

> *Mexicans.* Practically all Mexican laborers are of a racial mixture difficult to classify, though usually well recognized in the localities where they are found. In order to obtain separate figures for this racial group, it has been decided that all persons born in Mexico, or having parents born in Mexico, who are not definitely white, Negro, Indian, Chinese, or Japanese, should be returned as Mexican.

The Mexican race instruction was one of four paragraphs of instructions that dealt with individuals of mixed race.[17] The intent was to reserve the white category for those whose ancestry was overwhelmingly white. The Mexican instruction was no exception. But the interest in classifying mixed-race people had never before resulted in classifying Mexicans as a distinct race. How did the Census Bureau come to add this "Mexican race" category? We can confidently surmise that it emerged as a result of the discussions about restricting Mexican immigration and the connection of that issue to racial status.

We are forced to rely on surmises such as these about the appearance of the new "Mexican race" category because historians have failed to unearth any direct paper trail that explains why it appeared in that year.[18] Nevertheless, one piece of new evidence can be offered in support of this surmise. In 1928, Albert Johnson arranged to join the House Census Committee. During this term, he had only two committee assignments: membership on the Census Committee and chairmanship of the Immigration Committee. It stands to reason that he would have pushed for the Mexican race category, and that his voice would have been very consequential. He was not merely a senior member of the majority party. He was also the most important and knowledgeable member of the House on matters of immigration, had served on the Immigration Committee continuously since 1912, and had shepherded both Quota Acts to passage. Johnson had been holding hearings on restricting Latin American immigration, and the racial makeup of the Mexican population was central to his approach.

We can be sure that by 1929 Johnson knew all about the *Rodriguez* decision. In February of that year, Secretary of Labor James J. Davis (himself a vocal restrictionist) sent Johnson a revealing letter marked "personal." Clearly, they had speculated about the issues of Mexican blood for a time.

> In our recent discussion of the various proposals that have been made with a view to amending the immigration Act of 1924 with respect to immigration from the New World countries, the natives of which are now exempt from quota limitations, you said that you had been asked to consider whether or not the provisions of that Act relating to the exclusion of persons ineligible to citizenship would be applicable to any part of the present immigration of Mexicans. This inquiry has also come to the Department [of Labor] from time to time and because of your interest I asked the Solicitor of the Department of Labor to advise me with regard to the matter.

Davis then quotes in full the solicitor's opinion, which covered five single-spaced pages. The solicitor considered the argument that Mexicans "are neither white persons nor Africans nor of African descent" (the acceptable categories under the statute in 1870). If this were so, they would not be "eligible to American citizenship" and hence could be excluded from immigration. But the solicitor rejected the final step of this argument about ineligibility for citizenship, relying heavily on the *Rodriguez* case. He therefore concluded that "native Mexicans cannot be denied permanent admission to the United States because of their ethnological status as a race."

He also added an intriguing observation to the reliance on *Rodriguez*.

> The Mexican people are of such a mixed stock, and individuals have such a limited knowledge of their racial composition that it would be impossible for the most learned and experienced ethnologist or anthropologist to classify or determine their racial origin. Thus making an effort to exclude them from admission or citizenship because of their racial status is practically impossible.

Here the solicitor seemed to put aside the *Rodriguez* decision and focus only on ethnology. *Some* Mexicans were predominantly white, but which ones? In a case of so much mixing, it would be impossible to rely on ethnological considerations.

By contrast, Johnson may well have thought that Congress could be convinced to put the onus of proof on the individual: could the immigrant prove that he or she was in fact primarily of white descent? And indeed, the position of the 1930 census instructions (quoted earlier) stressed that an individual is white only when the proportion of white origins is overwhelming. Moreover, Johnson may have thought the issue could be resolved at the level of the group, not the level of the individual. A population so mixed over so many generations might approximate a distinct race of its own. The closing lines of Secretary Davis's letter seem to point in that direction, for he mentioned that "Last year, 57,765 immigrant aliens of the Mexican race" were admitted. And it is worth recalling that the Bureau of Immigration's List of Races and Peoples was still referring to a "Mexican race." In any case, Johnson may have felt it was worth soldiering on with his effort to classify Mexicans as a distinct race despite Davis's letter, or perhaps he had already applied whatever pressure he could muster on the House Census Committee.

In the end, these efforts to restrict or terminate Mexican immigration in the late 1920s failed (although they did lead to increased policing along the southern border). The 1930 census was only a first step toward what would have been needed, and there could be no follow-up. Public concern over immigration had plummeted after the passage of the 1924 act. Then, with the coming of Depression, Democrats gained control of the House in 1930. Johnson himself lost the chairmanship of the House Immigration Committee in 1930—to the New York City defender of the immigrant, Democrat Samuel Dickstein. In 1932, his own Washington State electoral district finally rejected Johnson, ending his congressional career.

On the broad issue of restricting Mexican immigration, the majority of large farm employers in the Southwest apparently remained consistently opposed to it, probably more so than factory employers in the North had been when they considered immigration policy for southern and eastern Europeans between 1918 and 1924. Some historians maintain that these manufacturers had come to believe that long-run transformations reduced their industries' needs for unskilled workers. Other historians seem to assume that manufacturers' willingness to accept restriction simply fluctuated inversely with the business cycle: when demand was down, manufacturers gave more heed to the cultural concerns that they shared with so many other well-off Americans. It is true that even in Texas, some large employers reached the conclusion that they could do without the Mexican immigrant workers and that it was important to end the social and racial threats the continuation of such immigration created. Indeed, Texas Congressman Box on Johnson's committee hewed to this line and invited farm employers of the same persuasion to testify. But other Texas employers, and apparently the great majority of employers from California, argued that the immigrants were necessary for their economic survival.[19]

In the early 1930s Mexican American defense groups as well as the Mexican government protested the racial designation of Mexicans on the U.S. census, insisting that they be classified (as before) as white. President Franklin Roosevelt's State Department took the Mexican government's objections seriously—especially as international tensions in Europe and Asia rose in the 1930s. By comparison, in 1924 when the State Department's concerns about offending the Japanese Empire had failed to stem the movement for regularizing exclusion of its subjects, not only was that target immigrant population smaller and politically weaker, but State was up against Congress itself at the peak of its restrictionism. Congress then asserted that the executive branch was meddling. By contrast, rolling back a census race category could be handled by the executive branch with little congressional opposition, particularly since it had been added just before FDR's supporters arrived in Congress.

The struggle around the "Mexican race" category in the 1930 census also turned out quite differently from the 1910 struggle in which the U.S. Immigration Commission strongly urged the addition of a question that would classify people according to categories in the List of Races and Peoples. In the Mexican race episode, a racial category was added to the existing census question. But given the array of forces at work, the classification was swept away well before the next decennial census. If it had been meant to stimulate legislation to restrict immigration of Mexicans (on the basis of a nonwhite status), it failed. By contrast, the 1910 episode involving the List of Races and Peoples was rather more public and centered on congressional committees. That public attention mattered; it led to the American Jewish Committee doing everything it could to marshal protest. And then the prospect of simply *rejecting* what the Immigration Commission was suggesting led to counterprotests by the Slavic groups. In this context the Census Bureau was obliged to find a compromise. That compromise kept the bureau away from racializing European groups directly as it would do in 1930 with the Mexicans. But it accomplished much of the data collection that the Immigration Commission had wanted through the new mother-tongue question. And the mother-tongue data were indeed available over the subsequent decade and a half of increasing restrictionist feeling. In one sense, then, the 1930 episode revealed that the Census Bureau could be channeled toward expanding racialization, if not for Europeans as it almost was in 1910, then at least toward Mexicans. Albert Johnson's place on the House Census Committee at the time must have been a strong stimulus to this departure, but recent research by Brian Gratton and Emily Merchant also found relevant discussions among bureau personnel.[20] Nevertheless, the changing political context after 1930 ensured that the Mexican race episode at the Census Bureau did not have long-lasting, tangible effects. By contrast, the 1910 episode over distinguishing European races in the enumeration involved a milder action in the end (the addition of the mother-tongue question), and one that imposed no particular stigma, as the bureau's short-term racialization of the Mexicans probably did. On the other hand, the data collected with the mother-tongue question may have had more impact on subsequent restriction than did the Mexican race question in its time.

The Bureau of Immigration had removed "Mexican" from the List of Races and Peoples in mid-1937. And the Census Bureau had removed the 1930 Mexican race category before the 1940 census. This time federal officials, far from going their separate ways about racial classification, as they had in 1910, channeled the two classifications in the same direction. And this unity of action across the agencies probably attests to the role of international relations at least as much as to the Mexican American defense groups' protests. Mexicans would henceforth be classified on the List as "other white."

PART THREE

The Ethnic Group: Formulation and Diffusion of an American Concept, to 1964

CHAPTER 9

From "Race" to "Ethnic Group"

Organizing Concepts in American Studies of Immigrants, to 1964

PART III TRACES THE EMERGENCE of thinking about "ethnic group" and "ethnicity" from the end of the nineteenth century to the moment just prior to the end of the 1960s when these terms became household words. The present chapter deals with the shifting use of terms and meanings among social scientists and the intellectual efforts to confront the related tension between ethnic persistence and assimilation. The next chapter deals with the limited diffusion of the new ideas beyond a circle of social scientists in two case studies from the late 1940s and early 1950s.

The meaning of ethnicity that had emerged by the 1960s has itself undergone further modifications in the half century since then. These changes include, for example, the emphasis on boundaries rather than on cultural differences between groups. The discussion of group persistence versus assimilation has evolved as well—for example, in specifying structural factors that make group persistence so useful for immigrants and their children and in illuminating how some form of ethnic identification tends to persist through generations. Also, as the concepts of ethnicity and assimilation have been applied to new immigrant groups who arrived since the Hart-Celler Act (1965) and on the African American experience since the civil rights era, meanings were bound to shift somewhat.[1]

Nevertheless, these shifts in conception and research agendas since the 1960s build on basics that had themselves emerged between 1900 and 1960.

The common view is that in the course of those six decades interpretation of group differences turned away from biology and toward culture and social structure. Some of these earlier interpretations had given pride of place to biological transmission, while others had cavalierly tossed together biological and sociocultural transmissions. This older way of thinking was replaced by a resolute understanding that ethnic groupings are solely products of social and cultural dynamics. The shift away from biological determinism, in turn, transformed the meaning of assimilation as well. It became much harder to believe that groups could not eventually assimilate once a belief in biological transmission of a group's mental traits—such as intelligence, self-control, or assertiveness—was swept away. So too, intermarriage might remain the most important measure of assimilative tendencies, but no longer because of the physical amalgamation of different stocks.

In the broadest sense, then, the intellectual developments discussed in this chapter are about the shift from biological to sociocultural analysis and from reliance on the "race" to "ethnic group" term. However, this summary would be woefully incomplete and misleading. Both race and ethnic group were terms already in use in the late nineteenth century. Both terms at that time allowed for a combination of sociocultural as well as biological transmissions of mental traits. The shift that came over the first half of the twentieth century came gradually and with varying degrees of self-consciousness about both the terms and their meanings. In addition, a number of other terms came into play, particularly "nationality," "national origin," and "minority," but all of these were also legacies of earlier eras. None of them would have been particularly better or worse than "ethnic group" in helping social scientists abandon biological explanations. These alternative terms probably lost out to "ethnic group" in the end because they involved other ambiguities. Still, through the 1940s, American sociologists generally moved unselfconsciously between the terms "nationality" and "ethnic group" and some continued to add race as well.

Two kinds of intellectual influences also need to be reevaluated in connection with the shift to "ethnic group." First, when natural scientists began condemning the use of the race term in the late 1930s, they may have helped attract attention to the ethnic group term. But they were actually arguing that "ethnic group" could be used to convey a clear-cut *bio-*

logical meaning whereas race was hopelessly overused, conveying both cultural and biological meanings. Second, the contribution of Max Weber in sharpening the definition of the ethnic group, so often cited today, seems to have entered American social science only *after* the usage of ethnicity as a purely social-cultural reality was already well established.

Finally, the shift from race to ethnicity did *not* leave nonwhites behind. The scope of the ethnic group term was broad enough to routinely include American racial differences based on skin color. True, discussions typically acknowledged the vast influence of skin color in creating the highest boundaries between groups and recognized that these distinctions would last the longest, and perhaps indefinitely. But at the same time, such racial groups were conceived to be part of the continuum of ethnic groups. American blacks, in particular, were typically included among the American ethnic groups, from 1900 to the 1960s. Likewise, no analytic distinction divorced religion from ethnicity. Rather, for some ethnic groups, religion was the fundamental unifying feature. The Jews were often mentioned as an example. But in their case, the emphasis on other elements such as language was also important (at least for the large number of Jews who had come from eastern Europe). But other examples of ethnic groups defined unambiguously by religious cohesion could be given on occasion: Quakers and Mennonites, for example.

While the first theme of this chapter concerns the shift from race to ethnicity, the second explores how American social scientists dealt with the tensions between ethnic group persistence and assimilation. In the early part of the twentieth century, mass immigration (and the reliance on ideas of biological determinism) ensured that the loudest discussion would be about how well and how fully the republic would succeed in absorbing such a diverse multitude. But even during that early period Israel Zangwill, Horace Kallen, and I. B. Berkson were among those who took up a different anxiety: What hope was there for ethnic survival in later generations? Indeed, Berkson, a name generally unknown today, provided the typology of possible assimilation scenarios still familiar to social scientists from its presentation in Michael Gordon's immensely influential *Assimilation in American Life* (1964): Anglo-conformity, the melting pot, and cultural pluralism. Then, a dozen years after the end of mass immigration, Marcus Lee Hansen presented a clear-eyed, balanced, and eloquent statement on the possibilities and limitations of ethnic life through the generations and their meaning for American culture. It is remembered today, if at all, only crudely through the reference to one of his observations: the third generation seeks to remember what the second tried to forget. It merits a closer look.

But *why* did these authors believe that ethnic persistence would not win out? One good reason was the empirical record: with the exception of African Americans and other nonwhites, the record showed that over the course of two or three generations, American social dynamics provided the descendants of the Irish, Germans, and Scandinavians with a modicum of economic mobility as well as attendant sociocultural changes such as language loss, geographical mobility, and eventually intermarriage with descendants of earlier European arrivals. Moreover, the more recent immigrant groups from southern and eastern Europe, for all the differences in their experiences, did seem to be following along similar lines at least as far one might judge from the experiences of the immigrants' children. This empirical record, in turn, seemed to be expected by social theories. Modern economies (or even more broadly, modern life), especially in relatively free societies, seemed to move away from distant group origins and toward universalist identifications based on attained socioeconomic positions—or perhaps to class struggles based on those positions. Variant theories emphasized America's particular history—including not least its settlement by a diversity of peoples and its political system that eventually incorporated them as equals—as well as ample land and resources.[2]

And yet it will be critical to appreciate that already in the 1950s several authors, Will Herberg most famously, traced the persistence of particularistic loyalties. For the foreseeable future, ethnic groups might only be melding into somewhat broader communities—from a single to a triple melting pot of Protestant, Catholic, and Jew. Then in 1963 Nathan Glazer and Daniel Moynihan published *Beyond the Melting Pot.* Here was a strong caution about the force of universalist tendencies to dissolve ethnic communities—at least in their major urban centers and at least for the then-foreseeable future. Moreover, Glazer and Moynihan found an *explanation* for the ethnic group persistence in the fact that class, neighborhood, and politics reinforced ethnicity, so that far from a group held together only by traditional cultural outlooks, an ethnic group was *an interest group.*

By the mid-1960s, the ethnic group and ethnicity were well-established terms, at least among a subfield of American social scientists. Early in his pathbreaking *Beyond Ethnicity* (1986), Werner Sollors traced the history of the new term "ethnicity." As late as the early 1970s, Sollors points out, scholars reported seeking the origin and definition of the term in their dictionaries. Indeed, Sollors himself found the first usage of the noun form, "ethnicity," in Lloyd Warner's study of Newburyport, Massachusetts, in 1941: Warner and his coauthor had written that "the concept of ethnicity is not based simply on place of birth." Sollors recounts the eureka moment: "There was the word! . . . This was the Kunta Kinte of ethnicity scholarship!"[3] We will revisit Warner's usage and its significance shortly, but as late as the mid-1960s, neither "ethnic group" nor "ethnicity" were household terms. The diverse mobilizations during and after the civil rights era, first and foremost by African Americans, then also by Hispanics, Asians, American Indians, and finally white ethnics, were probably the most important factor in creating a wider recognition of ethnicity in the late 1960s and early 1970s. The descendants of immigrants as well as other minorities, it now seemed, might not assimilate as quickly as had been expected, if ever.[4]

The extent to which thinking at the Census Bureau was influenced by this new social science emphasis on ethnic persistence—rather than merely by ethno-racial advocacy groups—requires more research. But it is at least a fitting coincidence that (as discussed in Chapter 11) the bureau first tested a new question in 1969 that was meant to trace all respondents' ethno-racial origins back in time—farther back than their own and their parents' birthplaces. Indeed, like the race question, this new question about origins ignored how many generations of ancestors had been living in America.

Terms and Meanings Evolve, Not Necessarily Together

DRAWING ON ETHNOLOGY

The term "ethnic group" was by no means unfamiliar in the nineteenth and early twentieth centuries, at least among readers who delved into topics of ethnology or came across references to such topics, for example, in explanations of the List of Races and Peoples. However, this older term carried a very different meaning from the one that became common in America by the late 1960s.

In order to appreciate the extent to which the meaning of the term had changed, consider the later meaning, as it is in use in the early twenty-first century. Textbooks in the social sciences today inform the reader that an ethnic group is made up of members who believe themselves to have a common origin and derive some meaning for their lives from that belief.[5] The common origin of the group may be regarded as historically true or altogether mythical. The consciousness of belonging is key: it can be relatively weak or strong at a given moment, changing over time. But absent that consciousness—because it has not yet formed or because it has wholly disappeared—it is hard to understand the population as an ethnic group. The ties are likely to be reinforced by other social characteristics: class and occupational concentrations, religion, neighborhood, associations, prejudice of others against the group, or by group members against non-members. Group loyalties typically exist at some level of strength for several generations. The concept conveys no hint of biological transmission of mental traits. Biology might relate to this concept of ethnicity in reproducing physical characteristics that can make members of a particular ethnic group more recognizable to each other or to others in the society. Skin color is the prime example in the American context, but other features—blond hair, for example—may play a similar role. A contemporary definition of ethnicity would allow for, not require, even this reduced role for biology. Biological relationships, of course, also might be related to an ethnic group insofar as many or most of its members did in fact (and not merely in myth) descend from a common group of ancestors. But even if the group members do share such genealogical connections, it is the belief in their existence and importance rather than the actual biological transmission of anything, much less particular mental traits, that is relevant to the definition.

The precise relationship between ethnicity and race in contemporary American social science is often uncertain. For example, in some discussions, the importance of racialization is to be found in distinctive boundaries imposed by a particular society. These boundaries are more rigid than those among ethnic groups. In such usage, races might be best defined as a subset of all ethnic groups. But alternatively, an individual race might be conceived to include multiple ethnic groups. At a minimum, we might consider race and ethnic group as overlapping concepts, sharing some features and not others.

We have already encountered the nineteenth-century usage of "ethnic group" in Chapter 1. The Greek root *ethnos*—people or nation or race—was the basis for numerous terms used in the study of human groups. In particular, since at least the eighteenth century, ethnology (and then also ethnography) described very broad fields of study with which anthropology has also been associated. One such field focused on what were considered "early" or "primitive" human types and communities across the globe. Comparisons among communities were meant to show both universal qualities held in all, and important differences from one to another. Frequently enough, the ancient or primitive groupings were described as "ethnic" groups. What held such a grouping together might be biological characteristics, social arrangements, or cultural productions, in any combination. And so the "ethnic group" term inherited from the nineteenth century bore a certain similarity to "nationality" in its second sense, as peoplehood. However, "ethnic group" also could call to mind a membership defined by the ethnologist and *not* necessarily found in the consciousness of group members, or in language. And in ethnology it was likely to refer to more ancient states of humanity than the "nation" that Johann Gottfried Herder had popularized.

In 1890, Daniel G. Brinton, an ethnologist at the University of Pennsylvania, published *Races and Peoples: Lectures on the Science of Ethnography* (1890).[6] Brinton explained at the outset of the book that the aim of his science "is to study the differences, physical and mental, between men in masses, and ascertain which of these differences are least variable and hence of most value in classifying the human species into its several natural varieties or types."[7] Chapter 1 covered "The Physical Elements" and Chapter 2 "The Psychical Elements." The latter included various emotions and instincts as well as language, religion, and arts. Chapter 3 took up "The Beginnings and Subdivisions of Races."[8] Among these subdivisions were branches, stocks, groups, peoples, tribes, and nations. But Brinton also recognized other terms, particularly "*Ethnos*, with its adjective ethnic . . . I know of no better word for it in English than a people, as I have already explained this word,—one of the elements of a stock all of whose members there is reason to believe, have a demonstrable relationship. Thus we should speak of the Aryan *stock,* made up of the Latin, Greek, Celtic and other *peoples.* The relationship among members of a *people* is closer than that between the members of a *Stock.*"[9]

Numerous authors drew from ethnology broad meanings of "ethnic group" in order to refer to immigrant peoples in America. Much more often than not, it appears that these authors felt no need to define the term. They were not in fact using a term in a new way, but rather were drawing on the usages already mentioned above. And in reference to immigrants to America in particular, they were much more likely to refer to the immigrants or their children and not to later-generation descendants (except perhaps to opine about eventual assimilation or amalgamation and its effects on the American population).

Under the cover of this "ethnic group" term, meanings changed over time, well before it seemed necessary to point out their implications. A brief look at four scholars illustrates this trend. The four publications examined here appeared in 1903, 1912, 1921, and 1931. The first two writers are unknown today, and the next two have the status of respected if rarely read pathbreakers in the study of American ethnic groups. These four writers took the term "ethnic group" for granted because it was a term in common use that had been inherited from the nineteenth century. Thus these authors did not think they were breaking new ground by using it. Yet to some extent they were increasing its applicability to sociocultural rather than physiological differences across human populations. Still, while considering the sociocultural, each of these four authors also gave at least a nod to the biological meanings of the old "ethnic" term. Nor was the move from physiological to sociocultural emphases particularly linear; it seems more pronounced in the 1903 than the 1912 and in the 1921 than in the 1931 work.

When Frederick A. Bushee published *Ethnic Factors in the Population of Boston* (1903), his work came with an enthusiastic introduction by William Z. Ripley, who had published *The Races of Europe* only four years earlier. Ripley saw Bushee's new work as a "study of racial phenomena." He stressed Bushee's data on differences in vital statistics and in degeneration (criminality, defectiveness, and dependency) across the "ethnic stocks" of Boston. The eventual goal of such comparisons was "to strip off the overlaying and confusing facts of social environment, laying bare the phenomenon of race alone." Bushee himself wrote that his purpose was "to point out various desirable and undesirable qualities" of Boston's "various ethnic groups," and in connection with the undesirable, he indeed devoted much attention to "degeneration."[10] Yet far from "laying bare the phenomenon of race alone," as Ripley had it, Bushee seems to have focused on just what Ripley wanted to strip away. Bushee explained how *social* conditions in the home country and in Boston led to the observed rates. In his hands, the term "ethnic group" generally referred to nothing more specific than an immigrant population from a particular country of origin. Moreover, Bushee regularly replaced the "ethnic group" term with "nationality," at least when referring to European immigrants. Bushee also included blacks in his usage of "ethnic group," yet when he did so, the alternative term he applied was more likely to be "race" than "nationality." He also sought to trace the extent to which ethnic group traits persisted into the later generations of immigrant descendants. Not surprisingly, however, their fate was a relatively minor theme in a work published in 1903, when new immigrants, who were arriving daily, were the preoccupation.

About a decade after Bushee's monograph, A. E. Jenks, a professor of sociology at the University of Minnesota, published "Ethnic Census in Minneapolis" in the *American Journal of Sociology*. The paper establishes early on that "the term 'race' we cannot wisely use here, so I use the word 'people' for such groups of persons as are known by the name of Swede, Irish, Pole, etc."[11] In contrast with this self-awareness, Jenks never defined the term "ethnic" in his paper, perhaps seeing it as a broad term covering historical origins. In any case, his exposition tells us something about how he thought about these groups. The purpose of his ethnic census was to study rates of "ethnic amalgamation," a process competing with "ethnic cohesion." There are two sorts of forces at work in determining the rates of amalgamation and cohesion: "cultural factors" and "hereditary factors." The hereditary factors influenced behavior over generations: "Even after direct trace of one's ethnic descent is lost, there is frequently a hereditary residue remaining with the individual among an otherwise amalgamated people—which residue has lasted as hereditary factors from one or other or both of the original ancestral people before amalgamation began."[12] Jenks explains the relative fecundity of individuals resulting from such "amalgamation" by these hereditary residues; he simply does not consider any competing cultural explanations. Thus the paper's conclusion is titled "Law of Fecundity for

Certain Peoples," and reads in its entirety: "The Irish blood tends to increase fecundity and Scandinavian blood tends to decrease fecundity of other peoples in amalgamation."[13] It is hard to believe that Jenks meant blood in a metaphoric sense here, or at any rate a metaphor for nonbiological processes. He had already distinguished hereditary from cultural factors and described how the former could survive "even after direct trace of one's ethnic descent is lost." Thus the cultural elements can be part of the study of ethnic groups, but for Jenks, the ethnic concept remained heavily freighted with biological characteristics of peoples.

Julius Drachsler had come to the United States with his parents from east-central Europe at the age of thirteen. He grew up in New York City, attending public schools and the City College of New York. Active in Jewish social work and social research, he also completed a Columbia University PhD in sociology in 1921. The same year, he published his doctoral dissertation, a classic empirical study of intermarriage in New York City, with a focus on the patterns of the first and second generations. A year earlier, he had published *Democracy and Assimilation: The Blending of Immigrant Heritages in America*. This was a more reflective, less empirical volume than the dissertation, surveying a good deal of writing on the topics in the title. He referred to the "blending" of the title as "ethnic fusion," most critically through intermarriage. But, he contended, even without the biological fusion resulting from intermarriages, cultural assimilation might proceed quite far.[14] In fact, for Drachsler the real significance of the "ethnic group" was in sociocultural dynamics. Those dynamics would eventually bring social and cultural assimilation and then fusion at the biological level as well. And his work included much criticism of biological determinism.[15]

Bessie Bloom Wessel also focused on "ethnic fusion" in *An Ethnic Survey of Woonsocket, Rhode Island* (1931). Drachsler had suggested that intermarriage rates would function as an empirical measure of fusion's progress. Wessel, however, defined "fusion" numerically in terms of several demographic parameters—each operating over several generations—to serve as an index of group mixture at the biological level. These parameters included the numbers of each ethnic group arriving in the city, and a variety of ethnic-specific demographic rates such as fertility, mortality, intermarriage, and geographic mobility out of the city.[16]

Wessel's innovative method was to assess these outcomes through a survey of the public school population. For the schoolchild and each parent, her survey recorded birthplace (country and province), languages spoken, and "nationality or race (example: English, French Canadian, Irish, etc.)." The survey also recorded country of birth for each of the four grandparents. In addition, teachers were asked to check off a discretely printed C or J at the bottom corner of the questionnaire if the respondent was colored or Jewish, respectively. Thus the research design provided information on the outcome of three generations of intermarriage patterns dating back in time from the mid-1920s.[17]

Wessel's interest in ethnic fusion drew on the longstanding interest in the future "American race"—the American population that would result from the amalgamation of the great European migrations of past decades—and occasionally with a mention of the non-European admixtures that might also eventually intermarry. But Wessel's interest also had a more specific stimulus in the political struggle over immigration restriction that had just ended in the Second Quota Act. That legislation rested on the expectation that the "national origins" of the current American (white) population could be adequately estimated. The results of the complex estimation were made available in 1929. She wrote, "There has been a steadily increasing scientific interest in ethnic research. The very difficulties which the government experts encountered in an attempt to arrive at a plausible analysis of the national origins of the United States served to call increased attention to the inadequacy of our data on the subject of national composition."[18] She presented her project as a contribution to such knowledge.

Finally, Wessel also contrasted her demographic exploration with the much wider sociocultural goals that had guided a very different recent community study: Robert and Helen Lynd's *Middletown*. Their study took in the whole of social life "and in its approach it incorporates most nearly the methods in use by anthropologists for the study of primitive culture in a given area." By contrast, "The emphasis in this volume . . . is more particularly upon those factors which play a basic part in determining the racial and cultural situation. It is therefore more particularly an inquiry into ethnic antecedents."[19] The ethnic dimension thus includes both "the racial and cultural situation." Moreover the ethnic and nationality dimensions seem to be the same: "The groups under investigation are referred to as ethnic groups or 'nationalities,' the term 'nationality' being used in its ethnic sense." But they can be distinguished from the "truly racial, i.e. hereditary characteristics."[20] Given all this, she added, "*Racial* is used in this monograph to refer to the stock which these ethnic groups represent. It is an adjective indicating the hereditary or biologic aspects of the problem. The use of this word does not signify that these groups [British, French Canadian, Jews, Italians and so on] ... may be called races."[21] Thus, she carved out the right to use "racial" as a synonym for the dimension of biological heredity, but she did not want to leave the impression that reference to that dimension implies a claim that immigrants are representatives of ancient, pure races. Given her attention to tracing the percentages of each group's origins over time, it may not be surprising that two of Wessel's earliest project papers were published in *Eugenics* and *Eugenical News*.

And yet, even though all of these elements pointed to concerns with biological factors, it seems safe to assume that Wessel, a Ukrainian-born Jew herself and a lifelong activist in immigrant educational and social work, was not inspired by negative views of the immigrant, whether stimulated by race theories, eugenics, or even physical anthropology. Besides her origins and community work, we also know that during her doctoral work in New York, she studied with Boas and Ruth Benedict. And her major work shows great respect for Julius Drachsler's earlier study of intermarriage; indeed, she approvingly quoted Drachsler on "generalizations that are superficial and often flippant, each based on more or less specious race theories."[22]

The importance of Wessel's discussions on heredity in ethnic fusion, however, should not be exaggerated. These discussions quite simply are not terribly important to the careful tracing of intermarriage rates and their outcomes in the school-age population that made her reputation. Her formulations about race and ethnic antecedents are more of a curiosity than a central feature of her work. Nevertheless, those formulations do show an effort to define a place for biological heredity in her meaning of ethnic fusion. As such, they are interesting as a demonstration of the long connection between an older ethnology and the uses of "ethnic group" as late as 1931.

It is worth asking, then, why in 1931 did Wessel's work nevertheless include the concern with the importance of hereditary factors for ethnic

study? Several explanations come to mind, and they are not mutually exclusive. First, the emphasis may have been simply the logical extension of
a focus on the outcomes rather than the rates of intermarriage. The rates
focus on discrete moments in time; the outcomes focus on subjects as the
products of long-term cumulative processes. She may have been intrigued
by the intellectual challenges of the estimation efforts required for the National Origins Act. Or, simply, she may have sought to justify the qualities
of her unique dataset—which recorded schoolchildren as the outcomes
of the long-term processes.

A second possible reason for Wessel's emphasis on the hereditary features of ethnic antecedents concerns her position in the chronology and
hierarchy of research and funding. Although her book appeared two years
into the Great Depression, the long research project on which it reported
actually had been conceived at about the time that the National Origins Act
of 1924 came into law. In 1926, Brown University received funding from the
Laura Spellman Rockefeller Memorial and the Rockefeller Foundation for
a project on "Ethnic Factors in Community Life." It was to be conducted
by Wessel "under the direction of a committee" composed mostly of social science faculty at Brown. "It plans a study of racial composition and of
racial and cultural fusion."[23] At that time Wessel held only an MA degree
and no regular professorial position at Brown. Her husband had died in the
influenza epidemic of 1918, leaving her alone with a child of three. Eventually, additional funding for the project followed her to Connecticut College, where she obtained a regular academic appointment. But the entire
project, including the preparation of the book, occurred before she held a
doctorate. Perhaps for these reasons "the author invited co-operative
council in the form of an Advisory Committee," wrote the chairman of
that committee, anthropologist Clark Wissler, in the foreword to the book.[24]
Besides Wissler, the advisory committee included Henry Pratt Fairchild
and Niles Carpenter.[25] Wissler and Fairchild, in particular, were well-
established academics, but they were also deeply involved not only with
the eugenics movement, but also with beliefs about the new immigrations
based on Nordic race theory.[26] It is possible that Wissler was exaggerating
the degree of choice Wessel had in inviting the advisory committee. Or
possibly Wessel knew that given her marginal academic role, especially at
the outset, she needed support. And if that support came from academics

such as Wissler and Fairchild, then that would be even more likely to establish her own credentials.

Finally, a more benign explanation is that Wessel had been impressed by the experience of the Lynds' *Middletown*, which Wissler had helped to get published and for which he had written a foreword. Indeed, Wissler may have helped the Lynds decide to study a place with "a small Negro and foreign-born population," so that instead of being forced to deal with "two major variables, racial change and cultural change," the authors could concentrate on the latter. Wissler was, in any case, known as someone who could get along with members of diverse intellectual circles. Whatever the origins of Wessel's advisory committee, her involvement with Wissler and Fairchild surely helps explain Wessel's grounding of the ethnic group discussion on a "racial" element as late as 1931—despite the influence of Drachsler (to say nothing of the influence of her social background).[27]

Bushee, Jenks, Drachsler, and Wessel were unselfconscious about the term "ethnic group," which they had inherited from nineteenth-century ethnology. In that context, the term typically contained a strong emphasis on physiological distinctions among groups and often a loose assumption about connections between those distinctions and group mental traits. Nevertheless, while not completely shedding these meanings, Drachsler, in particular, criticized biological determinism and emphasized sociocultural rather than biological processes.

The Chicago sociologist W. I. Thomas was much more influential at the time than any of these four, and he is better known today. We have already encountered Thomas's 1907 correspondence with Franz Boas on the similarity of mental equipment across all races (Chapter 2). When he took up issues of immigration and assimilation in the second decade of the century, Thomas stressed the exclusive role of sociocultural factors in creating differences in attitudes and values across groups. This focus was especially influential in his monumental work, written with Florian Znaniecki, *The Polish Peasant in Europe and America* (five volumes, 1918–1920).[28] The work presented immigrant and second-generation outlooks, social structures, and institutions in great detail. And yet Thomas discussed all of these themes primarily in terms of "race" and "nationality," terms at least as old as ethnology's use of the "ethnic group."

By 1920, an extramarital scandal led to Thomas's dismissal from the University of Chicago, and he never held another regular professorship after that. These circumstances in turn led the University of Chicago Press to cease publishing the later volumes of *The Polish Peasant,* and a commercial press took over the project. Finally, he had also drafted an overview of immigration and assimilation for a series on Americanization funded by the Carnegie Corporation and to be published by Harper & Brothers. But that plan, too, now had to be changed. Thomas's draft may have been edited by his colleagues Robert E. Park and Herbert A. Miller. In any case, it appeared under their authorship rather than his as *Old World Traits Transplanted.*

Old World Traits used the older terminology of race and nationality, but it turned decisively from biological to cultural explanation, and away from fears of inherent immigrant traits that would bring down American civilization. The work stressed that immigrant distinctiveness could not survive the New World's assimilatory processes. The work opened with the following declaration:

> During the past seventy years the various tribes, races, and nationalities
> of mankind have been examined in detail by the students of ethnology,
> and a comparison of the results shows that the fundamental patterns of
> life and behavior are everywhere the same. . . . All have a form of family
> life, moral and legal regulations, a religious system, a form of govern-
> ment, artistic practices, and so forth. . . . Formerly it was assumed that
> this similarity was the result of borrowing between groups. . . . But it is
> now recognized that similarities of culture are due, in the main, not to
> imitation, but to parallel development. The nature of man is everywhere
> essentially the same and tends to express itself everywhere in similar
> sentiments and institutions.[29]

But if "the nature of man is everywhere essentially the same," groups do indeed come to differ greatly in outlook, and the arriving immigrants are a case in point. The explanation is not in biology, and hence is not immutable; it is in the immigrants' "heritage," with different histories creating differences in "values" and "attitudes."

> Different races and nationalities attach values to different things, and
> different values to the same thing. This is the chief factor in the problem

of "Americanization," of harmonizing the life of the immigrants with our own. Every human group has developed in the course of its experience a certain fund of *values* particular to itself and a set of *attitudes* toward these values. . . . The object, the practice, the institution, is the value; the feeling toward it is the attitude. For the purpose of the present study we call the fund of attitudes and values which an immigrant group brings to America—the totality of its sentiments and practices—its "heritage."[30]

The work pleaded for an understanding of immigrant outlooks and the need for patience with immigrant institutions. While these institutions might seem to separate the immigrant from America, they actually provided a socially useful alternative to dislocation in the short run and an eventual bridge to American ways later. But neither institutions nor outlooks could be expected to last—even if, as we will see, some immigrant leaders and their children hoped otherwise.[31]

Old World Traits Transplanted, then, offered a self-conscious analysis of immigrant differences in terms of culture and showed that the end of the process would be assimilation. On the other hand, there was little discussion of the later stages in the process of such assimilation, particularly of the ethnic group in later generations. However, Thomas and Znaniecki did develop the conception of the Polish American community as a new social form (at about the same time *Old World Traits* appeared) in the fifth volume of *The Polish Peasant*.

A long chapter of that volume is titled "The Polish-American Community." Here the subject is "the formation of a new Polish-American society" that is not merely a diluted version of old village life in Poland. Instead, the Polish American community also draws from American society. And it is a *community* that is at issue, a social formation among individuals, not something within the mentality of a single individual. In the preface to this last of five volumes, the authors announce the significance of this new reality.[32]

> It is generally assumed that the main problems concerning the immigrants can be stated in terms of individual assimilation or non-assimilation. . . . The immigrant (or the immigrant's descendant) is

considered as still a Pole . . . or already an American, or somewhere on the way . . . and it is supposed that the essential thing to be studied in relation to him is how he makes this passage. . . . But, in fact if we look at the Poles in America not from the standpoint of Polish or American national interests but from that of an objective sociological inquiry, we find that the problem of individual assimilation is an entirely secondary and unimportant issue. . . . The fundamental process which has been going on during this period is *the formation of a new Polish-American society.* . . . The assimilation is not an individual but a group phenomenon. . . . And the striking phenomenon, the central object of our investigation, is . . . the creation of a society which in structure and prevalent attitudes is neither Polish nor American but constitutes a specific new product.[33]

Here Thomas and Znaniecki drew on the term "ethnic group"—among a variety of old terms—to describe the new society.

The nationalistic Polish tendencies of the local associations have thus not a political but a racial significance. Their aim is to preserve the cultural stock brought by the immigrants to this country—language, mores, customs, and historical traditions—so as to maintain the racial solidarity of the Poles as an ethnic group, independent of their political allegiance and of any economic, social, or political bonds which may connect each of them individually with their American milieu. . . . The only form of participation which are socially condemned are those which tend to incorporate him into American primary groups and to draw him away from his Polish *gens* that is, marriage, personal friendship, and all kinds of intercourse implying direct personal solidarity.[34]

This use of old terms may have made it harder for readers to grasp the full novelty of the discovery of the new type of society. Indeed, perhaps a concern that readers would miss the insight about a new ethnic society in the context of a fifth long volume explains why the authors highlighted the point in their introduction and italicized the key phrase, "formation of a new Polish-American society."

CAROLINE WARE AND LLOYD WARNER SELF-CONSCIOUSLY
LINK OLD TERM AND NEW MEANING

Caroline Ware gave special emphasis to the value of the culture concept for studying a variety of social phenomena, and particularly "ethnic communities." During the decade after 1930, she published three important pieces dealing with ethnic groups: a substantial article, "Ethnic Communities," in the *Encyclopedia of the Social Sciences* (1931); her major work of original research, *Greenwich Village, 1920–1930* (1935); and a methodological volume of essays, *The Cultural Approach to History,* which she edited and to which she contributed (1940). The notion of culture informs all three works as an approach to social analysis. She was inspired by the Lynds' *Middletown: A Study in Modern American Culture*—in both the method of participant observation and the demonstration of how aspects of a culture were interconnected.[35]

The article on "Ethnic Communities" was a self-conscious declaration that ethnic groups should no longer be subsumed under the old understandings of ethnology. Rather, they must be considered in the context of advanced societies, especially modern ones. They are best understood in terms of culture and minority status: "Ethnic communities are groups bound together by common ties of race, nationality or culture, living together within an alien civilization but remaining culturally distinct. . . . In its strict meaning the word ethnic denotes race; but when applied to communities in the above sense it is loosely used, in the absence of any more comprehensive term to cover the more general concept of culture."[36]

The essay surveys crucial features of ethnic communities, particularly in the history of Europe and North America. In the latter context, she includes both American black descendants of slaves and communities formed by voluntary immigration. The latter "developed and survived" in part through replenishment of newly arrived immigrants and in part as a result of discrimination by the host society. This discrimination tended to

> force them back into their ghettos, where they might seek their place among their own kind. Of low economic status, without an intelligentsia (except in the case of the Jews), leaderless and with a

tendency to lose successful members, since the price of success is often the severing of group ties, these immigrant communities hung on in most American cities, ignored by many and condemned by others as un-American. They have all developed certain characteristic features . . . mutual benefit societies . . . [specialized] food stores and restaurants . . . a church follows the first signs of prosperity [and eventually often school and press]. . . . Professional men of the group perform their sciences; traditional forms of entertainment develop; and the community becomes so complete that its members practically never leave it except to move from one such community to another. . . .

These communities consist of a solid, group conscious nucleus, surrounded by a fringe which is gradually being worn away by intermarriage, education, participation in such activities as sports and by economic change. They are torn within themselves by conflicts between the generations.[37]

But in the long run, once the replenishment of new arrivals has stopped (as it had in the United States in the 1920s), the ethnic communities that arose from voluntary immigration cannot be sustained because the conditions of modern industrial societies undercut their cohesion.

The force of economic pressure is constantly at work, breaking down isolation, producing physical mobility, causing contacts between members of different groups and rewarding those who are successful at the economic game, with scant regard for the group from which they come. The same factors which are wearing down cultural differences between nations are at work to eliminate ethnic communities within states. . . . The diffusion of a standardized material culture, elimination of distance and the common language of business are all at work to make the ethnic community a relic of a separatist age. Its greatest opponent is the unconscious pressure of an integrated economic society and a leveling material civilization.[38]

There is precious little room in this vision to doubt the effects of modernity, no hint here that social scientists might someday wonder at the tenacity of the ethnic phenomenon in the face of the influences Ware described.

The brief bibliography for Ware's article includes four citations to work on American groups; two show the debt to Thomas (*The Polish Peasant* and *Old World Traits Transplanted*). A third is also a product of the Chicago School: Louis Wirth's *The Ghetto* (1928), a historical survey of Jewish community life in delimited neighborhoods, and its re-creation in Chicago.[39] The fourth reference on America was to Wessel's *Ethnic Survey of Woonsocket*. Ware no doubt included it as an authoritative quantitative study of ethnic blending; she might have included Drachsler's study instead, which was closer to the spirit of her own work, but it was a full decade older than Wessel's book, and the latter in any case included copious reference to Drachsler's work.

It is worth pausing over the bibliography also to appreciate that for this article in the premier international reference work on social science, Ware did *not* cite Max Weber.[40] He had written a relatively short section in *Economy and Society* about "the ethnic group," which appeared posthumously in German in 1922. Weber explored in particular the basis for ethnic group cohesion and also how the social phenomenon differed from nation or race. Today the Weber piece is routinely mentioned in overviews of the topic. But these references to Weber are due to his characteristically strong theoretical formulations, not to any influence his article had on the development of the concept in America before the 1960s. Apparently only after the American concept had emerged by the mid-1960s did Weber's work on the subject gain attention. At any rate, *none* of the American texts surveyed in this chapter mentioned Weber's discussion. One reason surely was that the first English translation did not appear until 1968. Nevertheless, the language barrier was probably *less* important than a general American ignorance about most of Weber's work in the relevant period. Ware, for example, cites a number of other German works in the bibliography of her *Encyclopedia* article. Likewise, a 1947 article in the *American Journal of Sociology* on "The Nature of the Ethnic Group" referenced works published in both French and German without mentioning Weber.[41]

The absence of Weber's influence is also notable because Ware defined the group somewhat differently than Weber did. Ware placed the "cultural" connections among people at the center of the ethnic community, rather than a more narrowly defined sense of identity or belonging. Her definition did not deal unambiguously with the sense of a common historical origin, real or imagined, as the basis of ethnic cohesion. She refers less specifically to "common ties of race, nationality or culture."

Ware's big empirical study of Greenwich Village focused heavily on the neighborhood's Italian, Irish, and Jewish groups across two (and occasionally three) generations—and upon the cultural completeness of these communities: "Among the local people, the most fundamental social division was the ethnic one. . . . For practically every aspect of local life the several ethnic groups had separate institutions and distinctive ways."[42]

Finally, she took up the ethnic community again in a methodological context when she edited *The Cultural Approach to History*. "The concept of culture implies that any given society is an integral, though not necessarily a completely integrated, whole." The essays were arranged to show how the cultural approach could further understanding of a number of historical topics. One of these topics was "cultural groups" within American society. Ware wrote both an introduction to this section of the book as well as a summary of a roundtable discussion that had followed the individual papers. In these pages, she returned to many themes mentioned in the earlier *Encyclopedia* article, and she includes an extended quote from the passage in Thomas and Znaniecki's *Polish Peasant* in which they describe "the formation of a new Polish-American society." At the same time, she treats the ethnic communities as only one among a broad set of American cultural groups. She meant to draw attention to a continuum of ignored working-class cultural groups: "The issue of the status of cultural minorities is the issue of the status of workers. . . . The new urban industrial culture [is] developing in the hands of new Americans and old, peasant peoples and hill-billies."[43]

By 1940, Ware had been discussing "ethnic communities" for a decade or more. She may not have advanced the concept much beyond Thomas's formulations, however her *Encyclopedia* entry in particular served as a pithy and self-conscious discussion of how the term, now wrenched free of its origin in ethnology, had changed. And her own major research on the first and second generations in Greenwich Village served as a powerful example of such work.

During much of the decade after 1925, Lloyd Warner did graduate work at Harvard University in anthropology and also studied social psychological approaches to modern industry at Harvard's Business School. In 1930, he began a massive community research project on Yankee City. A large team spent years in Newburyport, Massachusetts, interviewing residents and learning about all aspects of the social structure. In 1935 Warner joined the faculty at the University of Chicago in anthropology and sociology, and it was from there that he published the five volumes of the Yankee City study. By the time the first volume appeared in 1941, Warner had also published other full-scale studies, and he held a prestigious professorship. The books in the Yankee City series naturally attracted much attention. The third volume, *The Social System of American Ethnic Groups* (coauthored with Leo Srole) appeared in 1945.[44]

Warner had already introduced the ethnic theme as a chapter in the first volume. Half of the city's population in 1930 was foreign born or the children of at least one foreign-born parent. Accordingly, besides studying many other dimensions of city life—social class, neighborhoods, the factory system, family, religion, politics, and so on—the researchers also divided the city into ten groups, "each of which had certain distinctive features." Besides the "Native, or Yankee," these include a variety of immigrant groups (Irish, French Canadian, Jewish, Italian, etc.) and "Negro."

> These groups, with the exception of the first, we have called "ethnics." The term "ethnic" as used in this study does not simply refer to foreign birth. Rather, it has a wider meaning. An individual was classified as belonging to a specific ethnic group if (1) he considered himself or was considered by the Yankee City community as a member of the group and (2) if he participated in the activities of the group. Our purpose . . . was to . . . study the ethnics in their relation to the larger community, to discover the nature of the social organization of the various sub-communities, and to evaluate the prevailing beliefs, attitudes and sentiments concerning ethnic individuals. Early in our stay in the community we were made aware of the force of these ethnic distinctions, of how these distinctions conditioned behavior by limiting and enlarging the participation and the social personality of the individual, and how quickly and directly barriers were set up on the basis of ethnicity. . . . The concept of ethnicity is not based simply on place of birth [but also on consciousness of membership by the member or others].[45]

The passage did not mention older meanings derived from ethnology.

The volume devoted exclusively to the ethnic group dealt with many aspects of the inner life of the groups—neighborhoods, family, church, language, schools, other voluntary associations. In particular, as the passage just quoted revealed, a principal reason for attending to ethnic groups had to do not with their inner life but with how they influence an individual's chances for upward mobility. The concluding chapter, "The American Ethnic Group," drives this point home. There the authors array the ethnic groups in terms of the relative strength of the barriers to upward mobility that each encounters. These barriers grow in strength with the distance between the old Yankees and each of the other groups. The greater the difference, the longer in generational terms total assimilation will take. The cultural differences, especially linguistic and religious, decline with time and generational standing. Still, full assimilation may take as long as six generations for some of these groups, particularly those of European origin who had a darker complexion. In the case of the Negro, the perceived biological differences will not go away no matter how much group members change in cultural or social behavior. Overcoming the race barrier depends in the end on the outlook of the dominant group, and that outlook may or may not change in the future. African Americans are indeed ethnic groups in Warner's usage, but they are ethnic groups with much less potential for advancement and group improvement.

Werner Sollors has observed that the Yankee City books include the first usage of the term "ethnicity."[46] Sollors focused on "ethnicity"—rather than "ethnic group"—in making this assessment. He may have done so for two reasons. First, "ethnic group," as we have seen, is an old term with a legacy of multiple connotations. Second, "ethnicity" implies an awareness of a variable for analysis—like social class, religion, or gender. Still, as we have seen in earlier sections of this chapter, numerous interwar authors—surely Thomas and Ware, and to a lesser extent Drachsler—were self-conscious about the American ethnic group as a new domain for study. So too were Berkson and Hansen, discussed shortly. Of those just mentioned, only Thomas and Hansen did not consistently rely on the term "ethnic group" to label the new subject.

Note too that the use of a new term need not involve much self-consciousness about arriving somewhere conceptually new. This seems true of Warner's use of the noun form "ethnicity," as opposed to his thinking about the new subject that both "ethnicity" and "ethnic group" captured. In several hundred pages about the ethnic groups of Yankee City, Warner and his coauthors mention "ethnicity" only in the few contexts already quoted and a very few others that are no more illuminating. Recall, in particular: "We were made aware of the force of these ethnic distinctions . . . and how quickly barriers were set up on the basis of ethnicity" and "the concept of ethnicity is not based simply on place of birth." In sum, Warner and his colleagues did indeed refer to a "concept of ethnicity." Yet the concept simply defined membership in the ethnic group; it is given no other task, and that task could be undertaken by reference to "ethnic group" without mentioning "ethnicity." Moreover, the latter term does not appear in the index, although scores of references to "ethnic groups" do. Thus Sollers's influential account of the origins of the first *usage* of ethnicity seems entirely accurate, but it may set too high a bar for judging new *meanings*. The meanings that ethnicity would capture had been emerging with the use of "ethnic group" over several decades before Warner wrote about "ethnicity." Similarly, if the challenge is to find a self-conscious use of the new meanings for "ethnic group"—the awareness of a new social form—it seems clear that Warner's work does indeed embody such self-consciousness. But the evidence that he did so is in his whole approach, and he shared that self-consciousness with many predecessors, in particular those already discussed here. And yet as an icon for, rather than the dating of, a conceptual departure, Warner's new wording can serve as well as any we will find.

WHY "ETHNIC GROUP" EMERGED FROM THE CONTINUUM OF RELATED CONCEPTS

Whatever the *conceptual* innovations of writers such as Drachsler, Thomas, Ware, and Warner, at least in the 1930s and 1940s the *terminology* for studies of the ethnic group remained in flux in influential books and the most prestigious sociological journal. The stress on social as opposed to biological processes in understanding "the ethnic group" was becoming more prevalent, but the terms used to capture this change were closer to Thomas's reliance on race and nationality than to the use most of the other writers just mentioned made of the "ethnic group."

T. J. Woofter's *Races and Ethnic Groups in American Life* (1933) appeared in a collection of papers on "Recent Social Trends in the United States" that President Hoover had initiated. Despite the title of Woofter's monograph, and the authoritative publication of which it was a part, the text offers very little by way of guidance for the reader about the difference between these terms; indeed, one is left to conclude that the author used them in overlapping and interchangeable ways.[47]

Three better-known examples can briefly serve to mark the limited diffusion of the turn from "race" and "nationality" to "ethnic group" or "ethnicity" before the end of the Second World War. These are *The Cultural Approach to History* (1940), which Caroline Ware had edited, William F. Whyte's *Street Corner Society* (1943), and Ruby Jo Reeves Kennedy's papers on intermarriage and "the triple melting pot" (1939–1944).

We have already considered Ware's own writing in the volume she edited in 1940. But the others engaged in the cultural history project had not absorbed her usage. When the American Historical Association first called for papers on the cultural approach, the announcement spoke of "nationality groups" as an example of a context in which to explore the new approach. And although Ware edited "Part Two: Cultural Groups," all of the papers that follow her introduction are subsumed under a second subheading, "Approaches to the Study of Nationality Groups in the United States."

Whyte's *Street Corner Society* was one of the most widely read sociological studies ever published. He was concerned with the young men within "the social structure of an Italian slum." Whyte had nothing to do with the biological determinism of the earlier period, nor did his work even mention concerns such as environment and heredity. It was a study of interpersonal dynamics, filled with vivid description and quotation of conversations. In this context, his informants typically spoke of their Italian origin in terms of race. Tony Cataldo argues with a club member at the settlement house about an upcoming election and says, "I don't go for this racial politics. I go for the best man no matter what his race is. . . . I'm for Kelly." And later, candidate Flanagan, speaking in the North End district, says, "This district don't have men that vote only because of their racial strain. For the immigrants of your race and my race I have no apology."[48]

But quite apart from the terms that were popular in the neighborhood, Whyte himself repeatedly spoke of racial rather than ethnic (or even "national origin" or "nationality") groups.

> As early as 1915, the racial composition of Cornerville [the North End] was practically the same as it is today. All but a few of the Irish families had moved out. The Jews who came in at the same time as the Italians had also been superseded, though many of them retained Cornerville business interests.[49] . . .
>
> From the time that the Italian immigrants got into street fights with their Irish predecessors there was bitter feeling between the races.[50] . . .
>
> Italians feel that the racial bond obligates other Italians to help them.[51] . . .
>
> When an Italian politician . . . sought to mobilize support for an Irishman, the racial feeling cut his influence to a minimum.[52]

Whyte studied, wrote, and interacted with major figures at Harvard and Chicago in the late 1930s and 1940s—including Lloyd Warner, deep into his own study of "ethnicity" and ethnic groups in Yankee City. Nevertheless, presumably the use of race in this loose, general way was not yet jarring to those with whom Whyte interacted. One reason it probably remained unrevised was that ultimately in *Street Corner Society* the terms were surprisingly marginal as Whyte was most interested in the interplay of different psychological types among his young men.

Ruby Jo Reeves Kennedy argued that the descendants of the immigrants would indeed melt—but not as Israel Zangwill's play had suggested. Instead, the descendants were intermarrying within the major religious groups: Protestant, Catholic, and Jewish. Kennedy could speak of "ethnic endogamy" and of the marriage patterns of "ethnic groups." But she uses these terms interchangeably with "national origins" and "nationality groups."[53] Moreover, the triple-melting-pot paper was her third on intermarriage published in *The American Journal of Sociology*. The earliest of the three papers, coauthored with her graduate school advisor, Maurice R. Davie, appeared in 1939. This paper referred only to "nationality."[54] Also suggestive is the context of Reeves Kennedy's middle paper on intermarriage, "Premarital Residential Propinquity and Ethnic Endogamy," published in 1943. But the next paper published in the same issue of the journal was called "Intermarriage among Nationality Groups in a Rural Area of Minnesota." Indeed, that other paper also had a table titled "Nationality of Parents . . ." in which the relevant column was headed "Ethnic Group."[55]

Part of the reason the terms "ethnic group" and "ethnicity" eventually came to prevail by the early 1960s had to do with the limitations of the terms in use until then. "Race"—especially when applied *within* "the color races"—had been challenged even before World War I by various social scientists and then for other reasons by geneticists, which will be discussed later in this chapter. And it had become a hot potato in the federal statistics system primarily as a result of the Jewish protests. When "race" differences among European peoples became a bedrock of the Nazi regime, the decline of the designation for European immigrant groups in America accelerated.

However, the "nationality" term also came freighted with competing usages—of political citizenship on the one hand and peoplehood on the other. Moreover, in general "nationalities" (in either sense) seemed to involve questions about "nationalism" and "nation-states." For both reasons, then, designating immigrants and their descendants as "American nationalities" did not seem to raise the right issues and associations.

One alternative term might have been "national origins." We have seen how race-oriented restrictionists exploited that term in Chapter 7. "National origins" was indeed a familiar term. But the restrictionists' use of it may well have been responsible for making it available in another way altogether. It became one among several terms for groups *against whom* discrimination was prohibited—as in "discrimination on the basis of race or color, religion, or national origin." In addition, "national origin" carried the same ambiguity as the "nationality" term. Moreover, to the extent that "national origin" did not convey peoplehood, it failed to capture the inner life of communities, with their distinctive social and cultural patterns. Just how dangerous any ambiguity about which of the two kinds of nationality an American ethnic group supported was on display in the discussions of Jewish groups concerned with "national minorities" in the aftermath of World War I (Chapter 6).

Finally, another term in wide use from the World War I years until around 1960 was "minority group." We should not be misled by its usage in our own time. Today, "minority" denotes particularly non-European groups (in the broad sense that also includes Latinos "of whatever race"). During that earlier four-decade period, perhaps even more than today, the term was used especially in connection with prohibited categories of discrimination— restrictions of opportunities and rights. It thus denoted groups who were vulnerable to discrimination from the majority on the basis of any of the categories mentioned earlier: race or color, religion, or national origin. But this association meant that "minority," too, like "national origin," carried baggage that helped limit its use. Its primary meaning did not call up associations with social and cultural patterns.

Writing at midcentury, Oscar Handlin concisely described the European origins of the term in discussions of national minorities. And this association raised for him other difficulties with the term in the American context.

> Ominously the term "minority" came into more frequent use [after World War I] as a description of various groups in the United States. The word had been borrowed from Europe, where it referred to such people as the Ukrainians in Poland or the Germans in Czechoslovakia. Discussion in the terms of the peace treaties had made it familiar to Americans. [But in Europe] it had been assumed that the preponderant majority of the population shared common traits of national origin. . . . In the United States, there was no majority in that sense; all the groups which considered themselves minority after 1918, added together, were more than a majority of the total population. . . . [And they] by no means acknowledged thereby that they were less American in nationality than anyone else. . . . Minority . . . therefore reflected an awareness on the part of some groups that they were underprivileged in access to opportunities.[56]

Handlin's "majority of minorities" were thus comprised largely of *white* Americans, although he surely meant to include nonwhites as well. The passage has a strange resonance of familiarity today not because of his own idea but because the *nonwhite* minorities of twenty-first-century usage are frequently discussed as the soon-to-be majority of Americans.

GUIDANCE FROM THE NATURAL SCIENTISTS? 1937–1951

Alarmed by the Nazi ascendency, a number of well-established geneticists and physical anthropologists sought to educate the public about race. They introduced the basic conclusions of modern genetics and argued that these, as well as the sloppiness with which "race" had been used for generations, made the term simply unintelligible. Moreover, there was no evidence that cultural differences (or mental traits generally) were related to observable physical differences among groups. The first book of this type was *We Europeans* by Julian Huxley and A. C. Haddon (1937). Another influential volume, Ashley Montagu's *Man's Most Dangerous Myth*, followed in 1942, and after the war the first and second UNESCO Statement on Race (1950 and 1951) articulated much the same message in a pithy form and on a very public stage. Most striking for our purposes was the suggestion, first proposed in *We Europeans*, to abandon the race term altogether—and replace it with "ethnic group."

> The word race as applied scientifically to human groupings has lost any sharpness of meaning. Today it is hardly definable.... There is still a lamentable confusion between the ideas of race, culture and nation.... In the circumstances, it is very desirable the term race as applied to human groups should be dropped from the vocabulary of science.... In what follows the word race will be deliberately avoided, and the term ethnic group or people employed.[57]

The message that the old uses of race had lost "any sharpness of meaning," coupled with the Nazi use of the term, certainly helped to delegitimize the term in the Allied countries. *We Europeans* may also have helped draw attention to "ethnic group" as an alternative term. Also, the impact of World War II meant that the accusation of racism could now be used strategically in the United States against forms of state-condoned discrimination.[58] The UNESCO Statements were certainly part of this transformation, as was *We Europeans* more than a dozen years before. True, the Quota Acts would not be swept away for more than a dozen years after the UNESCO Statement, but even proponents of retaining the quotas during the 1950s explicitly rejected Nordic racism (Chapter 10).

Granting all this, there is still a considerable irony here in connection with the eventual rise of the "ethnic group" term. The point to notice is that the natural scientists, horrified by the Nazis, had *not* discussed the ethnic group as a social and cultural entity. They had in mind the need for a new term in the study of the *physical* differences that are observed across very large collectivities of human beings around the world—a term to replace that aspect of the ethnologist's and anthropologist's earlier use of race. Consequently, any stimulus their work provided for the adoption of "ethnic group" as a term referring to American *sociocultural* groups would have been based on a misunderstanding. Consider first *We Europeans.*

> Let us turn to the criteria of ethnic grouping. . . . The more important . . . are . . . (i) hair-form and hair-colour; (ii) skin-colour; (iii) eye-colour and eye-form; (iv) stature; (v) head-form; (vi) nasal form; (vii) physiological and psychological characters; (viii) blood groups. . . . [But] psychological characters, such as colour-vision and acuity of sense perception, have not yet been properly defined in respect of their ethnic significance. . . . These issues are therefore outside the scope of this book.[59]

The same point applies to the 1950 UNESCO Statement on Race. The organization sponsored a short statement that an eminent group of scientists could sign, once more as a means of educating the public. That statement followed *We Europeans* in urging that the "race" term be replaced by "ethnic group." And once again, the latter term was to cover physical divisions of mankind.

> Most anthropologists agree in classifying the greater part of the present-day mankind into three major divisions ["Mongoloid," "Negroid," "Caucasoid"]. . . .
>
> Many sub-groups or ethnic groups within these divisions have been described. There is no general agreement upon their number, and in any event most ethnic groups have not yet been either studied or described by the physical anthropologists. . . . Whatever classification the anthropologist makes of man, he never includes mental characteristics as part of those classifications.[60]

As it happened, the 1950 UNESCO Statement came to be seen primarily as the product of social rather than natural scientists, and so a second statement by a different set of experts followed a year later. The 1951 (second) UNESCO Statement on Race held to the key points of the first—the revolution genetics had brought to scientific understanding and the stunningly diverse ways that the "race" term had come to be used. The new statement only modestly muted the emphasis on the absolute independence of physical groupings and mental traits. However, it deleted the call to abandon the "race" term and therefore also contained no discussion of "ethnic" or "ethnic group." The implication was that despite all the misuses of "race," there probably was a reasonable role for the term in the natural sciences; the point was to separate that role from all the others, not to dispose of the term.

Ethnic Group Persistence versus Assimilation across the Generations

THE DEBATE ABOUT ETHNIC SURVIVAL, 1909–1921

Beyond the changing terms and meanings associated with the ethnic group, a central intellectual preoccupation with ethnic life concerned the tension between group persistence in the American context and assimilation. Before the end of mass immigration in the 1920s, the issue was posed mainly in terms of the threat of immigration to American stability. Later, the more dominant question, especially to ethnic group members themselves, was whether ethnic societies and cultures could possibly survive through the generations. Could W. I. Thomas's "new social form," the American ethnic group, survive indefinitely, or were all its manifestations, however interesting and important, transitional and doomed not merely to evolve but to disappear? At least in his 1921 volume on Americanization, Thomas did indeed stress this transitional quality. But perspicacious observers were already thinking about this second question a dozen years earlier.

In particular, Israel Zangwill's *The Melting Pot* (1909) and Horace Kallen's "Democracy vs. the Melting Pot" (1915) defined two of the well-known views about the American future, assimilation versus ethnic pluralism. Discussion about each of these works raised crucial considerations about the long-term prospects for ethnic groups. Zangwill's play, so influential in the title's metaphor, did not in fact take up the details or stages of "melting."[61] But in presenting its two young immigrant protagonists who came from radically different backgrounds, it implied that we know enough to understand the essentials: David and Vera are inspired by universal American ideals and can therefore surmount group differences to find happiness together. Ancestral loyalties and prejudices were doomed in this fluid social and intellectual context. The mutual attraction of the protagonists would bring a biological as well as sociocultural blending: "America is God's Crucible, the great Melting-Pot where all the races of Europe are melting and reforming . . . Germans and Frenchmen, Irishmen and Englishmen, Jews and Russians—into the Crucible with you all! God is making the American."[62] Zangwill never quite sorted out the biological from the cultural processes by which God accomplishes the feat. But the play—and especially a later afterword—strongly suggest that Zangwill certainly did consider the biological dimension of the melting pot important for the character of American culture. Still, in the same afterword, he reflects that a good deal of assimilation can occur even without biological melding. Possibly he was responding to criticism when he chose to clarify the point in the afterword. Many Jews had attacked the play's positive portrayal of Jewish–gentile intermarriage and complete assimilation.

There is little concern with terminology in the play—"the races" of the immigrants covers the theme adequately. But we should also appreciate that a few years later, Zangwill confronted more closely the conceptual importance of terminology in a published lecture, *The Principle of Nationalities* (1917). Stimulated by the discussions the war accentuated, he wrote at some length about nationality as peoplehood and downplayed biological processes—at least for dynamics that operated within rather than between the color races. Such considerations led him to consider the eventual melding of nationalities—especially in the context of American immigration—as a sociocultural process.

> The Law of Contiguous Cooperation . . . at once begins to operate on the new elements. . . . The second and subsequent generations are far more fusible. Great is the Power of Place. The notion that Nationalities are immortal is obscurantist. . . . Of the two factors in our being,

Heredity and Environment, the latter is at least as important as the former. . . . If Nationality is so easily transferable, within the colour radius at least, . . . if America can make Americans out of Serbians and Bulgarians and Greeks and any old nationality it is because Bulgarians *are* Serbians and both of them Greeks; at any rate the traits of their common humanity exceed their differences. These quarrelsome races vanish in three generations, content that at least they are not dominated by each other.

Had Horace Kallen written a few years later, Zangwill's formulations here might have influenced the way Kallen confronted *The Melting Pot*. But when he wrote "Democracy vs. the Melting Pot" in 1915, Kallen was reacting to the play as part of what he thought was an excessive demand for Americanization. He argued that the persistence of races and nationalities in America was both the most natural and the most desirable future. Moreover, the meaning of "democracy," which was opposed to the "melting pot" in the essay, referred to the freedom of nationalities and races to express (through their own languages) their ancestral cultures. Through that democratic expression they would contribute to a richer American culture—to a "federation of nationalities." But if Zangwill had been short on details, Kallen was even more so. How the federation of nationalities would actually operate is explained only by the metaphor of a symphonic orchestra, in which each instrument contributes to the overall composition. Especially important in the present context is why Kallen felt so strongly that the descendants of the immigrants could avoid a fuller assimilation. Kallen seemed to rest his case on two assumptions. First, biological heredity supported ethnic cultural differences. This above all explains why Kallen had stressed (twice) in the essay that "We cannot change our grandfathers." Second, geographic concentration and isolation kept immigrants apart from each other. Kallen colossally overestimated this factor—at a time when the evidence was available to know better, and when others did know better.

Nevertheless, many readers were anxious, like Kallen, both about threats to ethnic survival and about the more intolerant calls for Americanization that emerged in the nationalism of World War I. John Dewey and Randolph Bourne, for example, were concerned about cultural expression and the potential of a more cosmopolitan and tolerant America.[63] From a different vantage point, Caroline Ware wrote in her "Ethnic Communities" article that intolerant Americanization drives stimulated ethnic pushback: "Leaders within immigrant communities have arisen to demand recognition for their groups, not merely for the exceptional individual. Such leaders are insisting that the amalgamation of ethnic groups into the American community must be by incorporation, not by suppression, and must proceed on the basis of respect for differences of inherited tradition and culture."[64]

Authors of Jewish origin in particular took up the question of long-term survival. Jews were most likely to have attained advanced education and to enter academic study at the time. This was so for some (such as Kallen and J. L. Magnes) who were descended from families of the German Jewish immigration who had been in the United States since the mid-nineteenth century. Also middle-class family origins and the attainment of advanced schooling were more common among the eastern European Jewish second generation than among other southern and eastern European immigrant groups.[65] Finally, Jewish writers were not merely sensitive to the issue of Jewish survival in America; they were familiar with similar issues from a century of modern European Jewish history. They explored both the terms of ethnic group survival in general and of Jewish survival in particular. They sought ways to explain how such survival could be tolerated in America and even be advantageous for the country's culture and political cohesion.

Judah L. Magnes, whom we encountered in connection with the controversies over the List of Races and Peoples, responded to the play in a sermon shortly after it first opened. Magnes did not deny that "the process he [Zangwill] describes is very largely going on. . . . I see children who are less Jewish than their parents. . . . I wonder how our leaders can be blind." And yet for Magnes there were also hopeful signs.

> Zangwill's description of the melting process by no means covers the whole situation. . . . There is a process of Jewish awakening. . . . Some have become Jewish nationalists [and some of those seek] . . . the strengths and consolation the Jewish religion offers. Many a religious Jew . . . now begins to understand the riches of [and the need for] Jewish national culture . . . [*contra* Zangwill, survival in America will

be enriched by a Zionist homeland:] America for the thousands who can live as Jews here, Zion for the thousands who must live as Jews there.[66]

But how does this vision sit with the need for American political and sociocultural cohesion? Here Magnes's statement is worth quoting at length because it shows a stunning similarity to the formulation Kallen would articulate some half dozen years later, near the end of "Democracy vs. the Melting Pot." Whether Magnes and Kallen directly influenced each other is unclear.

> It seems to be generally admitted at present that a man may be a good American no matter to what religious body he belongs. . . . But this exalted conception of freedom in America is being extended by the influx of large masses of those very nationalities whose presence here has given rise to the whole problem. They are making Americans realize that the America of the future is to be not a republic of individuals and religions alone, but a republic of nationalities as well. The Melting Pot is not the highest ideal of America. America is rather the refining pot. . . . Here at last the world is to be shown how men of varied religions and nationalities can learn to understand one another, and to work together in peace and in concord. . . .
>
> The hero of [Zangwill's] play is writing the great American symphony. If his symphony were really written, it would be a vast monotone. Its music, if any, would be that produced by one sound. The harmony of a symphony, however, is produced by a variety of distinct sounds blending into music under the artist's hand. The symphony of America must be written by the various nationalities which keep their individual and characteristic note, and which sound this note in harmony with their sister nationalities. Then it will be a symphony of color, of picturesqueness, of character, of distinction not the harmony of the Melting Pot, but rather the harmony of sturdiness and loyalty and joyous struggle.[67]

Magnes seems to have been indebted less than Kallen to a biological determinism, but in response to Zangwill, he provides only inspirational language to support the belief that over the generations ethnic groups persist. A brief look at three other American Jewish writers somewhat later (around 1920) shows a range of reactions to Kallen's essay. All three took the possibility of full assimilation for granted and had no belief that biological factors would slow the process. What they wondered about was ethnic survival.

Julius Drachsler, whom we encountered earlier, regarded Kallen as "a brilliant observer of immigrant life" who had nevertheless been "misled" by the "illusion of permanence" in "immigrant community life." In fact, "at the very base of the structure are forces at work . . . sapping its stability." Such forces include lack of group harmony and the waning of formal religion. "But the fatal disease . . . is the 'diluted' second generation. Silently, under the roof of every immigrant home there is going on a death-struggle between two worlds."[68] A reasonable hope is only that ideals and (cultural) strengths of many peoples will become part of American life over a long process of cultural assimilation.

Isaac Berkson published his doctoral dissertation completed at Teachers College, Columbia University—*Theories of Americanization*—at almost the same moment that Drachsler published his own Columbia dissertation. Berkson was committed to a career in Jewish education inspired by just the sort of reawakened religion and nationality (as peoplehood) that Magnes had invoked. Part of this reawakening he conceived to be the creation of a Jewish society in Palestine and eventually a Jewish state. Later he ended up working in Palestine for some years as an educational administrator.[69] His concern in the dissertation (his major work) was how a renaissance of Jewish culture could be balanced with a commitment to American democracy. The general form of the question concerned the survival and legitimacy of ethnic culture in American life.

> The question before us relates . . . to the particular kind of differentiation due to the retention of ethnic loyalties. The problem that faces us is whether ethnic distinctions are to be tolerated in America. The supreme difference from our point of view between the ethnic group and other classifications such as political parties, economic classes, geographic sections . . . is that the former is foreign and the latter indigenous. These ethnic distinctions—Jew, Italian, Pole—were formed under conditions of other times and places. . . . Further, if these foreign groups are to persist, under what limitations may they do so?[70]

When he referred to "theories of Americanization," he meant the competing theories about how the tension between ethnic persistence and assimilation might play out in the future. Berkson's work was not unknown at the time (Thomas's *Old World Traits*, for example, quoted from a prepublication copy). But the long-term influence of his writing was in contrasting three of these theories of Americanization. This delineation was incorporated four decades later into the discussion of assimilation scenarios in Milton Gordon's immensely influential *Assimilation in American Life*.[71] Berkson called these three theories "Americanization," "The Melting Pot," and "the Federation of Nationalities." In the first vision, the immigrant assimilates as quickly as possible into present-day American culture; in the second, all peoples (including the older American population) lose their distinctiveness but contribute something to a new American type; and in the third, the peoples of America remain distinct indefinitely. Berkson followed Kallen in the labeling of this third option. Milton Gordon would refer to it instead as "cultural pluralism," following Kallen's own popularization of that term years after his 1915 essay.

Berkson rejected the first two theories, Americanization and the Melting Pot, because they unnecessarily required the disappearance of the ethnic group. And he rejected Kallen's federation of nationalities because he saw that "The theory is based on the assumption of the ineradicable and central influence of race." He argued that race in fact had no such dominance, and consequently other cultures can—and assuredly did—lure the individual from particular ethnic loyalties: "The epigram, 'We cannot change our grandfathers' is but a sophism." Likewise, there was far too much mixing of groups in the same cities and even neighborhoods to believe that group concentration and isolation would ensure group survival.[72]

Berkson added a fourth theory of his own. The community theory, he wrote, "would make the history of the ethnic group, its aesthetic, cultural and religious inheritance, its national self-consciousness the basic factor. . . . [And that] must be acquired through some educational process."[73]

Berkson readily admitted the danger that cultural loyalties might be insufficient to preserve the ethnic community indefinitely. But he offered all he could, namely, a hope that some kind of ethnic schools would forestall that end. He also envisioned replenishment of cultural energy from the continuing arrival of immigrants from the old country.[74]

Harry A. Wolfson, then a young Harvard historian of medieval philosophy and later among the most renowned students of the subject, may seem an improbable contributor to this discussion. But he was an immigrant himself, a product of traditional Jewish culture and eastern European Zionism, as well as the study of Western philosophy. In 1918, after the Balfour Declaration and the British conquest of Palestine, he wrote a two-part essay, originally published anonymously in the *Menorah Journal*. Three years later he gave permission to the journal to reveal his authorship. This periodical had been publishing a wide variety of views on nationality as peoplehood, the "Jewish reawakening," and the blending of religion and culture. But Wolfson's two-part essay challenged a great deal that most writers had been taking for granted. He argued that a reawakening of cultural nationalism was indeed a necessary short-term goal for American Jews—because the Jews had no state of their own in which the reawakening could occur. But once they did get such a state—and in 1918 it looked as though they would— things would have to change in American Jewish life. Specifically, Wolfson rejected the invocations of Kallen and Magnes, mentioning both by name. A vibrant national Jewish culture would no longer suit the American scene. Those who wanted to be fully Jewish in cultural terms would move to Zion. The rest eventually would (and should) end up part of "a universal Jewish church" in America. This must be the inevitable outcome for American Jews because in America cultural and social assimilation were indeed inevitable; only a distinctive choice of a universal religion was compatible. Indeed, he preceded the analysis of the American Jewish condition with a brief analysis of American immigrant assimilation in general, which he titled, "the Cephalic index and baseball." The mention of the index was a reference to Franz Boas's study (described in Chapter 4) that even head form changed quickly in the New World. The reference to baseball was a wry comment that much more important than any role for biology in assimilation were social and cultural interactions. The ethnic group, then, could have an American existence, but only in the short term. But in all of this, Wolfson treated Kallen and Magnes gently. He was much more contemptuous of the Yiddishists (and especially their socialists), who hailed the triumph of the people's culture that had developed in the preceding decades, while they spurned the Hebraic culture of the Bible, other religious writings produced over two millennia, and the recent rebirth of Hebrew culture.[75]

The most prominent expert on immigrant and ethnic life at the time, W. I. Thomas, studied and criticized the work of cultural survivalists at the end of *Old World Traits Transplanted*. Indeed, he discussed Berkson directly. Thomas commented that he had no objection in principle to the success of their vision, but he saw it as unrealistic. It was understandable that such cultural loyalists would emerge, but their vision would fail in the course of a few generations. Ethnic survival would require one of three conditions. First, a great instrumental advantage in loyalty to the group, emphatically not the case in America. Second, an immigrant culture regarded as superior to that of the American mainstream; this, too, was not then the case nor likely to ever be so in an era of widespread interaction among groups. Third, a very thoroughgoing discrimination, but in fact discrimination was simply too weak to lead to immigrant group survival (although Thomas warned that Americanization programs were growing more coercive). Curiously, Thomas made no mention in that section of his work about the role of discrimination in retarding Asian assimilation. Replenishment by new arrivals also was not considered as retarding assimilation, perhaps because the First Quota Act was already at hand.[76]

In sum: group survival over the long term was impossible. Once again, whatever the terminology Thomas used, the emphatic turn from biological to sociocultural processes dominated his thought. In dealing with ethnic survival, he did not comment on Kallen's 1915 essay, "Democracy and the Melting Pot." Quite possibly he excluded Kallen from the cultural survivalist camp because, as Berkson stressed in the work Thomas had read, Kallen's views of the future rested on a biological process of transmission of cultural traits. Thomas, then, would not have thought Kallen qualified as an interesting example of a cultural survivalist.

M. L. HANSEN: THE MEANING OF ETHNIC LIFE TO EACH SUCCEEDING GENERATION, 1937

Marcus Lee Hansen helped transform American immigration history from the biography of illustrious individuals to the social history of mass movements. In 1937, approaching forty, he was a history professor at the University of Illinois in Urbana-Champaign, but he had barely a year before disease would end his life. The first part of his envisioned opus on immigration was published posthumously and won the Pulitzer Prize.[77]

Our interest is not in his major books but in a lecture, "The Problem of the Third Generation Immigrant," that he gave that year to a Swedish American historical society.[78] The lecture is known today above all for "Hansen's Law"—"What the son wishes to forget, the grandson wishes to remember."[79] But the "law" is only one insight into a broader sociological sketch of ethnic generations from immigration to assimilation. The "law" itself was important to his outlook, and his paper's title tended to push it into the limelight. Nevertheless, he did not write the essay in order to state the law but rather to grapple with much more profound issues about ethnic culture, identity, inevitable assimilation, and the historian's responsibility.

Written as a consideration of third and later generations of an *older* immigration, the lecture was first published by the Swedish American society to whom it had been addressed. Oscar Handlin and Nathan Glazer were instrumental in republishing it in 1952. By then they were already established second-generation intellectuals of the *newer* European immigration (from southern and eastern Europe). The published lecture would draw increasing attention in later decades, probably because the third generation of the southern and eastern Europeans were coming of age, and because at least some of this demographic were indeed wishing to remember, as the "law" predicted they would.[80] Perhaps, too, interest in the essay in still later decades has receded following the eclipse of that third generation's interest. But it would be a pity to lose sight of Hansen's essay simply because that transient demographic stage has passed.

What is often ignored in the pithy statement of the "law" is that Hansen did not think it was limited to *ethnic* generations. Hansen pointed out in an aside that the fascination with the Civil War in his time was another case in point. A year before, he noted "a granddaughter of the Confederacy" had written *Gone with the Wind*.[81] But he was especially interested in the third-generation immigrant. He urged his audience at the Swedish historical society to think about their own society and its tasks in the context of immigrant memories. The immigrant generation itself had been dying out.

Fifteen million are still part of the American population, but they are no longer immigrants. By one adjustment after the other . . . they became what the natives called "Americanized" (which was often nothing more than a treaty of peace with society). [The 1924 Quota Act and the Depression stopped the flow of new arrivals and removed] from the pages of magazines, from the debates in Congress and from the thoughts of social workers the well-known expression: the problem of the immigrant. Its going has foreshadowed the disappearance of a related matter of concern, which was almost as troublesome as the first, . . . "the problem of the second generation."

The sons and daughters of the immigrants were really in a most uncomfortable position. They were subjected to the taunts and criticisms [of "native Americans" and of "their elders"—parents, schoolmistress, truant officer, etc.]. . . . They were not slow in comprehending the source of all their woes: it lay in the strange dualism into which they had been born. . . . How to inhabit two worlds at the same time was the problem of the second generation. That problem was solved by escape. . . . The son . . . wanted to forget everything [language, customs, neighborhood].[82]

And so in organizational life: the immigrants created associations and preserved every scrap of evidence of the migration. "All this seemed useless to the son who cleared out his father's desk. . . . The second generation does not write any history."[83]

Then, however, appears the third generation. They have no reason to feel any inferiority when they look about them. They are American born. Their speech is the same as that of those with whom they associate. Their material wealth is the average possession of the typical citizen. [They look at recent immigrants, the] hordes who have been pouring through the gates and [they may suggest] that the onrush should be stemmed . . . usually prefaced with the remark that the recent immigrants are not so desirable as the pioneers that arrived in earlier times. [They perceive their own prosperity as] a sign of the hardy stock from which we have sprung; who were they [that hardy stock] and why did they come? And so their curiosity is projected back. . . . [In] the universities of the Middle West, where a large proportion of the students are the grandchildren and great-grandchildren of the nineteenth century immigrants [we observe] . . . the feeling of pride in which they study the history and culture of the nations from which their ancestors came.[84]

Indeed, Hansen wrote, the Swedes' own turn to experience this generational shift was commencing: "Whenever any immigrant group reaches the third generation stage in its development, a spontaneous and almost irresistible impulse arises which forces the thoughts of many people of different professions, different positions in life and different points of view to interest themselves in that one factor which they have in common: heritage, the heritage of blood."[85]

Hansen soon turned to historical study in particular. "What should be the attitude to the past? . . . Everyone accepts that self-laudation is not the end in view."[86] The third generation should try to write the history of the group, he said, "on broad impartial lines . . . and make a contribution to the meaning of American history at large."[87] Furthermore, he noted, "The [Swedish historical] society will not live forever. The time will come when membership will dwindle. . . . The constituency becomes gradually thinned out as the third generation merges into the fourth and the fourth shades into the fifth. . . . Men of insight . . . understand that it is the ultimate fate of any national group to be amalgamated into the composite American race."[88] Yes, "the ultimate fate of any national group" is to be amalgamated. The old cultural distinctiveness and loyalties will be lost. But "men of insight"—and he meant especially historians of insight—"will be reconciled to the thought that their historical activities will in time be merged . . . with the main line of American historiography itself." The third-generation mission must be to uncover the inner history of American immigration, "the mentality of the millions of persons who had not ceased to be Europeans and had not yet become accepted Americans."[89]

If the third generation can still express this mentality, it is also capable of avoiding a provincial self-adulation. Indeed, the two times he mentions the ethnic group explicitly it is in connection with avoiding that danger. To avoid it "should be on the minds of every writer who is tempted to generalize on the contribution of ethnic groups to the development of American life." Similarly, if the third generation of Swedish Americans could produce "a history of the Swedes in America that no one could accuse of being tainted with partiality," then it would accomplish "what no other ethnic group in America has been willing to do."

Hansen's essay set the historical tasks of his audience in the context of the third generation, but he also viewed that generation's task within an awareness of the oblivion that would eventually follow in the fifth or sixth generation. At the same time, he urges that the awareness of the generational pattern provides something more than despair that all will be forgotten in the end. The march to oblivion itself makes the group a part of the broad pattern of American history repeating in every group. Each specific group will disappear, but the awareness of participation in the process endures. We may wonder how much confidence Hansen had that the Swedes would indeed accomplish what every other group had been unwilling to do—abandon "self-laudation" for historical quality. But his own task was to clarify both the sociology of the generational challenge and provide the consolation of historical understanding.

Isaac Berkson may have been reasonably clear-eyed about ethnic assimilation over the generations, but he had hoped at least to forestall such outcomes through the ethnic school. W. I. Thomas believed not only that ultimate amalgamation was inevitable. He thought that views like Berkson's must be understood as a misguided hope, if perhaps interesting as a subject for the sociology of knowledge—a view likely to emerge at a particular stage in ethnic assimilation. And Thomas could hope to reassure the misguided nativist with this analysis of assimilation. Hansen, like Berkson, may regard the loss of group cultures and memories as tragic, but, like Thomas, he faces the inevitable. Yet, unlike Thomas, his interest is not to reassure the nativist but to find in historical understanding—shorn of the provincial self-laudation—how elements from the lost past join the broad development of American history.

That it was Hansen who formulated all this was no accident. It would have taken a seer to develop the details of later-generation ethnicity in connection with the Italians or Poles in the 1930s. By contrast, Hansen was familiar with the history of the older Scandinavian immigrations. And he was in the process of writing a multivolume series on the history of American immigration; the first volume, reaching to 1860, would deal with the oldest groups.

Not just his ethnic origin but also the moment at which he wrote broadened Hansen's perspective. As he notes, before 1930 it would have been very hard to envision the termination of ethnic replenishment. But the combination of the Quota Acts and the Great Depression had indeed terminated replenishment. It was not just that the older groups had late-generation descendants; now that was *all* they would have. Finally, the end of mass immigration from Europe also meant that the attention of observers was no longer riveted on stark contrasts between waves of new arrivals from a variety of countries and older-stock Americans. Nor was the very long debate about immigration restriction policy any longer demanding the attention and energy of anyone thinking about immigrants and their descendants; new issues could receive attention. He mentioned all these features of his time in the essay.

There was probably another reason Hansen had been drawn to themes of later-generation ethnic life. The National Origins Act of 1924 envisioned quotas that rested on a knowledge of the proportionate share of European American descendants that could be traced to each national origin. But Americans long removed from immigrant ancestors simply did not know their national origins; these would require research and estimation. Congress had left the calculations to the Census Bureau's chief statistician, Joseph Hill. Hill in turn recruited a board of academic experts to help him, and Hansen was the historian on that board. During the late 1920s, then, Hansen consistently confronted both the loss of ethnic consciousness among descendants and their blended origins. He had occasion to think hard about the long-term fate of ethnic groups sooner than, and in greater detail than, other scholars of immigrant life.

Increasing Diffusion of the Emergent Concept among Social Scientists, 1949–1964

In November 1952, the American Jewish magazine *Commentary* reprinted Hansen's lecture on the third generation. It appeared in a series called *The Study of Man*, which was the responsibility of Associate Editor Nathan Glazer. Oscar Handlin, then Harvard's specialist in the history of immigration, provided the introduction for the reprint.[90]

It was the achievement of Marcus Lee Hansen to have discovered the means of studying significantly the role of immigration in American history. . . . Hansen speaks, in the first instance, of the problems of writing the history of the specific immigrant group. But more generally he probes the whole question of group identification. . . . *Commentary* readers will be moved to ponder on the applicability to Jewish immigrants of Hansen's striking theses: his views on the second and third generation, . . . themes to which the immigrant historian should devote himself, and above all perhaps, his prediction of the limited survival span in America . . . of the effective *distinctive* life of the group.[91]

Handlin must have known of the Hansen essay for a dozen years or more. Hansen, a few years his senior, had been his intellectual partner in transforming the writing of American immigration history. Writing in particular for the Jewish readers of *Commentary*, Handlin added a passage that is hard not to read as his own and Glazer's personal concern with and admiration for Hansen's largest themes.

If one's own experience is any clue, one may predict that the first reaction of many Jewish readers to this essay will be one of surprise . . . at the uncanny similarities between patterns in the adjustment of other groups of settlers and those patterns which many have thought to be particular to the newcomers of the Jewish group. . . . The second reaction may come: to turn to the possible ways in which the Jewish group in America is after all exceptional and distinctive, and to consider whether, to what degree and how American Jews . . . can hope to escape the complete amalgamation which Hansen seems to predict.[92]

By the early 1950s, both Glazer and Handlin were writing extensively about American ethnic groups. Indeed, three years before his introduction to the Hansen reprint, Handlin had published another article in *Commentary*, "Group Life within the American Pattern: Its Scope and Limitations" (November 1949). In this article he reflected on the place of the voluntary association in "setting the limits and determining the scope of state action" in a democracy. Within the context of these larger concerns, much of Handlin's discussion turned on the role of the ethnic group in an impersonal society.

Membership in the ethnic group comes through the family. . . . Familial ties and common cultural, economic, social, and intellectual attitudes lead the group into a wide array of associational activities which express its awareness of its own identity. . . . A sense of inner responsibility for the group has produced innumerable charitable institutions. Like traditions give rise to cultural associations, and the desire for comradeship leads to purely social and fraternal societies. Common ideology and common interests sometimes encourage concerted political action as well.[93]

Handlin notes (much as Hansen had noted earlier) that "The problem of the role of ethnic groups was small in our consciousness until the 1930s" because the changing waves of immigrants kept the focus of attention on the first generation. Nevertheless, "Americans have not in these two decades grown less varied, but . . . so many Americans now face the problem of explaining to themselves the quality of their ethnic allegiances."[94]

The American groups are not maintained only or primarily as a response to prejudice: "while some ethnic groups are discriminated against, there is *no necessary connection* between prejudice and the existence of the ethnic group [italics added]."[95] The point was especially important for Handlin because he distinguished the ethnic group from the (vulnerable) European minority groups of the interwar period, as we have already seen.

Handlin also fleshed out his discussion of ethnic groups in 1952 when he testified before the President's Commission on Immigration and Naturalization. In connection with his brief testimony, he submitted a long document that was later published as two chapters of his essay collection, *Race and Nationality in American Life* (1957). The first part of the document demolished the evidence on race that Congress had relied on in passing the National Origins Act (1924). This evidence had come from the introductory overviews to the U.S. Immigration Commission's *Reports* (1911) and from Harry Laughlin's studies for Albert Johnson's House Immigration Committee in the early 1920s. The last part of Handlin's document for the President's Commission summarized evidence from contemporary science on the same issues. For example, he cited *We Europeans* as well as the 1950 UNESCO Statement. "Mankind is essentially one," races "differ from each other in the frequency of one or more genes which determine the hereditary concentration of physical traits," but "National, religious, geographic, linguistic and cultural groups do not coincide with race, and the cultural and social traits of such groups have no genetic connection with racial traits." And finally, "There is no evidence of any inborn differences of temperament, personality, character, or intelligence among races."

As we have seen, the first UNESCO Statement, like *We Europeans* before it, had also called for the elimination of the term "race" and for discussion of the *physical* differences among human groups in terms of "ethnic groups." The second UNESCO Statement (1951) had dropped this call as well as any discussion of ethnic group. By contrast, Handlin exploited these works to take an altogether independent direction. He defined the "ethnic group" as a purely social and cultural phenomenon: "Therefore it follows [i.e., from the 1950 UNESCO Statement] that the only meaningful basis upon which one can compare social and cultural traits is in terms of the ethnic group, which preserves its continuity to the extent that its culture passes from generation to generation through a common social environment. The inheritance of an ethnic group consists not of its biological characteristics, but of its culture."[96]

This discussion had appeared in Handlin's influential collection of essays in 1957, which had been titled *Race and Nationality in American Life*. But why "nationality"? The book never explains its title. Indeed in the several chapters on postwar themes, Handlin had discussed the American ethnic group at some length, and nowhere in the text did he speak of nationality in the sense of peoplehood. Probably he (or his publisher) had concluded that in 1957 "nationality" was still a more commonly understood term for peoplehood than was "ethnic group," at least among the wider readership Handlin hoped to reach.

In 1953, Glazer wrote an article for *Commentary* with a title remarkably like Handlin's from 1949: "America's Ethnic Pattern." He reexamined the old predictions of a melting pot and cultural pluralism in the light of "the main lines of assimilation of the various ethnic groups that make up the American population." Whatever "a nation of nations" had meant "for the earlier period of our history," it no longer was based on living culture but on a more self-conscious affiliation with origins.

> Today the "nations" that make up America no longer find much justification in the maintenance of language, religion and culture: they are

private or subconscious "nations" held together by a nostalgia which does not dare to become an ideology, a frame of mind which itself has no organic relation to their Old World past but is a reaction to the conditions of 20th-century America. What remains most questionable today in this history of assimilation is the status and future prospects of these ghost nations, built around ideologies of support of the home countries, and drawing their real strength from experiences in America which make their elements feel less than full Americans. Whether these empty nations are only given the illusion of a relatively vigorous life by recent developments in Europe, or whether the conditions of American life are not such as to maintain and strengthen them for some time to come: this is something that only the next twenty years can decide.[97]

Handlin, too, had discussed how American society stimulated ethnic association. But he had meant that such associations support the individual against the anonymity of an impersonal modern society. And he had emphasized how ethnic groups were not merely reactions to discrimination. For Glazer the associations also fulfilled an emotional need, but that need was a distinctly ethnic insecurity. The "ghost nations . . . [are] drawing their real strength from experiences in America which make their elements feel less than full Americans."[98]

Meanwhile, in the same years two other authors wrote enormously popular works on contemporary American life, and both stressed the social importance of ethnic groups. Samuel Lubell's *The Future of American Politics* (1951) concerned political trends of all kinds, but several of the most important trends derived from black–white relations or the experiences of descendants of immigrants. In considering the latter, he focused attention on two social patterns. The first was the "'coming of age' of the various urban 'minorities,'" in particular the children of the immigrants from southern and eastern Europe who were experiencing social mobility and cultural assimilation. The second was a close examination of isolationism in American life that Lubell found to be related to the later-generation German and Irish descendants, even when they themselves were not quite aware of the origin of their own beliefs. Lubell was not particularly concerned with progressing from these reflections to a theory of American ethnic groups. It was enough to understand the critical role that later-generation descendants of the immigrants were playing in contemporary politics. Glazer soon wrote a glowing review of Lubell's work for *Commentary:* "The best book yet written on American politics of the last twenty years; and if a better one should appear, it is hard to see how it could be anything but a further development of the basic pattern laid down by Lubell."[99]

In 1955, Will Herberg's *Protestant, Catholic and Jew: An Essay in American Religious Sociology* drew on discussions of American ethnic life in the work of Hansen, Ruby Jo Reeves Kennedy, Glazer, and Handlin. Herberg argued that the dominant American ideal was indeed the melting pot, and that the third generation eschewed ethnic separateness in principle. But in practice, much of its group life was still based on connections to the origin groups. So a subtle change took place in the nature of the group life of the third generation. The descendant of the immigrant is expected to give up "nationality, language, culture" of the forbearers: "One thing, however, he is *not* expected to change—and that is his religion. And so it is religion that with the third generation has become the differentiating element and the context of self-identification and social location."[100] Herberg spent remarkably little time defending the notion that the immigrant is expected to give up explicit ethnic (national origin) loyalties. An intriguing parallel is found in another book published in the same year as Herberg's: Marshall Sklare's *Conservative Judaism: An American Religious Movement.* Sklare explained much that was special about the Conservative movement in American Judaism in terms of a general American phenomenon, "the ethnic church." Here he made an argument very similar to Herberg's about ethnic loyalty expressed through the more acceptable religious community. But Sklare too said very little about *why* ethnic loyalty itself seemed unacceptable in America. The point is not that either author overlooked the question, but rather that each assumed it required no more than a few sentences.[101] Glazer also may have had in mind this reality when describing (in "America's Ethnic Pattern" [1953]) "a nostalgia which does not dare to become an ideology."[102]

This interpretation of religious themes through an ethnic lens was continued in Glazer's *American Judaism* (1957).[103] It rested heavily on the thesis that Judaism was the religion of a particular "nation," and that Jewish life in America was best viewed first through the lens of ethnic group life. In the introduction he offered two explanatory footnotes, back to back.

I use the word nation to refer to a group of people who feel they have a common identity and a common cultural heritage, who may feel they are of common descent, who may speak a common language, who may inhabit a contiguous stretch of territory, and who may on occasion form a nation-state. This usage is familiar to students of nationalism. "Nationality," "national group," "people," and "race" all have somewhat different connotations, but all of them have been used to refer to the same social reality.

The term "ethnic group" refers to an element in a population that feels itself, to some extent, part of a single nationality, nation, people, or race. In the United States, the Irish, Italians, and Poles, the French Canadians, Puerto Ricans, and Mexicans, the Negroes and the Jews, are all ethnic groups. So were the Germans in Czechoslovakia, the Hungarians in Rumania, the Boers in South Africa. An ethnic group may be a nation, or it may be only a fragment of a nation with slight ties to the main part, as is the case with most ethnic groups in the United States.[104]

But in 1963 the balance shifted when Glazer and Daniel P. Moynihan published *Beyond the Melting Pot: The Negroes, Puerto Ricans, Jews, Italians and Irish of New York City*.[105] However, this work, unlike Lubell's or even Herberg's, made race and ethnicity the absolute center of discussion. Moreover, as the title hinted, the book conveyed a new message. Many social scientists had thought, like Zangwill, Thomas, Drachsler, Ware, and Hansen, that the ethnic group could not long survive in the context of factors like occupational specialization and relatively meritocratic education and recruitment in modern society. But Glazer and Moynihan now argued that—at least for the special conditions of New York City and (it was implied) also other large ethnic communities—the ethnic group was surviving much longer and with more tenacity than expected. Furthermore, the book explained the tenacity: in the American city, the ethnic group operated as an "interest group," in which ethnic affiliation, social class, neighborhood, and political engagement were mutually reinforcing. Ethnic groups were persisting, then, and not only through indirect religious expressions. Back in 1952, Glazer had wondered whether or not American conditions would actually sustain the existence of "ghost nations" (the ethnic groups) for "some time to come." By 1963, he answered this question in the affirmative, and that was because the ghosts also functioned as interest groups in the contemporary city. The interests did not need to be grounded in the perpetuation of the immigrant generation's cultural distinctiveness. "The point about the melting pot," Glazer and Moynihan had written in the book's brief preface, "is that it did not happen. At least not in New York, and, *mutatis mutandis,* in those parts of America which resemble New York."[106] This "point" would be learned by many readers, especially in the 1970s and 1980s, when national attention focused on the many forms of white and nonwhite ethnic advocacy. This emphasis on ethnic persistence dovetailed with the new federal ethno-racial classifications developed for the 1980 census (discussed in Chapter 11). And yet the point of *Beyond the Melting Pot* began to be slowly *unlearned* as a reflection of contemporary America after the 1980s, especially as assimilative processes continued to operate on the children and grandchildren of the "white ethnic groups" who had gained such notice at the end of the 1960s.

By the time *Beyond the Melting Pot* was published in 1963, "ethnic group" and "ethnicity" were pretty well-established terms. The receding terminological flux can be observed also in Milton Gordon's *Assimilation in American Life* (1964).[107] From the perspective of the early twenty-first century, this work was described as "the most authoritative discussion of the concept [of racial and ethnic assimilation] in the post World War II era."[108] So it is worth remembering that it was subtitled *The Role of Race, Religion and National Origins.* And Gordon, unlike Handlin, explained the choice of terms: "When I use the term 'ethnic group' . . . I shall mean by it any group which is defined . . . by race, religion or national origin. . . . All these categories have a common social-psychological referent, in that all of them serve to create, through historical circumstances, a sense of peoplehood . . . and this common referent of peoplehood is recognized in the American public's usage of these three terms . . . and the term 'ethnic group' is a useful one for designation of this common element." Gordon added a note to this passage: "Some sociologists use the term 'ethnic group' to refer to a national origins group . . . [but we already] have a specific phrase, 'national origin' or 'nationality background' and we need the broader term because of the common sense of peoplehood running through race, religion or national origin."[109] Gordon's usage was thus a careful choice to define an expansive meaning for ethnic group, but one less common today: "the common sense of peoplehood running through race, religion or national origin."

Gordon's choice was typical. Today it is easy to fall into a narrow use of the "ethnic group" term, restricted to the descendants of immigrants, and even to descendants of white (European) immigrants. This restricted usage may have gained ground at the end of the 1960s when "the white ethnic" became an important term in the political culture (as described in Chapter 11). But it is important to understand that generally the social scientists who used the concept between the 1920s and the 1960s did *not* restrict the term to immigrants or white groups. Most explicitly treated African Americans as a particularly oppressed ethnic group. Certainly they may have been agnostic as to whether the long arc of history would bend to include the complete assimilation of the nonwhite groups and of African Americans in particular (Warner was especially explicit but even Zangwill dealt with the question). But they did not exclude such groups from the social and cultural concept of the ethnic. So, too, they included historical origin groups who cohere through religious loyalties. Ware, Handlin, and Gordon, for example, were explicit about this.[110] Attending to the broad initial meanings of the term emergent in the 1960s may help explain the difficulties that theorists and readers confront today in trying to specify the differences between race and ethnicity or to decide how well a variety of religious groups fit within the latter concept.[111]

CHAPTER 10

From Social Science to the Federal Bureaucracy? Limited Diffusion of the "Ethnic Group" Concept through the Early 1950s

DISCREDITING THE NAZI IDEOLOGY stimulated some sensitivity about extreme racist arguments at home in regard to both civil rights and immigration policy. Nevertheless, the restrictions and exclusions established in the National Origins Act of 1924 survived the war by more than a decade. A turn away from discussions about "races" came slowly too; in particular, "ethnic group" only became a common term in the political culture of the late 1960s. This chapter charts its slow diffusion through a close look at episodes in 1944 and 1952–1953.

Despite the tenacity of the National Origins Act, some modest reforms did occur between the time President Franklin Roosevelt came to power in 1932 and the end of World War II. Albert Johnson's efforts to close the "back door" of Mexican immigration, and the related introduction of the Mexican race category in the 1930 census, were reversed in the 1930s, along with the removal of the Mexican race category from the List of Races and Peoples. This change, in part a response to concerns raised by the Mexican government, was among the first of several ways in which international opinion influenced immigration policies, at least at the margins. Other examples followed during World War II. The complete exclusions of immigrants from some Asian countries (notably war allies) were replaced with tiny quotas—typically, one hundred admissions per year. Eventually, naturalization of Asian immigrants followed (Chinese in 1943, "races indigenous to India" as well as Filipinos in 1946). Finally, during the war temporary workers from the Americas were admitted (1943–1944). This was the beginning of the *Bracero* program that continued long after the war.

Rethinking Race, Nationality, and Ethnic Origin: The YIVO Institute Episode, 1944

The YIVO was founded in Vilnius, Lithuania, in 1925. The name is an acronym in the Yiddish language for the institution's name: Yiddish Scientific Institute. After fleeing to Paris and then New York City during the war, the YIVO brushed up its title and presented itself to Americans as the YIVO Institute for Jewish Research. In the Jewish world of eastern Europe, YIVO had declared that it had twin purposes: first, to encourage serious research on the language, culture, history, and demography of its people; and second, to invigorate *popular* Jewish knowledge by training teachers and offering a cultural program for a broad audience. Once resettled in New York in the early 1940s, YIVO had to find its way anew. In the late 1930s, there had been some ten million Yiddish speakers living around the world, but most were born in eastern Europe. Although their interaction with the wider cultures of eastern Europe on the one hand and with the Jewish religion on the other varied, mother tongue and the relative cohesion it provided did ground Yiddish speakers as a distinct people. The YIVO leaders in New York had spent their lives grappling with the issues of this distinct people. They regarded claims like those of Simon Wolf and American Jewish Committee spokesmen (that Jews were simply a religious grouping) as the expressions of advanced assimilative trends among Jews in western Europe and the United States.[1]

In the midst of the destruction of eastern European Jewry during the war years, YIVO activists had other concerns. They found the American statistics on immigration extremely useful because those statistics singled out "Hebrews" from the various other eastern European peoples. The YIVO scholars may well have thought the List of Races and Peoples originated in racist thought and prejudice, as I. A. Hourwich had thought a generation before, but also like him, they appreciated having the data. They understood that there would be no return to the mass immigrations of eastern European Jews like those of 1905 or 1910. Nevertheless, thousands had arrived in the United States since Hitler's rise, and they hoped that many thousands more might yet be allowed in after the war.

However, in 1943, in a reaction to the Nazi enemy's emphasis on a Jewish race, the liberal commissioner of immigration, Earl R. Harrison, announced that henceforth the Hebrew designation would be removed from the List of Races and Peoples. Those who had been classified in the past as Hebrews would now be classified into whichever *other* category on the List seemed most appropriate. In making that classification, Harrison announced, "Religious beliefs should be disregarded but the language spoken by and the country of residence of the applicant may be taken into consideration. . . . Where such criteria are non-existent, such a person may properly be classified as a member of the White race, in the same way as persons recorded as belonging to the Mexican race have been recorded since July 20, 1937 as persons of the White race."[2]

The YIVO scholars were shocked rather than gratified. And although they were relatively recent arrivals in America, as was YIVO as an organization, the YIVO scholars became actively involved in scrutinizing the options for classification. First, they wrote to Commissioner Harrison for an explanation. He replied in April 1944, largely repeating the wording of his agency's instruction. Still, the reply is interesting. He wrote, "The immigration law requires that certain statistical data be kept in the cases of aliens arriving in the United States. One item to be recorded is race. For many years the term 'Hebrew' was one of the terms used in recording the race of entrants. After considerable study on the part of the Department of Justice and this Service [Immigration and Naturalization], it was found desirable to discontinue the use of the term."[3]

Harrison referred only to race, rather than to races and peoples. This formulation was not an oversight or even a simplification to essentials. Harrison made it clear that his answer referred to the legal basis for the List. And since 1903, successive recodifications of immigration law included "race" among the items of information that the passenger lists should provide. The Bureau of Immigration's later addition of "people" to the name of the question had nothing to do with the legal mandate; as we have seen, the Bureau of Immigration apparently made the addition because some immigrants were more comfortable with it.

Harrison's wording did not explain *why* "it was found advisable" for the Immigration and Naturalization Service (INS) to change the classification of Jewish immigrants after forty-five years. Nevertheless, the people at YIVO surely knew that the American Jewish Committee had long called for the change. At the same time, the YIVO leaders suspected that American opinion—that is, opinion among Jewish organizations, social scientists, and government officials—was divided and was certainly uncanvassed.[4]

Accordingly, YIVO sent out a remarkable questionnaire to some 200 relevant authorities. The two-page cover letter explained the context and asked three questions:

1. Do you think it is important to have exact data on the immigration of Jews into this county, or do you see any reasons for refraining from collecting those data?

2. If you do not approve of the decisions of the Immigration and Naturalization Service as to the deletion of the term Hebrew from the classification of immigrants, would you simply recommend a return to the previous procedure as far as the Jews are concerned, or if not, what change would you suggest?

3. Do you consider the classification according to "race" appropriate? If not what other designation would you suggest?[5]

The survey clearly hit a nerve. The YIVO received 140 responses to its 200 questionnaires, and while the wording of the *direct* responses was typically brief, a surprising number of respondents added extensive additional comments, often amounting to a half page or more in print. Those 140 respondents comprise a who's who of relevant experts and leaders from American social science, Jewish life, and government. Examples include Gordon Allport, Ruth Benedict, E. S. Bogardus, Max Horkheimer, Paul Lazarsfeld, and W. I. Thomas; there were many others.[6]

The YIVO leaders decided to publish the survey responses verbatim, and they included three extensive articles of their own. One dealt with the history of the Hebrew category on the List of Races and Peoples. A second summarized the thinking of the 140 respondents and evaluated suggestions on terminology. The third presented data to show how different Jewish immigrant patterns were from those of other groups and therefore how important it was to keep the counts separate.

The most interesting feature of the YIVO effort remains the answers provided by the 140 respondents. They do not lend themselves to easy summary. But most of the many issues they discussed need not detain us. Would data on Jews increase or decrease anti-Semitism? Should the federal government or private groups collect relevant data? Was there much point (given the likelihood of relatively small Jewish immigration in the future) of worrying about such data? Should "Hebrew" or "Jew" be the relevant term? And when respondents expressed opinions as to why the immigration authorities had acted, perhaps a half dozen (nearly all affiliated with the YIVO itself) insisted they knew who had been pressing the authorities all along: the American Jewish Committee and others of the old Reform Jewish elite descended from the mid-nineteenth-century German Jewish immigrants.

More pertinent for us was that, in answer to YIVO's third question, the great majority of the respondents thought that race was the wrong term to be using in the List—it was either a meaningless designation or one that should be reserved for the broad physical divisions of mankind, in particular those related to color. But, then, what term might be substituted for conceptions related to peoplehood? Numerous respondents considered whether or not the federal government should ask about religion. This was, in the end, the simplest way to identify Jews. But did it violate the constitutional separation of church and state? Did it open the door to other such investigations (notably on the census)? Moreover, was a definition of group membership based on religion an anomaly of *Jewish* peoplehood in particular or one of broader applicability? Quite a number suggested a conference of government officials and/or social scientists to address the questions YIVO had asked in the survey.

Mother tongue had been the most relevant measure of group affiliation when the Census Bureau confronted similar questions in 1910. But those that mentioned mother tongue now were just as likely to note its limitations: assimilation in Europe meant that the government might need to ask about *parental* mother tongues. And yet, did affiliation with a people really end when the special language had disappeared? What, then, of Jews and other peoples in America (or in western Europe) who now spoke only the language of the majority? Was it really true that such people were now only Jewish in religion?

Some spoke of the need to capture the European meaning of nationality as peoplehood. For a few, this term itself seemed adequate. David Dubinsky, the leader of the Jewish garment workers, was a case in point. Writing in Yiddish in reply to the survey, Dubinsky thought "nationality" was the missing term on which the List of Races and Peoples could be reformulated, apparently unaware of the English term's ambiguity. But numerous other writers were well aware of that dual meaning.

A number commented that *any* appropriate concept would have to focus on "cultural affiliation." How, then, would such a concept handle assimilation? When raised, the reply was typically that one's "affiliation" was whatever one reported. The subjective reply had to suffice; affiliation could not be objectively imposed. But using a subjective response in turn meant that no clear or firm definition could be given for affiliations, that in some sense they were therefore unreliable. The discussion anticipated many of the issues that would resurface in the 1970s and 1980s around the Hispanic Origin and Ancestry questions introduced in the 1980 census and discussed in the next chapter.

The YIVO people seem to have been perplexed about the American government's reticence to ask about religion, whether for entering immigrants or for all residents on the census. They probably did know something of the American Jewish leaders' long insistence that this issue was wrapped up with church–state separation. But they meant to reexamine the point. Typical is the comment of one of the survey editors, Max Weinreich.

> We at the YIVO are contemplating a study . . . [of] the origin of the idea that the state should by no means inquire into the religion of the individual. . . . It is my contention that our aversion to inquiring about religion is a residue of former times, a fiction maintained nowadays merely because of conservatism. . . . Canada inquires after both religion and racial origin [with no rise in anti-Semitism]. . . . [And] the armed forces of the United States inquire into the soldier's religion.[7]

A few responses to the YIVO survey suggested that the "ethnic" or "ethnic group" concept should replace "races" on the List. Only 15 of the 140 respondents made this suggestion. About half of them were sociologists, but another 30 sociologists made no such mention of the "ethnic group" concept. It is striking that one of those sociologists that did not mention the concept was W. I. Thomas, who had sent a brief reply. More than two decades earlier his subtle and influential analysis had managed without use of the term, and he had not, it seems, adopted it since then.[8]

Max Weinreich, the YIVO research director, did pick up on the new terminology, thereby ending a long discussion of possible terms to replace "race" with the conclusion that "ethnic group" worked best. Weinreich's review had little influence in popularizing the term. His analysis covered nearly fifty pages, and his attention to the ethnic group was buried near the end. Moreover, the entire YIVO exercise probably did not interest very many readers. It helps us gauge the diffusion of the concept in the last years of the war, but it apparently contributed little to further diffusion.

The great majority of the responses came from people holding academic posts, and most of the rest were leaders in Jewish organizations. Four important federal officials also responded. Three of these were, or would be, high-ranking officials in the Census Bureau: Phillip Hauser, then an assistant director at the bureau; L. E. Truesdell, chief of the Population Division; and Conrad Taeuber, then a statistical analyst at the Agriculture Department but in the post–civil rights era a central figure at census, when the Hispanic Origin and Ancestry questions were developed. All three officials provided brief replies to YIVO, but all were to the point. Taeuber mentioned "the difficulty of distinguishing races and . . . [allocating] individuals to races," as reasons he was "inclined to agree" with the decision at the Immigration and Naturalization Service. He thought classification by country of origin and mother tongue the most attractive alternative to the List's classification by race. Hauser thought the data by race should be collected (as well as color data) perhaps using the Canadian question. Truesdell thought the data should be collected if it were reliable. And if the data were not reliable for Jews, it might as well be dropped altogether because the Jews constituted "nearly one half of immigrant aliens in 1941 (the last date for which I have figures at hand)." Data on country of origin would in any case be available. But "I certainly do not see any justification for making a classification by country of origin and *calling* it classification by *race*. In particular, I do not see any justification in discarding actual racial classification for Jews and retaining it for Negroes."[9]

On the one hand, each of these three responses from important officials in the history of the U.S. census suggests that the public official had no concern about speaking his mind. On the other hand, none of the three showed any recognition of an evolving "ethnic group" conception. To repeat, the same was true for the great majority, albeit not for all, of the academic responders.

The fourth federal official to respond was Stuart A. Rice, assistant director in charge of statistical standards in the Bureau of the Budget. As we will see in the next section, he still held the post nine years later, when his office grappled with the meaning of "ethnic classification." So his reply to the YIVO inquiry in 1944 is of some interest as background to the later federal discussions.[10]

Rice noted that someone at Immigration had informed him that the agency "discontinued the practice of listing Jews as a separate group on the ground that ... the Service ... has no legal authority to inquire as to an immigrant's religious affiliations." Moreover, "From various sources I have understood that there have been numerous protests against the previous practice of listing Jews and Hebrews as a racial group." He does not relate the two points, but his readers at YIVO no doubt did. At any rate, Rice's second formulation is also interesting in that it suggests that a high official, reasonably insulated from the specific issue, had no reason to know about the Jewish protests of the past. Nevertheless, if for some reason he did come to look into the matter, there were certainly those in government (especially, no doubt, at the INS) who did know the history. Rice proceeded to acknowledge that whatever the justice of the INS decision, it imposed a hardship on those who wanted statistics on Jewish immigrants. He then observed,

> One person whom I have consulted, and with whom I believe you have been corresponding, suggested that the adoption of a concept of ethnic origin might provide a basis for statistical classification which would permit the identification of various cultural groups without involving what to many persons appears as invidious discrimination in singling out one ethnic or religious group for special treatment.
>
> The issue which you present, as you well know, is one which has arisen in past years with reference not only to immigration statistics but also to an enumeration of the resident population of the Nation.[11]

A reasonable amount of exploration apparently put Rice in touch with an informant who linked the YIVO concerns to "cultural groups" in general and to "a concept of ethnic origin" in particular. Moreover, Rice intriguingly notes that "the issue which you present" is relevant also to the census enumerations. Although his first idea concerns cultural affiliation without mention of religion, his second seems to refer to a possible religion question for the U.S. census. He no doubt understood that various *other* Jewish organizations opposed any such question. He may have thought it worthwhile to explore those issues with a Jewish group that obviously had a different outlook on federal data collection. In any case, he concluded with an invitation.

> The Division of Statistical Standards is continually concerned with problems of this nature and we shall be glad, if you wish, to discuss with you and the Federal agencies concerned any suggestions you may advance for meeting the need for social statistics within the framework of the agencies' legal authority and at the same time avoiding the adverse public relations that have been produced by the use of certain statistical categories.[12]

As quoted earlier, Max Weinreich suggested that YIVO would pursue the invitation. If they did, nothing of consequence seems to have resulted. Likewise, there is no evidence that Rice thought back on his exchange with the YIVO scholars when his staff would struggle with the meaning of "ethnic classification" nine years later.

Federal Officials Interpret "Ethnic Classification," 1952–1953

Efforts to pass legislation admitting refugees fared better after than during the war. In 1948 the Displaced Persons (DP) Act admitted a maximum of 200,000 fleeing persecution, especially from Germany, Austria, and Italy. Their number would be charged against country quotas for future years. Another such act followed in 1953. Both were passed in the context of the Cold War, with an eye on America's international image and with sympathy for the victims of Communism.[13]

The crucial attempt to broadly reform immigration legislation during the early postwar period was made by means of the 1952 McCarran-Walter Act. But its authors refused to consider more than modest changes in existing laws. The act broadened the policy of establishing Asian quotas and naturalization that had started in the war years; at long last, nearly all traces of the 1790 "free white persons" prerequisites for naturalization disappeared. The act also substantially expanded the range of immigrants who could enter on a nonquota basis, particularly relatives of new citizens; earlier nonquota entrants included war brides and temporary workers, as well as all immigrants from the Americas (who had never been subject to the quotas of the 1920s). These small liberalizations were accompanied by some small new restrictive features, for example, concerning record-keeping to keep track of aliens.[14]

But the big question was what to do about the legacy of quotas and exclusions from the 1920s. The act's sponsors never contemplated touching the quotas or making more than token changes to Asian exclusion. Interestingly enough, the joint subcommittee report that led to the act explicitly and unequivocally rejected the Nordic race theory (which had enchanted so many in the 1920s) and any racial ranking of the quality of the world's peoples. Likewise, congressmen who argued for preserving the quotas did not do so on explicitly biological grounds. Recall that congressmen of the 1920s, too, had rarely justified restriction with reference to that theory; the difference now was that nearly everyone explicitly denied the claims of racial theory.

Why then preserve the quotas? First, everyone in Congress agreed on the need to preserve a low cap on *total* immigration; they differed only concerning the method for keeping it low. Those who campaigned to keep the quota system argued that the current law had served America well over nearly three decades of immense national challenges. Moreover, they insisted, the postwar standoff with the Soviet Union was hardly the moment in which to make social experiments. In addition, some legislators, while not drawing on hereditary differences, could still argue that arrivals who were socially and culturally similar to the American mainstream would assimilate most easily. Finally, quota supporters strongly insinuated that their opponents had ulterior motives: some were paid "professionals" working for the relevant immigrant or ethnic groups; others simply favored their own kind; still others had pink if not red loyalties and were either bent on admitting radicals or were naïve about such threats. It was not uncommon to claim that specific arguments voiced against the quotas in Congress had also appeared in the Communist Party newspaper, *The Daily Worker*.[15] President Truman vetoed the McCarran-Walter Act over the quota issue and expressed astonishment that quotas could be seriously discussed in 1952. But Congress found the votes to override, and the McCarran-Walter Act became law.

After the McCarran-Walter Act passed, a group of officials poring over its clauses noticed a requirement that visa applicants list their "ethnic classification." What, the officials wondered, did this term mean? Before discussing their efforts to find an answer, we need to appreciate that in the period since the war, the use of a similar term, "ethnic Germans," had become increasingly common.

"Ethnic Germans" was not a term Americans had introduced; it was an import from the European context—where the centuries-old eastward migration of German people was now intersecting with the realities of the Cold War. In the postwar context, the English-language term described German-origin people who had lived outside, generally east, of the German state. In the interwar years, these ethnic Germans had instead often been discussed (with other minority peoples of central Europe) as "national minorities." But in the postwar world, the term was no longer meaningful since the relevant states had expelled ethnic Germans. Nor could this population be described in English with the term "nationality," given the ambiguity about citizenship that the term conveyed. To refer to them only as "Germans" or "German people" would have been too inclusive, as those terms also referred to citizens of the German state itself. "Race" might also have worked in earlier times but not in the postwar world. Ironically, the ethnic German communities had often been stirred to Nazi sentiments in the Hitler years, and the German dictator had used their presence as an important justification for annexing territory, most famously in Czechoslovakia's Sudetenland. But with the collapse of Hitler's government, these ethnic Germans, well over ten million in all, were pushed westward, first fleeing the Red Army and later expelled by the postwar regimes in the east. Most of the latter expulsions occurred under the Soviet-dominated, Communist regimes. And it is this Cold War–era consideration that explains Congress's regular discussion of the "ethnic Germans" in the context of postwar refugee policy. Smaller numbers of "ethnic Greeks" and "ethnic Italians," from areas in Yugoslavia and other states that had come under Communist rule, were also included.

The mention of "ethnic Germans" and the related terms for other European groups of the war years ("ethnic Greeks," etc.) was novel in federal legislation. Such usage accounted for almost every mention of the term "ethnic" in federal governmental discussions during the late 1940s and early 1950s.[16] In the same years, the *New York Times* published a few articles that mentioned "ethnic" topics. Its first mention of "ethnic Germans" (July 25, 1947) occurred in an article about the postwar refugees, and the *Times* used the German term, *Volksdeutsche*, as well. The English use of the term may have been introduced by UN refugee organizations and imported into congressional discussions about refugee laws.

Consequently, the State Department had already worked out a definition of who would qualify as an "ethnic German" in 1949. The relevant individual had to have been born in "Poland, Czechoslovakia, Hungary, Rumania or Yugoslavia" and resided in Germany or Austria when the act was passed (June 1948). And he or she had to be "characteristically Germanic" based on several of the following criteria that would demonstrate "German ethnic origin":

a) Antecedents emigrated from Germany.
b) Use of any of the German dialects as the common language of the home or for social communications.
c) Resided in the country of birth in an area populated by persons of Germanic origin or stock who have retained German social characteristics and group homogeneity as distinguished from the surrounding population.
d) Evidences common attributes or social characteristics of the German group in which he resided in the country of his birth such as educational institutions attended, church affiliation, social and political associations and affiliations, name, business or commercial practices and associations, and secondary languages or dialects.[17]

The last three criteria establish that the first was insufficient: blood alone would not establish "ethnic origin." Rather, the State Department had established a thoroughly cultural and social meaning for "ethnic." And these German ethnic bonds had to be much stronger than was typical of bonds among ethnics who had been in America for several generations. Continuity of language use, community homogeneity, individual schooling, church, and economic position all pointed to much greater isolation from the majority population than was prevalent in America.

Thus "ethnic classification" probably entered the McCarran-Walter Act to cover the situation of "ethnic Germans." The congressional staff members who drafted the text of the act had thought it best to know whether visa applicants might qualify for special consideration under postwar refugee laws. But that clause of the act was so minor, the act so long, and the quota issue so much more compelling that congressional discussion never touched on the term.[18]

The Office of Statistical Standards within the Bureau of the Budget was charged with operationalizing the provisions in the act prior to its start date. Referred to by its initials OSS, it is not to be confused with the wartime intelligence agency that had used the same initials (the Office of Strategic Services). The OSS of our story came into being during the war years too. Faced with the growth of the federal bureaucracy in the New Deal and World War II, Congress passed the Federal Reports Act of 1942 to ensure that federal agencies did not burden individuals or businesses with overlapping requirements for information. One clause of this law directed the head of the Bureau of the Budget to review new data demands coming from the executive branch. An assistant director of the Bureau of the Budget headed the OSS: Stuart Rice, whom we encountered responding to the YIVO questionnaire in the preceding section. Had Rice thought to have his staff contact the YIVO scholars for help with their scrutiny of "ethnic classification," their effort might have taken a very different turn.

The deliberations over new terms in the McCarran-Walter Act were hardly a full-time job for any federal official. And yet more than a dozen individuals in the OSS, State Department, Immigration and Naturalization Service (INS), Census Bureau, Smithsonian Institution, and President's Commission on Immigration and Naturalization got involved trying to understand the act's reference to "ethnic classification." A committee and subcommittee coordinated by OSS struggled over the matter between August and December 1952. Then efforts died away, and by June 1953, the issue had disappeared. By then, Dwight D. Eisenhower had recaptured the presidency for the Republican Party (after two decades of Roosevelt and Truman), and the new executive branch had better things to do than follow up on opaque details left to them by outgoing officials. The new heads of the OSS concluded that they could simply ignore the "ethnic classification" requirement, and later still, they had that clause of the immigration law officially rescinded.

But before its unseemly demise, the "ethnic classification" term had perplexed officials for some time, and they showed erudition, intelligence, and energy in trying to interpret it. Fortunately, their internal correspondence and memos, first discovered and discussed by Margo Anderson and William Seltzer, have survived.[19]

The OSS appointed a subcommittee under the direction of one of its senior officials, Helen R. Jeter, to deal with the McCarran-Walter Act. The subcommittee included representatives from INS, State, and Census. This subcommittee in turn appointed a working group, chaired by one Harry Alpert, also of the OSS, to work exclusively on the meaning of the race and ethnic concepts in the act.

An early memo calling for a meeting of the subcommittee summarized the challenges.[20] The general context was the administrative legacy, since current usage should conform to past usage. In the past, aliens had been classified by "country of birth, nationality, race, country of last permanent residence and 'people.'" The recent DP legislation had added "German ethnic origin." The memo implied that there was a possible contradiction inherent in the new act.

> [It] abolishes all restrictions of race in naturalization procedure but retains race among the [data items to be collected]. . . . In addition, the new law requires "ethnic classification" and classification of "peoples indigenous to the Asia-Pacific Triangle." . . . [Moreover, in] the United States, there is no official precedent for a complete ethnic classification except the earlier Census classification by "mother tongue."
>
> It is [however,] doubtful whether language alone would now be considered a good basis for ethnic classification.

If the subcommittee could not avoid the definitional issue by simply relying on language (mother tongue) as a proxy for ethnic group, it would need to probe the concept itself in order to proceed.

> One of the first questions that must be addressed is whether every individual has an ethnic group?

> Any minority within a single nationality (citizenship) group (except a political party) may deserve consideration as an ethnic group. [An example: Serbs, Croatians, and Slovenians with Yugoslav nationality.] ... Such differences as now persist increasingly are cultural differences and it may now prove very difficult to assign every Yugoslav national to a particular ethnic group. [And probably only the ethnic Germans are relevant to American policy anyway.]

Might the term apply to people only in certain kinds of sociohistorical conditions? Similarly, would "ethnic classification" typically just duplicate the "citizenship" data? And even when it provided additional information, what use would it be? By tentatively defining an ethnic group as "any minority ... (except a political party)" within a state, the memorandum implied that not everyone actually had an ethnic group.

Part of the challenge was that the subcommittee had to focus on the meaning of the ethnic group *within Europe*. Thus American ethnic status was irrelevant to the subcommittee's issue—ethnic classification in Europe and especially the "ethnic German." When the subcommittee turned to research on American ethnic groups for illumination, they would find it difficult to make connections to the nature of other groups to whom the "ethnic" term was applied. Nevertheless, they did draw on readings and conversation about the use of the term in the context of American social science.

The subcommittee members recognized the crucial point that the ethnic group was bound up with cultural origins. Moreover, they were sensitive to the related dilemma: How stable were groups based on cultural origins? Could the current generation of Yugoslavs, for example, really be assigned to only one of the local ethnic groups, or did assimilation and intermarriage make such assignment impossible? And would language alone adequately identify a group? Probably not. True, mother tongue had sufficed for the European statisticians in the last quarter of the nineteenth century as well as for the American census takers in 1910, but generations of national integration had occurred since then. Finally, this early memo noted the use of "peoples" in the new law.

> The new immigration law refers to "peoples" presumably not synonymous with races. The Immigration and Naturalization Service has in use a classification "by race or people." ...

> This classification appears to be a combination of color, language, ethnic group, nationality and geographic group.

Four decades earlier, Interior Secretary Courtleyou's committee had also tried to tease out the underlying criteria for the categories found on the List of Races and Peoples, but that committee had come up with "language . . . locality . . . blood strain regardless of language." Living in a different age, the OSS subcommittee replaced the last with "ethnic group [and] nationality." In any case, the memo also asks: Can the classification of the List be abandoned in favor of a few significant ethnic groups? As Margo Anderson has demonstrated, however, the subcommittee never strayed far from the actual categories on the original List.[21]

From August to November 1953, the subcommittee and working group continued to refine the principles that lay behind an ethnic classification. An initial disclaimer began by underscoring "the preliminary character of this listing and . . . the need for further deliberations." It was soon expanded to cover "the inadequate state of knowledge, both conceptual and empirical, regarding ethnic groups."[22]

Eventually they got down to distinguishing among relevant concepts. They "interpreted *race* to refer to a classification of human groups in strictly physical anthropological terms." For immigration purposes, the color groupings of the "grand racial divisions" would be enough. By contrast,

> *Ethnic Classification*, with accent on cultural and social criteria, will necessarily have to be more detailed in order to provide the statistical information desired for administrative and research purposes. . . .
>
> The Working Group was guided by the concept of an *ethnic group* as one based on common ties of language, religion, culture, ancestry and historical continuity and not necessarily on nationality or citizenship.[23]

The writers do not invoke (and may not have known) the usage of nationality as peoplehood. Still, their main point was to distinguish ethnic from racial classification by the "accent on [the] social and cultural" in the former.

Finally, in later meetings the subcommittee members added to these distinctions the observation that the choice of ethnic group was a matter of subjective identity: "*in accordance with his own group identifications*" [emphasis in original]. Yet they also insisted on a limit to subjectivity: membership in *multiple* groups was prohibited. A principle behind all data gathering was that categories must be "mutually exclusive; no individual should find himself in two or more groups."[24] But what of a child (or later-generation descendants) of people from two different groups? The assumption, apparently, was that each individual would self-identify as a member of only one category.

After all of this work, the purpose behind the act's requirement of race and "ethnic classification" continued to trouble Jeter's subcommittee. If the answer provided would not determine the fate of the visa application, why ask the question? Still, the OSS was not free to alter the terms of an act. So the subcommittee speculated about its purpose. Perhaps the results would be useful for adjusting the national origins quotas in the decades going forward; adjusting, that is, for modifications created by the new arrivals.[25] But this solution was to ignore the historical context of the old quotas. They were based on a blood quantum: the proportion of (white) American blood derived from each "national origin." And yet by the 1950s, the OSS committees were treating that blood quantum as a metaphor for *cultural* origins, which would not remain stable in the Europe sending new arrivals. But would not processes of *American* assimilation also transform the cultural significance of the blood-quantum metaphor? And if so, what was the remaining rationale for bothering with a quota based on national origins? One can only wonder about the unrecorded discussions among these federal officials—discussions among appointees of the Roosevelt and Truman administrations, all of whom were then serving a president who just vetoed the McCarran-Walter Act because it had not dropped the quotas.

What we do know is that Jeter and the people working with her did not rely only on precedents (such as the List of Races and Peoples) nor on their own interpretations. They did their best to read up on the relevant literature and to be in touch with academic and other authorities. Thus Jeter reports on a meeting with someone at the President's Commission on Immigration and Naturalization: "During the conference Mrs. Penton telephoned telephoned Dr. Oberg, anthropologist in the Institute of Social Anthropology, Smithsonian Institution. He gave her a tentative definition of an ethnic group, chiefly in terms of cultural isolation within another culture."[26] A few weeks later Alpert reported to an OSS colleague,

I did not succeed in getting in touch with Hans Zeisl [an émigré social scientist then at Columbia]. I did have a chance for an extended discussion with a sociologist and an anthropologist. The sociologist is the author of an outstanding book on ethnic groups in the U.S. and the anthropologist a student of Boas . . . [I] was told that neither sociologists nor anthropologists have developed standard definitions of ethnicity but that there would be widespread concurrence with the inclusion of the criteria used in the definition which follows.

> An ethnic group is one which (1) identifies itself as distinctive in terms of a common culture as manifested predominantly in common ties of language and religion; (2) has a sense of common ancestry and historical continuity; and (3) maintains a distinctive social organization in the sense that it maintains and supports distinctive community institutions such as churches, newspapers, clubs, fraternal orders, etc.

As might be expected, the anthropologist put the accent on culture, while the sociologist stressed social organization.[27]

Alpert, it would appear, was notably more familiar with the anthropology and sociology of the ethnic group by November 1952 than when he had authored the introductory memo back in August. Moreover, he now spoke not only of the "ethnic group" but also of "ethnicity." While Warner and Srole had briefly used the latter term for the first time several years earlier, it was apparently common enough by 1952 to have turned up in the conversations Alpert was having with his academic consultants. Had Alpert followed up with more American sociologists, their recent studies of ethnicity might have influenced the work of Jeter's group more fully, not least by highlighting how the connotations of "ethnic group" differed between the United States and central Europe.

Helen Jeter's people had been meeting for some three months by the middle of November 1952. Preliminary lists of groups had been circulated and discussed.[28] Still, her superior at OSS was dissatisfied with the available summary statements, and now the McCarran-Walter Act was set to take effect in a matter of weeks. Accordingly, Jeter wrote a new memorandum that eventually ran to twelve single-spaced pages.[29] Jeter had earned a PhD at the University of Chicago and had held a variety of impressive research and governmental positions. In connection with that work, she had also authored numerous scholarly papers. However, there is no evidence that she had been involved with the social science literature on race and ethnic classification prior to the months of OSS meetings.[30]

Jeter's synthesis was more explicit than earlier memos had been about both federal precedents and social science. And consequently her synthesis reveals what she read, where she found leads, and where she found only dead ends. Also, her later correspondence about the synthesis shows who gave her feedback. Thus we have something of a map of the relevant terrain she could cover.

Jeter concluded that there must be some connection between ethnic classification and the List of Races and Peoples. "Definitions of ethnic classification and ethnic group are difficult to find [but] . . . the term 'people or peoples' may be traced back to . . . the [Folkmar's 1911] *Dictionary [of Races and Peoples]*. . . . And that the new term 'ethnic classification' is closely related . . . [i.e.:] a way of classifying individuals that is neither by race (defined by color) nor by nationality (citizenship)." Indeed, she mentioned such connections to the List, the *Dictionary,* or other aspects of the U.S. Immigration Commission's *Reports* several times. Nevertheless, these were not direct precedents for usage of "ethnic." Only the State Department's statement on determining eligibility for "ethnic Germans" (cited earlier) used that term. But she sensibly concluded that the criteria for ethnic Germans could not be generalized to all visa applicants.

Consequently, she turned from precedent to the findings of "anthropologists, ethnologists and sociologists." In retrospect, her failure here was not to meet up with the sociologists or historians whose work we surveyed in Chapter 9, and that her supervisor, Stuart Rice, did not think to steer her to the YIVO scholars. The only sociologist she mentioned was T. J. Woofter's monograph of 1933, *Races and Ethnic Groups in American Life*— probably because it was published in a semiofficial context, "President Hoover's Committee on Social Trends." Woofter, she correctly noted, had not defined his terms, although she deduced that he had in mind sociocultural communities.

She spent more time on the "anthropologists" and "ethnologists." The task of ethnology, she reports, has been to describe human groups that are distinct from others in some way—physical, cultural, or both. But again her references are decidedly dated—Evans-Pritchard, Benedict, Boas, Ripley, and Hrdlicka. These last two had made their reputations by 1910.

> The "early purpose of ethnology" had been to classify "biological characteristics."
>
> That task finished for all practical purposes, ethnologists have now turned to other kinds of description and classification primarily that concerned with "culture" [she quotes Robert H. Lowie's 1937 *History of Ethnological Theory* for a definition of culture].
>
> . . . There has been a gradual transition in popular concept toward an "ethnic group" as a cultural group, although the ethnologists have not yet said that a cultural group is the *only* kind of ethnic group.
>
> . . . .
>
> The emphasis has turned so completely to culture that some research workers have begun to labor in a still newer field, social anthropology . . . [which takes up] the study of social behavior in all human society and not merely primitive societies.[31]

Thus despite the older references, she eventually supported the earlier memos' call for a classification system that would rest on sociocultural characteristics. At the same time, her need to find meaningful federal precedents as well as to master the relevant academic literature is understandable. But in retrospect, it is striking that she did not confront the possibility that the older federal discussions relied on understandings that the scholarship of her own generation rejected—understandings involving a stronger role for biological determinism in particular.

The writings of the United States Immigration Commission and even the List of Races and Peoples were after all only precedents of federal usage in discussions, not of laws passed by Congress. Perhaps had the UNESCO Statements played a larger role in subcommittee discussions the scrutiny of precedents from 1900 to 1910 might have loomed larger. The statements would eventually play their own strange role in this tale.

On the other hand, Jeter surely knew the fierce debate over the McCarran-Walter Act, President Truman's veto, and the ultimate failure to reject the quotas. Yet nothing in the paper trail suggests that the officials drew a connection between the condemnation of the quotas as racist and a document like Folkmar's *Dictionary*.

The basic historical works that did so much to draw the links between racial thought and the political and cultural history of the restrictionist movement before World War I were still unpublished. Oscar Handlin must have been preparing his own devastating critique of the Immigration Commission's *Reports* (including the *Dictionary*) at just about the time Jeter was writing. He had in fact presented that critique first to President Truman's committee on immigration reform in 1952. But few knew to look at the appendix of that committee's report, around page 1,850, to find Handlin's first version. The critique became influential only when he included it as a chapter in *Race and Nationality* in 1957. The other two crucial histories were John Higham's *Strangers in the Land* (1955) and Barbara Miller Solomon's *Ancestors and Immigrants* (1956).[32]

Jeter and her subcommittee may well have detested arguments about Nordic races and detested the quotas as well. But another way to state the influence of the three as-yet unpublished studies just mentioned is that Jeter's group very likely did not link Nordic theory and the quotas to the milder restrictionist writings of the Immigration Commission, and were probably less likely than later generations would be to treat the use of the race term as something of disturbing promise in itself. Indeed, it really was the work of the three historians just mentioned that tended to draw together the perception of the two eras of restriction, one around 1907–1911, the other around 1921–1924. Handlin's essay could not have made the point more strongly, because its first and second sections were respectively rejections of the Immigration Commission's *Reports* and of Harry Laughlin's studies of immigrant behavior for Albert Johnson's House subcommittee on immigration.

Now Jeter's memorandum went for review to the Smithsonian, where "several anthropologists in different branches of this institution" read it. But by limiting her inquiry to the Smithsonian, she did not get feedback from sociologists. In any case, the Smithsonian scholars approved her careful distinction between classifications of mankind on "biological or racial and on cultural grounds." Still, they noted, "The authorities you cite . . . are not the most eminent or altogether in current favor professionally." But "under the circumstances they should serve as well as any others."[33]

However, the Smithsonian correspondent would offer comments only on race. He seems to have known of the recent use of "ethnic group" for physical distinctions in the first UNESCO Statement on Race, but he may not have felt competent on the uses of the term in sociology or even social anthropology. Nor did the Smithsonian reviewer refer Jeter to others who could have commented from the perspective of those fields.

The letter from the Smithsonian's authorities ends with a declaration about popular misunderstandings over race—hewing close to the second UNESCO Statement (which preserved a meaning for race and ignored the ethnic group term): "Few people seem to comprehend that race is a bio-logical concept and entirely different from such things as political affilia-tion, religion and language. Our anthropologists feel that more emphasis on, and a fuller explanation of, this fact would result in more reliable in-formation about immigrants."[34]

Possibly the last sentence included a slap at the List of Races and Peoples, which was still in use by the federal government. But it was too broad a state-ment to help Jeter. Jeter and her staff had mastered only so much, had looked to an authoritative but also limited source for help, and had received only minimal direction from other social scientists. Perhaps she would have gone on to contact others. But a very unwelcome intervention from the State De-partment now derailed the OSS discussion for some time—in fact until the new president took office and his administration dropped the effort to make sense of "ethnic classification."

In order to understand the State Department move, we must first take a step back in time and note an earlier intervention from another source that set the stage. Even before Jeter had written her November 1952 memo, the OSS efforts to create categories for "ethnic classification" had become public. Jeter's committee members at first seemed to assume that they would include the Jews in their ethnic classification; by religion or by other cultural markers the Jews seemed to belong there. After all, the cul-tural definition of ethnic group might rest in part or in full on religious divisions. The assumption about listing Jews reached the Jewish press. Once more a familiar protest emerged along the old battle line drawn more than a half century earlier by Simon Wolf. But there were differences. At issue now was not the designation of Jews as a "race," but rather as a category on an "ethnic classification." The central principle invoked in those earlier Jewish protests had never been about identifying Jews by race but by religion.

Congressman Emanuel Celler, representing parts of Brooklyn and Queens, had written to the State Department and the OSS to protest the inclusion of "Jewish" as an "ethnic classification." Shortly thereafter, Congressman Jacob Javits, representing the Upper West Side of Manhattan, had done the same. And the B'nai B'rith Anti-Defamation League had also protested to the Bureau of the Budget, of which Jeter's committee was a part.[35]

By the 1950s the large majority of American Jews were of eastern European origin, descendants of the dense Yiddish cultural milieu there rather than from the German-origin Reform Jewish elite like Simon Wolf or the members of the American Jewish Committee. Both Celler and Javits represented many Jewish voters of such background, and Javits's parents were themselves from eastern Europe. And yet, while American Jews of eastern European descent may have tended to live with a greater sense of an ethnic community than had Wolf's people, they nevertheless tended to express their Jewish commitments as a matter of religion, especially in the public sphere. Consequently, the basis of the protest Celler, Javits, and others raised about a Jewish ethnic classification was virtually identical to that raised about the Hebrew race category.

Celler's letter protesting the "ethnic classification" for Jews focused on religion and demonstrates a certain perplexity about the concept of ethnicity. It was addressed to Secretary of State Dean Acheson with a copy to the director of the Bureau of the Budget. Celler argued that creating a category for Jews in an ethnic classification "is an unwarranted confusion between religious appellation and that of origin." Many of the old chestnuts reappear to make the point. How to classify people of Jewish origin who converted? No other religion is going to be listed. In any event, the requirement would oblige Jews to "state their religious affiliation" (even if the classificatory intent was to elicit ethnic membership). And "no definition is furnished as to what constitutes the various 'ethnic classifications.'"[36]

In addition to the constitutional arguments, Celler pointed out that great power rested with consular authorities in approving visas. Consequently, it was important to ensure that a consular official who wanted to deny a Jew entry could not rely on the excuse that the applicant had not mentioned his religion. An item supposedly gathered only for informational purposes could serve as an excuse to deny a visa. His argument about the consular authorities may well have triggered such concerns at Jeter's next OSS subcommittee meeting held two weeks later: "Several members of the Committee suggested that the value of statistics on the subject of ethnic group was not sufficiently great to warrant the chance of harm to individuals who might be subject to discrimination in the administration of the Immigration and Nationality Act." The subcommittee went on to agree at that meeting that "'Jewish' should not appear on the list as an ethnic group."[37]

On the big issue, then, Celler and his allies won. Still, it is worth pausing to wonder what he actually believed. The closing comment of the letter to Acheson read, "I am a Jew and were I asked for my race and ethnic classification I would say that I am white and American."[38] It seems unlikely that he thought of Jewishness as simply a religious identity; at any rate, it was not a religious identity of the type Simon Wolf had embraced. Only a few months after he penned the letter to Acheson, Celler published an autobiography (*You Never Leave Brooklyn*). One chapter is a paean to Zionism and the early Jewish state. "The Nazi terrors had brought me" from one who thinks of the Jewish State as "a good idea to one passionately dedicated." He reflects,

> I had never thought to define for myself my Jewshness. . . . It was . . . a fact. . . . We practiced Reform Judaism. . . . Religion was a communal rather than a metaphysical experience. . . . I knew only a few words of Yiddish . . . but [observing Yiddish-speaking Jews at pushcarts] the texture of their sound . . . accentuated my exclusion from the voluble, excitable stream of life and religion. One was the other, and the two could not be boxed apart.
>
> This, as I see it now, motivated my Zionism.[39]

Thus for the Yiddish-speaking immigrants, Jewishness seemed to consist of something more than religion as he knew it; he seems to come close to saying that another concept is needed to more fully describe the nature of the affiliation, but we cannot say that he was conscious of that in the autobiography: "life and religion. One was the other, and the two could not be boxed apart." Perhaps then we should take him at his word when he wrote to Acheson that being a Jew did not seem to bear on his race—"white"—

or his ethnic classification—"American." By the end of the 1960s, as we shall
see, the use of ethnic terms had become vastly less puzzling, and it would
have been strange indeed for a Brooklyn Jew to declare his ethnicity to be
"American."

In any case, the Celler letter and the other Jewish protests produced some
attention at the highest levels of the State Department, and they eventually led officials there to an almost comical blunder. Adrian S. Fisher, the
legal advisor to Secretary Dean Acheson looked into "ethnic classification."
He drew up a memo for Acheson.

> Under the 1924 Immigration Act a visa applicant is required to identify
> his race [in terms of the List] . . . which is drawn from a *Dictionary of Races
> and Peoples* compiled by the 1907 Immigration Commission. . . .
>
> Under [the McCarran-Walter Act] . . . a visa applicant is required to
> give his race *and ethnic* classification. . . . The Department is confronted
> with an urgent need for clarifying its position as to whether it
> approves of the use of the designations "Jew, Hebrew or Israelite" for
> purposes of race or ethnic classification. The Department has already
> let it be known that it objects to the use of the term "Jew" for racial
> identification. . . . [And similarly, since June 30, 1943] the term "Hebrew"
> has been eliminated by the [INS] in the classification of immigrants by
> race or people, and the race designation [for them is] the country of
> origin.[40]

But Fisher's summary of the situation still left the question of how to define ethnic classification. Like Jeter and the others at OSS, Fisher, too, had
been reading up on race and ethnic groups. But Fisher had been reading a
different set of writers from Jeter. In particular, he focused on heirs to the
tradition of Huxley's *We Europeans*. Those studies defined the ethnic group
in physiological terms reminiscent of the old ethnological studies. Thus
Fisher had read especially Ashley Montagu's book-length text accompanying the UNESCO Statement on Race, as well as works by William How-
ells, W. C. Boyd, Michel Leiris, and E. A. Hooton. Race there referred *only* to
broad *physical* divisions of humanity ("Mongoloid, Negroid and Caucasoid,
which is, by and large another way of saying yellow, black and white").
And so, Fisher remarked, "There are races, but they are not what most of

us think they are. A race is a population marked by certain inherited or physical qualities, but these qualities can and do fluctuate, and can disappear by reason of geographic and other forms of isolation. Race is not a matter of national, linguistic, religious or cultural traits, which serve most of us for racial classification."[41]

Adrian S. Fisher was a product of elite preparatory boarding schools, Princeton, and Harvard Law School. He had been an important official in the federal government since the war years, and would serve in the federal government for three decades more. Then approaching forty, he was a close confidant of Dean Acheson. Two months before Fisher's intervention in the "ethnic classification" discussion, Truman had appointed him a member of the President's Commission on Immigration and Naturalization.[42] Fisher felt it necessary to clarify, presumably for himself and for Secretary Acheson that "races are not what most of us think they are . . . not a matter of national, linguistic, religious or cultural traits." For good measure, he proceeds to quote a famous passage about this distinction from the second UNESCO Statement on Race. If nothing else, the Fisher memo provides additional evidence for the novelty and influence of the UNESCO Statement, and in particular that its message about race really did come as news to even the most well educated—even a decade and a half (and a world war) away from *We Europeans*.

Fisher urged in conclusion "that in dealing with race and ethnic classification we rely as closely as possible on modern scientific conclusions." As to race, the three major color groups would do (white, black, yellow). But as to ethnic classification? Here was Fisher's blunder. He blithely suggested that the State Department should follow "some adaptation of Montagu's tabulation." Montagu's summary did qualify as an up-to-date summary of "modern scientific conclusions" about the ethnic group—at least from the perspective of one branch of research.

And Montagu's classification of ethnic groups as subgroups of the major color divisions did have another notable feature: "Jew, Hebrew or Israelite does not appear in this list." All of this was "of course subject to the findings of the [OSS] Interdepartmental Committee." In the meantime, State could on its own follow the path the INS had adopted in 1943 and "*drop the term 'Hebrew'* from the list of terms now being used" (emphasis in original). This should be announced "as well as the fact that the Department looks with disfavor on the use of the terms Jew, Hebrew and Israelite for the purpose of race and ethnic classification."

Fisher had focused heavily on responding to the Jewish protest but could not have looked closely at "Montagu's tabulation." The problem was that Montagu had defined "ethnic group" much as Huxley had in *We Europeans*—entirely as populations defined by physical traits. There was a small difference: whereas Huxley had urged dropping the "race term" entirely and replacing it with "ethnic group," Montagu kept the "race" term for the major observable human divisions and defined the ethnic groups as subdivisions of these races. Montagu's ethnic groups therefore included: *under Mongoloid*, Classical, Artic, American Indian, and Indo-Malay; *under Caucasoid*, Mediterranean, Nordic, East Baltic, Armenoid, Pre-Dravidian, and so on. To make matters worse, Fisher had not copied out Montagu's list for Acheson (he cited only the pages on which the list appeared). Presumably, Acheson had better things to do than look up a list of biological subdivisions of humankind; he simply signed off on Fisher's memo, and it became the State Department's position.

The most revealing feature of Fisher's intervention is not the blunder itself but the fact that he had been reading a different part of literature relevant to discussions of race and ethnicity than Jeter had. In one sense, he made an excellent choice, reading truly recent and widely read authorities. And they led him to the important conclusion that "there are races, but they are not what most of us think they are." The trouble was that this same literature had directed him to a meaning of "ethnic group" (common enough in certain subfields) that was much farther from immigration forms than the meaning found in Jeter's reading.

Shortly after Acheson signed off on the Fisher memo, several mid-level State Department officials undertook the unenviable task of reporting to the OSS their agency's new position (use Montagu list). Now again, it turned out that different people had read in different fields. *No one* at the OSS meeting had yet read the Montagu text. But by the next day, Jeter had done so, and reported to an OSS superior. She perceptively distinguished between the UNESCO Statement and Montagu's long discussion; only the latter, she noted, included the listing of "ethnic groups." Moreover, Jeter understood immediately the significance of the State Department's reliance on Montagu's list.

He defines ethnic group as a subdivision of race and *entirely* in physiological terms. . . . Note that his list includes "Nordic" which I would think
would cause as much trouble in the U.S.A. as Jewish. (I wonder if
Secretary Acheson knew it contained "Nordic"). . . .

   My guess is that if you . . . offer the Montagu list to the Congressional
Committee they will say it is certainly *not* what they had in mind.

Jeter had also come to appreciate that terminology about the ethnic group
varied across the disciplines that the officials of her subcommittee had been
trying to master.

I have [recently] come to the conclusion that physical anthropologists
use the term "ethnic" in reference to racial classifications as related to
physical characteristics only . . . while sociologists use it for cultural
groups that may have no physical kinship. (Perhaps the social anthropologists are somewhere between, trying to combine race and culture,
I am not sure.)[43]

A standoff of several months now ensued between the State Department
and the other agencies. Then, the new Eisenhower administration took
office. The List of Races and Peoples (with minor modifications) accompanied a new visa application to guide responses. At the end of the fiscal
year following Eisenhower's election, Jeter left federal employment for
other fields.

PART FOUR

Incorporating the Legacies of the
Civil Rights Era and Mass Immigration
from the Third World

~

CHAPTER 11

Race and the Immigrant in Federal Statistics since 1965

THE PRECEDING CHAPTERS HAVE DEALT with the classification of immigrants arriving at the border, or with tracking the immigrants' and their children's progress in America. Federal classifications were typically bound up with discussions about immigration restriction. Were too many immigrants coming, and in particular the wrong kinds of immigrants? Thus federal classificatory efforts often seemed at best neutral and often antagonistic to immigrants. But the important questions about comparable classifications in more recent decades are best explored in terms of the wider counts of *all* Americans by historical origin, and the American census is the crucial context. Moreover, in this period the new classifications were bound up with new kinds of federal protection for ethnic and racial minorities. Consequently, these groups were likely to seek legibility in the eyes of the state.

This chapter concerns the period since 1965. It deals with two related themes. The first is the changing role of classification as a result of the civil rights era. First and foremost, black mobilization prodded the federal government into a vastly transformed role as a major protector of minorities. Hispanic, Asian, and American Indian mobilization followed; moreover, leaders of white ethnics also made an attempt in this direction. During and especially after the civil rights years, this transformed governmental role had a giant impact on the collection of federal ethno-racial statistics, above all because those statistics were necessary to establish

333

and act on current discrimination and more generally on patterns of minority underrepresentation in better jobs, places of residence, unions, political offices, and the like. For the group at the heart of civil rights mobilization, the need was simply to have more data using the existing race category, black. Evidence of black–white inequalities in local census areas or in specific corporations or unions involved new counts that employed familiar categories, not new definitions of black and white. The case was different, especially for the group we today know as Hispanics, and for white ethnic groups; it was also true to a lesser extent for Asians (all three rarely known by those covering labels before the late 1960s). For these groups a good deal turned on how they would be defined by the government.

The resulting advocacy for changed data collection began during the 1960s and gained force and direction in the next decade. Three major efforts to transform ethno-racial statistics since the civil rights years followed, culminating respectively in changes designed to take effect in the 1980, 2000, and 2020 censuses. As we shall see, the census was by no means the only venue in which these post–civil rights era reforms were implemented; for example, such reforms influenced data collection of employment patterns. Nevertheless, centering the narrative on the census is a useful way to illuminate the major themes, and much of the action in all three cases did in fact focus on the census.

The second major theme of this chapter concerns the return of mass immigration to the United States since 1965, with the abolition of the quota regimes and exclusions set in the early 1920s and the passage of the 1965 Hart-Celler Immigration Act. The trends began even earlier and it took some years after 1965 for them to become clear. But within a decade or so no one could miss the return to mass immigration, this time primarily from Latin America and Asia. Once again, the need for data to mark and measure the progress of the immigrants and their children linked this great development to federal collection of ethno-racial data.

These two crucial changes in American social life—the civil rights era and new mass immigration from the third world—had entered their second half century in the years running up to the 2020 census. Moreover, and crucially, these two great trends were not independent of each other, not least because so many immigrants and their children were also "minorities," in the current sense of being nonwhites (including Hispanics), and in the sense of being protected by federal legislation. Once again, the concept of legibility is of some use to us: statistical evidence could be marshaled to press for federal action; legibility was required for such results, but legibility in this context was by and large advantageous.

A further theme in this era, as these two major social changes played out, was the relation between concepts of racial permanence and expectations of ethnic assimilation, especially as both concepts applied to the descendants of relatively recent immigrants—the second and third generations, for example. We have already had many occasions to trace the tension between ethnic survival and assimilation, and how the understanding of that tension was influenced by notions of racial permanence in an era when race, color, biological determinism, and ethnic groups were overlapping concepts. In the post–civil rights era, the overlap between notions of race and ethnicity, not least in law, became especially important. Categories for Hispanics and Asians came to be critical not only in tracking descendants of recent immigration, but also for the protection of federally protected nonwhite minorities.

Black mobilization for the civil rights that came in the 1960s has no single start date. But if we trace its influence through the federal *responses* to that mobilization—in executive orders, laws, and Supreme Court decisions—a reasonable beginning is the executive orders forbidding discrimination by military contractors begun under Franklin Roosevelt. Early Supreme Court cases brought by the NAACP about segregated schooling eventually culminated in the unanimous *Brown* decision (1954). Three years later, the first civil rights act passed since Reconstruction created a relevant subdivision of the Justice Department.

Violent responses by Southern whites often followed federal enforcement efforts, particularly after *Brown*. Such responses in turn riveted attention, stimulating reflection and demand for more effective federal action. These patterns peaked in the mid-1960s after civil rights activists developed forms of nonviolent direct action. Sit-ins at segregated lunch counters and other facilities began in 1960—reaching 200 Southern cities during the first year. The following year the Freedom Riders began demanding integrated bus services. And similarly, local drives to register Southern black voters gained strength, often under dangerous conditions. These mobilizations, as well as marches and further efforts at school integration, brought more violent reactions from Southern whites that federal authorities could not ignore.

By June 1963, President Kennedy had felt it imperative to send an omnibus civil rights bill to Congress, and in August came the March on Washington. But the drive for Kennedy's bill stalled, and by November he had been assassinated. President Johnson saw his own reelection in 1964 as dependent on getting a civil rights bill through Congress while holding on to Southern support for a native son of Texas. During that same summer of 1964, civil unrest exploded in a number of black inner-city ghettos. Nearly all of these occurred in *Northern* cities, demonstrating the huge racial inequalities that existed there, too, even without Jim Crow. Protests these events surely were, but since they included looting and other violence, many perceived them as destructive riots and demanded the restoration of law and order in the ghettos. A different reaction demanded forceful government action to deal with the underlying racial inequality. The civil rights bill, gutted of voting rights, passed before the presidential election. Nevertheless, the compromises that had been made to secure passage increased bitterness within the Democratic Party and between Johnson's government and the black civil rights leadership. In addition, August 1965 brought the shock of the Watts riots in Los Angeles.

The election of 1964 had produced the strongest liberal, Democratic majority in Congress since Franklin Roosevelt's first terms.[1] It had pitted the "states' rights" conservative Republican Barry Goldwater against Lyndon Johnson's activist federal government. With the winds of victory at his back, Johnson introduced a plethora of social welfare programs. More important for our purposes were three key initiatives relevant to ethnicity and race, all enacted in 1965. Two responded especially to the black–white racial divide: the Voting Rights Act supplemented the Civil Rights Act passed the year before and the affirmative action program committed the federal government to do more than merely adjudicate claims of civil or voting rights violations. It would "affirmatively" require firms that wanted federal contracts to implement plans aimed at increasing the employment of underrepresented groups. The federal pressure would not need a court's verdict about discrimination at all, nor proof of discriminatory intent. The focus of affirmative action was at the *group* level, and the goal was to reduce group underrepresentation.

The third major initiative of 1965 that dealt with ethnicity and race was the Hart-Celler Immigration Act; it finally abolished the highly restrictive immigration legislation of 1924 (the National Origins Act). This change had been a long time in coming. The 1924 act had continued with minimal re-examination through the Depression and war years. Its provisions had been recodified in the McCarran-Walter Act (1952), and survived a dozen more years. But every president since FDR had argued that racist immigration policies looked terrible to the people of other countries, and especially to those in the third world, where the competition for hearts and minds was fiercest.[2] Later, in the civil rights era, proclamations of American belief in racial equality sounded like a bad joke when one thought about the quotas and exclusions of immigration law. The very language of the Civil Rights Act, and in many federal reports, executive orders, and state acts that preceded it, prohibited discrimination on the basis of "race, color, creed, or national origin." Asian exclusions rested on race, the quotas on national origins.

Another source of support for change in immigration policy lay in the demographic and social history of the era. The immigrant stocks that the quotas disparaged, the descendants of those who had arrived between 1890 and 1920, grew ever-more numerous among the electorate. These later-generation descendants also grew more assimilated, and their social-class position rose. By the end of the 1950s, many were in better working-class jobs (often unionized) or in the vast range of the middle class, as petty proprietors, managers, or even professionals. And they deeply resented the quotas. More of these descendants of the 1890–1920 immigrations now served in Congress. When Hart-Celler passed in 1965, there were ninety-two Catholics and fifteen Jews in the House of Representatives; eighty-nine of the former and all of the latter supported the bill. So, too, did all Catholics and Jews in the Senate.

The 1964 election itself was partly a product these same demographic changes; it focused and intensified them. But insofar as LBJ's victory was also a sympathetic reaction to the civil rights mobilizations and an ac-tivist federal response, those mobilizations can be said to have indirectly helped pass the Hart-Celler Act. The act replaced the quotas with two broad numerical caps, one for the Americas, the other for the rest of the world, and with a single additional cap that limited all countries to the same

maximum number of immigrant visas. The visas would be allotted everywhere based upon two kinds of preferences: needed job skills and family
reunification.

The Hart-Celler Act thus opened the contemporary era of renewed mass
immigration. And yet its impact upon third world immigration in particular and on the scale of immigration in general turned out to be far greater
than architects of the bill had expected. Over the years, the terms of new
immigration law made it possible for a variety of factors to vastly increase
the number of arrivals. Some of these factors were demographic—refugee
arrivals, demands for student visas, guest workers, and undocumented
arrivals.

Another factor was the system of over-cap preferences for family members. The over-cap system had been growing since the early 1950s, and it
was expanded again in 1957.[3] In fact, this feature of the last years of the
quotas made it easier for restrictionists to back down: the quotas, they now
argued, were no longer controlling immigration anyway. Over-quota arrivals in those quota years were made up of two large groups: close relatives of new citizens and all arrivals from the Western Hemisphere (these
latter had never been covered by the quotas). By the mid-1960s, nonquota
arrivals predominated.[4] Once Hart-Celler allowed for a base of immigrants from the third world, and other features of immigration policy
allowed for many arrivals on *non*immigrant visas (e.g., students or guest
workers who eventually sunk roots in America), the family reunification
programs would, over decades, amplify the number of third world arrivals dramatically.

Finally, migration northward across the Mexican border continued the
ebb and flow of its long history under this new immigration regime. A large
flow between 1910 and 1930 died out and was reversed in the Depression
decade, but it revived with demand in the war years. The federal *Bracero* program, first meant to meet war needs and then extended up to the time of
Hart-Celler, was meant to be a guest-worker program. The American demand for Mexican labor, the increasing Mexican American communities
in the United States, and the fluctuations of the Mexican economy made
for a large migration, some rotating, some permanent, that the end of the
guest-worker program could hardly eliminate. From the first years of the
twenty-first century to the Great Recession, for example, more than half

of the arrivals from Mexico were "undocumented"—people coming without legal documents for entry. Mexican migrants comprised about three-fifths of all undocumented migrants, other Latinos another fifth.[5]

How the Federal Census Tracked Origins and Descent
before the Reforms of 1980

By the mid-twentieth century, the varied census classifications for group origins could be understood only in reference to the long and complex history of pressures that had created them. A question on birthplace, that is country of birth, had been asked since 1850, the enumeration that first recorded information separately on each individual. Questions on the two parental birthplaces had been introduced in 1880. But no effort had ever been made to extend birthplace questions to still-earlier generations; a prohibitive level of detail would have been involved. Moreover, there was also a substantive rationale for reporting only two generations of origins, a rationale based on the perceived assimilation experience of the European (white) population. The American-born members of the European immigrant groups lost their ancestral language and many cultural practices. They typically experienced some upward mobility in the second generation and more of it in the third. Out-marriage, too, was not uncommon by the second and becoming the norm by the third generation. Consequently, often the third- and more often the fourth-generation descendant of a European group was *also* the descendant of one or several other European groups. For mixed-origin people, not only ethnicity but also generational standing (the number of generations that had passed since an immigrant ancestor) might well differ when traced through one parent rather than the other. It seemed sensible, therefore, that after two generations, those of European descent were reported as simply native born of native parentage. As we have seen (Chapter 6), the birthplace questions often had been supplemented since 1910 by a mother-tongue classification, originally in order to distinguish among the various peoples immigrating from each multinational empire.

The only other origin reported was race; Europeans were white. Actually, the "race" had originally been titled the "color" question. This label had been used from 1850 through 1880. In 1890, the question had no title; it was headed simply, "Whether white, black . . . [etc.]." In 1900 it was retitled as "color or race," and continued that way through 1940 (and so titled again in 1970). Since 1950 the "race" term alone has generally been used, although occasionally the label was dropped in favor of "This person is . . ." (followed by a list of categories from which to choose). Moreover, the choice of terms used in census reports could fluctuate between "color," "color or race," and "race" in a given year.[6]

"White" was the default racial category, the one that included the vast majority of the population. Only one other racial group included a considerable fraction of the American population before 1950: roughly one in nine Americans was reported to be black. And indeed, it was *only* the race question that identified the vast majority of blacks. Birthplace questions going back two generations told nothing of the origins of African Americans. They, like most whites, were native born of native parentage. To put this summary differently, all descendants of the forced immigration on which African American slavery had rested were being tracked without regard to generational standing. The great majority of these descendants remained distinct from the rest of the population, disadvantaged on the important socioeconomic indicators, subject to Jim Crow restrictions in the South and to other powerful discriminations in the North. True, despite myths about separate races, there had been plenty of interracial offspring; but insofar as they could be identified by enumerators, they were classified as nonwhite—either as black or (in most censuses prior to 1930) as mulatto.

In addition to whites and blacks, the census had long listed two other groups as races or color groups: East Asian race was (and is today) recorded by reference to the country of birth of the immigrant ancestor. Thus, Chinese, Japanese, Korean, and eventually others have been listed as separate races, like white and black. This anomaly in classification began when the 1870 census included "Chinese," as those immigrants became a focus of national attention. This was the first recognition of any color category for people from Asia. Later, other East Asian immigrant groups were successively included under the "color" (or later the "color or race" or "race") question as *their* numbers grew and attracted attention: Japanese, Koreans, and Asian Indians. Like everyone else, descendants of East Asian immigrants were also tracked for two generations through the birthplace and parental-birthplace questions; thereafter these birthplace questions only returned the information that the individual was native born of native parentage. However, because East Asian *race* categories designated countries of immigrant origin, the descendants from these origins were *also* tracked (on the race question) from arrival through all subsequent generations at the level of country of origin—and without regard for generational standing.[7] The result was the first recording of country-level origins past the second generation. In the case of the Chinese, the 2020 census will mark 150 years of this practice.

Consistency might have predicted that the Chinese group would instead have been categorized in 1870 under the "color question" as "yellow" or at least "East Asian." But "Chinese" may have been the more common term for the group in the United States. In any case, the choice of a new term underscores that administrators felt they could not classify the Chinese under either of the two categories for which the color question had been created—white or black—and that the new arrivals were numerous enough (and subject to enough policy debates) to require a separate count. Beyond that, the choice to include a "color" category called "Chinese" shows how administrative practicalities could not always wait upon conceptual clarity. Moreover, once a particular administrative practice had been established it could grow by accretion. Thus initially, in the 1870 and 1880 censuses, the few *non*-Chinese among East Asian immigrants were simply classified racially as Chinese. In 1890, when numbers rose to meaningful levels, "Japanese" was added as a distinct category to the "color" question. Possibly, census officials recognized in that year a practical need to distinguish between two peoples within one color grouping. They may have had in mind the notion that color groupings could be thought of as "grand racial divisions" within which various peoples could be distinguished if needed and those could be referred to as races. True, no covering name was given for the "grand racial division" that included both the Chinese and the Japanese. But this was also the first time in the five decades of collecting census data at the individual level that the relevant census question did not have a covering label at all. Moreover, the immediately subsequent census (1900) labeled the question "color or race," possibly to anticipate any criticism that Chinese and Japanese did not refer to colors and that no covering color label for these categories was given.

In the census's "color or race" question the Asian groups designated by country names were always listed consecutively as each new category was added. By 1970 the question included five such country race categories: Japanese, Chinese, Filipino, Hawaiian, and Korean. In 1980, the bureau added four more: Vietnamese, Asian Indian, Guamanian, and Samoan. By then, the federal government had also officially acknowledged an "Asian" covering category; in the 1990 enumeration that label was finally added to the census form. Under it were listed the nine specific Asian national origin race categories from 1980 plus a tenth, "Other Asian or Pacific Islander."[8]

Before leaving the anomalous history of the Asian country race categories, two observations may be helpful. First, there is another usage of "color or race" that has long resonated in American history, but it seems to be entirely independent of that in the census question. Acts passed by Republican majorities during the post–Civil War Reconstruction referred to "race, color, or previous condition of servitude" when prohibiting discrimination against African Americans. Crucially, the phrase appeared in the Fifteenth Amendment, guaranteeing the right to vote (which passed Congress in 1869 and was ratified the following year) and in the Civil Rights Acts of 1866 and 1875.[9] The specific wording was probably a reaction to Southern state government initiatives of the same years to reassert controls over freed blacks and to President Andrew Johnson's weak federal enforcement of racial equality. Including all three terms would help eliminate any chance that Southern state legislatures might write their laws in a way Congress had failed to block. It does not appear that the usage of both "race" and "color" in these Reconstruction-era acts was clarified by definitions that would distinguish one term from the other.

Later, such legislation was weakened by the end of Reconstruction (1877), the U.S. Supreme Court case that drastically restricted the federal reach in civil rights cases (1883), and then by the disfranchisement of blacks in Southern states (1890–1910). Nevertheless, the phrase was not forgotten, and the important measures of the civil rights era would include it in modified form—for example, in the 1941 Executive Order 8802, and the 1957 and 1964 Civil and the 1965 Voting Rights Acts. By then there was no need to mention "previous condition of servitude." But both color and race were mentioned as impermissible categories of discrimination. Other kinds of forbidden discriminations were added, so that the phrase typically found in that legislation was a variant of "race, color, creed [or religion], or national origin." State legislation at the time experimented with various formulations of the other forbidden categories. Thus, New York State legislation in 1938 and 1941, respectively, included "race, creed, color or religion" and "nationality." A 1945 act in the state listed national origin and defined it to include "ancestry"; a Philadelphia act of 1948 included both these terms. And "several other northern states passed similar legislation."[10] During the second half of the 1960s, sex came to be a listed category as well.

The second observation about the anomalous history of the Asian country race categories is that its early history around the turn of the twentieth century bears certain resemblances to the way color, race, and peoplehood were treated on the List of Races and Peoples, created in 1898. The extensive debates about the List that have survived make it clear that the debaters exploited the various relevant concepts: color, grand racial division, race, nationality, and people. But these concepts were hardly differentiated in the categories of the List. Many categories referred to races (or peoples) who were the dominant group from a particular country and whose designation was a variant form of the country name—German, French, Greek, Mexican, Chinese, Japanese. But other category names did not refer to races and peoples that had this characteristic—Northern and Southern Italians, Hebrews, Bohemian and Servian, Croatian and Slovenian, Irish, Poles, and so on. True, the races and peoples from Europe could be considered part of the "white" color grouping, of a single "grand racial division." But that fact was nowhere designated in the List; nor were its East Asian categories (Chinese, Japanese, Korean) to be found under any covering label. Finally, the List included one grand racial division as a category—"African (black)." But this category did not serve as a covering label for any subcategories.

Recall that the U.S. Immigration Commission urged that the List become part of a census race classification. At that time, the "color or race" question, as it had been labeled in 1900, already included categories of a mixed nature—"black, white, [American] Indian, Chinese, Japanese." The commission's idea could be seen as extending the example of including detailed "race" data of the type already represented by the census Chinese and Japanese categories to European groups. Recall too that the commission used the List to track European origins through two generations only, while it tracked specific Asian (Chinese, Japanese, etc.) as well as African origins without regard to generational standing. And yet, had the List become part of the census in 1910, it is not inconceivable that European races and peoples might have come to be treated in the same way as the Asian country races in later censuses—given the mounting pressure for restriction in the years 1910–1924, and the role of biological determinism in discussions of restriction. The 1909 testimony of Commission Secretary W. W. Husband before the Senate's Committee on the Census does not suggest he had thought through the issue. But the fact that he brought Daniel Folkmar, who was more committed to views about the long-term influences of immigrant group differences, suggests the potentials. Possibly too, the precedent of the Asian country race categories smoothed the way for the Mexican race category in the 1930 census.

Finally, consider the race category treatment of the American Indian in the successive census race questions. When the 1870 census color question first went beyond black and white to include the "Chinese" category, it also added a category for the American Indian. This category, too, has appeared continuously since. A single American Indian category was eventually supplemented by a line on which the respondent could specify a tribal affiliation. Eventually, in the context of post–civil rights era group activism, this arrangement made the American Indian category resemble the Hispanic and Asian covering labels while the tribal information resembled the country of origin information.

The American Indian group differed in a crucial respect from the other "color or race" categories. Few Americans had origins in more than one of the census racial categories. Consequently, the challenge of how multiracial individuals should be classified by race or color was typically handled as a matter of marginal exceptions for which imperfect procedures would suffice—with the notable exception of black–white mixtures that were allocated to distinct race categories for many decades (mulatto and others). But American Indians had a far larger proportion of interracial unions and multiracial descendants than any other race. Eventually, the tribes themselves developed rules for membership requiring a minimum "blood quantum" of tribal origin. That quantum was typically well below 50 percent. But the tribes generally supplemented the blood quantum with cultural characteristics reflecting lifestyle and community recognition of the individual's belonging. Such criteria did not pertain directly to the American Indian category in the federal census but by the time of the post–civil rights era reforms in federal ethno-racial classification such criteria did made it easier for the federal government to define a highly mixed group as members of a single race.[11]

The federal arrangements described here for tracking different kinds of origins—by birthplace and race—would all come under pressure after 1965.

Impacts of the Civil Rights Era on Advocacy and Classification

HISPANIC ORIGIN AND PAN-ETHNICITY

Hispanics and Asians emerged as *pan-ethnics,* that is, as aggregations of several national origin groups thought to be united into a broader, meaningful unity. That larger unity was important in demonstrating that a large clientele needed federal attention, a clientele found all across the country and likely to become an important voting bloc. And indeed, members of both pan-ethnicities also came to see themselves and be seen by others as part of a wider, more powerful collective than they had been before. The emergence of these pan-ethnicities was a story about classification insofar as they aggregated national groups for presentation. But crucially, the national origin components of the aggregation had been available and continued to be so after the covering category was introduced.[12]

In one sense, the classificatory reforms that were introduced in the 1980 census can be viewed as reflecting the success of the movement for Hispanic and Asian pan-ethnicity. The less dramatic change was that an Asian cover label was applied to all the Asian country race groups. The new Hispanic Origin question amounted to a much greater departure; it was surely the single most important element in that set of 1980 reforms. Nevertheless, the Hispanic Origin question itself, as well as the other 1980 reforms, also changed conceptions of ethno-racial classification in ways that were at least as important as and quite independent of pan-ethnicity. No new census origin question before or after has ever dealt with only one kind of origin: Hispanic origin? No / Yes; if yes, from which national origin? In fact, a *second* new question was introduced with Hispanic Origin, the Ancestry question, which differed from Hispanic Origin only in asking for detail about *all* origins (not only Hispanic). The crucial departure inherent in both the Ancestry and Hispanic Origin questions was that they *pertained to all generations of immigrant descendants*—much as race categories did. By thus ignoring generational standing, the Hispanic Origin and Ancestry questions privileged the assumption that one's immigrant origins continued to matter for society no matter how *distant* these origins were in time, nor how *complicated* the origins had become as a result of intermarriages in prior generations of family history.

Against this background, the choice to record Hispanic origin and ancestry through an undefined number of generations was an important departure that can only be understood in its historical context. Ethnic origins, it was said, continued to influence life chances well past the second generation—especially for groups defined as nonwhite races and also for Mexican Americans and the descendants of the southern and eastern European immigrants. Consequently, the Census Bureau needed to count these groups past the second generation. Critically, officials and advocates expected that the *third- and later-generation members* would numerically dominate the new origin counts. After all, immigration had been low since the 1920s, and it was not expected that the number of new Hispanics and Asians would reach the levels they actually attained during later decades. Nevertheless, the march toward a giant immigration from the third world was already well underway by the end of the 1970s, and that immigration would make the people who populated the Hispanic and Asian categories increasingly *recent immigrants* and their American-born children. The categories, innocent of generational standing, would therefore end up playing a strange role in the understanding of group difference, conflating long-term, multigenerational ethno-racial gaps with the effects of being a new immigrant.

In one respect the creation of Asian rather than Hispanic pan-ethnicity is the more intriguing case. Chinese, Japanese, Indian, Pakistani, and other East Asian immigrants differed in language and religion, and their ancestral countries had often fought each other. Even the European Imperial powers that dominated many of them in recent centuries had differed. Thus Asian pan-ethnicity cannot be explained as capturing a shared cultural origin in the region of origin. It is, rather, the claim of a shared discrimination against these Asian groups in the American context that is the major basis for cohesion, and the attendant cultural unity in the American context (including but not limited to the history of immigrant exclusion) created by that experience. These considerations also help explain why the Asian pan-ethnic group does not in fact include all Americans with origins in Asia. It covers only origins in East Asia.

Nevertheless, the coming of the Asian pan-ethnic label did not mark as full a departure from earlier federal classification as the Hispanic Origin question did. Recall that Asian immigrants and their descendants had been listed by national origin under the "color" or "race" question in every census since 1870. The addition of a covering label finally included in the 1990 census amounted to only a minor change in the enumeration, even if it provided political and cultural standing.

By contrast, an American census had only once listed any Hispanic group as a race—the 1930 census listed "Mexican race." Nor did the 1980 reform create a place for Hispanics in the race question. Hispanic Origin was instead introduced as a distinct new question that purportedly concerned "ethnicity." But as with race, the census question on Hispanic origin dealt with ethnicity without regard to generational standing.

During the two decades prior to 1980, Mexican, Puerto Rican, and Cuban organizations increasingly jointly pressed for the 1980 Hispanic Origin question. Leaders of these groups could hardly fail to be profoundly affected by black mobilization. Black lawyers, members of Congress, leaders of mainstream organizations, and young direct-action radicals—all seemed role models to activists in other groups, especially given the new federal responsibilities to minorities. Now some agencies investigated individual complaints of discrimination, others examined group underrepresentation, and still others offered new funding for programs that targeted vulnerable populations. Minority appointments within the federal bureaucracy itself—across a wide range of agencies—also became a priority, and when achieved, they helped strengthen the federal sensibility for those new responsibilities.

At the same time, leaders of nonblack groups had to be concerned that the civil rights mobilization might direct federal energy only to black–white inequalities. True, the new legislation prohibited discrimination by "race, color, religion, sex, or national origin." But the visible, long-term struggles for such legislation had been conducted almost exclusively by and for blacks, with their white allies. However necessary and laudable the improvement of black conditions obviously was, what of the condition of other minorities? Would they receive only token attention?

Mexican Americans were concentrated in the Southwest, Puerto Ricans in the New York City area, and the newer Cuban group around Miami; each could be dismissed in Washington as a regional issue. Together they would have a better claim to federal attention—by virtue of both national presence and greater numbers. When the National Council of La Raza, then representing only Mexican Americans, moved its base of operations from the Southwest to Washington, DC, it reflected this understanding. So, too, did the group's increasing interaction with Puerto Rican organizations. The Puerto Rican population had increased tenfold between 1940 and 1960. Eventually La Raza redefined its clientele as all Hispanics.[13]

Demand for more federal data about these peoples had initially been especially strong in the Mexican American organizations. A critical feature of their concern with data was an insistence on tracking Mexican Americans beyond the second generation. Group leaders argued that the analogy of European immigrants simply didn't hold for the Mexican Americans of the Southwest. First, the earliest Mexican settlers in the area were not "immigrants" into an Anglo-American civilization at all but long-settled residents of a conquered area. Of course, later migrants had indeed crossed a formal international border when coming from Mexico, even if one barely maintained during its early history. But their descendants were unlike those of Europeans. Across the entire century since the time of the American conquest, advocates insisted, the Mexican Americans of the Southwest had suffered far more active discrimination than the Europeans had in the North, and they remained more isolated in geography, economic conditions, and language. Thus, despite having many generations' standing in the country, the group's disadvantages circa 1965–1975 were strongly related to their Mexican origin. From a numerical standpoint, these later-generation descendants made the Mexican Americans "America's second-largest minority." But they were also "the invisible minority," and a critical focus of the early advocacy was how to identify Mexican Americans of the third and later generations around 1970, those who were not identified through the birthplace and parental-birthplace questions.[14]

This conundrum had been haunting the bureau for several census cycles. We have already seen how restrictionist motives had created the 1930 census's "Mexican" race category, and how the 1930s brought successful opposition from Mexican American defense organizations, the Mexican government, and eventually the State Department. In the 1940 and 1950 census cycles, the information available on those of Mexican and European descent had been the same: birthplace and parental birthplaces, and classification as white on race. The *later*-generation Mexican Americans remained unidentifiable among all native-born whites of native parentage.

Conrad Taeuber had been an important Census Bureau official involved in the internal discussions and the debates with advocates until his retirement in 1973. In an interview conducted years later, he recalled how "the matter of the identification of what we now call Hispanics became a real political issue." However elliptically, he touched on the three key issues: first, the "Mexican race" legacy of 1930; second, the mixture of discrimination and isolation in creating a distinctive later-generation group; and third, the fact that the census parental-birthplace questions failed to identify this group.

> *Taeuber.* . . . As you recall, the 1930 Census had identified Mexicans as a separate race category. That did not go over well with the government of Mexico, and later the Census Bureau went to identifications of Spanish surnames as a way of identifying what we now call Hispanics. . . . With the continuing racist problem, and there was a problem primarily because the descendants of the people who were living in the area . . . when we took a large chunk of Mexico away from them. . . . The descendants of those people are still to a large extent speaking Spanish, and still to a large extent in Spanish-speaking churches. Irrigation, agricultural—it hasn't really moved out—they preserve their culture. Identifying them as native born of native parentage didn't quite do it. . . . We argued that we had native born of foreign parentage; that gives us Mexicans of first and second generation, gives us some Puerto Ricans of first and second generation, but we couldn't get away from the people in New Mexico, Arizona, and South Texas.[15]

The Census Bureau did try to get at this issue during the 1950s and 1960s with special post-enumeration counts of Spanish surnamed respondents in selected areas (particularly in the five states with high concentrations of Mexican Americans). The bureau collected common surnames from telephone directories of Mexico (as well as Puerto Rico and Cuba). After the census, clerks went through the schedules identifying respondents with qualifying names. This method had the advantages of being an "objective" count. But it was objective only in the limited sense that it rested on a clearly defined criterion rather than on the respondent's self-identification as a group member. By contrast, self-identification was *not* "objective" because it was based on varied, unstated, and possibly poorly defined criteria. But did the "objective" criterion fully capture the relevant population? Spanish surname did not include families who had changed their names, and it did not include the families of women who had married individuals who were not of Spanish descent. Crucially, the surname criterion would also miss all later generations of families that had involved either sort of name change.

Name changing and out-marriage typically reflected some degree of acculturation. So the surname criterion might be said to eliminate the more assimilated group members. If the argument for keeping track of distant origins was that those origins continued to handicap group members, were the people who did not have Spanish surnames really relevant to such handicaps? But no one knew: there was no way to count. In any case, whether distant historical origins handicapped current-day group members was a matter of more or less rather than of yes or no.

Another obvious strategy was to count the "Spanish-speaking" population. The objections here were very similar to those raised in connection with Spanish surname. If an American of Mexican descent no longer knew Spanish, did it follow that his or her life chances had ceased to be handicapped by that origin? Better, it seemed, to think in terms of "Spanish-speaking origins."

Self-identification did not have the disadvantages of these other methods and was not limited by generational standing. This was a rationale based on the effects of discrimination and isolation; two other considerations also supported the same conclusion. First, the larger the count, the stronger the political claim. Second, group pride was gratified both by the larger count, and by the claim that many later-generation descendants were loyal to their origins. Still, the census procedure for counting Spanish surnames in the Southwest was continued in 1960. The subjects were classified as "white persons of Spanish surname." This was the summary (and favorable evaluation) of the scholar and organizational activist George I. Sanchez. And the Census Bureau had apparently expected to continue the same approach into the 1970s as well.[16]

Yet by the late 1960s, established Mexican American leaders were formulating demands for better approaches. First, young activists and then ever-more leaders generally were dismissing George Sanchez's definition of white standing as wrongheaded in the American sense of whiteness. It rested heavily on the treaty rights that were left over from the mid-nineteenth century, rights that, in any case, often had been ignored.[17] The demand was now clearly for *self-identification* to capture the largest possible number of the later-generation population. After all, wasn't that exactly what was being done for blacks, Asians, and American Indians?

In any case, the census procedures of the late 1960s and early 1970s (those resting on special post-enumeration counts of the Spanish surname group) also had many other obvious disadvantages: they covered only five states, and even there the evidence came from only a sample of the population (restricting its use in studying local areas). Finally, the bureau quite simply did not intensively use the raw data it did have on the Spanish surname population: it produced relatively few relevant tables, and advocates found that requesting others was a frustrating process.[18]

In 1967, members of President Johnson's cabinet urged the Census Bureau to collect more information on "ethnic origin, particularly the identification of Mexican-Americans."[19] By 1969, the bureau had also begun to test questions that relied on self-reports rather than Spanish surname. At the same time (1969), it began testing the *general* (rather than Hispanic) version origin questions that would evolve into the Ancestry question. These questions spoke of "ethnicity," "ethnic origin or descent," or "Spanish/Hispanic origin or descent."[20]

In 1969, Herman Gallegos, the executive director of the Southwest Council of La Raza, perceptively argued that just such self-identification was permitted for "several other minority groups," including Filipinos, Hawaiians, and Koreans, but not for "Spanish-surnamed, Spanish-speaking minorities." Gallegos was referring here to the categories of the *race* question and drew the implications clearly: "The question titled 'Color or Race' [should] be changed to read 'Race, Color, or Ethnic Origin'" and it should provide "a breakout of the groups of Spanish heritage such as Mexican-Americans, Puerto Ricans, Cubans, Central Americans, South Americans, etc."[21]

Neither Johnson's cabinet members in 1967 nor Gallegos in 1969 were asking to define Mexican Americans (or all Spanish-origin groups) as a race. Rather, by the late 1960s the concept of "ethnic origin" had diffused vastly further than it had in the early 1950s when Helen Jeter's group pondered it. Not only social scientists but also federal officials and advocacy groups were used to it.

And yet the Spanish-origin groups could not be counted under the race question, given the earlier history of Mexican Americans and race as well as the present attempts at coalition building among various Spanish-origin groups with different compositions of color groups. But neither did Gallegos's proposed alteration of the "Color or Race" question to one on "Race, Color, or Ethnic Origin" prevail. Possibly there was pushback from the black organizations, who were uncomfortable with the change in nomenclature. And in any case, would a single question continue to require "Mark one [category] only"? If so, both black and Hispanic leaders would have had reason to worry about smaller counts than with two independent questions. Finally, Hispanic leaders would have had reason to oppose the Gallegos-type solution when they believed they could successfully hold out for a separate question focused explicitly on their clientele; that approach would stimulate the largest identification with the group.

Meanwhile, the Census Bureau officials were skeptical about trying to capture ethnic membership. How could a respondent even be expected to *know* all his or her relevant origins? How would he or she choose which of many possible origins to list? Would all who qualify even identify with the terms indicated on the form? And what of the *strength* of ethnic ties? Merely answering a question about origins did not imply that the ties had the same relevance for all. In other words, while advocates spoke of the isolation, discrimination, and continued distinctiveness of groups past the second generation, bureau officials wondered about levels of assimilation, intermarriage, and multiple origins in that the same population.

By the late 1960s, Spanish-origin organizations were routinely finding congressional allies. At the end of that decade, the Nixon White House apparently caught the Census Bureau off guard. It announced that the 1970 census would include a nationwide question on "Spanish Origin."[22] It was too late to put the question on the form that would go to all households (the "short form" for the 100 percent enumeration), but it was added to the form that would ask more detailed questions of a 5 percent sample of households (the "long form"). The question eventually asked, "Is the person's origin or descent Mexican, Puerto Rican, Cuban, Central or South American, Other Spanish," or none of those.

But this effort ended up as one among many features of Census Bureau work that were bitterly criticized—and attracted lawsuits—during the early 1970s over undercounts of the poor and minorities (not just Hispanics), lack of Spanish-language forms, and a general lack of attention to the Spanish-origin population. Additional pressure came in 1973 from a U.S. Commission on Civil Rights report, *To Know or Not to Know: Collection and Use of Racial and Ethnic Data in Federal Assistance Programs*, which argued that "distinctions based on national origin rather than race are seen as the meaningful ones."[23] President Nixon replaced the director of the Census Bureau; the new director created closer links to various ethnic and racial groups, including Hispanics in particular, with boards of ethnic stakeholders.[24]

Congressional advocates submitted several bills across the first half of the 1970s and held hearings concerning the need for better data. In 1971 and again in 1973, Puerto Rican and Mexican American members of Congress submitted bills that would require more data collection on the Spanish-origin population. The second of these cited "racial, social, economic, and political discrimination" that prevented the group from enjoying the "basic opportunities they deserve as American citizens." They could not "lift themselves out of the poverty that they now endure" because the lack of "regular, nationwide evaluation" prevented policymakers from making an accurate assessment of their "urgent and special needs."[25] These efforts eventually lead to congressional hearings on the data collection needs of "Spanish-speaking Americans" in 1974–1975.

All this made government officials acutely aware of the need to resolve the problem of collecting data on ethno-racial origins. One locus of bureaucratic energy was the Office of Management and Budget (OMB) that

President Nixon had authorized in July 1970. From its earliest days, the OMB officials saw that they would have to take on the challenge of systematizing race and ethnic data collection. By 1971, as historian Benjamin Francis-Fallon describes, the OMB reported that

> The "proliferation of statistical collection activities" in dozens of federal agencies had led to "wide disparities in the quality of data and the standards used," trouble with comparability, "overlapping collection activities," and other "operational inefficiencies." One agency would report as many as 15 ethnoracial categories while another reported as few as one ("minority"). Most agencies reported minorities according to five categories, but used "various categories for persons of Spanish heritage. Federal managers saw a situation in desperate need of direction.... [An OMB official] predicted that "the specification of categories will be a necessity." ... [Then] government departments and committees ... would "no longer have to waste time in trying to reach agreement on minority categories to be reported."[26]

In June 1976, Congress passed a bill urging the Office of Management and Budget to "develop a Government-wide program for the collection of data with respect to Americans of Spanish origin or descent." As Francis-Fallon notes, that this was "the only law of its kind, mandating data collection for a specific ethnoracial group." It called for "a reliable and comprehensive socioeconomic profile" for Spanish origin "on par with that available for the general population of the United States."[27] In 1977, the OMB released Directive #15: *Race and Ethnic Standards for Federal Statistics and Administrative Reporting.*

OMB DIRECTIVE #15

The wording of the short Directive is instructive and worth a close read. It restated the old arrangements of the race question, introduced the Hispanic origin group along the lines Congress had set out the preceding June, and still allowed agencies to have some leeway in choosing procedures to follow. However, accomplishing the first two goals meant that the specifics set out in the directive are best explained as codifying the peculiar legacies of past arrangements, however inconsistent, and bringing in a category to define Hispanics as something other than a race, rather than stating any other clear principles, for example about ethnicity as a companion category to race.

Very near the beginning of the Directive the text notes what might be called the usual disclaimer: "These classifications should not be interpreted as being scientific or anthropological in nature, nor should they be viewed as determinants of eligibility for participation in any Federal program."[28] The categories do not derive their meaning from science: What do they mean?[29] The absence of any definition for ethnicity is particularly striking; this concept, after all, was nearly novel in connection with federal law and directives, even if it was widespread in popular discussion by 1977. By contrast, every census had had a race (or color) question.

The remainder of the text includes two major sections.

1. Definitions.

   The basic racial and ethnic categories for Federal statistics and program administrative reporting are defined as follows:

   a. *American Indian or Alaskan Native.* A person having origins in any of the original peoples of North America and who maintains cultural identification through tribal affiliation or community recognition.

   b. *Asian or Pacific Islander.* A person having origins in any of the original peoples of the Far East, Southeast Asia, the Indian subcontinent, or the Pacific Islands. This area includes, for example, China, India, Japan, Korea, the Philippine Islands, and Samoa.

   c. *Black.* A person having origins in any of the black racial groups of Africa.

   d. *Hispanic.* A person of Mexican, Puerto Rican, Cuban, Central or South American or other Spanish culture or origin, regardless of race.

   e. *White.* A person having origins in any of the original peoples of Europe, North Africa, or the Middle East.

Presumably the reason the categories had to be defined while the covering concepts (race and ethnicity) could be left undefined was practical:

people would be assigned directly to categories; category definitions were the rules for assignment. Yet those category definitions were hardly straightforward. It is true that all five rest in part on reference to regions (and sometimes countries) of the globe. But in the case of the ethnicity category (d), the reference to countries and region is solely to origin in a cultural, and perhaps national sense. Thus an Hispanic is "a person *of* Mexican [or other listed countries'] . . . culture or origin." By contrast, for each of the four race categories the reference to region is to "a person having origins in any of the original peoples of that region." What distinguishes these "original peoples of . . ." is not stated explicitly, but it would seem to be *physical* traits; hence the contrast with ethnicity and hence the additional descriptor of color for race category (c). A few years later, the *Procedural History* of the 1980 census presented its own version of the usual disclaimer: "The concept of race used in recent censuses reflects self-identification by respondents; it does not denote any clearcut, scientific definition of biological stock."[30] But the disclaimer seems to leave as plausible the impression that the self-identity and nonscientific classification pertains to biological stock.

There are two other elaborations of the geographic reference for race categories. In category (b) the text adds *examples* of countries within the relevant region: "This area includes, for example, China, India, Japan . . ." The examples seem redundant, but they may be there to acknowledge the century-long use of Asian national origins as race categories, particularly in the census: for example, the Chinese, Asian Indian, and Japanese race categories. But this link between OMB examples and census Asian national origin race categories seems to imply that for the OMB, too, the "original peoples of . . ." these Asian countries are each to be taken as a distinct race. The other elaboration of geographic reference cuts in the opposite direction. In category (a), region is supplemented by the requirement of maintaining cultural membership. But cultural membership seems to be what defines the ethnicity category.

The second major section of the Directive offers two acceptable ways to use these categories. "To provide flexibility, it is preferable to collect data on race and ethnicity separately," giving eight possible combinations (four races, two ethnicities).

a. *Race*:
  –American Indian or Alaskan Native
  –Asian or Pacific Islander
  –Black
  –White
b. *Ethnicity*:
  –Hispanic origin
  –Not of Hispanic origin

And of specific concern, "When race and ethnicity are collected separately, the number of White and Black persons who are Hispanic must be identifiable, and capable of being reported in that category." But the Directive also accepts "a combined [race and ethnicity] format" of five categories:

  –American Indian or Alaskan Native
  –Asian or Pacific Islander
  –Black, not of Hispanic origin
  –Hispanic
  –White, not of Hispanic origin

Note that the underlying concepts of race and ethnicity are related in quite different ways in these two formats. The "preferable" arrangement presents them as entirely independent of each other; someone in either "ethnic category" (Hispanic or non-Hispanic) can be in any of the four race categories. This is not the case for the "combined format." There, Hispanics cannot appear in the black or white race categories (the smaller number of Asian or American Indian mixes with Hispanic origin are ignored). Consequently, the counts in the black and white categories would be lower than in the "preferable" arrangement. This was probably perceived as a relatively minor threat to black numbers because Mexicans in particular had been so systematically assigned to the white race in the past. Also, everyone surely understood that the Census Bureau would use the more detailed "preferable" option.

It is taken for granted that the four race categories and the two ethnicity categories (Hispanic, non-Hispanic) are complete and mutually exclusive. But how, in this framework, is the multiracial individual to be classified? "The category which most closely reflects the individual's rec-ognition in his community should be used for purposes of reporting on persons who are of mixed racial and / or ethnic origins." By Census 2000 a multiracial interest group had successfully challenged the assumption that a person actually had to be fitted into only one category. And then in that new context of multicategory assignments, it would be possible too, in the twenty-first century's second decade, to reopen the question of the connection between "ethnicity" and the race categories.

Before leaving the Directive, it is important to understand how frail its presentation of "ethnicity" as a new concept for federal data collection really was. The political pressure was not to enshrine "ethnicity," it was to "develop a Government-wide program for the collection of data with respect to Americans of Spanish origin or descent" (as the congressional bill phrased the goal). There were reasons (discussed earlier) why a Hispanic origin race seemed a poor solution; hence "Hispanic origin" had to be something else. Also, the Directive did note, "In no case should the provisions of this Directive be construed to limit the collection of data to the categories de-scribed above." The OMB would be happy with additional detail on eth-nicity (as well as race) groups; and the Census Bureau would soon provide both. "However, any reporting required which uses more detail shall be or-ganized in such a way that the additional categories can be aggregated into these basic racial / ethnic categories." And this interagency comparability to the basic list of five groupings was important not least because they com-prise the minimum categories that all levels of government need to track for "civil rights compliance . . . and equal employment reporting."

There was always something lame in the OMB announcement of two required categories of ethnicity, Hispanic and non-Hispanic. Notwith-standing the announcement that agencies could add more ethnicities, it was clear that only the four race categories and Hispanic counted for the fed-eral efforts to address group underrepresentation under the programs set up in the 1960s. The public may indeed have been familiar with the term "ethnicity" by the 1980s, and would soon speak of Hispanics and "Hispanic origin." But it is less clear that the public knew then (or knew decades later) that "Hispanic origin" was an "ethnicity." In fact, the introduc-tion of the Hispanic Origin question as an ethnicity was weirdly reminiscent of events that transpired two-thirds of a century earlier. Recall that in 1910,

Census Director Durand introduced the mother-tongue question as the alternative to counting immigrant groups as "races." He did so by stressing a new terminology for the counts, in particular that mother tongue was the measure of "nationality" (in the sense of peoplehood). And yet, in questionnaires and then in its publications the bureau rarely if ever mentioned nationalities, only mother tongues. And likewise, after 1980, it became simpler and more relevant to speak of Hispanic origin than of ethnicity. People may speak of "ethno-racial" origins but few probably realize that the government proclaims that it collects data on several races and one ethnicity.

THE WHITE ETHNICS AND THE ORIGIN QUESTION

The OMB mandated an "ethnicity" question on Hispanic origin in time for the 1980 census. It read in part, "A person is of Spanish / Hispanic origin or descent if the person *identifies* his or her ancestry with one of the listed groups. . . . Origin or descent (ancestry) may be viewed as the nationality group, the lineage, or country in which . . . ancestors were born." The question was on the "short form" that went to every American household. As the OMB also permitted federal agencies to gather more ethno-racial information than the mandated ethnicity and race categories, the Census Bureau added an *Ancestry question.* This was a generalized form of the Hispanic Origin question, that is, gathering information on the specific ethnic origins of all Americans—rather than assigning most of them into the residual "Not of Hispanic origin" category. As such, Ancestry was the only census question that produced data on these origins for whites who were three or more generations removed from immigrant forbearers. Respondents were asked to report "the ancestry group with which the person *identifies.* Ancestry (or origin or descent) may be viewed as the nationality group, the lineage, or the country in which . . . ancestors were born." As a question of lesser importance than Hispanic Origin, Ancestry was not asked on the 100 percent enumeration, but only on the "long-form" questionnaire sent to a sample of households.

Why did the Ancestry question come into being? Three considerations seem relevant. Census Bureau officials had been uncomfortable about introducing a new origins question that focused on only one ethnic (or panethnic) group—Spanish origin. It would have been a dramatic departure from the bureau's past treatment of origins and one hard to justify on demographic grounds. Partly for this reason, no doubt, the bureau had begun testing *general* at the same time as *Spanish* origin questions. This dual testing track was visible as early as 1969, long before OMB Directive #15. A second reason for the Ancestry question's success was political pressure, in this case from the white ethnic organizations. A third, closely related reason was a perceived continuum of historically disadvantaged groups along which fell blacks, other nonwhite minority groups, and the white ethnics.

The descendants of southern and eastern Europeans in particular pressed for the information that the Ancestry question eventually provided. Their families had experienced discrimination as "the wrong kinds" of European races, and they had experienced these travails more recently than had descendants of earlier European immigrants. And so their groups claimed that the connections between ethnic origins and life chances were stronger for them than for descendants of the northern and western European immigrations, much as the Mexican American groups were claiming about their clientele compared to descendants of any European immigration. The pressure for such data did not derive only from an interest in the group's life chances. Ethnic pride played a role, too, related in part to resentment at the increasing attention the federal government was giving to black and other nonwhite minority groups.

It was in the late 1960s that "white ethnic" became a familiar term. It applied loosely "to the mostly Catholic [or Orthodox Christian] immigrants or persons with ancestry from eastern or southern Europe ... while Jews and Catholic Irish Americans are on the boundaries." WASPS and Scandinavians were excluded.[31] Until the 1960s, the white ethnic groups had had precious little incentive to demand that the federal government pay more attention to them. Over the decades (and generations) their cultural distinctiveness had declined and their economic condition had been improving. Still, most lived in the Northern cities, many in working-class neighborhoods close to where great numbers of black migrants from the South had been settling since the 1940s. This uneasy proximity accentuated their tendency to refer to themselves simply as whites, rather than as Italian, Polish, or Slovak. The rapidity and completeness of this identity shift from (for example) Italian to white should not be exaggerated. There is no reason to claim that the identities and loyalties as members of specific national origin groups were suddenly lost. A person could easily define oneself as white or Italian American, depending on the specific social context.[32]

John Skrentny's authoritative study, *The Minority Rights Revolution,* illuminates how reverberations from the white ethnic movement came into the process by which four protected groups eventually were defined as legally eligible for affirmative action. In 1967 the undersecretary of Housing and Urban Development gave a speech on the problems of the "average white ethnic male"—economic insecurity, life adjacent to a black ghetto, observing antiwar protests at the universities (which violated his values), and generally feeling neglected. Various foundations, universities, and other organizations created a "National Project on Ethnic America." By 1971, the Ford Foundation was providing nearly $1 million for efforts to alter a situation in which "great numbers of working-class Americans have not been at the center of recent social concerns" and to increase understanding of "the continuing role of ethnicity in American life." In 1969 *Newsweek* reported on "The Troubled American Majority" (with much attention to the white ethnic) and in 1970 on "Rising Cry: Ethnic Power." In 1972 *Congressional Quarterly Weekly Report* examined "Campaign '72: The Rising Voices of Ethnic Voters."[33]

The concerns of the white ethnic leaders were not identical to those of the Hispanic leaders described earlier, but there were some general similarities. On the one hand, the unapologetic assertiveness of black leaders could be something to emulate; on the other, assertiveness, and especially the ghetto disorders, were resented. Also, the white ethnics were struck that several minority groups *other than blacks* were emerging as entitled to affirmative action remedies.[34] They expressed an ethnic pride of their own and a demand for attention to the economic needs of their own clientele. They felt that the economic standing of their communities was relatively low, and that a history of discrimination helped explain why.

Another partial parallel with Hispanic mobilization had to do with a concern for late-generation ethnicity that survived into the third generation and beyond. The overwhelming majority of the southern and eastern Europeans had actually arrived during the quarter century between about 1890 and 1913. Mostly young adults, these immigrants' *children* had come into the world during roughly the first quarter of the twentieth century, and their *grand*children by about 1940–1960. Thus, in the late 1970s, the second generation was concentrated in the later-middle-age brackets or beyond; many third-generation members were in young adulthood.[35] If the 1980 and later censuses were to follow the progress of southern and eastern European ethnics, they would have to take counts that went past the second generation. Of course, this disappearance of the third and later generations from view in the census was nothing new in the history of European immigration to America: descendants of British, Irish, German, and Scandinavian immigration waves had all passed through such a process, appearing by 1970 only as part of the giant group listed as "native whites of native parentage." And yet that was cold comfort to the white ethnics, not least because they believed theirs was a European immigrant epic distinctly marked by discrimination.

Recall finally the evolution of thinking among the American social scientists culminating in *Beyond the Melting Pot* (1963): "The point about the Melting Pot . . . is that it did not happen." This view of large ethnic communities like those in New York City rested on the notion that a variety of factors—class, neighborhood, immigrant origins, and local politics—reinforced each other in group loyalties. Glazer and Moynihan did not mean to limit the generalization to the descendants of the city's two large southern and eastern European groups—Italians and Jews. Their study also covered two non-European groups whose people had nearly all come to New York more recently—African American arrivals from the South and Puerto Ricans. And it included the Irish, who had predated any of these in the city. There is no need to argue that this book was a necessary condition for the federal ethno-racial classifications to change. Pressure from the ethno-racial advocacy groups of the 1960s and 1970s provides an adequate explanation for the change. Moreover, Glazer and Moynihan were not discussing "Hispanics" but Puerto Ricans. Nevertheless, the book did set out a view that could only have encouraged the perspective that groups tend to persist for a long time, and by no means only nonwhite groups. "At least in New York . . . and those parts of America that resemble New York."[36]

One focus of white ethnic mobilization in 1965–1966 was for inclusion in the affirmative action programs. Of course, white ethnics could sue under civil rights law against "discrimination on the basis of . . . religion or national origin." But inclusion as a protected group would have meant that white ethnic individuals would not have to file suit and prove acts of discrimination. Instead, group counts would be used to show their group to be underrepresented in various attractive social positions, and then federal authorities could exert informal pressure or bring legal action for change. All this came down to a very specific point of detail, particularly in connection with underrepresentation in employment. The Equal Employment Opportunity Commission (EEOC) began to investigate group underrepresentation at firms. Clearly, blacks would be on the specified list of protected minorities to be counted, but which other groups would be? A Polish American organization urged the EEOC to include their people. But the suggestion was rebuffed. Not only was the form already running out of room, but also, "once we take care of them, where do we put Italians, Yugoslavs, Greeks, etc. who are sure to want to be separately identified?"[37] The white ethnic continuum posed the challenge of the slippery slope precisely because arguments against homogenizing all whites into a privileged elite were familiar.

At a federal hearing an Italian American leader made the broader point to the EEOC chairman that not all minority groups who had suffered were listed. Omitted were "minority groups such as Italian-Americans, Polish-Americans, German-Americans, Irish-Americans, Jewish-Americans, and others." Some congressmen also supported the claim.[38] The members of these white ethnic groups had often been listed among "minorities" well into the 1950s—either in ethnic terms or as Catholics and Jews. Then too, the Civil Rights Act explicitly prohibited discrimination in employment on the basis of "race, color, religion, sex, and national origin." How then was the decision made to exclude the white ethnics from the minorities protected by the EEOC and for affirmative action? How did it come about that Hispanics, Asians, and American Indians would join blacks on that list but the white ethnics would not? Skrentny illuminates the interplay of minimal data, assumptions, federal officials, politicians, and ethnic organizations. He summarizes: "There was some undefined standard of oppression and victimhood that guided national policy relating to affirmative action. . . . Women, Asians, Latinos, and American Indians had suffered like blacks and thus could be analogized to them. White ethnics had not suffered enough and the analogy did not work."[39]

Skrentny acknowledges that Nathan Glazer and Arthur Mann argued at the time for a different explanation: that the white ethnics generally were well on their way to assimilating into a (white) mainstream. Consequently the leaders of the white ethnic organizations who argued otherwise really lacked a meaningful clientele. But Skrentny counters that the link between leaders and clientele was complex for all groups. In general, white ethnics had "advocates in Congress and in the White House. Politicians wanted their votes and saw them as an economically disadvantaged group." The white ethnics failed to be listed with the four nonwhite groups partly because of "standard of oppression" just mentioned; they also failed, Skrentny suggests, because politicians could relate to them in terms of their other identities such as class, religion, union membership, and so on. In the end, the white ethnic failure meant that "National policy therefore racialized [white] ethnics as privileged whites and they remained close but just outside the minority rights revolution."[40]

Skrentny also calls attention to an interesting incident that happened a few years earlier, when Eisenhower's President's Committee on Government Contracts proposed specific minorities on whom employers should report hires. The list of minorities originally included Jews. However, black groups had argued that Jews were not disadvantaged, and the committee's survey director had concurred that in terms of "social recognition and economic progress, Jews had done well." The major Jewish organizations involved, including the Anti-Defamation League (ADL), the American Jewish Committee, and the American Jewish Congress had not objected.[41] Skrentny notes that they no doubt wanted to avoid a struggle with black civil rights organizations. But there was a wider context of considerations operating above all for Jews and to a lesser extent for Catholics.

The case of the Jews is clearest, and it runs through the narrative of Jewish protests against legibility described in earlier chapters. Originally defined by the Reform elites of German Jewish origin like Simon Wolf or the early leaders of the American Jewish Committee, it rested heavily on the principled insistence that the constitutional church–state separation forbade taking account of an individual's religion. This position captured the way these Jewish elites identified as Jews: as members of a distinct enlightened religion, they were "Americans of the Mosaic persuasion." Yet most eastern European Jews who arrived between 1880 and 1920 were embedded much more fully in a Jewishness that involved many cultural characteristics. As such, one might think it would have been more natural for them than for the old German Jewish elite to consider being a protected minority. But the social and institutional history followed a very different path.

First of all, assimilation over the course of two generations radically reduced the distinctiveness of descendants of eastern European Jewish immigrants. Secondly, as noted in Chapter 10, many of these descendants of eastern European Jews defined themselves almost exclusively in religious terms even if their identity with Jewish peoplehood was actually strong. Finally, the major Jewish defense organizations continued to rest much of their advocacy on the separation of church and state; after all, whatever else, Jews were also a religious group.

The histories of the major Jewish defense organizations themselves reflected both the demographic history and the self-definitional issues of the group. The AJC had been founded by a self-recruiting German Jewish elite in 1906. By the 1950s, the leadership was still drawn from that group but over half the membership was now of eastern European Jewish origin, taming somewhat the earlier positions; now, for example, support for Zionism and Israel especially in the post-Holocaust years was a given. Following a somewhat similar trajectory, German Jews had founded the B'nai B'rith brotherhood in the mid-nineteenth century. It had always represented a much lower level of elites, primarily local business people, than the AJC. By the 1950s, it, too, found its membership increasingly among the children of the eastern European Jewish immigration. In 1913 B'nai B'rith founded an offshoot, the Anti-Defamation League, which focused on opposition to discrimination—especially discrimination against Jews but increasingly in the postwar era against any group. By contrast, the American Jewish Congress had been founded in opposition to the elitist, Reform outlooks of the AJC in the World War I era. The congress had always drawn on Jews from eastern Europe much more heavily than the other two organizations had. If the committee represented a national economic and professional elite, was self-recruiting, and worked quietly behind the scenes, the representatives of congress were elected by a large membership and emphasized openness and assertiveness in the American political scene.[42]

The AJC and its predecessors had been central in the movement against immigration restriction for well over a half century. And by the postwar era, all three major organizations (AJC, ADL, and Congress) were participating in both Jewish and general antidiscrimination and civil rights work. They had been very prominent among those testifying at various federal committees investigating discrimination.

Their activism on church–state separation was very strong in the postwar period. The protests of Celler and Javits over "ethnic classification" described in Chapter 10 were a continuation of the earlier ones about immigrant identification. The American Jewish Congress, with its legacy of assertiveness, was especially willing to engage in the public role of litigation and brought numerous church–state cases to court. These cases were especially common in connection with schools—school prayer, release time for religious instruction, support for religious schools, and so on. In fact, in the decade and a half just prior to the passage of the 1964 Civil Rights Act, the American Jewish Congress had challenged and won an historic array of church–state cases at the Supreme Court that raised the wall of separation considerably.[43]

Also, in the mid-1950s, the American Jewish Congress had led the fight to oppose a question on religion on the U.S. census. The Census Bureau had supported the inclusion of the question, and had proceeded so far as to include a test question in a Current Population Survey (CPS). The American Jewish Congress's pressure against even releasing the results of that preliminary survey was such that most of the results were in fact withheld. The grounds, as always, were that the American government had no right to inquire into the religious beliefs of its people.[44]

The fear of practical repercussions of such legibility went well beyond the constitutional objection. In 1910, when those fears stood out in connection with the List, they seemed to refer both to the threat of immigration restriction and to "fanning the flames of bigotry" in the public. This latter would be the outcome of presenting Jewish concentrations that would be viewed as unattractive, such as high rates of work in "unproductive," nonmanual occupations, or of residence in the biggest eastern cities. By the mid-1950s, mass immigration was a thing of the past, and the fear of popular bigotry was expressed in terms that had moved up the social-class ladder. Kevin M. Schultz captures these fears in his detailed discussion of the mid-century struggle over a census religion question.

Rabbi S. H. Markowitz of Philadelphia [asked] . . . "Do you want the following questions answered by no less an authority than the U.S. government? 1. What is the average Jewish income? 2. How many Jewish bankers are there in the U.S.? . . . 3. Where do Jews live?" Sociologist Marshall Sklare was concerned about "the problem of cross-tabulations . . . the most sensitive [cross-tabulation] from our point of view would be running religion against income." A memo from the American Jewish Committee pointed out "The possibilities for mischief of cross-tabulating religion and income are obvious." [These "possibilities for mischief" were turning up] just as society was beginning to lose its long-standing suspicions about Jews.[45]

In sum, whether on the constitutional grounds or from broader fears of legibility to the government or the gentile public, there was no diminution of Jewish opposition to being identified in government surveys as Jews during the postwar period; if anything the American Jewish Congress's recent court cases could be seen as the high point of such opposition over the course of seven decades.

Of course, major Jewish organizations could easily support specific investigations into anti-Semitism in the workplace or elsewhere. But supporting a federal category for Jewish counts in the workplace? And to have any traction, workplace counts would have to be compared to federal census counts of Jews. The weight of this legacy made it intellectually and politically impossible for the Jewish organizations to now pivot to the latter policy of embracing such counts.

But more than inconsistency was at issue. A real trade off was involved: if leaders of Jewish organizations had in fact chosen to argue for including Jews as a protected group, they would have had to give up the claims to a "religion-blind" public domain. In purely self-interest terms, would this trade really be an advantage? And would the average Jew consider it as such? Skrentny came across a Jewish Labor Committee representative who did consider the possibility of Jewish protected status. Apparently his reflections went nowhere.[46]

Later, there would be cases in which discriminatory actions against Jews were prosecuted under laws prohibiting *racial* discrimination. At first the mainstream Jewish organizations were hesitant to support this legal strategy since it seemed to bring the affirmation of a Jewish race a step closer, but they eventually came around. Nevertheless, noting that discrimination against Jews could be racial in nature was a long way from advocating legibility through federal counts of Jews. Later there also would be some Jewish individuals (or even a few small groups) who wondered, in print or on the internet, why Jews were not an acceptable category under the census Ancestry or even race questions. One suspects that such commentators were often unaware of the giant role that the Jewish mainstream organizations had played in ensuring those prohibitions. Even writers who were aware of that history are best analogized to the Zionists of 1910, or to the YIVO intellectuals of the 1940s, who criticized the American Jewish Committee's opposition to a Hebrew race. Jews may indeed feel vastly more at home in early twenty-first-century America, compared to a century or even half a century earlier. But that feeling has not produced demands from mainstream Jewish organizations for legibility in federal classifications.[47]

The huge difference in the third quarter of the twentieth century between Jewish and black well-being and between anti-Jewish and anti-black discrimination mattered here. Many more people would have found it sensible to trade the (greatly flawed) "color-blind" constitution for black protected status than would have traded the "religion-blind" constitution for Jewish protected status. For the vast majority of Jewish actors, resisting legibility remained the best outcome. For the nonwhite groups, legibility since the civil rights era was a vast improvement over earlier situations—not least because in earlier federal classification systems all of them except later-generation Hispanics had been legible anyway. Now their legibility in the enumerations (and on affirmative action forms) held out some promise of federal action on their behalf.

The situation for Catholic groups was less clear cut. In particular they had fought the Jewish organizations both on religious schools and on a religion question for the U.S. census.[48] However, identifying a religious—rather than an ethnic—background for counts of protected groups may well have raised historical complexities and trade-offs for Catholics as well as for Jews. Moreover, Skrentny notes that politicians who thought about the white ethnics found they were thinking about people they routinely approached as Catholic, working class, or union member. Likewise, their identity as Catholics could confuse and complicate how white ethnics themselves felt about the federal workplace counts.

Thus the white ethnics were in fact (in Skrentny's perceptive formulation) "close but just outside" relevant discussions of minority rights. These white ethnics therefore did have some presence in the discussions concerning the importance of ethnic descent past the second generation—in terms of levels of well-being and loyalty to origins.

The *Bakke* case on affirmative action in higher education admissions called attention to this continuum of ethno-racial minority groups at the end of the 1970s. The case concerned admissions policy at the University of California Davis Medical School. Affirmative action admissions policies at institutions of higher education did not come about as a matter of federal mandate. They were initiated by the institutions, often prompted by student demands. They typically entered the arena of the courts when an unsuccessful white applicant brought suit claiming that racial discrimination in favor of nonwhites had led to his or her rejection. The courts, and ultimately the U.S. Supreme Court, then had to decide whether the affirmative action admissions policies themselves violated civil rights laws. The *Bakke* case was the crucial turning point in such litigation.

Many white ethnic groups filed briefs opposing the UC Davis Medical School's affirmative action policy. A particularly important brief was filed on Bakke's behalf by three Polish organizations. This brief argued that the university did not consult data about which groups had suffered most. Instead it "began with a list of preferred groups already in mind without a comprehensive study of which ones had been discriminated against." Yet national origin as well as race was a prohibited basis of discrimination; it was therefore plausible that good data on underrepresentation would show that Polish Americans should be on the list of groups that had suffered most. Nor was race-based discrimination *more* prohibited than that based on national origin.[49]

The *Bakke* decision was famously split, but Justice Powell's opinion provided the crucial swing vote and governed the decision. Powell hesitated to embrace the university's defense—namely, that preferential admissions were acceptable because they redressed prior discriminations against ethno-racial minority groups. He instead supported an admissions policy that considered race as one of several relevant factors in order to attain the educational goal of a diverse student body. Racial origin, he noted, might function the way musical talent did in considering the mix.

Powell's famous concerns about the redress defense sound eerily like those in the Polish American brief. He wrote:

> The difficulties entailed in varying the level of judicial review according to a perceived "preferred" status of a particular racial or ethnic minority are intractable. . . . The white "majority" itself is composed of various minority groups, most of which can lay claim to a history of prior discrimination at the hands of the State and private individuals. Not all of these groups can receive preferential treatment and corresponding judicial tolerance of distinctions drawn in terms of race and nationality, for then the only "majority" left would be a new minority of white Anglo-Saxon Protestants. There is no principled basis for deciding which groups would merit "heightened judicial solicitude" and which would not. Courts would be asked to evaluate the extent of the prejudice and consequent harm suffered by various minority groups. Those whose societal injury is thought to exceed some arbitrary level of tolerability then would be entitled to preferential classifications at the expense of individuals belonging to other groups. Those classifications would be free from exacting judicial scrutiny. As these preferences began to have their desired effect, and the consequences of past discrimination were undone, new judicial rankings would be necessary. The kind of variable sociological and political analysis necessary to produce such rankings simply does not lie within the judicial competence—even if they otherwise were politically feasible and socially desirable.[50]

Powell also commented in a note that

> The University is unable to explain its selection of only the four favored groups—Negroes, Mexican Americans, American-Indians and Asians—for preferential treatment. The inclusion of the last is especially curious in light of substantial numbers of Asians admitted through the regular admissions process.[51]

In sum, during the late 1970s, the conception of a continuum of minority groups, explicitly including the white ethnic groups, was being forcefully expressed at the highest governmental level. The point is not that the case or Powell's formulation necessarily had a direct impact on deliberations at the Census Bureau; it is enough that the conception of the continuum was familiar at the time. Policy-oriented demographers at the Census Bureau would have been aware of the continuum. Such awareness may have given bureau officials a strong rationale for not limiting counts of distant ethnic origins to Hispanics while ignoring other groups.

To recap the broader argument, three factors help account for the introduction of the Ancestry question: (1) the sense that if ethnic origins were a reasonable topic for the census, counts should not be limited to Hispanics; (2) the political pressure from white ethnic groups; and (3) the perceived sense of a continuum extending across the white ethnic and nonwhite minority groups. And crucially: groups along this continuum did not seem to fully assimilate by the third generation.

How strong was the drive for the Ancestry question? This is not easy to answer. In an oral history interview, Louis Kincannon, who was working at the OMB in the years before 1980 and would later serve as director of the Census Bureau, recollected the period in which the bureau was finalizing the 1980 questionnaire. He noted that the Ancestry question was saved by President Carter's White House staff in an election year.[52] And further, he recalled only moderate support for the question from Census Bureau officials. But it is worth attending to his description on that point:

> Given the objective in the Carter Administration of reducing Federal paperwork, we [OMB] just about had to cut something out . . . [and one question we urged be cut] was ancestry. . . . Essentially, it was not a very scientific question; it was sort of an opinion poll—"What would you like to be identified with?"—you know, the Poles or the Scots or the whatever. Since it didn't have any scientific basis and didn't have any objective answer that you could evaluate, we took a rather dim view of it. In fact, informally, the Census Bureau didn't seem to express much enthusiasm for it. It had been a substitute for a question called "mother tongue," which had been used traditionally to analyze and monitor immigrant population. So we recommended eliminating . . . [the Ancestry question] and some others. The political people in the Carter Administration [rejected most of our recommendations for cutting

questions. . . . The ethnic desk in the White House insisted that the ancestry question go on the census.[53]

Kincannon's recollections indeed suggest that presidential politics saved the Ancestry question—"the ethnic desk." He is less definitive on the attitude of Census Bureau officials to that question. The notion that the Ancestry question "had been a substitute for a question called mother tongue" may well have been a common view at the Census Bureau. Like ancestry, mother tongue had been a way to explore historical origins through a measure other than birthplaces. But ancestry was much more inclusive in reaching back in time more than two generations; mother tongues rarely did.

Kincannon may well have been right that bureau officials had no great faith in the Ancestry question. But they probably lacked the same faith in the Hispanic Origin question too, and (as we observed earlier) for just the reasons Kincannon mentioned about Ancestry: "not a very scientific question . . . sort of an opinion poll . . . didn't have any objective answer." If, notwithstanding these limitations, Hispanic Origin was going on the census questionnaire, bureau officials may well have reasoned, the more general form of the question should be there too.

THE CENSUS ORIGIN QUESTIONS, 1980

To appreciate how fully Ancestry was a generalized Hispanic Origin question, consider now the full instruction that accompanied each in the 1980 census.

Question 7. Hispanic Origin
A person is of Spanish / Hispanic origin or descent if the person *identifies* his or her ancestry with one of the listed groups, that is, Mexican, Puerto Rican, etc. Origin or descent (ancestry) may be viewed as the nationality group, the lineage, or country in which the person or the person's parents or ancestors were born.

Question 14. Ancestry
Print the ancestry group with which the person *identifies*. Ancestry (or origin or descent) may be viewed as the nationality group, the lineage, or the country in which the person or the person's parents or ancestors

were born before their arrival in the United States. Persons who are of more than one origin and who cannot identify with a single group should print their multiple ancestry (for example, German-Irish).[54]

Both questions concern the group with which the respondent "identifies." Both relate the identification to the same three terms (ancestry, origin, or descent). Both define the meaning of these three concepts with identical words (last sentence, Hispanic Origin; second sentence, Ancestry).

In a world of single origins, there would be little advantage to a Hispanic Origin question distinct from the Ancestry question. But in American society, with its intermingling of peoples, many respondents list not only multiple origins, but they list *only some* of their origins. The Hispanic Origin question forces attention to *one particular origin:* are you Hispanic— yes or no?

The results lived up to expectations: notably higher numbers of people identified as Hispanic on the specific rather than the general question. This advantage was energetically preserved. In the understated words of an early history of the two questions during the 1980s, two bureau officials commented, "The Bureau also considered a combined Hispanic origin and ancestry question but did not test this approach based on the advice received through consultations." A footnote clarified: "Participants at a 1985 Conference . . . strongly recommended that the Census Bureau not test a combined Hispanic/ancestry question because the proposed question would be confusing and divisive to the public."[55] And yet, by 1980, the race question had come to resemble at least two crucial features of the new Ancestry and Hispanic Origin questions: all three relied on subjective identity and all ignored the respondent's generational standing in America.

The instructions to the Ancestry question included one more line of text: "A religious group should not be reported as a person's ancestry." With the long history of Jewish protests that church–state separation was violated if such data were collected (most recently over the religious question for the 1960 census), there was no desire to deal with yet another. But the instruction no doubt also anticipated parallel problems with other religious choices: for example, Catholic or Greek Orthodox ancestry.

When the bureau added Hispanic Origin and Ancestry, it also *eliminated* two relevant questions: mother's birthplace and father's birthplace.

Parental birthplaces had been reported in every enumeration from 1880 through 1970. The most obvious reason for dropping them now was to limit the total number of questions. Also, the pressure of the ethnic advocacy groups, and hence the attention of politically sensitive officials, was on the two *new* questions and late-generation subjective identity. If origin is more important than progress toward assimilation, then information on generational status may seem expendable. But losing that information was a fateful turning point. Despite decades of massive immigration and the rise of a new second generation that followed 1980, the bureau failed to reinstate it.

The reforms to ethno-racial inquiries in the 1980 census included one other important feature, rarely if ever noticed. The 1980 race question was not in fact labeled as such. Instead, the printed question read, "Is this person . . ." followed by boxes, each with the name of a race category. Thus the form simply presented categories of origin—without reference to any label that signaled a classificatory concept ("race" or any other).

All Americans received the census questionnaire with the race question. And the U.S. census carries authority as an institution of study and reporting. It holds up a mirror to the nation, one that is often amplified by the media. We may not have a good way to measure how much influence that presentation carries, but there is no reason to assume that it carries none. Dropping the classificatory label might have suggested that the categories found in this question cannot be easily related to one covering concept. Instead, something else unites them: historical origins have all influenced people's historical experiences and particularly life chances, no matter how differently they have done so.

It is unlikely that the Census Bureau had *meant* to signal such a message by dropping the "race" term at the time. The *Procedural History* of the 1980 census explains the decision on narrow grounds: "The word 'race' was not used on the 1980 census questionnaires; instead, the lead-in to item 4 was 'Is this person—.' This departure from most recent censuses was made at the suggestion of the Bureau's advisory committees, which had noted that some of the categories listed in the question are not generally considered racial groups."[56] The *Procedural History* does not tell us *which* categories under the race question perplexed the advisory committees. Probably they were referring to the new Pacific Island categories: Hawaiian, Guamanian, and

Samoan. But of course the recognition that "some of the categories listed in the question are not generally considered racial groups" takes one down the path to the broader understanding of their heterogeneity. In any event, the "race" label was reinstated for the very next decennial census (1990), in an effort "to make the intent of the question clearer and improve reporting."[57] The same challenge of how to label the census race question would resurface some forty years later, in the reform effort for Census 2020.

MULTIRACIAL ORIGIN AND CENSUS 2000

Recall that through the late 1990s one could report membership in only one race. The list of races was, to the statistician, complete and nonoverlapping. The convenience of this arrangement was more than statistical: it ignored the messy realities of interracial unions and especially unions between blacks and whites. These, of course, had a very large place in the history of American racial boundaries. To some extent, this same simplification of origins operated for civil rights protections as well: membership in only one race made antidiscrimination and affirmative action issues easier to deal with. Nevertheless, at the end of the 1990s, a protest movement eventually led the OMB to revise its Directive #15 so that it officially allowed people to report membership in multiple races.

Recall that the treatment of mixed origins had differed across the decades depending on the kind of origins. Parental birthplaces, listed prior to 1980, had always allowed for "mixed parentage," as it had been called. The child with one parent from Ireland and the other from Germany listed two parental birthplaces on the census. Similarly, a person could list as many origins as he or she wished on the Ancestry question. The Census Bureau tabulated a maximum of three of these the first time the question was asked (in 1980) and two since then.[58]

In the long history of the "color or race" question prior to 2000, only black–white combinations had ever been listed, and those were used only long ago. From 1850 through 1920, the mulatto category was an option in every census except one (1900). The 1890 census had actually listed three levels of black–white mixture: mulatto, quadroon, and octoroon.[59] Since 1930, only black and white categories were listed, accompanied by the instruction to count any noticeable quantity of African origins in the black category. The instruction about blacks in the 1930 census is occasionally discussed as the triumph of "one drop rule." But 1930 is very far along in American history to seek recognition of that concept. All the census classifications of blacks, whites, and black–white mixed race people across the decades should be seen as ways of preserving the count of the unmixed *white* stock. The early interest in separate counts of the mixed race population had been stimulated by speculation concerning how differences between the black and white races affected mixed-race offspring (for example, speculation about the supposed low fertility of such offspring). The discrete counts of the black–white mixed race population did not imply any a failure to recognize that any admixture of black and white blood removed the individual from the white stock. Nor did the discrete counts arise from a parallel concern with black racial purity.[60] Insofar as the one drop rule reflected concern with the purity of the white race, it can be said to have operated in the censuses of 1850 through 1950, either through separate counts of black–white mixed race people or through counts that included these mixed race individuals in the black population.[61]

By 1930, the Census Bureau also instructed enumerators to count mixtures other than black and white in the category in which he or she most easily fit. Later, this guideline was generalized to all groups. Later still, particularly from 1960, such decisions were left to the respondent. As the bureau came to rely more heavily on the mailed census form during the decades after 1950, self-reporting quickly became the principle factor in racial identification.

In retrospect it is hardly surprising that the issue of mixed-race unions would come up at some point after the civil rights revolution, and indeed after the *Loving* case (1967) ruled state laws against miscegenation unconstitutional. But politics no doubt did much to determine at which point it came up, and it made strange bedfellows in the ensuing debate. A small number of mixed race couples and their organizations spoke up for recognition, some asking for a single new race question category, "multiracial." Eventually these people received the support of Republican House Speaker Newt Gingrich and others who may well have hoped to dilute the political power of the Black Caucus in Congress and civil rights advocates generally. On the other side, just such expectations triggered the anxious opposition of civil rights advocacy groups to the changes in federal race data. One factor that certainly heightened concern was the uncertainty about the number of people who had identified as African American under the old question but might cease to do so if a "multiracial" category was added to the census race question. Alternatively, how many who had identified as African American might now list themselves as both white and black if respondents were instructed to "Mark one or more" of the traditional categories?

Whatever the mix of political forces that pressed the federal government to take up the multiraciality issue when it did, the federal bureaucracy succeeded in making a relatively independent and important contribution. First, the Census Bureau and the OMB rejected the proposal to add a single new race category for all multiracials; this option was inadequate given the range of mixed race combinations. Second, the Census Bureau extensively tested of the new instruction, "Mark one or more." Results showed relatively small shifts in minority group responses. Thus, for example, the large fraction of African Americans who knew they had some white progenitor generations back (not least a slaveholder) did not regard this legacy as making them multiracials in the terms of the race question.

Not long after the OMB replaced the instruction to "Mark one [category] only" with the instruction to "Mark one or more," the Department of Justice headed off potential new challenges to civil rights legislation by declaring that for purposes of civil rights law, a mixed-race person was to be counted in the minority race category. If this decision at Justice had an arbitrary quality, it also brought a certain poetic justice since the "one drop rule" had so long placed the mixed-race individual in the black column. The decision also avoided the alternative: endless case-by-case challenges as to who qualifies as a minority group member for evaluating discrimination or underrepresentativeness. The Justice Department's simplification did not affect the counts of mixed origins reported in the census.[62]

Although the focus of political attention remained on multiracials and the race question, the fact is that conceptually the challenge posed by mixed origins confronted the Hispanic Origin question too. The census asked whether a person was of Hispanic origin. Options read: No, not of

Hispanic origin, Yes, Mexican, Yes, Puerto Rican, etc. And the respondent was instructed to mark one category. There was thus no way for the respondent to indicate that he or she had *both* Hispanic *and* non-Hispanic origins. Beginning with Census 2000, when the instruction on the race question was changed to "Mark one or more," the Hispanic Origin instruction appears to have changed in a more ambiguous way. The earlier instruction to mark one category was deleted. But no explicit instruction was added to indicate that it was permissible to mark *more* than one category. Looking back from 2017, a major Census Bureau review of the race and Hispanic Origin questions noted that (since the 2000 reform),

> while the reporting of multiple races is permitted, reporting multiple Hispanic origins or a mixed Hispanic / non-Hispanic heritage in the current Hispanic origin question is not permitted. This differential treatment recognizes interracial unions and multiracial individuals but does not recognize the existence of Hispanic / non-Hispanic unions and individuals or those with a diverse Hispanic heritage.[63]

Only on the Ancestry question were all combinations of multiple origins permitted from its introduction in 1980: for example, German and Irish, Chinese and Korean, German and Korean, African and Irish. This consideration did not stop the advocates of multiracial reporting from demanding the change in the race question itself, nor the OMB from agreeing to the change. The point is that reporting multiple origins under a single, politically charged question can be important to the respondent as well as to the public's understanding. This is what was not permitted in the race and Hispanic Origin questions prior to 2000.

Why, then, was the Hispanic Origin question not more of a target for the same reform as the race question in the late 1990s, a reform that would have allowed the Hispanic origin individual to also be a non-Hispanic individual? The reasons surely have to do with the political contexts of the debate. Probably the *minor* reason had to do with the concerns of advocacy groups over the size of Hispanic counts, the insistence on avoiding anything that would reduce the number of Hispanics counted or complicate the meaning of the count. This minor consideration alone might well have been enough to ensure that the Hispanic Origin question would not be altered in the late 1990s. But such a change for the Hispanic Origin question was simply never the subject of public attention at all.

The *major* reason that attention focused where it did surely had to do with the refusal of the publicized families to accept the iconic American simplification that if they declared themselves (or their children) to have white origins it meant that they could not also have black origins. The case of Hispanic / non-Hispanic origins may have been logically similar, but historically and politically it was altogether different.

A Generation On: Mass Immigration and the Legacy of the 1980 Classifications

RACE AND IMMIGRATION: INTERTWINED IN A NEW WAY

The reforms of 1980 always had to serve a dual purpose, classifying both race and new immigrants. The classification could never meet the need for both kinds of information—about race and immigration—equally well. But the limitations of the compromises made for 1980 have come to seem far more important after another forty years of mass immigration.

Hispanic Origin and Ancestry shared the fixed character of race question categories. Above all, these questions ignore the length of time since an individual's immigrant ancestors arrived in the United States—whether one generation back or twenty. And second, race and Hispanic Origin both originally ignored by design the simple fact of intermarriage. Ancestry did not do so by design, but it could not possibly fully reflect all the ethno-racial blending in the pasts of most individuals. The reform of 2000 changed this initial design only for the race question. These limitations had always been inherent in the race question; they seemed acceptable for the new questions in 1980 because the Hispanic Origin and by extension the Ancestry question were designed to offer the compensating advantages of the race question. Specifically, they were designed to supplement the parental-birthplace questions by tracking origins over a longer historical period—farther back, that is, than the second generation. This feature was particularly important, as we have seen, for the Mexican Americans of the Southwest.

However, the categories constructed with that historically race-oriented perspective were soon classifying primarily *recent* immigrants and their children. Given the increasingly huge third world immigration in the decades after 1970, the majority of the individuals counted in the Asian and Hispanic categories—many tens of millions—were now first- or second-generation members. What mattered for the substantial majority of Asian and Hispanic families was not the impact of many generations of American descent, as it was, for example, for African Americans or American Indians. It was instead much more about how *recent immigrant* status related to social inequalities.

Of course, we have witnessed earlier federal classifications in which racial and immigrant status had been intertwined, and the dilemmas of this most recent variant will seem vaguely reminiscent. However, the central question about race and immigration in the 1890–1925 period had been: How much and for how long would immigrants of different racial origins exhibit qualities inherent to their race? A century on, the new central question about race and immigration seemed to be: How much and for how long will Asian and Hispanic Americans—who turn out to be mostly immigrants and their children—suffer inequalities, some of which may be related to racial or race-like discriminations and some of which are related to that recent immigration status? Drawing on W. E. B. DuBois's aphorism ("the problem of the twentieth century is the problem of the color-line"), the political scientist and former director of the Census Bureau Kenneth Prewitt noted, "The problem of the twenty-first century is the problem of the color line as it intersects the nativity line."[64]

Asian and Hispanic immigrants shared the origin categories of protected minorities, but they also shared needs of immigrant families from most *any* background to establish themselves in the American social structure. For example, a majority of the new immigrants arriving after 1970 came without advanced educational attainments or wealth. Moreover, they entered a very different American economy than had earlier waves of immigration, with fewer low-skill jobs in manufacturing or agriculture, and with growing income inequality. Recall too that large numbers of Hispanic immigrants in the early twenty-first century face American life with *undocumented status*. They cannot rely on the law for protection but must fear its scrutiny even when accessing services such as health care or education. This status therefore increases the handicaps of the immigrants and their children.[65]

Above all, how would the American-born children of recent immigrants fare in this new America? If there is one thing that is clear from the experience of immigration it is that there is something special about the second generation, situated at the transition point between immigrant past and American future. How is the present-day transition from immigrant to American families different from what it was in the past? In particular, has the transition process become slower and harder because of the changed nature of the economy? Moreover, is the nonwhite status of so many present-day immigrants a decisive factor? Or has the civil rights revolution and related cultural transformations made the nonwhite status of recent immigrants drastically less important than it had been for the Chinese, Japanese, or Mexicans in the century after 1850? Has it made today's racial discrimination against immigrants rather more like the racialization of the Irish in the 1850s or the southern and eastern Europeans after 1890—bad enough, surely, but not as bad as the discriminations against nonwhite immigrants of that earlier time? Then too the post-1965 immigration is bimodal in the sense of including a nontrivial fraction of arrivals, especially but not exclusively from Asia, who arrive from a much higher class and educational background than had characterized the nineteenth- and early twentieth-century arrivals from the same countries. These differences would of course influence their children's trajectories.[66] The combination of such factors helps explain the relatively high rates at which native-born Hispanics and especially Asians were marrying non-Hispanic whites—rates that recall the rates among the native-born children of southern and eastern Europeans in the past. By contrast, these rates are much higher than those among African Americans, contradicting, at least in this respect, the expectation of an analogy based on racial minority status.[67]

Questions about the social patterns of the vast new second generation help us appreciate the loss incurred when the parental-birthplace questions were discarded (removed as part of the 1980 reforms). Those questions would have made it possible to identify the American-born children of the immigrant. In their absence, the second generation cannot be distinguished from all other American-born Hispanics or Asians (indistinguishable, that is, from the descendants of much earlier arrivals). Comparisons between all American-born Hispanics or Asians on the one hand and non-Hispanic whites on the other too easily leave the impression that differences observed are due to race or race-like status rather than to the impact of more recent immigration itself. The observed differences, that is, are too easily interpreted as the result of being "Asian" (or, for example, Chinese) or "Hispanic" (or, for example, Mexican) rather than to generational standing and immigrant parents' resources. The danger of such misinterpretation is of course much worse if all Hispanics or Asians, whether native or foreign born are included in the comparison to non-Hispanic whites.

By 2010, there was evidence that the great immigration of recent decades would also affect the composition of the black race category in unexpected ways. Relatively significant numbers of black immigrants had been arriving for a century, but mostly from the Caribbean. However, in the most recent decades the immigration of Africans, and especially of graduate students and professionals, took on a new significance: without the parental-birthplace questions, the American-born children of these people, often highly successful in school, were being identified simply as native-born blacks. In the absence of the parental-birthplace questions, the census does not allow us to distinguish the native-born blacks who are the children of immigrant African professionals and those who are the descendants of American slaves. There have, of course, been important gains in educational attainment and class standing among the latter since the Second Reconstruction; in the words of a recent scholar, their situation was "somewhere between Jim Crow and Post Racialism."[68] But judging where between those two poles should not be confused by including the high attainments of the new African second generation.

The intertwining of race-like and immigration status is also helpful in understanding peculiarities of ancestry data. Above all, the interpretation of that evidence turns on the amount of time various ancestries have been settled in the United States. The more recent the immigration experience, the less likely that ancestry will be mixed. Ironically, this feature makes ancestry data very useful for some of the *newest* immigrant groups— namely, those who are non-Hispanic white or black and second generation. Examples include Egyptians and Nigerians. Since the parental-birthplace questions were dropped in 1980, only the Ancestry question (and mother tongue) provides origin information on their first American-born generation. Indeed, for this reason, the Arab-American Institute came to the defense of the Ancestry question when it was considered for removal from the 2000 enumeration.[69] By contrast, for descendants of most European immigrants, and especially for those the farthest removed from immigration, the specific ancestry or ancestries reported are likely to be one or two among a great many that might be mentioned if family lore were complete and space on the form sufficient. The farther back in time the European immigrant experience, the less social significance the report of ancestry can generally have, notwithstanding the race-like fixity the answers seem to suggest.

Recall that in 1980 this question was welcomed especially for preserving information on the descendants of the southern and eastern Europeans, prevalent in the white ethnic movement prior to 1980. However, by 2010, even the descendants of that last European immigrant wave, were three, four, or five generations from the relevant immigrant ancestor. A fourth- or fifth-generation descendant of *any* European stock is overwhelmingly likely to also be the descendant of multiple *other* stocks as well, most commonly from Europe. Indeed, such descendants typically cannot know much about their messy lines of descent; they report about whatever ancestor is known. This long assimilative process not only guarantees multiple rather than single ethnic origins; it also raises skepticism about the *strength* of any reported self-identification. Also, meaningful connections between ethnic origins and life chances become harder to find. All these considerations are even more important for the descendants of arrivals from northern and western Europe, since they are mostly descended from *still-earlier* immigrant arrivals—decades or centuries earlier—than those from southern and eastern Europe.

Americans of the 2020 era who could claim at least one ancestor, and often several, from southern or eastern Europe no longer lived in the social context of Glazer and Moynihan's *Beyond the Melting Pot*, written some two decades prior to the 1980 census. The authors had stressed that ethnicity had not died out, "at least not in New York City," and by implication not in other large eastern American metropolises. As late as 1980, the ethnic reality they had described in 1963 may still have been moderately strong in such places. But even in 1980, ever fewer of the descendants of southern and eastern European immigrants lived in such communities—to say nothing of the vast number of Euro-Americans descended from the earlier immigrants who had come from northern and western Europe. By the 2020 era—two generations on from *Beyond the Melting Pot*—vestiges of that older ethnic tenacity surely still existed, concentrated among the old ethnic populations of cities that had absorbed great concentrations of immigrants, and that had also been replenished with modest numbers of new arrivals who settled there. But far higher proportions of the descendants of the 1890–1920 immigrants have moved on to very different places, schools, and jobs. In those new environments, many of these people have found partners descended from origins other than their own and produced offspring who were still less likely to have strong ties to one European national background.

Thus forty years of social change related to both immigration and race helped to make some features of the federal ethno-racial classification system appear more problematic for 2020 than they had in 1980. Nevertheless, the stimulus for a third round of post–civil rights era reforms came principally from another problem with the classifications, largely independent of all those just described. Since the introduction of the Hispanic Origin question in 1980, very large numbers of Hispanics had failed to report themselves in any of the four broad race categories—white, black, Asian, or American Indian—that the OMB had designated. Instead, most of these people identified themselves as "Some Other Race," a category found on the race question since 1910 but that had always been numerically inconsequential prior to 1980 and subject to post-enumeration recoding. By 2010 some twenty million respondents chose "Some Other Race"; as nearly all were Hispanics, they accounted for four in ten from the group. While most other Hispanics reported themselves in the white race category, the choice for many seemed the least unreasonable of the offered options rather than a natural fit. These choices made it clear that the four OMB race categories did not seem relevant to tens of millions of Hispanics. Indeed, a major Census Bureau review noted that "if no major questionnaire changes are implemented, SOR [Some Other Race] may be the second largest 'race' group in 2020,"[70] more numerous, indeed, than blacks.

After the "Mexican Race" episode of 1930, the bureau instructed that "Mexicans are to be regarded as white unless definitely of Indian or other nonwhite race."[71] But in the era of respondent-completed census forms, the bureau could no longer rely on an enumerator to designate a Mexican American respondent as white. Instead, some fraction of Mexican Americans (both native and foreign born) described themselves as members of "Some Other Race." Apparently, the Census Bureau, following the post-1930 instruction, recoded these self-reports to white. Then, in 1980, having introduced the new question on Hispanic Origin, the Census Bureau decided that the race choice by respondents of that origin should no longer be recoded.

How much of the widespread Hispanic tendency to list oneself in "Some Other Race" *preceded* the introduction of Hispanic Origin in the census and in public awareness? If it was very widespread prior to the 1970s, for example, it may well have reflected concepts of race that were somewhat different in Mexico or Latin America than in the United States. But if the proportion of Hispanics choosing "Some Other Race" grew during the 1970s or later, then the growth may reflect primarily something about the *American* context—and particularly the changes that accompanied the prevalence of the Hispanic origin concept itself. Indeed, G. Christina Mora described how the Census Bureau itself helped in the "racialization" of Hispanics, a role no doubt then also popularized in the media.

> The Census Bureau reported data on Hispanics mainly by comparing Spanish / Hispanic-origin respondents to two newly defined populations, non-Hispanic whites and non-Hispanic blacks . . . [making] Hispanic pan-ethnicity seem race-like. These racial analogies soon became a staple of most census reports. . . .
>
> By describing Hispanics through racial comparisons, the bureau insinuated that a person might be Hispanic if he or she was neither white nor black.[72]

Unfortunately, the *number* of such recodes remains unknown for the three censuses from 1940 to 1970. In the absence of more knowledge than is now available about the census recoding practices prior to 1980, it is impossible to conclude whether or not the pattern Mora described was the primary source of Hispanic respondents' choice of "Some Other Race."[73]

In any case, Census Bureau officials were especially uncomfortable with the huge numbers reporting "Some Other Race." This category was, after all, not one the OMB had mandated in Directive #15. Recoding a few people from that category was one thing; recoding tens of millions (and on what basis?) was quite another. Moreover, it was discomforting to have to report that so many Americans could not find a place in the OMB race categories—so many that by the next census choices for "Some Other Race" might well outnumber all the OMB races except white. This bizarre situation underscored limitations in the federal (that is, OMB) use of race, as indeed the multiracial challenge had done in the second round of reforms.

Nevertheless, the bureau tended to formulate this challenge in terms of a fairly narrow technical problem. Many federal agencies required complete age-race-sex tabulations for planning purposes. These are based on the race categories mandated by the OMB Directive #15. The Census Bureau therefore does indeed reallocate "Some Other Race" responses to the four OMB race categories. This was the reason that a review of ethno-racial classification was once again undertaken, the third since the civil rights era. Thus, a problem estimated to affect perhaps a tenth of Americans in 2020 opened a broad review of the way race and ethnic origin are presented to the American population as a whole. A similar situation had triggered the change at the end of the 1990s, when a very much smaller proportion of Americans had insisted on their right to be listed as both white and black.

REFORMS PROPOSED FOR CENSUS 2020:
A PARTIAL FIX FOR THE 1980 REFORM

Popular mobilizations led to the 1980 and 2000 reforms, the former by Hispanics, the latter by multiracials.[74] By contrast, the initiative to change the classifications for the 2020 census seemed to reflect a more even balance of bureau officials and group advocates in confronting the long-standing problem of Hispanics responses to the race categories.

The clear alternative to the separate race and Hispanic Origin questions was a single query with five broad ethno-racial categories: white, black, American Indian, Asian, and Hispanic Origin. The bureau also tested the impact of urging respondents to "Mark all that apply," rather

8. What is Person 1's race or ethnicity?
Mark all boxes that apply AND print ethnicities in the spaces below.
Note, you may report more than one group.

☐**WHITE** – *Provide details below.*
    ☐ German   ☐ Irish   ☐ English
    ☐ Italian   ☐ Polish   ☐ French
Print, for example, Scottish, Norwegian, Dutch, etc.

[ ][ ][ ][ ][ ][ ][ ][ ][ ][ ][ ][ ][ ][ ][ ]

☐**HISPANIC, LATINO OR SPANISH** – *Provide details below.*
    ☐ Mexican or   ☐ Puerto   ☐ Cuban
       Mexican American   Rican
    ☐ Salvadorian   ☐ Dominican   ☐ Colombian
Print, for example, Guatemalan, Spaniard, Ecuadorian, etc.

[ ][ ][ ][ ][ ][ ][ ][ ][ ][ ][ ][ ][ ][ ][ ]

☐**BLACK OR AFRICAN AMERICAN** – *Provide details below.*
    ☐ African   ☐ Jamaican   ☐ Haitian
       American
    ☐ Nigerian   ☐ Ethiopian   ☐ Somali
Print, for example, Ghanaian, South African, Barbadian, etc.

[ ][ ][ ][ ][ ][ ][ ][ ][ ][ ][ ][ ][ ][ ][ ]

☐**ASIAN** – *Provide details below.*
    ☐ Chinese   ☐ Filipino   ☐ Asian Indian
    ☐ Vietnamese   ☐ Korean   ☐ Japanese
Print, for example, Pakistani, Cambodian, Hmong, etc.

[ ][ ][ ][ ][ ][ ][ ][ ][ ][ ][ ][ ][ ][ ][ ]

☐**AMERICAN INDIAN OR ALASKA NATIVE** – *Print, for example,*
Navajo Nation, Blackfeet Tribe, Mayan, Aztec, Native Village of
Barrow Inupiat Traditional Government, Tlingit, etc.

[ ][ ][ ][ ][ ][ ][ ][ ][ ][ ][ ][ ][ ][ ][ ]

☐**MIDDLE EASTERN OR NORTH AFRICAN** – *Provide details below.*
    ☐ Lebanese   ☐ Iranian   ☐ Egyptian
    ☐ Syrian   ☐ Moroccan   ☐ Algerian
Print, for example, Israeli, Iraqi, Tunisian, etc.

[ ][ ][ ][ ][ ][ ][ ][ ][ ][ ][ ][ ][ ][ ][ ]

☐**NATIVE HAWAIIAN OR OTHER PACIFIC ISLANDER** – *Provide*
details below.
    ☐ Native Hawaiian   ☐ Samoan   ☐ Chamorro
    ☐ Tongan   ☐ Fijian   ☐ Marshallese
Print, for example, Palauan, Tahitian, Chuukese, etc.

[ ][ ][ ][ ][ ][ ][ ][ ][ ][ ][ ][ ][ ][ ][ ]

☐**SOME OTHER RACE OR ETHNICITY** – *Print details.*

[ ][ ][ ][ ][ ][ ][ ][ ][ ][ ][ ][ ][ ][ ][ ]

Figure 1.
"Optimal" Origin
Question Proposed
for the 2020 Census

Source: Kelly Mathews
et al., *2015 National
Content Test Race and
Ethnicity Analysis
Report: A New Design
for the 21st Century*
(Washington, DC:
Government
Publishing Office,
2017), 88.

than "Mark one or more," thereby doing as much as it could to stimulate more reports of multiple origins. The respondent could choose any number of these categories (see Figure 1), but could avoid choosing any of the OMB *race* categories. A directed feature could still be discerned in the new question's Hispanic Origin category—in connection with the examples provided for *other* major categories. Under "Black" (and "White"), there were no examples of a Spanish Caribbean origin group (neither in the check-off boxes nor among the suggestions for the write-in line).[75]

The crucial feature of the change to a single question would be that those identifying as Hispanics would no longer need to also find an appropriate race category. Tests showed that faced with the two-question format, about 55 percent of Hispanics reported themselves as white and almost 40 percent more as Some Other Race. In the combined-question format, roughly 70 percent report as *only* Hispanic (the choice unavailable in the two-question format), 25 percent as white, and virtually none as Some Other Race.[76] These changes in Hispanic responses could also be expressed in terms of the distribution of all American responses: the proportion of Hispanics would be virtually unchanged, the proportion selecting "Some Other Race" would drop to a negligible level, and the proportion of all Americans identifying as white would decline slightly, by perhaps three percentage points.[77]

From one vantage point, the combined ethno-racial question could be said to finally merge Hispanic origin (as well as the new MENA category, discussed shortly) into the basic list of OMB races. From another perspective, the new question amounted to a step in the direction of creative ambiguity, even reminiscent of the convenience of having dual terms in the title of the List of Races and Peoples (of which W. W. Husband had remarked in 1908 that were both were included because some immigrants preferred one term, some the other).

Also tested was the addition of a line under each of the recognized OMB categories. Here the respondent would be urged to report more narrowly defined origins. For American Indians and Asians, such origins would be like those requested in the past on the race question: tribal membership and specific country race categories, respectively. For Hispanics, the specific origins would be the country categories requested before on the Hispanic Origin question. For blacks and whites, the specific origins would be those requested in the past on the Ancestry question. For example, blacks might list simply African American, and/or Jamaican, Haitian, or Nigerian. Whites might list Irish and/or German.[78]

Finally, the bureau explored how different labels for the combined new race/ethnicity question would influence respondents. It might be labeled "Race and Ethnic Origin," or it might not be labeled at all. If unlabeled, as in the 1980 census, the specific categories it might simply be introduced with a prompt such as "This person is . . ." or "Which categories describe Person 1?" The bureau's Nicholas A. Jones, who directed the impressive analysis and testing program, summarized the issue.

> Recent Census Bureau qualitative research found that the terms "race," "ethnicity," and "origin" are confusing or misleading to many respondents, and they mean different things to different people. . . . Removal of the term "race" from the question . . . [did not influence] either unit or item response rates. Recent cognitive research tested an open-ended instruction ("Which categories describe you?") and found that respondents did not have issues with understanding what the question was asking. Therefore, an alternative option being explored tests the removal of the terms "race," "origin," and "ethnicity" from the question stem and instructions. Instead, a general approach asks, "Which categories describe Person 1?"[79]

Note that Jones took up two important but discrete issues here. First, he reported that "the terms 'race,' 'ethnicity,' and 'origin' are confusing or misleading to many respondents, and they mean different things to different people." Second, he also reports that "respondents did not have issues with understanding what the question was asking" when *all* such terms were dropped.

By early 2017, the bureau could report that its detailed testing of alternatives indicated "optimal" choices. These were the combined race and ethnicity question, the write-in line for specifying detail, the instruction to "Mark all [the categories] that apply," and finally to "use the Race/Ethnicity terminology for the combined question" rather than simply drop the labels altogether ("which categories describe person 1?").[80] The "optimal" choice in each case meant that the large-scale test results had shown that this alternative produced the fewest numbers reporting "Some Other Race," the least disruptions to any related categories, and the most detail in reporting.

However, on the last choice, the decision to retain "the Race/Ethnicity terminology for the combined question," the bureau authors felt the need to elaborate. First, the decision here was *not* based solely on the field testing. Rather, "The results of this research *in conjunction with previous qualitative research* indicate that it is optimal to use the Race/Ethnicity terminology for the combined question" (emphasis added). Second, the three alternatives tested in the field—"Race/Ethnicity," "Race/Origin," and no terms— seem to have worked equally well.

> But a decision needed to be made about which terminology should be employed for future data collections. NCT cognitive and usability research indicated that the use of "categories" in data collections conducted in Spanish caused some confusion among Spanish-speaking respondents who thought "categories" presented a more hierarchical ordering of groups rather than a list of options.[81]

Jones's earlier update had stated that qualitative testing showed that "the terms 'race,' 'ethnicity,' and 'origin' are confusing or misleading to many respondents, and they mean different things to different people." Moreover, the decision to describe continued use of these problematic terms as the "optimal" alternative rested not on the sophisticated analysis of the large and carefully constructed survey data, but rather on other, presumably less authoritative, evidence that the report did not detail directly or cite beyond the sentences quoted here. A briefing from the same period provides slightly more detail: the testing involved forty Spanish-speaking respondents' reaction to the unlabeled version of the race/ethnicity question that was tested—namely, "Which categories describe person 1?" The results "show a pattern of respondents linking the word '*categoría*' to a hierarchical order or ranking, rather than to a natural list of options."[82] Ironically, the earlier wording of the *un*labeled question in 1980 did not even use the word "category" but simply prompted "This person is . . ." Similar wording had been used in 1960 (and in the enumerator-based census of 1890 as well). But the wording "This person is . . ." had not been tested in the 2015 survey. The omission was hardly surprising; the testing program involved dozens of combinations of question format, wording, write-in line, and three variants of terminology.

These appear to be the circumstances in which bureau officials faced the reality that "a decision needed to be made about which terminology should be employed." Going forward, the American population would continue to encounter the "Race / Ethnicity" label when it completed the 100 percent enumeration. The path *not* chosen was to avoid the poorly understood labels ("Race" and "Ethnicity") altogether. This matter of labeling might seem trivial but it is better regarded as consequential. Consequential because the race term still carries biological connotations, but consequential too because the race term remains at the heart of civil rights concerns and legal redress. The bureau's field tests could not provide a clear basis for the decision on labeling the new combined question.

In any case, officially, the bureau's race and ethnicity branch was merely reporting on the results of tests. Recommendations for policy changes were the OMB's responsibility. Still, it seemed likely that most or all of the "optimal" alternatives mentioned here eventually would be adopted by the OMB as well.

Two major features of the 1980 reform were left untouched by the Census Bureau's third effort to modify ethno-racial classification since the civil rights era: the Ancestry question and the parental-birthplace questions. The new Race / Ethnicity question's subcategories and write-in lines might well produce roughly the same information as the Ancestry question. If so, the case to eliminate the latter would be strong. It would be stronger still if the parental-birthplace questions were in fact reinstated in the near future since the new immigrant groups, most of whose members had arrived since 1965, would no longer need to rely on the Ancestry question to track their second generation.

For groups with long histories of immigration (Mexicans, Chinese, etc.), the Ancestry data were useless for identifying their second-generation members since these could not be isolated from the later generations. For these groups, only the reinstatement of the parental-birthplace questions would allow the second generation to be identified. But the push for that reinstatement was left for another day. The simplest of bureaucratic reasons probably helps explain the failure to review the Ancestry and parental-birthplace questions. First, both these inquiries were the responsibility of a different Census Bureau office than the one carrying out the review. Also, in the case of the parental-birthplace questions, reinstating questions would involve a modest increase in enumeration costs. There were also reasonable substantive arguments for leaving the review of Ancestry and parental birthplace for the future. Whether Ancestry would indeed be redundant would be clearer when the responses to the combined race / ethnicity question came in. Moreover, both Ancestry and parental birthplace would not appear on the 100 percent enumeration that comes but once a decade, but only on the annual American Community Survey involving 1 percent of the population. The rich array of social indicators against which the second generation's progress could be measured only appear in that 1 percent survey.

Finally, the Census Bureau considered a quite separate reform of ethnoracial classification: whether to recommend that the OMB add a sixth required category for race and ethnic data collection: Middle Eastern and North African (MENA). Under existing OMB procedures, such a person was part of the undifferentiated white race category: "a person having origins in any of the original peoples of Europe, North Africa or the Middle East." Past mobilization for some such classification had existed since at least the 1990s, originally typically around Arab American identification, and possibly a common language origin, much like the Hispanic category. However, a related designation might include other Middle Eastern groupings, such as Turks and Iranians, as well as minority peoples across the region. Also, could the category be meaningfully defined without involving the census and OMB with religious classification? MENA claims about both discrimination and cultural origins had much to do with Islam. On the other hand, by no means was every individual in the MENA or the narrower Arab American group a Muslim. During a review in the 1990s the OMB concluded that there was then too little consensus as to the parameters of the group for it to attain a category of its own. Still, the OMB encouraged further discussion and study. In the meantime, the various groups that MENA would eventually cover were identified only in the Ancestry question and of course, for those of the immigrant generation, also in the birthplace question. In the years after the 9 / 11 attacks, the domestic reaction ratcheted up the concern with discrimination against the peoples captured under the MENA label. The very fact that the MENA category was included among the issues the Census Bureau investigated in the 2015 field tests demonstrated that the various advocacy groups had sufficiently unified under a pan-ethnic label to overcome the hesitations that the OMB had expressed in the 1990s.[83]

The tests confirmed that "the optimal" alternative for producing federal statistics on the group was indeed to create a distinct ethno-racial category for them—distinct from the undifferentiated American "white" race.[84] But if enhanced legibility would produce the best data, the advocacy groups were decidedly aware that legibility also stimulated anxieties in MENA communities. There was a potential for legibility to be misused, not least by a federal government eager for any information that might help counter terrorism; such misuse had been perceived on occasion since 9/11.[85] Here was a case that fell somewhere between the Jewish and the post–civil rights minority-group positions.

Donald Trump's election transformed the political context for the decision about the MENA category and about the 2020 ethno-racial classificatory reforms in general. Recall the anti-Muslim sentiments that Trump had injected into the campaign and then the early efforts of his administration to ban visas for arrivals from various Muslim countries. Likewise, the campaign had stimulated antagonism toward undocumented immigrants and then his administration aggressively pursued their deportation. Then he pardoned the former Arizona sheriff convicted of ignoring federal court orders to cease discriminatory actions against Mexican Americans. Trump also endorsed slashing immigration levels generally. Eight months into this presidency, it would have been foolhardy to guess how the classificatory reforms would fare. Meanwhile, the Census Bureau also faced congressional attacks, especially from Republicans, on large budgetary issues—limits on Census 2020 that could weaken its legitimacy (for example, for congressional redistricting) and on the American Community Survey (ACS, sent annually to 1 percent of Americans), which provides rich data on well-being and inequality. Moreover, the Census Bureau's director had resigned and the administration had not yet nominated a replacement.[86] But would these broader struggles over budgeting, the ACS, and a director at least ensure that the narrower matter of ethno-racial classifications would not become a subject of struggle? Again, who could say, given President Trump's erratic reactions and his frequent efforts to energize his electoral base? Rejecting the MENA category would withhold recognition from a community in which Arabs and Muslims predominate, but even adoption of the new combined Race / Ethnicity question was hardly a sure thing.

Recall the anomaly in how the census has dealt with the "Color or Race" of Americans with East Asian origins: by recording an immigrant ancestor's country of origin as a race category (for example, "Chinese") and preserving the information in respect to all later-generation descendants. The anomaly might have remained a curious minor peculiarity inherited from earlier times; it might eventually have been removed. Instead it first survived into the late twentieth century and then through three periods of post–civil rights era reforms. This outcome dovetailed reasonably well with notions of Asian pan-ethnicity and with the way the OMB Directive #15 (1977) envisioned classifying the individual Asian groups under the pan-ethnic heading. Soon after (in 1990), the census form included "Asian" in the race questions, as a covering label for nine race categories named for countries in East Asia. The recording of Asian now paralleled closely those of Hispanic origin, even if (in federal terms) the Asians were found under the race question and Hispanics under a question about ethnicity. Both provided pan-ethnic as well as country-of-origin data and provided both no matter how far back in time the respondent's immigrant ancestors had arrived. And both resembled the race classification for American Indians, for whom one category acted as a covering label under which tribal membership could be added by the respondent. Following this distinction strictly, one might say that if Hispanicity was constructed as a pan-ethnicity, Asian was a pan-race (and so too was American Indian). But the similarities mattered more than the differences. Meanwhile, the new Ancestry question would create a parallel method of recording under yet another kind of classification, meeting the demands of white ethnic leaders as well as the discomfort of census officials with the Hispanic Origin question that addressed only one ethnic grouping, albeit a pan-ethnic one.

These reforms of 1980 changed the way immigration and race were entwined in the federal system and the resulting popular culture. First, in Hispanic Origin, Ancestry, and the East Asian race categories, country of origin was now to be regarded as noteworthy no matter how far back in time ancestors had arrived in the United States. But second, with the re-sumption of immigration, huge numbers of *new* arrivals would populate the Hispanic and Asian categories. Consequently, the innovation to ig-nore generational standing, while attending to ethno-racial origins no matter how distant, collided with the need to track the fate of families that had arrived much more recently. One result has been a tendency to com-pare all members of the various origin groups—all Hispanics with non-Hispanic whites, for example—as though group origins alone, and not also relatively recent immigration histories determined social position. This tendency was accentuated further because the questions that could distinguish the *second-* from *third- and later-*generation descendants (that is, the parental-birthplace questions) were discarded with the 1980 census reforms.

The 1980 reforms had left in place the notion that descendants of mul-tiracial unions could report themselves in one race only. This restriction had applied, by the way, to the descendants of Asian country-of-origin race designations as well; thus one could not report both Filipino and Chinese origins. And it applied as well to the new Hispanic Origin ques-tion; one could not report both Dominican and Salvadorian origins. This system was dismantled for the race, but not the Hispanic origin, question in the 2000 reform.

The third ethno-racial classification reform effort (meant to take effect with the 2020 census) addressed problems resulting from the 1980 reform, especially (in the bureau's view) that large fractions of the Hispanic popu-lation could not find a meaningful way to list themselves in one of the OMB race categories. Another way to see the problem was that the con-cepts of race and ethnicity were a long way from self-evident. And by the second decade of the new century, the Hispanic origin classification was rarely defined in the way the OMB had sought to define it in 1977: as an ethnic status independent of race. The point is not to decide whether or not Hispanic origin had come to be a race in America. But it had indeed come to designate a group origin typically distinguished from other cat-egories of origin that the census listed as races. From yet another perspec-tive, by the time of the reforms for the 2020 census, Hispanic origin had broken free of the ethnicity concept under which the OMB had introduced it some forty years earlier. And this outcome might be compared to the way the Census Bureau had introduced mother tongue by means of the "nationality" concept. Hispanic origin, like mother tongue, had needed much less than forty years to shake off the concept that had been employed to contextualize and justify it.

Conclusion

MUCH OF THIS BOOK explored the creation and evolution of federal ethno-racial classifications—most notably the List of Races and Peoples, the National Origins Act of 1924, and the U.S. census. These classification schemes almost never resulted from the quiet deliberations of experts, free from political pressure. In at least three cases—the List, the 1910 census mother-tongue question, and the 1970 census Spanish origin question—they were produced in trying circumstances, and they were produced at the very last possible moment. Moreover, they emerged from entirely different sectors of the government: the List emerged from the midlevel of the Bureau of Immigration, the mother-tongue question from the director of the Census Bureau, and the Spanish origin question from President Nixon's office. And while federal officials often initiated change, as in those cases or in the reforms proposed for the 2020 census, the pressure of advocacy groups counted for much in the run-up to the federal actions—the most striking of which was in the case of the Hispanic Origin question, and in a more complex way with multiracial origins in Census 2000. In many instances, advocacy groups protested federal initiatives and, within limits, shaped outcomes. The most obvious case concerns the many Jewish protests over the List's Hebrew category across a half century, "ethnic classification" in the McCarran-Walter Act, and the religion question in the 1960 census. Another example is the brief Slavic counterprotest over the "race" classification in the 1910 census.

None of the classification schemes emerged as a straightforward application drawn from the natural or social sciences. Officials often said as much when introducing them. In fact, across the entire period of time covered here, the disavowal of scientific meanings for terms used in the classifications has been surprisingly consistent among officials who rolled them out, especially (but not exclusively) in connection with race. Race was not to be understood as defined in biology, ethnology, or anthropology. Safford and McSweeney had already included that disavowal in their first draft of directions for the use of their List. Daniel Folkmar included another in his *Dictionary*. The "Brief Statement of the Investigations" that introduced the Immigration Commission *Reports* added still another. More recently, the OMB Directive #15 (1977) and reports on reform efforts for 2020 offer the reader similar reminders. The meanings that the terms *should* be understood to convey typically did not accompany these disclaimers.

All of these episodes in the history of classification schemes have arisen from the social needs and pressures of their times, and they were shaped imperfectly by struggles in politics and the bureaucracy. It could not have been otherwise, but it is a service of history and social science to illuminate relevant cases. Doing so may help dispel illusions about the nature and authority of the classifications and about the limits of their utility, while still leaving us able to appreciate and profit from that utility. It is no small irony to recall at the end of this work that the counts of immigrants found in the categories of the List of Races and Peoples or in the 1910 census mother-tongue question have enriched the work of American social historians since the 1960s, even as they have wondered about the worldview that drove the creation and use of the List.

Still, to say that social needs and pressures shaped the classifications is not to say that they were not shaped by ideas—however vaguely stated or variously grasped. The problem of interpretation is especially great with the "race" term. What it *meant* in various contexts has been a constant challenge to interpret, and this was especially true for discussions of race and immigration. Henry Cabot Lodge's detailed and articulate formulations over a half century, most of them at the center of the immigration policy debates, illuminate the broader intellectual issues that racial theory addressed and assumptions on which it rested—even as different exponents incorporated the issues and assumptions into a continuum of viewpoints.

Like so many others, Lodge was typically vague about how any *particular* racial characteristic was transmitted across generations: through the blood, which he certainly believed was often important, or through processes of socialization, which he agreed could be operating as well. One likely reason for his willingness not to elaborate even further on this balance between explanations based on blood and socialization rested on the view that socialization could eventually become part of the legacy in the blood—through Lamarckian or Darwinian processes. Moreover, a cavalier approach to the time frames involved for such processes made it much easier to wave away challenging complexities: particular instances in group differentiation might have come in the "historical" or "zoological" period. This way of thinking apparently made the line between social and biological processes blurry rather than bright. It followed that there was not much value in thinking too much about *which* process—social, biological, both—was dominant at a particular moment. Not only was the answer unknowable, but it was also not terribly significant because the social shaded into the biological over the course of time. Some thinkers, like Madison Grant, relied more heavily on biological transmission. At the other end of the continuum, a few came early on to rule out biologically based mental differences among human groups. The brief 1907 correspondence between W. I. Thomas and Franz Boas is a striking instance. But for the most part, that era differs from our own because we reject the older hypothesis of biological transmission for group differences in character and values. The notion that social and cultural transmission could *also* account for such differences was common enough in the earlier period—although often, it seems, with the added thought that sociocultural could eventually become biological transmission.

When it came to immigration policy, Lodge's big speech (1896) had left no doubt that race differences in mental attributes—self-discipline, assertiveness, ability for self-government—mattered immensely to the success of absorbing arrivals in the immigrant generation as well as in the long-term racial composition of their descendants. And yet Lodge also believed that the balance of numbers was crucial, that the Anglo-Saxon blood and culture working in America could assimilate many immigrants of other origins. By contrast, Madison Grant saw in every undesirable addition to the bloodstream a degradation to it, and he thought socialization a fatuous delusion. Grant's and Harry Laughlin's more complete biological determinism have dominated historians' discussions of the outlooks behind the eventual passage of the Quota Acts in the 1920s.

In *Strangers in the Land* (1955), John Higham, the most influential historian of American nativism, built up to Grant's views in his chapter "Towards Racism: The History of an Idea." Higham concluded that chapter with the comment, "This, at last, was racism." And although Higham stayed focused on the period and place of his subject, the associations to Nazi ideology were difficult to miss. They would be detailed in Jonathan Spiro's able biography of Grant published a half century after Higham's work (2008).[1] But it is too easy to conclude from the structure of Higham's chapter that racism requires Grant's formulations to have mattered—either because views such as Lodge's seem messier, vaguer, and too close to an old romanticism to be called twentieth-century racism or because legislators would not have been convinced to pass the Quota Acts without Grant's influence. The actual impact of Grant's and Laughlin's distinctive forms of "scientific racism" on the passage of the Quota Acts needs to be reconsidered. Nordics in one theory were more or less the Teutonics and Anglo-Saxons in the other, and the undesirables were also the same in both. The distinctive features in the later arguments, however welcome they were to those looking to curb immigration, were not particularly determinative of legislative victories. Albert Johnson, who headed the congressional push, may have enjoyed the attention of Grant and Laughlin, and his House committee certainly encouraged Laughlin's studies as those of an ally. But committee members did not need those studies to make a case that they, and Congress as a whole, had supported for some time.

One peculiar characteristic of the race arguments, especially in connection with immigration, bedevils efforts to make historical sense of that period: contemporaries drew two different distinctions between desirable and undesirable races. The race concept typically sorted among Europeans, favoring Anglo-Saxon, Teutonic, Nordic, northern, and western; but it also sorted between Europeans and others, that is, between white and nonwhite races. Consequently, it will always be important to approach the uses of race in American life by bearing the dual nature of racial differences in mind—and least through the 1920s, often into the 1950s and beyond. I have referred to this duality as the difference in race differences. Typically all

European arrivals were considered "white on arrival," as Thomas Guglielmo put it, even if some European groups were racially undesirable white arrivals. There were many white races, and the differences among them meant everything to the republic's future. Being white did not make the races of southern and eastern Europe desirable additions to the polity.

To say that over time such undesirable European races "became white" is best glossed to mean that they, and especially their descendants, were perceived to be ever-less different from Americans who had descended from the white races that had been regarded as desirable at an earlier date, such as 1850 or 1900. This process of distinct white races evolving into an ever-larger and less internally differentiated people was driven especially by social class mobility and cultural assimilation—and was typically accelerated by the arrival of a large *new* group that was regarded as undesirable. For the immigrants from southern and eastern Europe, this process progressed far during the two generations that followed the 1921 and 1924 Quota Acts, and it continued thereafter too. Two large nonwhite migrations accelerated the process of white melding. First, the black move from the South to the cities of the North began in earnest in World War I, grew greatly in World War II, and continued into the civil rights era. To some extent, the low education and rural work experience they brought from the Jim Crow South were like those of the Europeans who immigrated to the Northern cities. But the black migrants encountered a uniquely severe and consistent discrimination there, especially in residences and labor markets. The new black–white contrast in the northern cities tended to reduce the perception of the differences among white groups. Later, the post–1965 third world immigrations also accelerated the sense of a single white race, even as it diversified the nonwhite population.

Preconceptions about a unified white race that are a product of our own time will distort an evaluation of race divisions *among* white people that existed during the three decades prior to the Great Depression, and even about the period of transition from then to the new millennium. Nevertheless, to stop with that conclusion does not yet explain how this difference in race differences was understood circa 1895–1930, particularly how the two kinds of race differences could be compared by contemporaries—on the one hand *among* white races and on the other *between* white and nonwhite races.

Both types of race differences were critical to the immigration restriction struggles, but Asian flows were cut off on the basis of origins well before the European quotas of the early 1920s—in the Chinese Exclusion Act (1882), Gentlemen's Agreement (1908), and Asiatic Barred Zone (1917). Moreover, in the first and third measures, Asian groups were excluded completely, and this process would be extended in the 1924 act. By contrast, even the 1924 act did not quite exclude southern and eastern Europeans.

That National Origins Act of 1924 preserved the earlier Asian exclusions and extended them more fully and explicitly to Japan. Congress considered these provisions against Asians while it simultaneously debated "national origin" quotas for racially desirable and undesirable Europeans. But typically the two discussions were compartmentalized. In the debates over desired and undesired white races, there was usually no mention of nonwhite immigration. In the debates over the Japanese clauses, there was almost never a mention of the continuum of white race desirability. Even more striking, nearly all of the staunchest anti-quota congressmen who had denounced immigrant racialization were silent about the parallel racialization of the Japanese, or else they explicitly supported that exclusion.

Both of these racial features of the struggles over immigration— differences among white races and between them and others—must be grasped together without minimizing the distinctive character of the other. But it is unreasonable to expect that debaters in Congress or elsewhere would clarify and elaborate on both racial distinctions at once. I have tried to find cases when individuals violated the compartmentalization and approached a self-conscious discussion: Theodore Roosevelt ruminating on Japanese versus Russians or Turks, Madison Grant and Lothrop Stoddard comparing the kinds of racial threats, Sidney Gulick seeking a restriction policy fair to Japanese but aware of difficulties of assimilation, Justice Sutherland's aside on the most swarthy of the Europeans in writing the *Thind* opinion, and Albert Johnson's efforts to explore Mexicans' mixed racial origins as a way to move their classification out of the white column. More historical work on such self-conscious efforts to discuss the difference in race differences would be helpful. The cases just mentioned, however, suggest that the most straightforward understanding of these two conceptions of racial divides is that the color races were regarded as being *further apart* from each other than were any two races within one of the grand divisions, notably within the family of white races.

This difference in race differences lies at the heart of diverse questions in both American history and sociology. Its broadest formulation asks how each kind of race difference actually operated as a boundary in American daily life—whether in law or in the social behavior of hiring, home rentals, seating in theaters and restaurants, dating, or marriage.[2] That broad formulation must be seen as asking how to specify the nature of each type of racial discrimination. If we are told that European immigrants also suffered from racial discrimination, can we specify carefully how nonwhite groups—and above all African Americans—suffered a different kind of racial discrimination? I will return to one feature of that discussion in a moment. But for the most part, I have focused on a much narrower question: How explicitly did historical actors discuss two kinds of race differences, and how self-conscious were they about how the conceptual distinction related to the meaning of race and to their policy prescriptions, especially for immigration?

If most of my attention has been on this narrower intellectual discussion, the chapter on the Quota Acts bears on the wider matter of how different kinds of racial distinctions operated in American social and institutional history. Sociologist Cybelle Fox and historian Thomas Guglielmo have distinguished, generally correctly in my view, between the *impacts* of the white–nonwhite racial boundaries and the weaker boundaries among white races in this period, noting in particular that divisions among white groups were rarely institutionalized. Two important examples are that the federal census never enumerated white races separately and that American law did not distinguish among them. We should recall in passing here how close the 1910 discussion (about incorporating the List of Races and Peoples into that year's enumeration) came to violating the generalization about the census, but in the end it did not. Moreover, in domestic law, the truth of Fox's and Guglielmo's second generalization that law did not distinguish among white races seems clear cut and obviously very important.

Both kinds of racial difference—among Europeans and between them and nonwhites (particularly East Asians)—shaped the American immigration law defined in the 1920s. The quotas were a legal and institutional structure imposed by the United States against some white races and in favor of others. True, they did not affect *domestic* legal and institutional history. In fact, the quotas may have accelerated the full assimilation of the immigrants from southern and eastern Europe by insuring that no mass of *new* arrivals would replenish their ethnic consciousness or the hostility of older-stock Americans. But the fact remains that in federal *immigration* law, race distinctions among whites glaringly and drastically affected immigration flows for forty years. Immigration law had discriminated against East Asians for much longer still—most notably in the case of the Chinese for over eight decades by 1965. Moreover, as noted, while the southern and eastern Europeans were restricted, the Asians were excluded. But it is also true that those new legal restrictions on Europeans reduced their number by a vastly greater number than any laws had ever reduced Asian flows. The 1925 quota for Italians was 6,203; Italians admitted in 1914, the last year before the war, had numbered 283,738. This reduction of 98 percent amounts to practical exclusion—although even the tiny Italian immigration numbers after 1925 remained higher than those of the Asian arrivals.

The shift away from classification based on the old and varied uses of race took place across a long period. For the study of American immigrants and their descendants, that transition can be captured in the transition from the meaning of "race" in 1900 to that of "ethnic group" in 1960. But especially before the 1940s, the shift in ideas was gradual and uneven. The shift in terminology paralleled that in ideas quite imperfectly, not least because a third term, "nationality" (in the sense of peoplehood), tended to precede "ethnic group" in the meaning the latter eventually assumed. Both terms, "nationality" (as peoplehood) and "ethnic group," had been available in the late nineteenth century. But at that time these terms, much like race, conveyed the possibility of transmission of human difference through either socialization or "blood." Moreover, a writer like Thomas could work within the framework of the old terms (race and nationality) while abandoning biological in favor of social explanations for behavior. This messy shift in terms and meanings can also be seen in the slow diffusion of new terms beyond a small circle of writers in the late 1940s and early 1950s, even in academia or among the most highly educated federal officials.

In 1910, thinking about the tension between ethnic group persistence and assimilation had focused mostly on whether the immigrants could be successfully absorbed; especially after the cessation of mass immigration in the 1920s, assimilative possibilities seemed clear, but those of group persistence much less so. This theme, as well as the intellectual and political rejection of the older racial thought, was common in works on immigrants and their descendants in the early 1960s. But these developments were soon overtaken by the watershed years around 1965, when the civil rights era transformed minority group standing. Neither "ethnicity" nor "ethnic group" seem to have been household words before the late 1960s, and then apparently became so when attention focused on "white ethnic groups" that reacted to the later phases of the civil rights era. Attention to the tension between ethnic survival and assimilation seemed to tilt in the direction of survival.

Following passage of the major new civil rights legislation and creation of the affirmative action programs, the ethno-racial minorities—blacks in the first instance, but also other nonwhites and even, it seemed, those "white ethnic groups"—sought to press the federal government for data that would illuminate group inequality and therefore serve as a goal to federal action. These groups exploited their existing "legibility" in federal data gathering, or demanded to be made legible or made more legible. The contrast between the goals of these advocates after the 1960s and the earlier struggles of mainstream Jewish organizations to avoid legibility could not have been greater. Dominant Jewish organizations had perceived safety in avoiding legibility (to the government and to gentile majority opinion). They did not modify this position as it applied to their own clientele in the post–1965 period, whether because of their long opposition to religious enumeration made such a shift impossible or because the social-class profile of American Jews was higher than that of the other relevant groups.

Advocacy on behalf of ethno-racial minorities eligible for federal protection led to the first of three post–civil rights era reforms in the 1980 census classifications. New origin questions (Hispanic Origin and Ancestry) preserved immigrant origins across all generations since arrival, no matter how far back, as the race question categories had always done. This tracking addressed a claim that far from losing out to assimilation, ethnic life persisted well past the second generation and continued to determine life chances and cultural distinctiveness among many—Mexican Americans in the Southwest, Asian Americans, and the grandchildren of southern and eastern European immigrants.

This new effort to enumerate members of groups, no matter how many generations of their families had lived in the United States, soon collided with an altogether different phenomenon of gigantic numerical importance—the resumption of mass immigration, now dominated by arrivals from Latin America and Asia. So the counts devised for tracking late-generation descendants of earlier immigrations increasingly included large proportions from new immigrant families. Did the counts show that long-resident families of Mexican Americans had not reached parity with native-born Americans, or did they show that new immigrants and their children had not done so?

But if the 1980 reform tracked immigrant origins through all generations, as earlier classifications had only tracked races, the reforms of 2000 that swept away the restriction to "Mark one [race] only" made reporting race categories more like the unproblematic reporting of two different parental birthplaces or multiple ancestries. The lines distinguishing *kinds* of origins were getting fuzzier or at least shifting. Bureau research for the 2020 census questions discovered that many people found race, ethnicity, and origin confusing, and the terms meant different things to different people. Its conclusion that a combined race / ethnicity question would be optimal was also a step away from older distinctions among kinds of origins.

Clearly, *some* historical origins mattered to a great many Americans' identity and also affected their life chances—most especially designation in terms of major OMB categories or a recent immigrant group. At the same time, specific countries of origin became less meaningful after several generations in America, especially for people of distant European immigrant ancestry melding into the single white population. But in its turn, the (non-Hispanic) white population was forming increasing numbers of unions with Hispanics and Asians and even, although still at a decidedly lower rate, with African Americans. The broadest categories of the combined race / ethnicity question were the large, old OMB race and Hispanic Origin categories (American Indian, Asian, black, Hispanic, non-Hispanic white). But Americans would be urged to "Mark all that apply" so that the mixture of these origins would be underscored by the census results too.

The meaning of more *specific* origins that respondents would provide under any of these five OMB categories would vary greatly with the respondent's family history. The huge number of Americans with at least one European ancestor who arrived six or twelve generations back usually would provide no more than an inkling of the whole range of ancestors' origins. Typically the origins remembered were those of the one or two most recent immigrants in that family tree or the ones most memorialized. Tens of millions of other Americans, whose immigrant origins extend back only one or two generations, would be apt to write in specific country origins closely tied to life chances. The value of these different kinds of responses across a large and diverse nation would have to be teased out. But that challenge itself would underscore the vast range of ways that race and immigration have mattered across the trajectories to the present.

Notes

Abbreviations

AJCA	American Jewish Committee Archives, New York City
AJHS	American Jewish Historical Society, Center for Jewish History, New York City
ARCGI	*Annual Reports of the United States Commissioner General of Immigration* (Government Printing Office, Washington, DC)
CR	*Congressional Record* (followed by date of remarks and page number), permanent hardbound edition (Government Printing Office, Washington, DC)
FB / APS	Franz Boas Papers, American Philosophical Society, Philadelphia (microfilmed)
USICR	United States Immigration Commission (1907–1911), *Reports* (41 vols.; Government Printing Office, Washington, DC, 1910–1911)
USNA	United States National Archives, Washington, DC

1: Creating and Refining the List, 1898–1906

1. All figures on the size of immigration flows were calculated from Susan B. Carter et al., eds., *Historical Statistics of the United States,* Millennial Edition (New York: Cambridge University Press, 2006), table C-89; Aristide R. Zolberg, *A Nation by Design: Immigration Policy in the Fashioning of America* (New York: Russell Sage Foundation; Cambridge, MA: Harvard University Press, 2006).
2. Thomas M. Pitkin, *Keepers of the Gate: A History of Ellis Island* (New York: New York University Press, 1975), 33–39.
3. *USICR* 39:43.
4. Edward P. Hutchinson, *Legislative History of American Immigration Policy, 1798–1965* (Philadelphia: University of Pennsylvania Press, 1981), 536–39.

5. Edward F. McSweeney to Thomas Fitchie, June 18, 1898 (in a cover letter to Safford's report), File 52729/9, Entry 9, Record Group 85, Bureau of Immigration Papers, USNA. On the origins of the List, see also Charles B. Forcey, "Powderly, Terence Vincent," *American National Biography Online;* Harry J. Carmen et al., eds., *The Path I Trod: The Autobiography of Terence V. Powderly* (New York: Columbia University Press, 1940); Victor Safford, *Immigration Problems: Personal Experiences of an Official* (New York: Dodd, Mead and Co., 1925); Patrick Weil, "Races at the Gate: A Century of Racial Distinctions in American Immigration Policy (1865–1965)," *Georgetown Immigration Law Journal* 15, no. 4 (2001): 625–48; Nathan Goldberg, Jacob Lestchinsky, and Max Weinreich, *The Classification of Jewish Immigrants and Its Implications: A Survey of Opinions* (New York: Yiddish Scientific Institute–YIVO, 1945), 90–94.

6. McSweeney to Fitchie, June 18, 1898.

7. Victor Safford to the Commissioner of Immigration, June 8,1898, File 52729/9, Entry 9, Record Group 85, Bureau of Immigration Papers, USNA. All quotations from Safford's report refer to this item.

8. McSweeney to Fitchie, June 18, 1898.

9. McSweeney to Fitchie, June 18, 1898.

10. Jonathan J. S. Rodgers to Terence Powderly, June 22, 1898, File 52729/9, Entry 9, Record Group 85, Bureau of Immigration Papers, USNA.

11. Edward F. McSweeney, Jonathan J. S. Rodgers, Richard K. Campbell, and Victor Stafford to Terence V. Powderly, June 26, 1898; Edward F. McSweeney and Victor Stafford to Terence V. Powderly, June 28, 1898; and Telegram, Jonathan J. S. Rodgers to Terence V. Powderly, June 29, 1898. All from File 52729/9, Entry 9, Record Group 85, Bureau of Immigration Papers, USNA.

12. McSweeney, Rodgers, Campbell, and Stafford to Powderly, June 26, 1898, 2.

13. McSweeney, Rodgers, Campbell, and Stafford to Powderly, June 26, 1898, 2–3.

14. McSweeney, Rodgers, Campbell, and Stafford to Powderly, June 26, 1898, 7.

15. United States Industrial Commission, *Reports* (Washington, DC: Government Printing Office, 1901), 15:131, 91–92.

16. The supplemental form is available on the microfilm reels for the port of New York Passenger Lists but not on the reels for the few other ports that I could easily check. This could mean that it was not in use at those other ports, or for some reason not microfilmed for those ports.

17. Kevin Kenny, *The American Irish: A History* (New York: Pearson Education, 2000), chaps. 2–3; Diane Ravitch, *The Great School Wars: New York City, 1805–1973; A History of the Public Schools as a Battleground of Social Change* (New York: Basic Books, 1974), chaps. 3–7.

18. All quotations from the "instructions" in the text are from the draft that appears to be the last, probably drafted by Safford in late September.

19. See, for example, *The Encyclopedia Britannica,* 11th ed., "Ethnology and Ethnography," 9:849–51.

20. McSweeney, Rodgers, Campbell, and Stafford to Powderly, June 26, 1898, 6.

21. Quoted in Marian L. Smith, "Race, Nationality and Reality: INS Administration of Racial Provisions in U.S. Immigration and Nationality Law Since 1898,"

Prologue 32, no. 2 (Summer 2002) at https://www.archives.gov/publications /prologue/2002/summer/immigration-law-2.html.

22. See, for example, *USICR, Vol. 5 (Dictionary)*, discussed in Chapter 4.
23. U.S. Industrial Commission, *Reports*, 15:91–92.
24. Terrence V. Powderly, "A Menacing Irruption," *North American Review* (August 1888): 165–74.
25. *ARCGI*, 1898, 33–33.
26. *ARCGI*, 1899, 5.
27. Pitkin, *Keepers of the Gate*, chap. 3.
28. *ARCGI*, 1899–1903. See, for example, 1902, table III and discussion of it.
29. *ARCGI*, 1903, 42, 73.
30. Husband to Wheeler, December 15, 1908, included in correspondence of Husband to Max Kohler, March 14, 1927, in the latter's papers at AJHS. Paul Schor, *Compter et Classer: Histoire des Recensements Americains* (Paris: Editions de l'Ecole des Hautes Etudes en Sciences Sociales, 2009), 266n5, cites another copy of the 1908 letter in the William W. Husband Papers, Chicago Historical Society, Chicago.
31. Daniel G. Brinton, *Races and Peoples: Lectures on the Science of Ethnography* (New York: NDC Hodges, 1890), 99.
32. Madison Grant to T. Roosevelt, May 27, 1918, as quoted by Thomas G. Dyer, *Theodore Roosevelt and the Idea of Race* (Baton Rouge: Louisiana State University Press, 1980), 17.
33. U.S. 57th Cong., 2d Sess. Senate Hearing, "Regulation of Immigration" (Washington, DC: Government Printing Office, 1902), Vol. 4421, Doc. 62, p. 422.
34. U.S. 57th Cong., 1st Sess., Senate Hearing, "Immigration of Aliens" (Washington DC: Government Printing Office, 1902), Vol. 4264, Doc. No. 2119, pp. 140; 143–44.
35. All quotations from the instructions in the text are from the printed forms of the indicated year (in the National Archives microfilm series for the Passenger Lists).
36. *ARCGI*, 1904, 162.
37. *ARCGI*, 1908, 62.

2: Immigration—Especially European—through the Lens of Race

1. John A. Garraty, *Henry Cabot Lodge: A Biography* (New York: Alfred A. Knopf, 1953); and especially for race and immigration issues, William C. Widenor, *Henry Cabot Lodge and the Search for an American Foreign Policy* (Berkeley: University of California Press, 1980). See also Barbara Miller Solomon, *Ancestors and Immigrants: A Changing New England Tradition* (Cambridge, MA: Harvard University Press, 1956), chaps. IV and VI.
2. J. Laurence Laughlin, ed., *Essays in Anglo-Saxon Law* (Boston: Little, Brown and Co., 1876).
3. Henry Adams, "The Anglo-Saxon Courts of Law," in Laughlin, ed., *Essays in Anglo-Saxon Law*, 1–2.
4. Adams, "The Anglo-Saxon Courts of Law," 1–2.

5. Henry Cabot Lodge, "Anglo-Saxon Land Law," in Laughlin, ed., *Essays in Anglo-Saxon Law,* 55–56.

6. "Lecky's England," *Literary World,* June 1878, 3–4. I follow Widenor, *Lodge,* e.g., 59–60, 358, for the attributions of anonymous articles to Lodge.

7. Lodge, "Lecky's England," 3–4.

8. Lodge, "Lecky's England, 4.

9. Lodge [anonymously], "Limited Sovereignty in the United States," *The Atlantic Monthly* 43 (February 1879), 185.

10. Lodge, "Limited Sovereignty," 189.

11. Alexander Keyssar, *The Right to Vote: The Contested History of Democracy in the United States* (New York: Basic Books, 2000), chap. 5.

12. Garraty, *Lodge,* 117–18; Widenor, *Lodge,* 60.

13. CR, June 26, 1890, 6543.

14. CR, June 26, 1890, 6543–44.

15. Garraty, *Lodge,* 119.

16. "The Civilization of the Public School: A Reply," reprinted in Henry Cabot Lodge, *Speeches and Addresses, 1884–1909* (Cambridge, MA: Riverside Press, 1909), 57–64; quotation from 62.

17. Keyssar, *Right to Vote,* 85–86, 376.

18. Joel Perlmann and Robert A. Margo, *Women's Work: American Schoolteachers 1650–1920* (Chicago: University of Chicago Press, 2001), 34–35, 61–70.

19. Edward P. Hutchinson, *Legislative History of American Immigration Policy, 1798–1965* (Philadelphia: University of Pennsylvania Press, 1981), 101–2; CR, February 19, 1891, 2956.

20. U.S. 52nd Cong. 1st Sess., Senate Committee on Immigration and House Committee on Immigration and Naturalization, Acting Jointly, "Hearing on House Bill 401 to Amend Various Acts in Relation to Immigration April 23, 1892" (Washington, DC: Government Printing Office, 1892), 740.

21. Lodge, "Distribution of Ability in the United States," *Century* (September 1891); reprinted in Henry Cabot Lodge, *Historical and Political Essays* (Cambridge, MA: Riverside Press, 1892), 168–88; quotation from 165.

22. Cf. John Higham, *Strangers in the Land: Patterns of American Nativism, 1860–1925* (New Brunswick, NJ: Rutgers University Press, 1955), 141n.

23. Lodge, "Distribution of Ability in the United States"; Garraty, *Lodge,* 143.

24. Thomas C. Leonard, *Illiberal Reformers: Race, Eugenics & American Economics in the Progressive Era* (Princeton, NJ: Princeton University Press, 2016), 142–43.

25. Edward Bemis, "Restriction of Immigration," *The Andover Review* 9 (March 1888): 251–64; quotation from 262.

26. CR, February 19, 1891, 2956; Henry Cabot Lodge, "The Census and Immigration," *Century,* September 1893.

27. Higham, *Strangers in the Land,* 147; Dyer, *Theodore Roosevelt and the Idea of Race,* 143ff.

28. Henry Cabot Lodge, "Lynch Law and Unrestricted Immigration," *North American Review,* 152, no. 414 (May 1891): 602–12.

29. CR, February 19, 1891, 2956.

30. *New York Times*, March 18, 1896, 3; Henry Cabot Lodge, ed., *Selections from the Correspondence of Theodore Roosevelt and Henry Cabot Lodge, 1884–1918* (New York: C. Scribner's Sons, 1925), 1:216.

31. CR, February 19, 1891, 2956.

32. Henry Cabot Lodge, "Restriction of Immigration," CR, March 16, 1896, 2817–20; reprinted in Lodge, *Speeches and Addresses*, 243–66; quotation from 251. All following quotations from the speech cite page numbers in the reprinted version.

33. "Restriction of Immigration," 252.

34. Elazar Barkan, *The Retreat of Scientific Racism: Changing Concepts of Race in Britain and the United States between the World Wars* (Cambridge: Cambridge University Press, 1992), 235.

35. "Restriction of Immigration," 253.

36. "Restriction of Immigration," 252–53.

37. "Restriction of Immigration," 254.

38. "Restriction of Immigration," 256.

39. "Restriction of Immigration," 261.

40. "Restriction of Immigration," 263–64.

41. "Restriction of Immigration," 259.

42. "Restriction of Immigration," 261.

43. "Restriction of Immigration," 261–62.

44. Carter et al., eds., *Historical Statistics of the United States*, table C-89. Figures for Hungarians and Greeks estimated from residual categories of other eastern and other southern Europeans, respectively.

45. "Restriction of Immigration," 262–63.

46. "Restriction of Immigration," 264.

47. Higham, *Strangers in the Land*, 155–56.

48. "Restriction of Immigration," 265.

49. "Restriction of Immigration," 266.

50. Claudia Goldin, "The Political Economy of Immigration Restriction in the United States, 1890–1921," in *The Regulated Economy: A Historical Approach to Political Economy*, ed. Claudia Goldin and Gary D. Libecap (Chicago: University of Chicago Press, 1994), 223–58, see 227; Higham, *Strangers in the Land*, 101–5.

51. Higham, *Strangers in the Land*, chap. 6; Oscar Handlin, *Race and Nationality in American Life* (Boston: Little, Brown, 1957); Ivan Hannaford, *Race: The History of an Idea in the West* (Washington, DC: Woodrow Wilson Center Press, 1996).

52. Leonard, *Illiberal Reformers*, 91–98.

53. Barkan, *Retreat of Scientific Racism*, 235. See also Lancelot Hogben, *Genetic Principles in Medicine and Social Science* (London: Williams & Norgate Ltd., 1931), 166–68, discussed by Barkan in this context.

54. Barkan, *Retreat of Scientific Racism*, chap. 6.

55. M. A. DeWolfe Howe, *James Ford Rhodes: American Historian* (New York: D. Appleton and Co., 1929), 120.

56. David R. Roediger, *The Wages of Whiteness: Race and the Making of the American Working Class* (New York: Verso, 1991); Noel Ignatiev, *How the Irish Became White* (New York: Routledge, 1995); Matthew Frye Jacobson, *Whiteness of a Different*

Color: European Immigrants and the Alchemy of Race (Cambridge, MA: Harvard University Press, 1998); Thomas A. Guglielmo, *White on Arrival: Italians, Race, Color and Power in Chicago, 1890–1945* (New York: Oxford University Press, 2003); and Cybelle Fox and Thomas A. Guglielmo, "Defining America's Racial Boundaries: Blacks, Mexicans and European Immigrants, 1890–1945," *American Journal of Sociology* 118, no. 2 (September 2012): 327–79.

57. Fox and Guglielmo, "Defining America's Racial Boundaries"; Stephan Thernstrom, *The Other Bostonians: Poverty and Progress in the American Metropolis, 1880–1970* (Cambridge, MA: Harvard University Press, 1973); Stanley Lieberson, *A Piece of the Pie: Blacks and White Immigrants since 1880* (Berkeley: University of California Press, 1980); Joel Perlmann, *Ethnic Differences: Schooling and Social Structure among the Irish, Italians, Jews and Blacks in an American City, 1880–1935* (New York: Cambridge University Press, 1988).

58. Theodore Roosevelt to Cecil Arthur Spring Rice, June 13, 1904, in Elting Elmore Morison, ed., *The Letters of Theodore Roosevelt* (Cambridge, MA: Harvard University Press, 1951–1954), 4:832.

59. Gary Gerstle, *American Crucible: Race and Nation in the Twentieth Century* (Princeton, NJ: Princeton University Press, 2001), 17–24, includes a description of Roosevelt's more typical distinctions among white races in his *Winning of the West* (1890).

60. William Z. Ripley, *The Races of Europe: A Sociological Study* (New York: D. Appleton and Co., 1899).

61. Higham, *Strangers in the Land.*

62. Higham, *Strangers in the Land*, 155, 157.

63. Madison Grant, *The Passing of the Great Race, or the Racial Basis of European History* (New York: Charles Scribner's Sons, 1916), 150.

64. Grant, *Passing of the Great Race*, 197.

65. Grant, *Passing of the Great Race*, 29.

66. Grant, *Passing of the Great Race*, 61.

67. Grant, *Passing of the Great Race*, 69–71.

68. T. Lothrop Stoddard, *The Rising Tide of Color against White World-Supremacy* (New York: Charles Scribner's Sons, 1920).

69. W. I. Thomas, "The Mind of Woman and the Lower Races," *American Journal of Sociology* 12, no. 4 (January 1907): 435–69.

70. Franz Boas, "The Mind of Primitive Man," *Journal of American Folklore* 14 (1901): 1–11.

71. Thomas to Boas, May 14, 1907, FB / APS.

72. Boas to Thomas, May 18, 1907, FB / APS.

73. Barkan, *Retreat of Scientific Racism.*

3: First Struggles over the List

1. For general treatments, see Hasia Diner, *A Time for Gathering: The Second Migration, 1820–1880*, vol. 2 of *The Jewish People in America* (Baltimore: The Johns Hopkins University Press, 1992) and Gerald Sorin, *A Time for Building: The Third Migration, 1880–1920*, vol. 3 of *The Jewish People in America* (Baltimore: The Johns Hopkins University Press, 1992).

2. Available at https://en.wikipedia.org/wiki/Pittsburgh_Platform. For a recent evaluation, see Eric L. Goldstein, *The Price of Whiteness: Jews, Race and American Identity* (Princeton, NJ: Princeton University, 2006), 29–30, 248.

3. Mitchell B. Hart, ed., *Jews and Race: Writings on Identity and Difference, 1880–1940* (Waltham: Brandeis University Press, 2011).

4. *USICR*, 42:266.

5. Naomi W. Cohen, *Jews in Christian America: The Pursuit of Religious Equality* (New York: Oxford University Press, 1992); Jonathon D. Sarna and David G. Dalin, *Religion and the State in the American Jewish Experience* (Notre Dame, IN: University of Notre Dame Press, 1997); see especially Sarna's introductory essay.

6. *Church of the Holy Trinity v. United States*, 143 U.S. 457 (1892).

7. For rich evidence and insight on related topics, see Goldstein, *The Price of Whiteness*, esp. chap. 4; cf. 108 on the formulations of this paragraph.

8. James C. Scott, *Seeing Like a State: How Certain Schemes to Improve the Human Condition Have Failed* (New Haven, CT: Yale University Press, 1998). I am grateful to Derek J. Penslar for reminding me of the legibility terminology and suggesting that it would conveniently capture arguments I was making about the Jewish organizations' discomfort with the List that seemed to extend beyond any specific constitutional issue.

9. Cyrus Adler to Mayer Sulzberger, December 14, 1909, in Ira Robinson, ed., *Cyrus Adler: Selected Letters* (Philadelphia: Jewish Publication Society of America, 1985), 1:177.

10. Partha Chatterjee, *The Politics of the Governed: Reflections on Popular Politics in Most of the World* (New York: Columbia University Press, 2004), esp. chap. 3, and Eugene M. Avrutin, *Jews and the Imperial State: Identification Politics in Tsarist Russia* (Ithaca, NY: Cornell University Press, 2010), discuss group reactions other than resistance to being "seen." I am grateful to Sunmin Kim and Derek J. Penslar for directing me to the first and second, respectively.

11. John C. Livingston, "Simon Wolf," *American National Biography Online*; Esther L. Panitz, *Simon Wolf: Private Conscience and Public Image* (Rutherford, NJ: Fairleigh Dickinson University Press, 1987).

12. Nathan Glazer, "Social Characteristics of American Jews, 1654–1954," *American Jewish Yearbook* 56 (1955): 3–42; Simon Kuznetz, "Immigration of Russian Jews to the United States: Background and Structure," *Perspectives in American History* 9 (1975): 35–124.

13. Union of American Hebrew Congregations, *Thirty-Seventh Annual Report* ("Secretary Nagel's Address," January 18, 1911), 6627, 6633.

14. *ARCGI*, 1899, 13.

15. Cited in Simon Wolf, *The Presidents I Have Known from 1860 to 1918* (Washington, DC: BS Adams, 1920), 259–63.

16. Simon Wolf, "Report of the Board of Delegates on Civil and Religious Rights" (November 14, 1899) in Union of American Hebrew Congregations, *Twenty Sixth Annual Report* (January 1900), 4121–24.

17. "Memorandum, July 7, 1903" (author unknown; National Archives, RG 85, Entry 9, file 52363 / 25), notes that "For some time they [immigrants] were also

recorded by religion, which latter practice was discontinued on January 1, 1900."

18. Wolf, "Report," 1899, 4121–22, and Wolf, *Presidents*, 238. See also "Memorandum" [n.d., no author; referred to as "A" in the covering "Memorandum"], RG 85, Entry 9, file 52363 / 25, USNA.

19. Wolf to Cortelyou, October 13, 1903, RG 85, Entry 9, file 52363 / 25, USNA. Reprinted [n.d.] in Union of American Hebrew Congregations, *Thirtieth Annual Report* (January 1904), "Meeting of the Board of Delegates on Civil and Religious Rights," 5030–51; letter reprinted, 5042–43.

20. Wolf's correspondence with the Jewish authorities was reprinted in Union of American Hebrew Congregations, *Thirtieth Annual Report*, 5042–50.

21. "Memorandum in Reference to Compilation of Hebrew Statistics," 1903 (unsigned and undated, but citing Wolf's letter "of October 12").

22. Union of American Hebrew Congregations, *Thirtieth Annual Report*, 5043.

23. Union of American Hebrew Congregations, *Thirtieth Annual Report*, 5045.

24. Union of American Hebrew Congregations, *Thirtieth Annual Report*, 5047.

25. Union of American Hebrew Congregations, *Thirtieth Annual Report*, 5050.

26. Union of American Hebrew Congregations, *Thirtieth Annual Report*, 5050.

27. Union of American Hebrew Congregations, *Thirtieth Annual Report*, 5044.

28. Union of American Hebrew Congregations, *Thirtieth Annual Report*, 5050.

29. Union of American Hebrew Congregations, *Thirtieth Annual Report*, 5047.

30. Union of American Hebrew Congregations, *Thirtieth Annual Report*, 5046.

31. Union of American Hebrew Congregations, *Thirtieth Annual Report*, 5044.

32. Union of American Hebrew Congregations, *Thirtieth Annual Report*, 5043–44.

33. Philip Cowen to Frank P. Sargent, November 12, 1903, RG 85, Entry 9, file 52363 / 25, Bureau of Immigration Papers, USNA.

34. Unsigned Memorandum, July 7, 1903, RG 85, Entry 9, file 52363 / 25, Bureau of Immigration Papers, USNA.

35. Unsigned Memorandum, July 7, 1903.

36. Unsigned Memorandum, July 7, 1903.

37. Unsigned Memorandum, July 7, 1903.

38. S. N. D. North to George B. Cortelyou, July 14, 1903, RG 85, Entry 9, file 52363 / 25, Bureau of Immigration Papers, USNA.

39. "Memorandum by Mr. Hunt, Department of State," n.d. [referred to as "B" in the covering "Memorandum"], RG 85, Entry 9, file 52363 / 25, Bureau of Immigration Papers, USNA.

40. Unsigned Memorandum, n.d. [referred to as "A" in the covering "Memorandum"], RG 85, Entry 9, file 52363 / 25, Bureau of Immigration Papers, USNA.

41. Unsigned Memorandum, n.d. [attached as the covering memorandum to "accompanying memoranda marked A and B"], RG 85, Entry 9, file 52363 / 25, Bureau of Immigration Papers, USNA.

42. S. N. D. North to George B. Cortelyou, July 31, 1903, RG 85, Entry 9, file 52363 / 25, Bureau of Immigration Papers, USNA.

4: *The United States Immigration Commission, 1907–1911*

1. *USICR*, 1:14; Oscar Handlin, *Race and Nationality in American Life* (Boston: Little Brown, 1957), chap. 5; and Robert F. Zeidel, *Immigrants, Progressives and Exclusion Politics: The Dillingham Commission, 1900–1927* (DeKalb: Northern Illinois University Press, 2004).
2. Zeidel, *Immigrants, Progressives and Exclusion*; Zolberg, *A Nation by Design*, 232–38.
3. Husband to Wheeler, December 15, 1908.
4. These comments were eventually published in *USICR*, vol. 41.
5. The extensive quotations from this hearing appear in order, from *USICR*, 41:265–75.
6. *USICR*, 41:271.
7. Copy of letter from Kadimah Society to USIC, February 9, 1910, AJCA. Also the Baltimore Federation of American Zionists protested on February 2, 1910, to Friedenwald, AJCA.
8. Bernard G. Richards, secretary of the Jewish Community of New York (the Kehillah) to Friedenwald, February 18, 1910, AJCA.
9. Mack to Friedenwald, December 15, 1909, AJCA.
10. Friedenwald to Kadimah Society, February 25, 1910; Sulzberger correspondence, AJCA.
11. USIC, "Brief Statement of the Investigations of the Immigration Commission, with Conclusions and Recommendations and Views of the Minority," *Reports*, 1:5–49; section on "Racial Classification of Immigrants," 17–20.
12. *USICR*, 1:17–20.
13. *USICR*, 1:17.
14. *USICR*, 1:18.
15. *USICR*, 1:19–20.
16. Husband to Wheeler, December 15, 1908.
17. John S. Gilkeson, *Anthropologists and the Rediscovery of America, 1886–1965* (New York: Cambridge University Press, 2010), 31–32; Marshall Hyatt, *Franz Boas, Social Activist: The Dynamics of Ethnicity* (Westport, CT: Greenwood Press, 1990), 106–13; see also George W. Stocking Jr., *Race, Culture and Evolution: Essays in the History of Anthropology* (Chicago: University of Chicago Press, 1968).
18. *USICR*, vol. 38, *Changes in Bodily Form of Descendants of Immigrants*.
19. Boas to Simkovitch, March 15, 1906, FB/APS.
20. The initial approach to Jenks does not appear in the Boas correspondence. The first mention of a connection is in Boas to Husband (January 4, 1908 [probably 1909]): "Professor Jenks told me he would mention the matter [clerical assistance] to you" (FB/APS).
21. Francesco L. Nepa, "E. A. Goldenweiser," and Piero Matthey, "A. A. Goldenweiser," *American National Biography Online*.
22. Reprinted in Philip Davis and Bertha Schwartz, eds., *Immigration and Americanization: Selected Readings* (New York: Ginn and Co., 1920), 216–23; quotations from 217 and 222.

23. E. A. Goldenweiser, "Walker's Theory of Immigration," *American Journal of Sociology* 18, no. 3 (November 1912): 342–51.

24. Eric Goldstein, "Maurice Fishberg," *American National Biography Online;* W. W. Husband, "U.S. Immigration Commission, 1907–10" (bound volume, Chicago Historical Society), 13. Fishberg's acquaintance with Boas is reflected in the Fishberg-Boas letters in the Boas Correspondence (FB/APS).

25. Roland P. Falkner to I. A. Hourwich, December 22, 1911, in I. A. Hourwich Papers, Houghton Library, Harvard University.

26. Jeremiah W. Jenks, "The Character and Influence of Recent Immigration," in *Questions of Public Policy: Addresses Delivered in the Page Lecture Series, 1913, Before the Senior Class of the Sheffield Scientific School, Yale University* (New Haven, CT: Yale University Press, 1913), 2.

27. Mae Ngai, *Impossible Subjects: Illegal Aliens and the Making of Modern America* (Princeton, NJ: Princeton University Press, 2004), chap. 1.

28. Daniel Folkmar, *Lecons d'Anthropologie Philosophique: ses Application a la Morale Positive* (Paris: Librarie C. Reinwald, 1900). This was an expanded version of the original thesis, published the preceding year as *L'Anthropologie Philosophique: Consideree comme Base de la Morale* (Paris: Librarie C. Reinwald, 1899). James R. Glenn, "Folkmar, Daniel," in Christopher Winters, ed., *International Dictionary of Anthropologists* (New York: Garland Press, 1991), 203–4; Handlin, *Race and Nationality*, chap. 5 as well as the annotated original version, Oscar Handlin, "Memorandum by Oscar Handlin, Associate Professor of History, Harvard University Concerning the Background of the National-Origin Quota System," United States, 82nd Congress, 2nd session, House of Representatives, President's Commission on Immigration and Naturalization" *Hearings* (Washington, DC: Government Printing Office, 1952), 1839–63 (see also his "Statement," 327–33); and *Who's Who in America: A Biographical Dictionary of Notable Living Men and Women in the United States*, vol. 13 (Chicago: A. N. Marquis and Company, 1925).

29. Folkmar, *L'Anthropologie Philosophique* (1899), 154–55; William Dalton Babington, *Fallacies of Race Theories as Applied to National Characteristics* (London: Longmans, Green and Co., 1895).

30. U.S. 61st Cong.,1st Sess., *Hearings before the Committee on the Census of the Senate on the Bill (H.R. 1033) to Provide for the Thirteenth and Subsequent Decennial Censuses* (Washington, DC: Government Printing Office, 1909), 29–42.

31. USICR, *Dictionary of Races and Peoples*, vol. 5; "The Races That Go into the American Melting Pot," *New York Times*, May 21, 1911, Sunday Magazine, 2.

32. USICR, *Dictionary*, "Introductory," 5:1–7; quotation from 3–4.

33. USICR, *Dictionary*, 5:54–55.

34. Franz Boas, "Race Problems in America," *Science* 29, no. 752 (1909): 839–49 (s.n.), quotations from 839 and 845.

35. Boas, "Race Problems in America," 849.

36. Boas to Jenks, January 29, 1909, FB/APS.

37. Husband to Boas, January 29, 1909, FB/APS.

38. Husband to Boas, September 29, 1909, FB/APS.

39. Boas to Husband, October 8, 1909, FB / APS.
40. Husband to Boas, October 12, 1909, FB / APS.
41. Boas to Husband, October 14, 1909; Husband to Boas, October 15, 1909, FB / APS.
42. Zeidel, *Immigrants, Progressives, and Exclusion*, 111.
43. Jeremiah W. Jenks, "The Racial Problem in Immigration," National Conference of Charities and Correction, *Proceedings XXXVI* (1909), 215–22; Jenks, "The Character and Influence of Recent Immigration"; Jeremiah W. Jenks and W. Jett Lauck, *The Immigration Problem: A Study of American Immigration Conditions and Needs* (New York: Funk and Wagnalls Company, 1911), e.g., 24–26, 35–38, 48, 265–66, 269. See also Handlin, "Memorandum," 1839–40.

5: *Urging the List on the U.S. Census Bureau, 1908–1910*

1. CR, January 8, 1909, 625.
2. Sulzberger to Friedenwald, January 11, 1909, AJCA.
3. Fulton M. Brylawski to Adler, January 11, 1909, AJCA.
4. Friedenwald to Sulzberger, January 12, 1909, AJCA; Brylawski to Friedenwald, January 14, 1909, AJCA.
5. Friedenwald to Guggenheim, January 12, 1909, AJCA; Guggenheim to Friedenwald, January 13, 1909.
6. Friedenwald to Guggenheim, January 12, 1909, AJCA.
7. Joel Conarroe, "Guggenheim, Simon," *American National Biography Online*.
8. Guggenheim to Friedenwald, January 13, 1909, AJCA.
9. U.S. 61st Cong., 1st Sess., Senate Committee on the Census, "Hearings before the Committee on the Census of the Senate on the Bill (H.R. 1033) to Provide for the Thirteenth and Subsequent Decennial Censuses" (Washington, DC: Government Printing Office, 1909), 29–42, quotation from 31.
10. Goldfogle to Friedenwald, January 15, 1909, AJCA; CR, January 20, 1909, 1153.
11. Friedenwald to Husband January 21, 1909, AJCA.
12. "Hearings before the [Senate] Committee on the Census," 29.
13. "Hearings before the [Senate] Committee on the Census," 30.
14. "Hearings before the [Senate] Committee on the Census," 30–31, 34.
15. "Hearings before the [Senate] Committee on the Census," 35.
16. "Hearings before the [Senate] Committee on the Census," 31, 34–35, 37.
17. "Hearings before the [Senate] Committee on the Census," 31.
18. "Hearings before the [Senate] Committee on the Census," 31–32.
19. "Hearings before the [Senate] Committee on the Census," 31.
20. "Hearings before the [Senate] Committee on the Census," 32–33.
21. "Hearings before the [Senate] Committee on the Census," 31, 33–34.
22. *New York Times*, March 7, 1910, 3.
23. Charity Organization Society of the City of New York, Department for the Improvement of Social Conditions (Conference Committee of New York), "Suggestions with Regard to Methods of Publication and Tabulation of the

Thirteenth Census," May 17, 1909; see also letter from Claghorn and Lawrence
Veiller to William B. Bailey, Census Bureau, 1909. Similar materials were sent
from Bureau of Statistics, Commonwealth of Massachusetts, to Bailey,
August 25, 1909. All at USNA, RG 29, Entry 145, Box 1.

6: The Census Bureau Goes Its Own Way

1. *The Encyclopedia Britannica*, 11th ed., "Nationality," vol. 19.
2. *Oxford English Dictionary* (Oxford: Oxford University Press, 1879–1928) cites
   Mill's usage; Walker Connor, *Ethnonationalism: The Quest for Understanding*
   (Princeton, NJ: Princeton University Press, 1994), 4–8.
3. *Meyers Großes Konversations-Lexikon*, vol. 14 (Leipzig: Bibliographisches Institut,
   1908), 442–43.
4. A recent survey, Joep Leerssen, *National Thought in Europe: A Cultural History*
   (Amsterdam: Amsterdam University Press, 2006), also cites the older literature.
5. William Z. Ripley, *The Races of Europe: A Sociological Study* (New York: D. Appleton
   and Co., 1899), chap. 2, "Language, Nationality and Race."
6. Henning Bauer, Andreas Kappeller, and Brigitte Roth, *Die Nationalitaten des
   Russicschen Reiches in der Volkszahlung von 1897, Quellenkritische Documentation und
   Datenhandbuch* (2 vols.; Stuttgart: Franz Steiner Verlag, 1991), vol. 1, chaps. 1 and
   3.; Rudolf Kleeberg, *Die Nationalitatenstatistik, ihre Ziele, Methoden und Ergebnisse*
   (Leipzig: Thomas and Hubert, 1915), especially chaps. 1–2.
7. Quoted in Bauer, Kappeller, and Roth, *Die Nationalitaten des Russicschen Reiches in
   der Volkszahlung von 1897*, 1:138–40.
8. Quoted in Bauer, Kappeller, and Roth, *Die Nationalitaten des Russicschen Reiches in
   der Volkszahlung von 1897*, 1:138.
9. Quoted in Bauer, Kappeller, and Roth, *Die Nationalitaten des Russicschen Reiches in
   der Volkszahlung von 1897*, 1:138–39.
10. U.S. 61st Cong., 1st Sess., Senate Committee on the Census, "Hearings Before the
    Committee on the Census of the Senate on the Bill (H.R. 1033) to Provide for the
    Thirteenth and Subsequent Decennial Censuses" (Washington, DC: Govern-
    ment Printing Office, 1909), 29–42, quotation from 37–39.
11. Premier Recensement General de L'Empire de Russie, "Liste de Recensement,"
    [Russian and French] (St. Petersburg, 1897 [?]); Francine Hirsch, *Empire of
    Nations: Ethnographic Knowledge and the Making of the Soviet Union* (Ithaca, NY:
    Cornell University Press, 2005), chap. 1, especially 38.
12. Isaac A. Hourwich, *Immigration and Labor: The Economic Aspects of European
    Immigration to the United States* (New York: G. P. Putnam's Sons, 1912).
13. Kathleen A. Shanahan, "I. A. Hourwich," *Dictionary of American Biography* (New
    York: Oxford University Press, 1999); Melech Epstein, *Profiles of Eleven: Profiles of
    Eleven Men Who Guided the Destiny of an Immigrant Society and Stimulated Social
    Consciousness among the American People* (Detroit, MI: Wayne State University
    Press, 1965), 255–68.
14. Daniel Folkmar, "The Duration of School Attendance in Chicago and
    Milwaukee," Transactions of the Wisconsin Academy of Sciences, Arts and

Letters, vol. 12, parts 1–2 (Madison, WI: State Printer, 1898), where Folkmar acknowledged Hourwich's help.

15. *The Day*, November 22, 1914, 5.

16. Isaac A. Hourwich, "The Jews in America: A Statistical Overview from the Recent Census," vol. 2 in Isaac A. Hourwich, *Oysgevelte Schriften* [Yiddish: Selected Works], 4 vols. (New York: [s.n.], 1917), 97–104.

17. Arthur A. Goren, *New York Jews and the Quest for Community: The Kehillah Experiment: 1908–1922* (New York: Columbia University Press, 1970); and Aryeh Goren, ed., *Dissenter in Zion: From the Writings of Judah L. Magnes* (Cambridge, MA: Harvard University Press, 1982).

18. Magnes to Hourwich, November 18, 1909, I. A. Hourwich Papers, Houghton Library, Harvard University. Hourwich's arguments are based on Magnes's restatements in his letters to Hourwich, November 18 and 24, 1909.

19. Magnes to Hourwich, November 24, 1909.

20. I. A. Hourwich, *The Day*, November 22, 1914, 5.

21. U.S. 61st Cong. [Senate], "Report 387: Amendment to Act Relating to Thirteenth and Subsequent Censuses March 14, 1910." The report includes the full text of Durand's letter.

22. CR, March 17, 1910, 3290.

23. CR, March 14, 1910, 3129–30.

24. CR, March 15, 1910, 3193.

25. I found no explanation as to why the instructions were changed (in the Bureau of Immigration papers at the National Archives). However, my search was largely confined to a few files with obviously relevant subjects (e.g., "Hebrew Race").

26. F. H. Larned to William J. Moxley, July 5, 1910; Benjamin Cable to Isi Fischer, May 29, 1911, both in RG 85, Entry 9, file 52363 / 25, Bureau of Immigration Papers, USNA.

27. Daniel Folkmar, "Second Memorandum to the Director *In re:* The Plan of Tabulating Only Five Countries by Mother Tongue," December 10, 1910, RG 29, Entry 200, file P-12, Records of the Bureau of the Census, USNA.

28. Daniel Folkmar, "Memorandum to the Director *In re:* Tabulation of Mother Tongue," September 6, 1910, RG 29, Entry 200, file P-12, Records of the Bureau of the Census, USNA.

29. Folkmar, "Second Memorandum to the Director: *In re:* Tabulation of Mother Tongue," September 10, 1910, RG 29, Entry 200, file P-12, Records of the Bureau of the Census, USNA.

30. J. H. Parmelee, "Memorandum for Dr. Hill," February 7, 1910, RG 29, Entry 200, file P-12, Records of the Bureau of the Census, USNA.

31. Wilcox, "Note: United States Census," American Statistical Association, *Publications*, 13, no. 3 (September 1913): 553.

32. Daniel Folkmar, "Memorandum to the Director: *In re:* Jewish Names," June 7, 1910, and E. H. Lewinski, "Report on Jewish Names," n.d., RG 29, Entry 200, file P-12, Records of the Bureau of the Census, USNA.

33. Joseph A. Hill, "Memorandum for the Director: *In Re* certain difficulties in the return of country of birth caused by disturbed conditions in Europe," February 5, 1919, RG 29, Entry 198, file 35, Records of the Bureau of the Census, USNA.

34. United States Bureau of the Census, *Thirteenth Census of the United States Taken in the Year 1910*: vol. 1, *Population: General Report and Analysis* (Washington, DC: Government Printing Office, 1912), 781.

35. Goldenweiser, "The Mother Tongue Inquiry in the Census of Population," American Statistical Association, *Publications*, 13, no. 4 (December 1913), 648–55.

36. *Thirteenth Census*, 959.

37. USICR, *Dictionary*, 5:55–56.

38. "Proceedings of the Anthropological Society of Washington: Meeting of February 21, 1911," *American Anthropologist*, n.s., 13, no. 2 (April–June, 1911): 316–17.

39. Franz Boas, *Race and Nationality* (New York: American Association for International Conciliation, 1915), 5–6.

40. Glen Levin Swiggett, ed., *Proceedings of the Second Pan American Scientific Congress* (I. Anthropology), vol. 1 (Washington, DC: Government Printing Office, 1917), 9–21.

41. Swiggett, ed., "Proceedings," 16.

42. Swiggett, ed., "Proceedings," 17.

43. Swiggett, ed., "Proceedings," 17–18.

44. Swiggett, ed., "Proceedings," 20.

45. Israel Zangwill, *The Melting Pot: Drama in Four Acts* (New York: Macmillan, 1909).

46. Swiggett, ed., "Proceedings," 20.

47. Swiggett, ed., "Proceedings," 21–22.

48. Oscar J. Janowsky, *The Jews and Minority Rights (1898–1919)* (New York: Columbia University Press, 1933), chap. 5.

49. Janowsky, *Jews and Minority Rights*, chap. 5; Sachar, *A History of the Jews in America*, chap. 8; Jonathan Frankel, "The Jewish Socialists and the American Jewish Congress Movement," *YIVO Annual of Jewish Social Studies* 16 (1976): 202–341.

50. "Minutes of the Conference of Delegates Appointed by the American Jewish Congress Organization Committee and the Conference of National Jewish Organizations, New York, July 18, 1916, 2–4, AJHS.

51. "Minutes of the Executive Organizing Committee for an American Jewish Congress, August 9–10, 1916." Cited in Janowsky, *The Jews and Minority Rights*, 185n32. AJHS holds a copy of the minutes of the Executive Committee, but the set from this date is missing.

52. David Kertzer and Dominique Arel, "Censuses, Identity Formation and the Struggle for Political Power," in *Census and Identity: The Politics of Race, Ethnicity and Language in National Censuses*, ed. David Kertzer and Dominique Arel (Cambridge: Cambridge University Press, 1998), 12.

53. Mara Loveman, *National Colors: Racial Classification and the State in Latin America* (New York: Oxford University Press, 2014), 11.

54. Paul Schor, "Mobilizing for Pure Prestige? Challenging Federal Census Categories in the USA (1850–1940)," *International Social Science Journal (ISSJ)* 183 (2005): 89–101.

55. Quoted in Schor, "Mobilizing for Pure Prestige?," 97.
56. Schor, "Mobilizing for Pure Prestige?," 97.
57. Paul Starr, "The Sociology of Official Statistics," in William Alonso and Paul Starr, *The Politics of Numbers* (New York: Russell Sage Foundation, 1987), 26.
58. Mae M. Ngai, *Impossible Subjects: Illegal Aliens and the Making of Modern America* (Princeton, NJ: Princeton University Press, 2004), 31.
59. Fox and Guglielmo, "Defining America's Racial Boundaries."
60. Kohler to Husband, March 7, 1927. See also Kohler, *Immigration and Aliens*, 309–405, especially 400–401.
61. Husband to Kohler, March 14, 1927, Kohler Papers, AJHS.
62. Husband to Wheeler, December 15, 1908.
63. *USICR*, 1:17–18.
64. "Proceedings of the Anthropological Society of Washington: Meeting of February 21, 1911," *American Anthropologist*, n.s., 13, no. 2 (April–June, 1911), 316.
65. Kohler to Husband, March 23, 1927, Kohler Papers, AJHS.
66. Ngai, *Impossible Subjects*, chap. 1; Fox and Guglielmo, "Defining America's Racial Boundaries."

7: The Second Quota Act, 1924

1. Gerstle, *American Crucible*, 82.
2. Jonathon P. Spiro, "Patrician Racist: the Evolution of Madison Grant" (PhD diss., University of California, Berkeley, 2000). See also Jonathon P. Spiro, *Defending the Master Race: Conservation, Eugenics and the Legacy of Madison Grant* (Burlington, VT: University of Vermont Press; Hanover, NH: University Press of New England, 2009); Higham, *Strangers in the Land*.
3. *CR*, January 30, 1914, 2610.
4. E. P. Hutchinson, *Legislative History of American Immigration Policy, 1798–1965* (Philadelphia: University of Pennsylvania Press, 1981), 160; *CR*, January 30, 1914, 2610; *CR*, Appendix for January 30, 1914, 96.
5. Higham, *Strangers in the Land*, 304–9.
6. Higham, *Strangers in the Land*, 312, 410n36. Spiro, *Defending the Master Race*, 203. See also Spiro, "Patrician Racist," 494n28.
7. U.S. House Committee on Immigration and Naturalization, *Hearings*, April 16–17, 1920 (Laughlin, "Biological Aspects of Immigration"), 1921; November 21, 1922 (Laughlin, "Analysis of the Metal and Dross in America's Modern Melting Pot"), 1923.
8. U.S. 66th Cong., 3rd Sess., House Report 1109, December 12, 1920.
9. Based on use of the search capabilities for digitized texts.
10. Calvin Coolidge, "Whose Country is This?," *Good Housekeeping* 72:2 (February 1921), 13–14, 106, 109.
11. Higham, *Strangers in the Land*, chap. 10 and 312–24; Zolberg, *Nation by Design*, 248–54.

12. *CR*, April 8, 1924, 5864.

13. *CR*, April 8, 1924, 5910.

14. *CR*, April 8, 1924, 5911.

15. U.S. House, The Committee of Immigration and Naturalization, *Hearings: Restriction of Immigration*, serial 1-A, 1924, 390–92.

16. Based on search results for "Nordic" and "Laughlin" in the digitized version of the *Congressional Record* during the debate on the 1924 act.

17. *CR*, April 2, 1924, 5413.

18. Higham, *Strangers in the Land*, 322.

19. *CR*, April 3, 1924, 5468.

20. *CR*, April 3, 1924, 5468.

21. *CR*, April 3, 1924, 5468.

22. Gerstle, *American Crucible*, 120–21.

23. *CR*, April 8, 1924, 5864. See also Christian Joppke, *Selecting by Origin: Ethnic Migration in the Liberal State* (Cambridge, MA: Harvard University Press, 2005), 41–42.

24. Gerstle, *American Crucible*, 120–21.

25. *CR*, April 3, 1924, 5462.

26. *CR*, April 3, 1924, 5462.

27. *CR*, April 4, 1924, 5568.

28. *CR*, April 9, 1924, 5945.

29. *CR*, April 16, 1924, 6473 and April 18, 1924, 6635.

30. *CR*, April 18, 1924, 6634–35.

31. *CR*, April 8, 1924, 5826.

32. *CR*, April 8, 1924, 6228.

33. *CR*, June 4, 1924, 10512.

8: *Immigration Law for White Races and Others*

1. Sidney L. Gulick, *Two Addresses by Prof. Sidney L. Gulick on a New Immigration Policy and the American-Japanese Problem* (New York?, s.n. 1914), 7.

2. Gulick, *Two Addresses*, 8.

3. Gulick, *Two Addresses*, 22–23.

4. Gulick, *Two Addresses*, 30–31.

5. Sidney L. Gulick, *American Democracy and Asiatic Citizenship* (New York: Charles Scribner's Sons, 1918), 102–4.

6. U.S. Congress, Senate Committee on Immigration, *Emergency Immigration Legislation: Hearings . . . on H.R. 14461, Part 11*, January 19, 1921, 534.

7. *Takao Ozawa v. United States* (260 U.S. 178, 1922).

8. *United States v. Bhagat Thind* (261 U.S. 204, 1923).

9. Ian F. Haney Lopez, *White by Law: The Legal Construction of Race* (New York: New York University Press, 1996); Mark S. Weiner, "'Naturalization' and Naturalization Law: Some Empirical Observations," *Yale Journal of Law and the Humanities* (Summer 1998): 657–66.

10. *Ozawa.*

11. *Thind.*

12. *Salt Lake City Tribune,* November 14, 1901; cited in Joel Francis Paschal, *Mr. Justice Sutherland: A Man against the State* (Princeton, NJ: Princeton University Press, 1951), 41.

13. *Thind.*

14. *Thind.*

15. Higham, *Strangers in the Land,* afterword (esp. 343–44); Gerstle, *American Crucible;* Ngai, *Impossible Subjects;* Zolberg, *A Nation by Design.*

16. Immigration from the Philippines, then under U.S. rule, was a special case; see Chapter 10.

17. U.S. Department of Commerce, Bureau of the Census, *Fifteenth Census Instructions to Enumerators* (Washington, DC: Government Printing Office, 1930), 26.

18. Ngai, *Impossible Subjects,* 50–55; Jennifer L. Hochschild and Brenna M. Powell, "Racial Reorganization and the United States Census, 1850–1930: Mulattoes, Half-Breeds, Mixed Parentage, Hindoos, and the Mexican Race," *Studies in American Political Development* 22, no. 1 (Spring 2008): 59–96; Schor, *Compter et Classer;* and especially Brian Gratton and Emily Klancher Merchant, "La Raza: Mexicans in the United States Census," *Journal of Policy History* 28, no. 4 (October 2016): 537–67. My own efforts in the Census Bureau and the (limited) House Census Committee records also turned up no "smoking gun."

19. Higham, *Strangers in the Land,* 315–18; Gerstle, *American Crucible,* 113; Daniel J. Tichenor, *Dividing Lines: The Politics of Immigration Control in America* (Princeton, NJ: Princeton University Press, 2002), 168–202; Zolberg, *Nation by Design,* 232–35, 248–60.

20. Gratton and Merchant, "La Raza."

9: From "Race" to "Ethnic Group"

1. Fredrik Barth, ed., *Ethnic Groups and Boundaries: The Social Organization of Culture Difference* (Boston: Little, Brown, 1969); Herbert J. Gans, "Symbolic Ethnicity: The Future of Ethnic Groups and Cultures in America," *Ethnic and Racial Studies* 2 (1979): 1–20; Mary C. Waters, *Ethnic Options: Choosing Identities in America* (Berkeley: University of California Press, 1990); Alejandro Portes and Min Zhou, "The New Second Generation: Segmented Assimilation and Its Variants," *Annals of the American Academy of Political and Social Science* 530 (November 1993): 74–96; Richard Alba and Victor Nee, *Remaking the American Mainstream: Assimilation and Contemporary Immigration* (Cambridge, MA: Harvard University Press, 2003); Stephen Cornell and Douglas Hartman, *Ethnicity and Race: Making Identities in a Changing World,* 2nd ed. (Thousand Oaks, CA: Pine Forge Press, 2002); Philip Kasinitz, John Mollenkopf, Mary C. Waters, and Jennifer Holdaway, *Inheriting the City: The Children of Immigrants Come of Age* (New York: Russell Sage Foundation, 2008); Tomas R. Jimenez, *Replenished Ethnicity: Mexican Americans, Immigration and Identity* (Berkeley: University of California Press, 2010).

2. For brief summaries, see Nathan Glazer and Daniel P. Moynihan, eds., *Ethnicity: Theory and Experience* (Cambridge, MA: Harvard University Press, 1975), introduction, and Werner Sollors, *Beyond Ethnicity: Consent and Descent in American Culture* (New York: Oxford University Press, 1986), 20–21. See also David Hollinger, *Postethnic America* (New York: Basic Books, 1995 [2005]), esp. chaps. 2 and 4, as well as discussions below, especially of W. I. Thomas and Caroline Ware.

3. W. Lloyd Warner and Paul S. Lunt, *The Social Life of a Modern Community* (New Haven, CT: Yale University Press, 1941), 220; Sollors, *Beyond Ethnicity*, 23–24.

4. Sollors, *Beyond Ethnicity*, 20–21; John D. Skrentny, *The Minority Rights Revolution* (Cambridge, MA: Harvard University Press, 2002), 275–304; Matthew Frye Jacobson, *Roots Too: White Ethnic Revival in Post-Civil Rights America* (Cambridge, MA: Harvard University Press, 2006), 19–37. See also Victoria Hattam, *In the Shadow of Race: Jews, Latinos and Immigrant Politics in the United States* (Chicago: University of Chicago Press, 2007).

5. For example, Cornell and Hartman, *Ethnicity and Race*.

6. Daniel G. Brinton, *Races and Peoples: Lectures on the Science of Ethnography* (New York: NDC Hodges, 1890), title page.

7. Brinton, *Races and Peoples*, 18.

8. Brinton, *Races and Peoples*, 7–8.

9. Brinton, *Races and Peoples*, 100–101.

10. Frederick A. Bushee, *Ethnic Factors in the Population of Boston* (New York: Macmillan for the American Economic Association, 1903).

11. A. E. Jenks, "Ethnic Census in Minneapolis," *American Journal of Sociology* 17, no. 6 (May 1912): 776–82. Quotation on 776.

12. Jenks, "Ethnic Census," 778–79.

13. Jenks, "Ethnic Census," 782.

14. Julius Drachsler, *Democracy and Assimilation: The Blending of European Heritages in America* (New York: Macmillan, 1920), and *Intermarriage in New York City: A Statistical Study of the Amalgamation of European Peoples* (New York: Columbia University, 1921); Charles S. Bernheimer, "Julius Drachsler: An Appreciation," *Jewish Social Service Quarterly* 4, no. 3 (March 1928), 220–25.

15. Drachsler, *Democracy and Assimilation*, 75–79, 211–14.

16. Bessie Bloom Wessel, *An Ethnic Survey of Woonsocket, Rhode Island* (Chicago: University of Chicago Press, 1931), 22.

17. Wessel, *Ethnic Survey of Woonsocket*, 14–18, 268–74.

18. Wessel, *Ethnic Survey of Woonsocket*, 5.

19. Wessel, *Ethnic Survey of Woonsocket*, 6.

20. Wessel, *Ethnic Survey of Woonsocket*, 18–19.

21. Wessel, *Ethnic Survey of Woonsocket*, 22.

22. Leo W. Simmons, "Bessie Bloom Wessel, 1888–1969," *American Anthropologist*, n.s., 72, no. 3 (June 1970): 555–57.

23. "News and Notes," *American Journal of Sociology* 31, no. 4 (January 1926): 529

24. Clark Wissler, "Foreword," to Wessel, *An Ethnic Survey*.

25. Wessel, *Ethnic Survey of Woonsocket*, ix.
26. Barkan, *Retreat of Scientific Racism*, 108–12.
27. Robert S. Lynd and Helen Merril Lynd, *Middletown: A Study in Modern American Culture* (New York: Harcourt, Brace and Company, 1929), 8; John S. Gilkeson, *Anthropologists and the Rediscovery of America, 1886–1965* (New York: Cambridge University Press, 2010), 77–80 on Wissler and the Lynds.
28. William I. Thomas and Florian Znaniecki, *The Polish Peasant in Europe and America* (Chicago: University of Chicago Press [vols. 1–2] and Boston: R. G. Badger [vols. 3–5], 1918–1920).
29. William I. Thomas [published with authors shown as: Robert E. Park and Herbert A. Miller], *Old World Traits Transplanted* (New York: Harper and Brothers, 1921), 1–2.
30. Thomas [printed as: Park and Miller], *Old World Traits Transplanted*, 3–4.
31. Thomas [printed as: Park and Miller], *Old World Traits Transplanted*, 296–308.
32. See especially, William I. Thomas and Florian Znaniecki, *The Polish Peasant*, vol. 5, Introduction and Part I (1918–1921), chaps. 2 and 3. See also William I. Thomas and Florian Znaniecki, *The Polish Peasant in Europe and America: A Classic Work in Immigration History* [selections edited with an introduction by Eli Zaretsky] (Urbana: University of Illinois Press, 1996), especially 107–9 and 119–21.
33. Thomas and Znaniecki, *Polish Peasant*, 5:x–xi.
34. Thomas and Znaniecki, *Polish Peasant*, 5:101–3.
35. Lynd and Lynd, *Middletown*; Caroline F. Ware, "Ethnic Communities," in *Encyclopaedia of the Social Sciences*, ed. Edwin R. W. Seligman, vol. 5 (New York: MacMillan Co., 1930–1935 [1931]), 607–13; Caroline F. Ware, *Greenwich Village, 1920–1930: A Comment on American Civilization in the Postwar Years* (Boston: Houghton Mifflin Co., 1935); Caroline F. Ware, *The Cultural Approach to History* (Port Washington, NY: Kennikat Press, 1940); Ellen Fitzpatrick, "Caroline F. Ware and the Cultural Approach to History," *American Quarterly* 43, no. 2 (June 1991): 173–89.
36. Ware, "Ethnic Communities," 607.
37. Ware, "Ethnic Communities," 611–12.
38. Ware, "Ethnic Communities," 612–13.
39. Louis Wirth, *The Ghetto* (Chicago: University of Chicago Press, 1928).
40. Werner Sollors, ed., *Theories of Ethnicity: A Classical Reader* (New York: New York University Press, 1996); John Hutchinson and Anthony D. Smith, eds., *Ethnicity* (New York: Oxford University Press, 1996); Richard Jenkins, *Rethinking Ethnicity: Arguments and Explanations*, 2nd ed. (Thousand Oaks, CA: SAGE Publications, 2008 [1997]); Cornell and Hartman, *Ethnicity and Race*.
41. E. K. Francis, "The Nature of the Ethnic Group," *American Journal of Sociology* 52, no. 5 (March 1947): 393–400.
42. Ware, *Greenwich Village*, 127.
43. Caroline F. Ware, "Cultural Groups in the United States," in Ware, ed., *Cultural Approach to History*, 62–73; quotation from 72–73.
44. W. Lloyd Warner and Leo Srole, *The Social Systems of American Ethnic Groups*, vol. 3 in the *Yankee City* series (New Haven: Yale University Press, 1945).

45. W. Lloyd Warner and Paul S. Lunt, *The Social Life of a Modern Community* (New Haven, CT: Yale University Press, 1941), 211–13, 220.

46. Werner Sollors, *Beyond Ethnicity: Consent and Descent in American Culture* (New York: Oxford University Press, 1986), 20–24.

47. T. J. Woofter, *Races and Ethnic Groups in American Life* (New York: McGraw Hill, 1933).

48. William Foote Whyte, *Street Corner Society: The Social Structure of an Italian Slum* (Chicago: University of Chicago Press, 1943), 162, 227.

49. Whyte, *Street Corner Society*, xvii.

50. Whyte, *Street Corner Society*, 195.

51. Whyte, *Street Corner Society*, 211.

52. Whyte, *Street Corner Society*, 217.

53. Ruby Jo Reeves Kennedy, "Single or Triple Melting Pot? Intermarriage Trends in New Haven, 1870–1940," *American Journal of Sociology* 49, no. 4 (January 1944): 331–39.

54. Maurice R. Davie and Ruby Jo Reeves, "Propinquity of Residence before Marriage," *American Journal of Sociology* 44, no. 4 (January 1939): 510–17.

55. Lowry Nelson, "Intermarriage among Nationality Groups in a Rural Area of Minnesota," *American Journal of Sociology* 48, no. 5 (March 1943): 585–92. The reference is to table 1.

56. Handlin, *Race and Nationality*, 135–36. A briefer formulation appeared in the 1949 essay, "Group Life within the American Pattern."

57. Julian S. Huxley and A. C. Haddon, *We Europeans: A Survey of "Racial" Problems* (New York: Harper, 1936), 107–8; Ashley Montagu, *Man's Most Dangerous Myth: The Fallacy of Race* (New York: Columbia University Press, 1942).

58. I am grateful to Paul Schor for this formulation.

59. *We Europeans*, 114, 142–43.

60. UNESCO, *Four Statements on the Race Question* (Paris: Oberthur-Rennes, 1969), 31–32.

61. Israel Zangwill, *The Melting Pot: Drama in Four Acts* (New York: Macmillan, 1909).

62. Zangwill, *The Melting Pot*.

63. Horace Kallen, *Culture and Democracy in the United States*, with a new introduction by Stephan J. Whitfield (New Brunswick, NJ: Transaction Publishers), ix–lxix.

64. Ware, "Ethnic Communities," 612.

65. Perlmann, *Ethnic Differences*, chap. 4.

66. Judah L. Magnes, "Sermon Delivered at Temple Emanuel, New York, October 9, 1909," in *Dissenter in Zion: From the Writings of Judah L. Magnes*, ed. Arthur A. Goren (Cambridge, MA: Harvard University Press, 1982), 103–8.

67. Magnes, "Sermon . . . October 9, 1909."

68. Drachsler, *Democracy and Assimilation*, 75–84; quotations from 75, 77, 79.

69. Isaac B. Berkson, *Theories of Americanization: A Critical Study, with Special Reference to the Jewish Group* (New York: Teachers College, Columbia University, 1920), 52; Henry Franc Skirball, "Isaac Baer Berkson and Jewish Education" (PhD diss., Teachers College, Columbia, 1977).

70. Berkson, *Theories of Americanization*, 52.

71. Milton Gordon, *Assimilation in American Life: The Role of Race, Religion and National Origins* (New York: Oxford University Press, 1964).

72. Berkson, *Theories of Americanization*, 81, 88, 92; Horace Kallen, "Democracy versus the Melting Pot," *The Nation*, February 18 and 25, 1915.

73. Berkson, *Theories of Americanization*, 98.

74. Berkson, *Theories of Americanization*, 107.

75. El. Lycidas [H. A. Wolfson], "Pomegranates," *Menorah Journal*, pts. 1 and 2 (Feb. and June 1918, respectively). The Cephalic index quote is from pt. 2, 162; the critique of Kallen and Magnes from pt. 2, 163–67. On the *Menorah Journal*, see Daniel Greene, *The Jewish Origins of Cultural Pluralism: The Menorah Association and American Diversity* (Bloomington: Indiana University Press, 2011).

76. Thomas [printed as: Park and Miller], *Old World Traits Transplanted*, 296–308.

77. Marcus Lee Hansen, *The Atlantic Migration, 1607–1860: A History of the Continuing Settlement of the United States*, edited with a foreword by Arthur M. Schlesinger (Cambridge, MA: Harvard University Press, 1940) and *The Immigrant in American History* edited with a foreword by Arthur M. Schlesinger (Cambridge, MA: Harvard University Press, 1940).

78. M. L. Hansen, *The Problem of the Third Generation Immigrant* (Rock Island, IL: Augustana Historical Society, 1938).

79. Hansen, "Third Generation," 9.

80. Peter Kivisto and Dag Blanck, eds., *American Immigrants and their Generations: Studies and Commentaries on the Hansen Thesis after Fifty Years* (Urbana: University of Illinois Press, 1990).

81. Hansen, "Third Generation," 10.

82. Hansen, "Third Generation," 6–7.

83. Hansen, "Third Generation," 10.

84. Hansen, "Third Generation," 10–11.

85. Hansen, "Third Generation," 12.

86. Hansen, "Third Generation," 13–14.

87. Hansen, "Third Generation," 14.

88. Hansen, "Third Generation," 14, 17.

89. Hansen, "Third Generation," 17–18.

90. M. L. Hansen, "The Third Generation in America: A Classic Essay in Immigration History," [Abridged version of *The Problem of the Third Generation Immigrant*, ed. Oscar Handlin], *Commentary* (November 1952): 492–500.

91. Handlin, introduction to "Third Generation in America," 492–93.

92. Handlin, introduction to "Third Generation in America," 493.

93. Oscar Handlin, "Group Life within the American Pattern: Its Scope and Its Limits," *Commentary* (November 1949): 415.

94. Handlin, "Group Life within the American Pattern," 416.

95. Handlin, "Group Life within the American Pattern," 413.

96. Handlin, *Race and Nationality*, 152. See also Handlin, "Statement" [and Memorandum], 327–33 and 1839–63.

97. Nathan Glazer, "America's Ethnic Pattern," *Commentary* (April 1953): 402. See also the version "American Ethnic Groups: From Culture to Ideology" in *Freedom and Control in Modern Society*, ed. Monroe Berger, Theodore Abel, and Charles H. Page (New York: Van Nostrand, 1954).

98. Glazer, "America's Ethnic Pattern," 408.

99. Lubell, *Future of American Politics*, chaps. 3, 4, and 7; quotation from pp. 1–2. Nathan Glazer, review of *Future*, in *Commentary* (July 1952): 87–92; quotation from 87.

100. Will Herberg, *Protestant Catholic and Jew: An Essay in American Religious Sociology* (Garden City, NY: Doubleday, 1955), 23.

101. Marshall Sklare, *Conservative Judaism: An American Religious Movement* (Glencoe, IL: Free Press, 1955), esp. chap. 1, sec. d, "The Ethnic Church and Religion as a Vehicle."

102. Glazer, "America's Ethnic Pattern," 402.

103. Nathan Glazer, *American Judaism* (Chicago: University of Chicago Press, 1957).

104. Glazer, *American Judaism*, 3–4.

105. Nathan Glazer and Daniel Patrick Moynihan, *Beyond the Melting Pot: The Negroes, Puerto Ricans, Jews, Italians and Irish of New York City* (Cambridge, MA: MIT Press and Harvard University Press, 1963).

106. Glazer and Moynihan, "Preface," *Beyond the Melting Pot*.

107. Gordon, *Assimilation in American Life*.

108. Alba and Nee, *Remaking the American Mainstream*, 4.

109. Gordon, *Assimilation in American Life*, 27–28.

110. Besides the preceding Gordon quotation, see, for example, Handlin, *Race and Nationality*, 153, and "Group Life within the American Pattern," 413.

111. See, for example, Sollors, *Beyond Ethnicity*, 36–39; Hollinger, *Postethnic America*, 33–39; Cornell and Hartman, *Ethnicity and Race*, chap. 2.

10: *From Social Science to the Federal Bureaucracy? Limited Diffusion of the "Ethnic Group" Concept through the Early 1950s*

1. Cecile E. Kuznitz, *YIVO and the Making of Modern Jewish Culture: Scholarship for the Yiddish Nation* (New York: Cambridge University Press, 2014).

2. Goldberg, Lestchinsky, and Weinreich, *Classification of Jewish Immigrants*, 10.

3. Goldberg, Lestchinsky, and Weinreich, *Classification of Jewish Immigrants*, 7.

4. Goldberg, Lestchinsky, and Weinreich, *Classification of Jewish Immigrants*, 7.

5. Goldberg, Lestchinsky, and Weinreich, *Classification of Jewish Immigrants*, 11–12.

6. Goldberg, Lestchinsky, and Weinreich, *Classification of Jewish Immigrants*, 12–13.

7. Goldberg, Lestchinsky, and Weinreich, *Classification of Jewish Immigrants*, 147–49.

8. Goldberg, Lestchinsky, and Weinreich, *Classification of Jewish Immigrants*, 36. Replies that suggest ethnic group explicitly: numbers 10, 12, 23, 24, 39, 51, 63, 70, 77, 80, 86, 91, 93, 103, and 128.

9. Reply Numbers 29, 49, and 82, "The Replies," in Goldberg, Lestchinsky, and Weinreich, *Classification of Jewish Immigrants*.

10. Goldberg, Lestchinsky, and Weinreich, *Classification of Jewish Immigrants*, 73–74.
11. Reply Number 129, "The Replies," in Goldberg, Lestchinsky, and Weinreich, *Classification of Jewish Immigrants*.
12. Reply Number 129, "The Replies," in Goldberg, Lestchinsky, and Weinreich, *Classification of Jewish Immigrants*.
13. Roger Daniels, *Guarding the Golden Door: American Immigration Policy and Immigrants since 1882* (New York: Hill and Wang, 2004), especially chap. 5; Zolberg, *Nation by Design*, 9; David Scott FitzGerald and David Cook-Martin, *Culling the Masses: The Democratic Origins of Racist Immigration Policy in the Americas* (Cambridge, MA: Harvard University Press, 2014), chap. 3.
14. Waters and Ueda, *New Americans*, appendix.
15. Stephen T. Wagner, "The Lingering Death of the National Origins Quota System: A Political History of the United States Immigration Policy, 1952–65" (PhD diss., Harvard University, 1986), chaps. 2–3 and especially 90, 121, 183, 252; Daniels, *Guarding the Golden Door*, chap. 6; Divine, *American Immigration Policy*, chaps. 8–9.
16. Revealed by a search of the term in *Proquest Congressional*.
17. *CR*, April 5, 1949, appendix, A2011.
18. U.S. 82nd Cong., 2d Sess., Joint Committee on the Judiciary, *Comparative Print of the Texts . . . Public Law 414* (Washington, DC: Government Printing Office, 1952), Sections 222(a) and 231(a) of the new act.
19. Anderson kindly shared with me the documents she had photocopied. She discussed these documents in Margo Anderson, "Race and Ethnic Classification in the McCarran-Walter Act," in *Immigration and the Legacy of Harry S. Truman*, ed. Roger Daniels (Kirksville, MO: Truman State University Press, 2010). They were originally "retrieved as part of a larger project with William Seltzer (Fordham University)" who discovered them (Anderson, "Race and Ethnic Classification in the McCarran-Walter Act," n8). All of the documentary sources discussed in the remainder of this section are those Anderson shared with me. All cited are from Entry 148, Statistical Records Relating to Particular Subject Areas, 1940–1968 (40.7); Box 352, Immigration and Naturalization (1949–1961) to 750 Miscellaneous (Welfare); Folder: Race and Ethnic Classification; Records of OMB, RG 51, USNA, MD.
20. Subcommittee on International Migration Statistics, "Notes for a Meeting," August 1, 1952.
21. Anderson, "Race and Ethnic Classification."
22. "Working Group on Ethnic Classification to Sub-Committee on International Migration Statistics," August 12, 1952 (first quote) and September 24, 1952 (second quote);
23. "Working Group . . ." September 24, 1952.
24. Subcommittee on International Migration Statistics, Minutes of Meeting, October 3, 1952.
25. Subcommittee on International Migration Statistics, Minutes of Meeting, October 3, 1952.
26. Helen R. Jeter, "Note for Files," RE. Meeting with Penton on September 24, 1952.

27. Harry Alpert to Mr. Mills (c.c. Mr. Rice), November 3, 1952. In the "Minutes of Meeting," October 3, 1952, definitional disagreements among subcommittee members are mentioned several times.

28. Anderson, "Race and Ethnic Classification," presents the various versions of the lists.

29. I follow here Margo Anderson's sensible conclusion from the internal references in the materials that Jeter and her staff prepared in the long summary memo ("Race and Ethnic Classification"). All references to Jeter's long memo of November 14 that follow are to Office of Statistical Standards, "Definition and Classification of Population Groups under the Immigration and Nationality Act of 1952, Draft for Discussion, November 14, 1952."

30. Obituary in *The Washington Post*, March 12, 1998, cited in http://www.findagrave .com/cgi-bin/fg.cgi?page=gr&GRid=32150113 [accessed June 22, 2015]. Obituary in *University of Chicago Magazine*, October 1998. http://magazine.uchicago.edu /9810/html/deaths.html [accessed June 28, 2015].

31. Office of Statistical Standards [Jeter], "Definition and Classification of Population Groups . . . November 14, 1952."

32. Handlin, "Statement" [and memorandum], 327–33 and 1839–63; Handlin, *Race and Nationality*, chap. 5; Higham, *Strangers in the Land*; Barbara Miller Solomon, *Ancestors and Immigrants: A Changing New England Tradition* (Cambridge, MA: Harvard University Press, 1956).

33. A. Wetmore (Secretary, Smithsonian) to Stuart A. Rice (OSS), December 15, 1952.

34. Wetmore to Rice, December 15, 1952.

35. Celler to Acheson, September 15, 1952 (folder: Immigration and Naturalization). See also Jewish Telegraph Agency (JTA), "Government to Draw up Race Lists for Visas," September 24, 1952. http://www.jta.org/1952/09/24 /archive/government-committee-to-draw-up-race-lists-for-visas [accessed Jun. 29, 2015].

36. Celler to Acheson, September 15, 1952.

37. Subcommittee on International Migration Statistics, "Minutes of Meeting," October 3, 1952.

38. Celler to Acheson, September 15, 1952.

39. Emanuel Celler, *You Never Leave Brooklyn: The Autobiography of Emanuel Celler* (New York: John Day, 1953), 114–15.

40. Fisher to Acheson, December 3, 1952.

41. Fisher to Acheson, December 3, 1952.

42. "Adrian S. Fisher," Wikipedia, https://en.wikipedia.org/wiki/Adrian_S._Fisher.

43. Jeter to T. J. Mills, December 23, 1952; see also Jeter to Files, February 3, 1953.

11: *Race and the Immigrant in Federal Statistics since 1965*

1. Wagner, "Lingering Death."

2. Wagner, "Lingering Death," chaps. 2–3; Daniels, *Guarding the Golden Door*, chap. 6; FitzGerald and Cook-Martin, *Culling the Masses*, chap. 3.

3. Waters and Ueda, eds., *New Americans*, appendix.

4. Wagner, "Lingering Death," 424–25, 473; Daniels, *Guarding the Golden Door*, chap. 6.

5. Neil Foley, *Mexicans in the Making of America*, esp. chaps. 5–8; Douglas S. Massey, Jorge Durand, and Nolan J. Malone, *Beyond Smoke and Mirrors: Mexican Immigration in an Era of Economic Integration* (New York: Russell Sage Foundation, 2002). See also the valuable Pew studies, such as Jeffrey S. Passel and D'Vera Cohn, *Trends in Unauthorized Immigration: Undocumented Inflow Now Trails Legal Inflow* (Washington, DC: Pew Hispanic Center, 2008), accessed at http://www.pewhispanic .org/files/reports/94.pdf/.

6. The forms are conveniently shown at https://www.census.gov/history/www /through_the_decades/questionnaires/. The question included no label in 1980 and on at least some subsamples in 1960. See also Paul Schor, *Counting Americans: How the U.S. Census Classified the Nation* (New York: Oxford University Press, 2017), especially chaps. 12 and 16.

7. Forms, instructions, and questions are presented at http://www.census.gov /history/www/through_the_decades.

8. OMB Directive #15, *Race and Ethnic Standards for Federal Statistics and Administrative Reporting*, May 12, 1977; available at http://wonder.cdc.gov/wonder/help /populations/bridged-race/directive15.html. See also https://www.census.gov /history/www/through_the_decades/questionnaires/.

9. Eric Foner, *Reconstruction: America's Unfinished Revolution, 1863–77* (New York: Harper and Row, 1988), 199–201, 243–59, 446–49.

10. Wagner, "Lingering Death," 407–11.

11. C. Matthew Snipp, "American Indians: Clues to the Future of Other Racial Groups," in *New Race Question*, ed. Perlmann and Waters, 189–214.

12. Dina Okamoto and G. Cristina Mora, "Panethnicity," *Annual Review of Sociology* 40 (2014): 219–39.

13. G. Christina Mora, *Making Hispanics: How Activists, Bureaucrats and Media Constructed a New American* (Chicago: University of Chicago Press, 2014), chap. 2.

14. Benjamin Francis-Fallon, "Minority Reports: The Emergence of Pan-Hispanic Politics" (PhD diss., Georgetown University, 2012), chaps. 5, 10; Mora, *Making Hispanics*, chap. 3.

15. Robert Voight, "Oral History: Conrad Taeuber" (interview conducted April 12, 1989), https://www.census.gov/history/pdf/taeuber_oral_history.pdf.

16. Francis-Fallon, "Minority Reports," chap. 5.

17. Francis-Fallon, "Minority Reports," 164.

18. Mora, *Making Hispanics*, 80.

19. Francis-Fallon, "Minority Reports," 168.

20. Namepeo McKenney and Aruthur R. Cresce, "Measurement of Ethnicity in the United States: Experiences of the U.S. Census Bureau," in Statistics Canada and U.S. Bureau of the Census, *Challenges of Measuring an Ethnic World: Science, Politics, and Reality* (Washington, DC: Government Printing Office, 1993); see also the codebooks for the November 1969 and November 1979 CPS Surveys ("Technical

Documentation"), and U.S. Bureau of the Census, *Current Population Report,*
Series p-20, No. 213, "Persons of Spanish Origin in the United States: November,
1969," and Series p-20, No. 221, "Characteristics of the Population by Ethnic
Origin: November, 1969" (Washington, DC: Government Printing Office, 1971);
Charles E. Johnson Jr., Consistency of Reporting Ethnic Origin in the Current
Population Survey (Bureau of the Census Technical Paper 31) (Washington, DC:
Government Printing Office, 1974); Stanley Lieberson and Mary C. Waters, *From
Many Strands: Ethnic and Racial Groups in Contemporary America* (New York: Russell
Sage Foundation, 1988), chap. 1; Joel Perlmann and Mary C. Waters, "Introduction," in *New Race Question,* ed. Perlmann and Waters, 9.
21. Francis-Fallon, "Minority Reports," 169n26.
22. Francis-Fallon, "Minority Reports," chaps. 5, 10; Taeuber, "Interview."
23. Francis-Fallon, "Minority Reports," 341–42.
24. Mora, *Making Hispanics,* chap. 3; Francis-Fallon, "Minority Reports," chaps. 5, 10.
25. Francis-Fallon, "Minority Reports," 343.
26. Francis-Fallon, "Minority Reports," 339–40.
27. Francis-Fallon, "Minority Reports," 347.
28. All quotes from the Directive are from United States Office of Management
and Budget, "Statistical Directive #15: Race and Ethnic Standards for Federal
Statistics and Administrative Reporting," *Federal Register* 42, no. 1926 (May 13,
1977).
29. Barry Edmonston, Joshua Goldstein, and Juanita Tamayo Lott, eds., *Spotlight on
Heterogeneity: The Federal Standards for Racial and Ethnic Classification—Summary of a
Workshop* (Washington, DC: National Academy Press, 1996), 36–37; Lawrence
Wright, "One Drop of Blood," *The New Yorker,* July 25, 1994, 46–55, 54.
30. U.S. Census Bureau, *1980 Census of Population and Housing: Procedural History*
(Washington, DC: Government Printing Office, 1986), chap. 12, p. 19.
31. Skrentny, *Minority Rights Revolution,* 275.
32. Guglielmo, *White on Arrival.*
33. Skrentny, *Minority Rights Revolution,* 278–81 and 296.
34. Skrentny, *Minority Rights Revolution,* chap. 19.
35. Perlmann, *Italians Then, Mexicans Now,* 13–36, and Joel Perlmann, "Ethnic Group
Strength, Intermarriage and Group Blending" in *Studies in Contemporary Jewry* 25
(2011): 49–61.
36. See discussion in Chapter 9.
37. Skrentny, *Minority Rights Revolution,* 290.
38. Skrentny, *Minority Rights Revolution,* 281–83, 293–95.
39. Skrentny, *Minority Rights Revolution,* 289–90.
40. Skrentny, *Minority Rights Revolution,* 275–314.
41. Skrentny, *Minority Rights Revolution,* 283.
42. Howard M. Sachar, *A History of the Jews in America* (New York: Alfred A. Knopf,
1992), 262–67, 410–12, 468–83, 674–76; Stuart Svornkin, *Jews Against Prejudice:
American Jews and the Fight for Civil Liberties* (New York: Columbia University
Press, 1997); Gregg Ivers, *To Build a Wall: American Jews and the Separation of Church
and State* (Charlottesville: University Press of Virginia, 1995), chap. 2.

43. Naomi W. Cohen, *Jews in Christian America: The Pursuit of Religious Equality* (New York: Oxford University Press, 1992); Jonathon D. Sarna and David G. Dalin, *Religion and the State in the American Jewish Experience* (Notre Dame, IN: University of Notre Dame Press, 1997); Ivers, *To Build a Wall*; Svonkin, *Jews Against Prejudice*; Kevin M. Schultz, *Tri-Faith America: How Catholics and Jews Held Postwar America to Its Protestant Promise* (New York: Oxford University Press, 2011), chaps. 5–7.

44. Svonkin, *Jews Against Prejudice*; Schultz, *Tri-Faith America*; Leo Pfeffer, "An Autobiographical Sketch," in *Religion and the State: Essays in Honor of Leo Pfeffer*, ed. Jaimes E. Wood Jr. (Waco, TX: Baylor University Press, 1985), 487–534, especially 501–2. I am grateful to Johnathon Sarna for alerting me to Pfeffer's memoir.

45. Schultz, *Tri-Faith America*, 167.

46. Skrentny, *Minority Rights Revolution*, 283–84.

47. Goldstein, *Price of Whiteness*, 224–27. Cf. 224.

48. Schultz, *Tri-Faith America*, chap. 7.

49. Skrentny, *Minority Rights Revolution*, 275–314.

50. U.S. Supreme Court, *Regents of the University of California v. Bakke*, 438 U.S. 265 (1978), 295–97.

51. Cited in Skrentny, *Minority Rights Revolution*, 175 (*Bakke*, footnote 45).

52. Peter Skerry, *Counting on the Census? Race, Group Identity, and the Evasion of Politics* (Washington, DC: Brookings Institution Press, 2000), 37; Nathan Glazer, "Reflections on Race, Hispanicity and Ancestry in the U.S. Census," in *The New Race Question*, ed. Perlmann and Waters, 318–26, especially 322–24.

53. Frederick G. Bohme, "Oral History of C. Louis Kincannon," 1992 available at https://www.census.gov/history/pdf/Kincannon_Oral_history.pdf.

54. U.S. Census Bureau, *1980 Census of Population and Housing: Procedural History*, chap. 12, pp. 12, 15. Available at https://www.census.gov/history/www/through_the_decades/overview/1980.html.

55. McKenney and Cresce, "Measurement of Ethnicity," 181, 200.

56. U.S. Census Bureau, *1980 Census of Population and Housing: Procedural History*, chap. 12, p. 10.

57. McKenney and Cresce, "Measurement of Ethnicity," 174; U.S. Census Bureau, *Census of Population and Housing: Procedural History* (Washington, DC: Government Printing Office, 1996), available at https://www.census.gov/history/pdf/1990proceduralhistory.pdf, 12–10, 14–16.

58. Lieberson and Waters, *From Many Strands* 1988, 7–8; http://www.census.gov/population/censusdata/pc80-s1-10/pc80-s1-10.pdf.

59. http://www.census.gov/history/www/through_the_decades/questionnaires/and http://www.census.gov/history/www/through_the_decades/census_instructions/.

60. Margo J. Anderson, *The American Census: A Social History*, 2nd ed. (New Haven, CT: Yale University Press, 2015), 46–49.

61. See instructions at http://www.census.gov/history/pdf/1950instructions.pdf.

62. Perlmann and Waters, eds., *New Race Question*, 17–18; Kim Williams, *Mark One or More: Civil Rights in Multiracial America* (Ann Arbor: University of Michigan Press, 2008); Wright, "One Drop of Blood."

63. Kelly Mathews et al., *2015 National Content Test Race and Ethnicity Analysis Report: A New Design for the 21st Century* (Washington, DC: Government Publishing Office, 2017), 4.

64. Kenneth Prewitt, *What Is YOUR Race?: The Census and Our Flawed Efforts to Classify Americans* (Princeton, NJ: Princeton University Press, 2013), chap. 9, "The Problem of the Twenty-First Century Is the Problem of the Color Line as It Intersects with the Nativity Line."

65. Hirokazu Yoshikawa, *Immigrants Raising Citizens: Undocumented Parents and their Young Children* (New York: Russell Sage Foundation, 2011); Frank D. Bean, Susan K. Brown, and James D. Bachmeier, *Parents without Papers: The Progress and Pitfalls of Mexican American Integration* (New York: Russell Sage Foundation, 2015).

66. See, for example, Xiao-Huang Yin, "China: People's Republic of China," Jennifer Holdaway, "China: Outside the People's Republic of China," and Pyong Gap Min, "Korea," all in Waters and Ueda, eds., *The New Americans*, 340–54, 355–70, 491–503, respectively. On the sociological debates about the fate of the new second generation see, for example, Alejandro Portes and Ruben Rumbaut, *Immigrant America: A Portrait*, 3rd ed. (Berkeley: University of California Press, 2006); Joel Perlmann, *Italians Then, Mexicans Now: Immigrant Origins and Second Generation Progress, 1890–2000* (New York: Russell Sage Foundation and Levy Economics Institute, 2005), and Philip Kasinitz, John H. Mollenkopf, Mary C. Waters, and Jennifer Holdaway, *Inheriting the City: The Children of Immigrants Come of Age* (New York: Russell Sage Foundation and Harvard University Press, 2008).

67. See, for example, the data and related discussion over Richard Alba, "The Myth of a White Minority," *The New York Times*, June 11, 2015, op-ed page; Richard Alba, "The Likely Persistence of a White Majority: How Census Bureau Statistics Have Misled Thinking about the American Future," *The American Prospect* (Winter 2016): 67–71; and comments by Kenneth Prewitt, William Darity Jr., Harold Meyerson, Frank D. Bean, and Richard Alba in "Prospect Debate: The Illusion of a Minority Majority America," February 2016, http://prospect.org /article/prospect-debate-illusion-minority-majority-america; Herbert J. Gans, "The Census and Right-Wing Hysteria," Sunday Review, *The New York Times*, May 11, 2017, https://www.nytimes.com/2017/05/11/opinion/sunday/the-census -and-right-wing-hysteria.html; and William H. Frey, "The Census and Diver- sity," Letter, Opinion Pages, *The New York Times*, May 22, 2017, https://www .nytimes.com/2017/05/22/opinion/the-census-and-diversity.html?_r=0. See also Joel Perlmann and Mary C. Waters, "Intermarriage and Multiple Identities," in Waters and Ueda, eds., *The New Americans*, 110–23.

68. Lawrence D. Bobo, "Somewhere between Jim Crow and Post Racialism: Reflections on the Racial Divide in America Today," *Daedalus* 140, no. 2 (Spring 2011): 11–36.

69. For a good example, see Helen Hatab Samhan, "Not Quite White: Race Classification and the Arab-American Experience," in *Arabs in America: Building a New Future*, ed. Michael W. Suleiman (Philadelphia: Temple University Press, 1990), 222–24.

70. Mathews et al., *2015 National Content Test Race and Ethnicity Analysis Report*, 4. Merarys Rios, Fabian Romero, and Roberto Ramirez, "Race Reporting among Hispanics: 2010" (Working Paper No. 102, Population Division, U.S. Census Bureau, 2014), http://www.census.gov/content/dam/Census/library/workingpapers/2014/demo/POP-twps0102.pdf; Nicholas Jones, "Update on the U.S. Census Bureau's Race and Ethnic Research for the 2020 Census," *Newsletter*, April 2015, http://www.census.gov/people/news/issues/vol3issue6.html.

71. http://www.census.gov/history/pdf/1940instructions.pdf, 43.

72. Mora, *Making Hispanics*, 114–15.

73. The IPUMS datasets, on which researchers typically rely for these enumerations, discusses related differences in its general and detailed versions of the Race variable. See https://usa.ipums.org/usaaction/variables/RACE#comparability_section. I am grateful to Tim Moreland at IPUMS for helpful clarifications. On the relevance of Latin American understandings of race in this context, see especially Clara Rodriguez, *Changing Race: Latinos, the Census and the History of Ethnicity in the United States* (New York: New York University Press, 2000).

74. Edmonston, Goldstein, and Tamayo Lott, eds., *Spotlight on Heterogeneity*, 28–29, 47, 53–54; Williams, *Mark One or More*.

75. Rios, Romero, and Ramirez, "Race Reporting among Hispanics: 2010"; Elizabeth Compton, Michael Bentley, Sharon Ennis, and Sonya Rastogi, "2010 Census Race and Hispanic Origin Alternative Questionnaire Experiment," U.S. Census Bureau, 2013, https://www.census.gov/2010census/pdf/2010_Census_Race_HO_AQE.pdf); Mathews et al., *2015 National Content Test Race and Ethnicity Analysis Report*.

76. The proportions for Hispanics choosing "Some Other Race" in various question formats can be calculated from Mathews et al., *2015 National Content Test Race and Ethnicity Analysis Report*, Table 5. The proportion of the decline for Hispanics reporting as white can be estimated from that table and information in Karen R. Humes, Nicholas A. Jones, and Roberto R. Ramirez, "Overview of Race and Hispanic Origin: 2010" (2010 Census Brief #2; March 2011), https://www.census.gov/prod/cen2010/briefs/c2010br-02.pdf, Tables 1, 2 and 10. See also Compton et al., "2010 Census Race and Hispanic Origin," 43.

77. Mathews et al., *2015 National Content Test Race and Ethnicity Analysis Report*, Table 5.

78. Mathews et al., *2015 National Content Test Race and Ethnicity Analysis Report*, 88; Jones, "Update."

79. Jones, "Update."

80. Mathews et al., *2015 National Content Test Race and Ethnicity Analysis Report*, executive summary and 84, 86.

81. Mathews et al., *2015 National Content Test Race and Ethnicity Analysis Report*, 80; repeated in its entirety in the conclusion (86) and again in the executive summary.

82. Beverly M. Pratt, "Evaluating Alternative Instructions and Terminology," in the presentation "2015 National Content Test Results and Recommendations"

(presented at the Applied Demography Conference, San Antonio Texas, January 12, 2017), 36, http://demographics.texas.gov/Resources/Presentations /ADC/2017/2017_01_12_2015NationalContentTestResultsandRecommendati ons.pdf.

83. Edmonston, Goldstein, and Tamayo Lott, eds., *Spotlight on Heterogeneity*, 33; OMB, "Standards for the Classification of Federal Data on Race and Ethnicity," *Federal Register* 62, no. 131 (July 9, 1997): Notice, 36932–36; Williams, *Mark One or More*, 29; Samhan, "Not Quite White"; and her presentation to the 2015 Forum on Ethnic Groups from the Middle East and North Africa (Census Bureau, May 29, 2015), https://www.census.gov/library/working-papers/2015/demo/2015 -MENA-Experts.html.

84. Mathews et al., *2015 National Content Test Race and Ethnicity Analysis Report*, 72.

85. Anny Bakalian and Mehdi Bozorgmehr, *Backlash 9 / 11: Middle Eastern and Muslim Americans Respond* (Berkeley: University of California Press, 2009), esp. chap. 6 and appendix A. Rashmee Roshan Lall, "Time for MENA Americans to Stand Up and Be Counted," *The Arab Weekly*, October 9, 2016, http://www.thearabweekly .com/Opinion/6654/Time-for-MENA-Americans-to-stand-up-and-be -counted.

86. Phil Sparks, "August 2017 Update," *The Census Project*, https://thecensusproject. org/updates/august-2017-update/. See also comments of Kenneth Prewitt, October 27, 2017, at https://www.pbs.org/newshour/show/the-2020-census-is -at-risk-here-are-the-major-consequences.

Conclusion

1. Higham, *Strangers in the Land*, 157; Spiro, *Defending the Master Race*, chap. 14.

2. On the latter, see Thomas A. Guglielmo, *White on Arrival: Italians, Race, Color and Power in Chicago, 1890–1945* (New York: Oxford University Press, 2003), and Fox and Guglielmo, "Defining America's Racial Boundaries."

Acknowledgments

What a pleasure to finally thank those who helped! My research efforts have been based at the Levy Economics Institute of Bard College, where I have taught. I am grateful to Dimitri B. Papadimitriou and Leon Botstein, presidents of the institute and the college, respectively, who ensured that I had the time and supportive atmosphere in which to work. The staff of the institute, including its ever-helpful librarian, Willis C. Walker, as well as Elizabeth Dunn, Kathleen Mullaly, and the late Susan Howard, provided solutions to countless problems. I am also grateful to the staffs at major research libraries and archives—Harvard, the U.S. National Archives (especially Marian L. Smith), the Chicago History Museum, the Center for Jewish History, and the Archives of the American Jewish Committee.

Comments and encouragement from other scholars helped greatly over the long term. These included participants too numerous to mention at conferences where I presented my evolving work. Faculty colleagues at Bard also heard several on-campus talks, read drafts that eventually morphed into chapters, and offered suggestions and encouragement. I am especially grateful to colleagues Mario Bick, Yuval Elmelech, David Kettler, Cecile E. Kuznitz, and Allison McKim for comments over the years, to say nothing of friendly colleagueship. Students in several of my Bard classes also read drafts, and their reactions provided insight in an enjoyable way. My student Patrick Nevada served superbly as a research assistant and eventually coauthored a working paper with me that served as an early draft of Chapter 11.

I was also fortunate to have colleagues and friends throughout the land and across the disciplines who offered specialized aid over the years. Long before I ever imagined that the whiteness theme might turn up in my research, conversations with Noel Ignatiev had sensitized me to its place in the history of American labor and immigration. Later, a conversation with Gary Gerstle helped me define directions for a book. Margo J. Anderson, Cecile E. Kuznitz, Stephan R. Lehmann, Tim Moreland, Ann Morning, Derek Penslar, Kenneth Prewitt, Jonathan D. Sarna, and Mark S. Weiner promptly and expertly answered queries. Margo Anderson also kindly turned over photocopies of a batch of manuscripts she and a colleague had discovered at the National Archives, and these came to form the basis for the second part of Chapter 10.

When I had written a draft of what I thought might be the whole book—Part I and Chapters 7 and 9—I was immensely fortunate to get thoughtful readings at this critical stage from Nathan Glazer, David Hollinger, Mara Loveman, Paul Schor, and Roger Waldinger. Besides comments on particular topics, their suggestions about structure and emphasis made a real difference, not least in urging me to follow ethnoracial classification through the civil rights era and into the present. Later still, Sunmin Kim commented thoughtfully on all the chapters, taking up specifics as well as issues of focus and presentation that he thought I could still find useful. After yet more revision, my son, Noam Perlmann, acted as an "intelligent lay reader" to catch discussions that might be unclear except to an expert, and his suggestions eventually went much further, providing several hundred improvements in the clarity of argument and force of expression. Finally, at Harvard University Press, Michael Aronson read a draft, arranged for a contract, and shepherded the manuscript through the early stages. After Michael's retirement from the press, Andrew Kinney took over as my editor and has provided general guidance for the book and extensive helpful comments on every chapter. All of these people have made the book better. But I could not fully incorporate all of their good advice, and of course I alone am responsible for its limitations.

Index